# Engaging with Literature of Commitment

# Volume 1

# C ROSS
## ULTURES

### Readings in Post / Colonial
### Literatures and Cultures in English

148

SERIES EDITORS

Gordon Collier    Bénédicte Ledent    Geoffrey Davis
(Giessen)           (Liège)           (Aachen)

CO-FOUNDING EDITOR
†Hena Maes–Jelinek

# Engaging with Literature of Commitment

## Volume 1

### Africa in the World

Edited by
Gordon Collier, Marc Delrez, Anne Fuchs,
and Bénédicte Ledent

Amsterdam - New York, NY 2012

Cover image:
MatseLuca (Matsemela Manaka, South Africa, & Luca Gansser, Switzerland)
*Festival Speciale Africa 2* (1988; acrylic on jute, 100cm x 80cm)
© Luca Gansser Studio, Lugano

Cover design:
Inge Baeten

The paper on which this book is printed meets the requirements of "ISO
9706:1994, Information and documentation - Paper for
documents - Requirements for permanence".

ISBN: 978-90-420-3508-9
E-Book ISBN: 978-94-012-0784-3
© Editions Rodopi B.V., Amsterdam – New York, NY 2012
Printed in The Netherlands

FOR GEOFF ◄❖►

# TABLE OF CONTENTS

## WHAT IT'S ALL ABOUT

## CODA

# ACKNOWLEDGEMENTS

The Editors wish to thank all of the contributors to this volume for their readiness, under difficult logistical circumstances, to submit tailormade material, and for having borne up, with great patience, during the protracted period of gestation involved in birthing this dizygotic twin.

A special debt of gratitude is owed to the artists Winifred Belmont and Luca Gansser, and to the family of Matsemela Manaka, for their gracious generosity in permitting their artwork to be used for the covers of the two volumes.

A particular vote of thanks to Ingrid, wife of our honoree, Geoffrey V. Davis. As fully qualified keeper of the books and Divine Messenger, Ingrid proved to be an indefatigable worker behind the scenes throughout the process.

# A MEMORY TRIP
## Partly in Tandem, Partly Quadrilogical

SCENE: There are four interlocutors (GORDON Collier, MARC Delrez, ANNE Fuchs, and BÉNÉDICTE Ledent), sitting together after their months – indeed, years now – of highly rewarding slog (sorry: change that to 'editorial work') preparing a suitably massive tome in honour of Geoffrey V. Davis. At times losing sight of the man himself when engaged in tidying up the intricacies of this or that essay on that subject or this author, at other times having his image reflected back at them by the appreciative passing comments of contributors, this quadrumvirate (doesn't Latin have a word that can embrace two women as well as two men?) has decided to pool the resources of memory to see if they can come up with something more substantial than a few 'enigma variations' on this solidly unchanging if protean figure. Memories being subjective and selective, their formulation can hardly jettison the experiencing self altogether – which goes some way to explaining why comparatively subdued modesty alternates with unbridled egocentricity in the following. Let the conversation commence.

◄❖►

GORDON: How do we kick off here? Or, rather, when? You're clearly the *grande dame*, Anne; maybe —

ANNE: — Thanks for drawing attention so subtly to my seniority, Gordon, but appearances can deceive, though I will have something to say about the when and where, and temporal precedence, a bit later on. You kick off, perhaps.

GORDON: Well, Geoff has been a stable and originary presence in my life, and in Rodopi's book series Cross/Cultures and *Matatu*; but where and when did it all begin? Picture a mild, warm, sunny June day in 1985, with a high blue sky for a Sistine ceiling. I am sitting, in the company of my customary solitary self, on the bottom-burnished wooden slats of a bench on the top deck of an excursion vessel chugging through the waters of West Berlin – Havel,

Wannsee, Glienicker Lanke – the murmurous drowse of conference sessions thrust aside to make room for the primary reality of disengaged *plein-air* rubbernecking. I have escaped from the confines of the Eighth Conference on Commonwealth Language and Literature, "North–South Tensions in the Commonwealth," being held, under the auspices of the Freie Universität, at Schloss Glienicke, a palatial heap on generous parkland. A stocky, ruddy-faced, long-haired young man sitting opposite me leans amiably and amicably across, and we engage in conversation; I notice, with pleasure, that he has a touch of Lancashire in his accent. Because he is a stranger to me, but clearly a participant in this conference run by our eccentric, sibylline, already legend-enshrouded hostess, Edith Mettke, I am unguarded in my pronouncements. It seems clear to me from what this young man says that this is the first such conference he has attended, which fact encourages me to (figuratively speaking) reach down my superior index finger to touch his, infusing him with the life-breath of ill-digested facts about the history of 'our' New Literatures in English organization, to which I have belonged since its inception in 1977. Subsequent to the boat-trip, I must have spent some more time together with Geoffrey V. Davis (I had surreptitiously checked the conference programme; the onomastic resonance of that middle initial would emerge only much later), but I also recall something that I never cease to observe with envious irritation: in any larger gathering of people, there was little hope of having Geoff all to myself; he is a nuclear element in his own social quantum system – wherever he goes, he attracts the particles of other people effortlessly, creating an atmosphere of conversational good-will.

What, for me, was magnetic about that first meeting, and what has kept the iron filings of my otherwise vacillating self inclined towards Geoff ever since, was his straight-shooting honesty and openness. Having, as a comparatively early-generation New Zealander, inherited a long legacy of suspicious prejudice about patrician airs, I felt and still feel that I could trust him. Thinking myself, at the time, to be the possessor of deeper truths about 'Commonwealth literature', I chose to think him infectiously innocent, but I learned quickly that one judges Geoff thus at one's peril. I know of nobody who wears his wide learning so lightly (another 'Northern' trait), and with such good humour. His enthusiasms (for German *Exilliteratur* – which charmed me, as I had studied German at university; for classical music – though his investment in opera was beyond me) have always been conveyed as a sharing of his pleasure, as dispatches from the front, never as covert one-upmanship.

Just in case any of you are tempted to put the record straight at this point – I have intimated that I misjudged Geoff's 'Commonwealth literature' experience in a solipsistic, semi-autistic, Bishop Berkeley and the cat and the Eye of God sort of way: because Berlin was the first time I met Geoff, and because he looked so endearingly wet behind the ears, and because I had been Comm.-litting since the mid-1970s, I assumed that Berlin was his baptism of fire. (I also put him as much younger than I was, when, I eventually discovered, I am older than him by barely two months.) There are two revelations that put me well off-beam. One is the tiny irony that I presented no paper at Berlin but Geoff did, and an accomplished, seasoned traveller's one at that (and I hadn't even attended that session).[1] The other – and it was some time before I realized this: Geoff was a consummate global player on at least two fronts quite some time before Berlin. A fascinating detail – and the briskly detailed memoir by Hamish Walker and Michael Senior attests amply to this – is the fact that his very earliest writings, 1979–82, were some eight reports on his experiences in the People's Republic of China. Memento traces of his trips to China are all over his apartment. A Northern boy (Southport schooling) and an Oxford scholarship student, he took his undergraduate degrees in French and German (he is also fluent in Russian, which helps with *Boris Godunov*), and his doctorate, taken at Aachen, was on Arnold Zweig.[2] Academically, then, first base for Geoff was as a Germanist, but of a very special breed,

---

[1] The title was "Life on the Black Side of the Fence: Forced Removals and the Migrant Labour System in Recent Black South African Literature." It was published in *Tensions between North and South*, edited by Edith Mettke (Würzburg: Königshausen & Neumann, 1990): 73–91, though the five-year gap between paper and publication of the proceedings must have been too much for Geoff to bear, and it also came out in another, more thematically relevant critical collection a year earlier – *Current Themes in Contemporary South African Literature*, edited by the redoubtable Lehmann & Reckwitz (Essen: Blaue Eule, 1989): 125–56. This is the only occasion I know of where Geoff has betrayed any signs of crafty opportunism and overt auto-cannibalism.

[2] See Zweig's own celestial lucubrations in the present volume, as mediated by Debby Vietor–Engländer. The doctorate emerged as his first book, *Arnold Zweig in der DDR: Entstehung und Bearbeitung der Romane "Die Feuerpause", "Das Eis bricht" und "Traum ist teuer"* (Bonn: Bouvier, 1977), which was followed by his co-edition (with Dave Midgley and Heino Müller – the former of whom wrote a Zweig monograph that Geoff reviewed earlier in *German Life and Letters*, 1984) of the 1987 Cambridge International Arnold Zweig Symposium (1988).

those who combine 'exile literature' with 'East German' literature.[3] Not only that, but he was a consummate cosmopolitan, travelling far further afield than I had dared do.[4] A red thread clearly runs through his research in German literature, and that is the question of liminality and marginalization, and the surmounting of this condition. And this red thread, or Hansel's breadcrumbs, can be traced further, into Geoff's loyal and authoritative engagement with the apartheid literature of South Africa, which follows closely on his 'Germanist' publications – his earliest articles on German topics date from the early 1980s, as do those on South Africa.[5] An early and much-appreciated high point of these foundational years of Geoff's critical production is the two volumes he brought out with Michael Senior, *South Africa: The Privileged and the Dispossessed* (1983–85). Geoff has a very special, scarcely describable gait – you would know it was him approaching you even at dusk and at two hundred metres distance. It must come from all the amazing leg-work he and Michael put into that book, which I would be tempted to call a precocious achievement, were it not for the fact that all of the fruits of his research, up to the present, are based on this kind of wide-ranging, omnivorous, and panoptical thoroughness.

BÉNÉDICTE: Your first memory of Geoff is concrete and discrete but, paradoxically, fuzzy around the edges. For my part, it's difficult to remember exactly when I first met Geoff. All I know for sure is that in my mind he is, in

---

[3] For me uncanny, if for others banal: in the early 1970s, before being kindly disabused of my hobby by Michael Hamburger over coffee, I was obsessively translating Christa Wolf, Johannes Bobrowski, Volker Braun, Rainer Kunze, and Peter Huchel. So Geoff and I were both looking across the border, if from different angles.

[4] He gave papers at conferences on East German and émigré literature in St. Louis, Missouri (1980), Houston (1980), Dundee (1983), New Hampshire (1982, 1984, and 1986), Cambridge (1987), and New Orleans (1987). And that's just for starters.

[5] His first-ever 'postcolonial' article was related to his first and continuing area of active interest, South Africa, "Kapstadt: Glanz und Elend dicht beisammen," *Aachener Nachrichten* (14 March 1981). Two interviews with South African writers were published in 1982 (with Gladys Thomas and Matsemela Manaka). One article is a kind of crossover with his interest in East German culture: "'Erkennt Ihr, warum wir Euch lieben?': The GDR and the States of Southern Africa in the 1980s," in *The GDR in the Eighties*, ed. Ian Wallace (Dundee, 1984): 45–70. This essay came out of the Dundee conference, where Geoff will have consolidated his friendship with the Germanist Ian Wallace, which became a creative partnership and a co-presence in different series published by Rodopi.

one way or another, so inextricably linked with my professional life that it seems I have somehow always known him. Looking back, however, I think that the first time I came across Geoff was in Cambridge in the late 1980s, probably during the 1987 Michaelmas term, at one of the 'International English Literature Seminars' that Tim Cribb was holding every second Friday evening at Pembroke College. At the time, postcolonial literatures did not enjoy the widespread success they now have – at least not in Cambridge – and these seminars were a cosy affair, with just a small group of enthusiastic participants listening to speakers including Wilson Harris, Ben Okri, and scholars from around the world. If I'm not mistaken, the first of these meetings that Geoff attended during a research stint at the famous university was a discussion of the South African Guy Butler's narrative poem *Pilgrimage to Dias Cross* led by the redoubtable Shakespeare and Renaissance drama scholar, Professor Muriel Bradbrook. I don't think I got much of a chance to actually speak to Geoff on that particular occasion, but I knew from the start who he was, for Hena – Geoff's life-long friend, who was also my doctoral supervisor – had already spoken highly of him to me.

ANNE: Geoff was born two roads away from where I now have a flat back in my home town in the Midlands. From 1944 to 1951 I travelled daily on my school bus past the nursing home where his mother had given birth to him. This perhaps explains why meeting him for the first time at a conference in the South of France[6] was like meeting up with an old friend; it may be that many people have this impression with Geoff, who, though far from naive, *a-priori* treats everyone as an equal and worthy of both his confidence and his confidences.

After a short, militant, but highly incongruous march with others down the Promenade des Anglais in Nice, advocating a renewed boycott by the French

---

[6] This conference was held in 1988 at Nice (where my husband and I were teaching) and organized by Jacqueline Bardolph under the aegis of EACLALS. The proceedings were edited by Jacqueline and published as *Short Fiction in the New Literatures in English* (Nice: Faculté des Lettres, Université de Nice–Sophia Antipolis, 1989). Gordon notes that, thanks to Geoff's many friends in France, Cross/Cultures was not far away: in 1997, Jacqueline convened another short-fiction conference at Nice, the proceedings of which were published as a memorial volume, edited by Jacqueline but redacted after her death by André Viola (also no longer with us) and Jean–Pierre Durix under the title *Telling Stories: Postcolonial Short Fiction in English* (Cross/Cultures 47; Amsterdam & Atlanta GA: Rodopi, 2001).

of South African Outspan oranges, we agreed to keep in touch. Our next meeting, also in 1988, was in Grenoble at the house of Jacques and Neela Alvarez–Péreyre, where Geoff arrived with a strange and tragic East German friend called Tommie (but that's another tale) in tow. We talked and talked for a long weekend, about communism (my husband, Michel, who belonged to the French P.C., was present), about the Berlin Wall, about Israel, but mainly about South Africa. Both Geoff and I were committed not only to the 'literature of commitment' but also to the anti-apartheid movement. Strangely enough, we had both left early research interests concerned with Germany and the Second World War (I had written my Doctorat d'Université dissertation on "Theatre in Paris during the German occupation" and Geoff, of course, had been working on German exile literature) for South Africa. With Alvarez–Péreyre we outlined a huge project dealing with the whole of South African literature. Needless to say, the project in question never even reached the stage of a book proposal, but for me (and I hope for Geoff) that weekend turned out to be an important stepping-stone in life.

The immediate consequence was all in my favour; a neophyte compared with Jacques Alvarez–Péreyre, who had numerous translations and publications to his credit, including *The Poetry of Commitment in South Africa*, and, equally, compared with Geoff, who, as Gordon states, had already published his book for schools on South Africa with Michael Senior, I had just written a book I was trying to get published. In his incredibly generous way, Geoff devoted much time and thought to this problem and eventually persuaded Rick Takvorian, whom Geoff knew in his capacity as artistic director of the Ludwig Forum in Aachen, and who had been entrusted as general editor with a series of volumes on contemporary theatre by Harwood, to take me on.[7] This is important, in that, through these initial contacts of ours, in particular with Robert Robertson (Harwood's London agent), Geoff subsequently brought out two more volumes on South Africa with Harwood.

MARC: Fortunately, there is such a thing as fictional truth. Of all four participants in this quadrangular conversation I am the youngest, which is perhaps why I tend to be the least focused on retrieving the actual facts of the past. My

---

[7] Harwood is an academic publisher, in the 1980s part of Gordon & Breach, later to become Taylor & Francis, and today taken over by Routledge. Harwood published the first edition of my book *Playing the Market*, on Johannesburg's Market Theatre, in 1990 (with the encouragement of Michel and Geoff, a revised edition appeared in the Cross/Cultures series in 2002).

perception of Geoff consists essentially of intuitive impressions – sensory snapshots, as it were – which have etched in my mind the indelible and unmistakable signature of his unassuming personality. Geoff is so *clear*. No repressed rancour there, no hidden agenda, no manipulative obliquities.… Let us put it like this: not even his most gracious compliments can be construed as flattery. No matter how consistently supportive he tends to be. His belief in people, perhaps an offshoot of his ingrained humanism, certainly pollinates and propagates in a cascade of unimagined consequence. There is a puzzle here, to do with the persuasiveness of a man who invariably expresses his views with absolute modesty. Yes, it is a paradox, surely, that the overt acknowledgement of his normality should create the conditions in which so many achievements of daunting magnitude may begin to be contemplated. Many a conference, many a book, owes its existence to Geoff's unassuming presence, which constitutes a facet of his incredible enthusiasm. Indeed, such benevolence, such a capacity for *warming* to others, can only be grounded in a form of genuine humility. Thus Geoff possesses the ultimate qualities of the literary critic: a brand of unpretentiousness that borders on negative capability, coupled with an insatiable curiosity fed by good-will and respect for the intention of the text – to the point that one could overlook the underlying erudition and intelligence.…

It is relevant that – in fictional memory – his first words to me were spoken in apology. In retrospect, this seems astonishing, since he had after all done me the favour of including, in his *Crisis and Creativity* volume, a most juvenile article of mine (but a misprint had sneaked into the title during the editing process). As this was a book of proceedings originating in the 1988 Aachen–Liège conference, which Geoff co-organized with my then doctoral supervisor, Hena Maes–Jelinek (and, as you said, your own, Béné), it follows that I must have caught sight of him lazing in the sunshine, at coffee-break time, on the lawns of the *château* at Colonster. Little did I know at the time that I would later be enlisted in the team (together with Geoff himself, Peter Marsden, and Béné) responsible for the organization of a replay of that memorable *Ur*-script. This collaboration, which eventuated in the GNEL/ASNEL Conference held in Aachen and Liège in May–June 2000, was to lay the foundations for multiple professional friendships and for a series of further projects similarly triggered by Geoff's optimistic yearning for those academic crops which he saw stored up in the dark cracks of future time. I do not wish here to beautify the picture by suggesting that our behind-the-scenes preparatory meetings consisted of anything else but sheer hard work all round, but it is the case that Geoff's geniality, along with Pete's valiant wit, served to allay any doubts we lesser Liège colleagues might have entertained about the soundness of our common venture. It must be remembered that the 2000 conference was a cross-border affair, which generated its own difficulties – such as having to smuggle in, inside a big diplomatic-looking Mercedes, Jamaican poets who did not have a visa for Belgium —

GORDON: — Déjà vu! That also happened at the 1988 conference; I sat in the front passenger's seat, and my idol Eddie Brathwaite, from Barbados, sat with saturnine mien in the back, solicitously attended to by Christine Pagnoulle.

MARC: Like the 1988 one, the 2000 venue turned out to be rather grand, with its 330 delegates and no fewer than thirty invited creative writers from all five continents! A pattern was set here, with Geoff brimming with ideas and enthusiasm and desire to invite all the most impoverished writers of the world, and the rest of the team anxiously rehearsing budgetary availabilities. As Béné, who subsequently officiated as the purse-bearer of EACLALS and then ACLALS for over a decade, and also Ingrid ('The Wife'), will probably confirm, Geoff qualifies for the title of official, card-carrying treasurer's nightmare.

BÉNÉDICTE: You can say that again!

GORDON: Apropos money, his enthusiasms will make him bolt like an exhilarated pony in the direction of ever-new challenges, even when penniless and stuck in some current task.

These ever-new challenges... I recall two conferences, the chronology of which puts us in tandem: the one you mentioned first, Marc – the 11th Commonwealth Literature conference (1988), "Crisis and Conflict in the New Literatures in English," convened by Geoff and by Hena Maes–Jelinek at Liège – and the 12th (1989), "Them and Us: Cross-Cultural Perspectives on the New Literatures in English," convened by me at Giessen. Just look at that Aachen–Liège conference, a nightmare of logistics, and calculate how little time had elapsed between what I took to be his mid-1985 initiation into the mysteries of The Organization and the mid-1988 venue. The latter was a large affair but (okay, this is a pissing contest) not so large as my Giessen conference of the following year, in a much smaller, single location, wellnigh unrepeatable, one might think. Or, at least, re-stageable only with some diffidence. The 1988 Aachen–Liège occasion yielded at least three volumes of selected conference proceedings. One volume was entitled *Crisis and Conflict: Essays on Southern African Literature* (Essen: Die Blaue Eule, 1990), and was edited by Geoff. The other two – and Marc has adverted to these – were *Crisis and Creativity in the New Literatures in English*, edited by Geoff and Hena Maes–Jelinek, and *Crisis and Creativity in the New Literatures in English: Canada*, edited by Geoff alone. The latter two books appeared as volumes 1 and 2 of a new book series called "Cross/Cultures: Readings in the Post/Colonial Literatures in English" under the imprint of Editions Rodopi (Amsterdam and Atlanta GA, now Amsterdam and New York). My own hands-on involvement in Cross/Cultures started only with volumes 5 and 6, the latter of which, *US/THEM: Translation, Transcription and Identity in Post-Colonial Literary Cultures* (1992), was the outcome of the above-mentioned 12th conference. But if I look at the masthead of volume 1, I see that the series co-editors are Gordon Collier (Giessen), Hena Maes–Jelinek (Liège), and Geoffrey Davis (Aachen). It makes sense, in terms of the Aachen–Liège conference, for Geoff and Hena to be on the editorial board, but I have no clear recollection of how I got to be there. Much the same applies in the case of *Matatu*, which is a predominantly Africa-oriented journal, and where it was only logical that its Africanist founding editor, Holger Ehling, should have two Africanists, Geoff and Frank Schulze–Engler, as his co-editors, and where it was less logical to include me, from volume 12 onwards, as Caribbean editor. The main thing is: Geoff was always there, and I moved up profitably through the ranks in his generous wake.[8]

It was at the 12th conference in Giessen that a New Literatures Association was formally instituted. With a few early exceptions, selected proceedings from further conferences (the venues for which were agreed on at annual general meetings) have appeared in the Cross/Cultures series under the sub-series title "ASNEL Papers." I mentioned that the ambitious 1988 Aachen–Liège conference seemed unique, unrepeatable. But we have also collectively intimated the grip on Geoff of his recklessly generous enthusiasm. Behold the three volumes of ASNEL Papers 8, 9.1, and 9.2, co-edited by Geoff – these were the belated outcome of that massive, astounding repeat performance at the same bicephalous venue of Aachen and Liège, "Towards a Transcultural Future: Literature and Society in a 'Post'-Colonial World" (2000). By the time (2005) the proceedings of the first conference finally made their way down the birth canal into the light of print, Geoff was co-editing either with

---

[8] He was co-editor of *Matatu* from its very first issue in 1987, the first six issues being published under Holger Ehling's imprint (Göttingen, then Frankfurt), before the series was taken up by Rodopi in 1990.

his fellow *genius loci* at Aachen, Pete Marsden, or with you, Béné, and you, Marc, two of Hena Maes–Jelinek's acolytes at Liège and now professors there in her stead and her tradition.

BÉNÉDICTE: This combination of crystal-clear data and fuzziness is getting to be a habit with you, Gordon. But with this synergy of place and time, conferences and publishing outcomes, there is clearly a Germany/Belgium connection fairly firmly in place.

That Geoff is good company but also a bon vivant was further confirmed for me, after the Pembroke College meeting that I mentioned earlier, when more occasions for collaboration presented themselves. The first of these was that second Aachen–Liège conference under the auspices of ASNEL/GNEL, which I was involved in co-organizing along with Geoff, Marc, and Peter Marsden. Working with this team proved to be extremely gratifying – on both the human and the scholarly/logistical level – even if the management of a congress with more than three hundred participants and several dozen writers proved, as Marc has already suggested, to be an occasional source of anxiety, particularly under Geoff's visionary and at times unrealistically generous leadership. However, his wildest ideas, for example the staging of Wilson Harris's *Jonestown* in a German museum, came off to everybody's satisfaction and the three edited collections of essays that followed this gigantic conference owe much to his creative determination.

But what about the 'French connection', Anne? I'm interested in hearing how that developed further.

ANNE: It's typically less French than South African. In 1991 we set off together for Johannesburg, where we stayed with my friends Malcolm Purkey and Pippa Stein, and in three mad weeks we met, interviewed, and commissioned articles from the numerous contributors to the forthcoming *Theatre and Change in South Africa* volume.[9] I still have visions of Geoff resolutely eating his picnic lunch at the bottom of a mountain while I travelled up in a ski-lift to eat mine with Stephen Gray at the top, and pleading with him not to go so fast as he strode ahead through down-town Jo'burg. But on the whole he was a delight to work with and his charm and natural friendliness worked wonders in putting our interviewees at ease.

---

[9] *Theatre and Change in South Africa*, ed. Geoffrey V. Davis & Anne Fuchs (Contemporary Theatre Studies; Amsterdam: Harwood Academic, 1996).

By this stage in his life, all kinds of other things were happening: he had just met Ingrid, future wife for Geoff and future friend for the Fuchs family; with others, as Gordon recounts, he had founded and was increasingly involved in Rodopi's Cross/Cultures series; and then there was Matsemela Manaka, who tended to arrive either in Aachen or in Nice and announce in a piteous tone: "Geoff" – or "Anne," depending on the destination arrived at – "I'm at the railway station." 'So what?' we may have thought occasionally, but in fact always rushed in a state of high excitement to pick up our South African playwright, musician, and artist friend. Geoff edited, once more for Harwood, *Beyond the Echoes of Soweto*, a compilation of Matsemela's plays and other work.[10] Matsemela took part in the session on South African theatre that Geoff and I organized at an MLA conference in Chicago,[11] and, incidentally, I think it was here that we met Marcia Blumberg for the first time. Among other artists represented in Geoff's spacious eyrie flat (that those of us around the eighty mark have some difficulty in attaining these days), Matsemela has pride of place, and it was his work, of course, that appeared on the front cover of what the Germans and French call Geoff's '*Habilitation*'.

BÉNÉDICTE: You mentioned that Chicago conference, Anne, and Geoff's close international friendships, all of which prompts me to think further, and a bit closer to home, about my contacts with Geoff. In the weeks, months, and years that followed that first Cambridge meeting, I got to cross Geoff's path more and more often, notably at the Jubilee Conference on Commonwealth Poetry, held at the Commonwealth Institute in London in November 1987, then at the Aachen–Liège conference that he co-organized with Hena in June 1988 and where I gave my very first paper, which, like Marc's, was later to be edited by the same team and appear in the first volume of the Cross/Cultures series.[12] To the budding researcher that I was then, Geoff came across on all these occasions as a very accessible person who, in spite of his already impressive scholarship, was most willing to listen to and encourage his younger colleagues.

---

[10] Matsemela Manaka, *Beyond the Echoes of Soweto: Five Plays*, ed. Geoffrey V. Davis (Contemporary Theatre Studies; Amsterdam: Harwood Academic, 1997).

[11] Modern Language Association (MLA) Annual Convention, Chicago, 27–30 December 1990.

[12] *Crisis and Creativity in the New Literatures in English*, ed. Geoffrey V. Davis & Hena Maes–Jelinek (Cross/Cultures 1; Amsterdam & Atlanta GA: Rodopi, 1990).

I remember the same generosity in the years that followed when, several times during the writing of my doctoral dissertation, Geoff sent me copies of difficult-to-find articles. It was only in 1996, when we were elected onto the board of EACLALS with Hena, who became the chair of the association, that I was given an opportunity to collaborate with him more concretely. I have a memory of long but always fruitful board meetings in Liège during which I acted as a kind of buffer between Hena's down-to-earth manner and Geoff's more idealistic approach to all the matters that we had to decide upon. During the three years of that most rewarding partnership, I got to know Geoff better, not only his bigheartedness but also his insatiable intellectual curiosity and enthusiasm for all things artistic, whether literature, music, drama or film. Geoff is still one of the few people I know who regularly crosses one or several European borders just to go to a play, an opera or a concert, be it in Brussels, Amsterdam or London. No wonder he is also a tireless academic globetrotter, who has attended countless conferences on all five continents. I remember meeting him at such venues as Jamaica in 1992, Zimbabwe in 1999, and Canada in 2007 and listening to his always passionate appreciation of the country that he was visiting as well of the keynotes and papers that he had heard.

GORDON: The "spacious eyrie flat" that you mentioned, Anne, and that all of us know well – it prompts other fond memories. My personal library is insanely larger than his (okay, this is a pissing contest again), but I had more delight in grazing his groaning bookshelves at Johanniterstrasse 13 than in any bookstore. There was always some discovery – something arcane and valuable that I hadn't known about, or books that I myself also possessed that made us kindred souls, or items I didn't have and was tempted to steal. Our reading, I found, was voracious and catholic and sometimes off the wall, though not so much as Geoff's flat, part of which once collapsed from the weight of all those tomes.

Whenever I got him on the phone (and this has been corroborated by other members of my family), his voice would sound weary, worn down by the incredible burden of the multifarious tasks he took upon himself, and by – to me, a cautious stay-at-home soul – endless bank-account-devouring trips to all parts of the globe. But this wasn't weariness, and never complaint, for Geoff, although he has an acute sense of justice, has never been a self-absorbed whinger (to use an Australasianism for a chronically dissatisfied Englishman in the colonies). He gets the job done. Not only does he do this, but the essays he writes are always spot-on, modest, yet deep in their implications.

The red thread of liminality and dispossession, and indeed globality, can be traced yet further, as we see his energies bundled for a further leap into the beyond, this time shortly after Berlin, when, in 1986, he attended the Triennial Conference of the Association of Commonwealth Literature and Language Studies at the National University of Singapore. This seems to have been his second 'Commonwealth' conference. In the same year, on a Faculty Enrichment Grant, he had already made a research trip to Canada; there was a second trip in 1989. Thus, as far as 'Commonwealth' travel is concerned, too, Geoff was a global player early in the game. Even before this (and Berlin) he is 'everywhere'. His first non-South African piece of 'postcolonial' writing on a specific region dates from 1985 (a report on the British Australian Studies Conference at Warwick for ACOLIT). His earliest Canada pieces, in 1986–88, are brief reports, his first article on Canada being a handbook survey (1991) on history as reflected in Canadian literature. Both the Australian and the Canadian material evince an awareness of the liminal condition, as does his sole essay on a New Zealand topic (also 1991), which focuses on ethnic otherness.[13] For all Geoff's continuing 'on the ground' investment in the literature and culture of South Africa, Canada, Australia, and latterly black Britain, the twin apotheosis (to dare an oxymoron) of his commitment to honouring liminal but postcolonially central themes must surely be the symposium on Aboriginal Australia he mounted together with Dieter Riemenschneider at Düsseldorf in 1993,[14] and the ambitious ongoing series of Chotro conferences on India's scheduled peoples and the world's Indigenes.[15]

---

[13] See "'Real Historical Fiction': Kanadische Geschichte im Spiegel der englischsprachigen Literatur Kanadas," in the handbook *Kanada: Gesellschaft – Landeskunde – Literatur*, ed. Geoff Davis & Axel Wieger (Würzburg: Königshausen & Neumann, 1991): 201–18, and "*Other Halves*: Geschichtsbewußtsein und ethnische Problematik im zeitgenössischen neuseeländischen Film," in *Neuseeland im pazifischen Raum*, a collection of Aachen talks edited with Werner Kreisel, Jürgen Jansen & Peter H. Marsden (Aachen, 1992): 271–94.

[14] *Aṟatjara: Aboriginal Culture and Literature in Australia*, ed. Dieter Riemenschneider & Geoffrey V. Davis (Cross/Cultures 28; Amsterdam & Atlanta GA: Rodopi, 1997).

[15] *Indigeneity: Culture and Representation*, ed. G.N. Devy, Geoffrey V. Davis & K.K. Chakravarty (New Delhi: Orient BlackSwan, 2009).

Apart from our joint editorial work on Cross/Cultures and *Matatu*, an experimental joint conference presentation on Australian film,[16] and a gloriously adventurous journey we took together to Canada, I have been an admiring bystander at the expanding circles of Geoff's involvement in national and international organizations, including the running of the German Association GNEL/ASNEL, the European EACLALS, and the worldwide ACLALS. Like the Aachen–Liège conferences, some of these presidencies have been repeat performances – these organizations know the best man when they see him. But I don't know how he does it all.

BÉNÉDICTE: Those organizations – oh, those organizations! There was more event organization in the decade following Aachen–Liège No. 2, notably after Geoff was elected chair of EACLALS in 2002 and chair of ACLALS in 2007. Marc and I joined him on the board of both associations and in the course of this alliance of several years we were involved more or less directly in the running of several international conferences, in Malta (2005), Venice (2008), Windsor (Cumberland Lodge) (2010), and Cyprus (2010). All of these undertakings meant holding numerous meetings, mostly in Liège or in Aachen, in that book-lined top-floor flat in Johanniterstrasse, during which we tried to stick to our agendas but also discussed literature over food and drinks – thereby indulging at one go Geoff's voracious appetite for books and for good cheer. As Geoff's recent re-election as the head of EACLALS confirms, he is the ideal person to run such an association. Well-organized, dynamic, and now free of teaching duties, he also shows an uncommon devotion to the Commonwealth – taken here in its institutional sense, of course, but also in the more literal meaning of general good.[17] Geoff has

---

[16] Geoff and I gave a paper together, at a symposium on Australian studies held at Oberjoch in October 1990, which became "Die ikonographie der Landschaft im australischen Film," in *Mensch und Natur in Australien*, ed. Gerhard Stilz (Bern: Peter Lang, 1991): 197–221, revised and translated as "The Iconography of Landscape in Australian Film," *Australian and New Zealand Studies in Canada* 6 (Fall 1991): 27–41. Another joint venture was our long interview with the Australian poet Geoff Goodfellow, published in *Kunapipi* 14.3 (1992): 27–48.

[17] One example of Geoff's 'interconnections': he was an official guest of the Republic of Zimbabwe in 1991, edited, together with Mbongeni Malaba, *Zimbabwean Transitions: Essays on Zimbabwean Literature in English, Ndebele and Shona* (Matatu 34; Amsterdam & New York: Rodopi, 2007), and currently shuttles between Aachen and London to advise on a government commission on culture and Zimbabwe–UK relations.

indeed worked relentlessly for the benefit of the community of postcolonial scholars. His selflessness should be a model for the upcoming generation of academics, who all too often tend to get involved only when personal advancement is at stake.

ANNE: That selflessness is even reflected in the subject of the bulk of his own writing, from his early collaboration with Michael Senior to his magnum opus, *Voices of Justice and Reason*, which sums up admirably not only Geoff's corpus on South Africa but, perhaps even more so, the voice of the man himself, always just and reasonable (in his writing at least!).[18] Never alarmed by my own family's more robust style, he has spent many intellectually stimulating short holidays with us (before Michel's death in 2005) in Nice, Aachen, England, and the Cévennes. If Geoff is often the life and soul of the party, he has also the surprising faculty of becoming completely still, quiet, and invisible, which is what I have experienced when watching plays, listening to music or even doing interviewing with him. This perhaps is due to his amazing powers of concentration on the subject in hand. His whole-hearted enthusiasm for Commonwealth literature was, right up to his retirement and indeed after, appreciated by his students (a group of whom he regularly escorted both to South Africa and for a week in Wales every year) to an extent that I only realized when I met those he had brought to Mandelieu in 1995 for the conference on New Francophone and Anglophone Theatre. We met at conferences – New Delhi, Paris, London, and Manchester; Aachen, Berlin, Bad Boll, and Tübingen. In Tübingen, I came across Bruce King, who, like Geoff himself, had, for a semester, been an associate professor in France. When he asked what I was doing at that moment, I told him about my increasing enthusiasm for black-British theatre, and he suggested I might like to publish a book on the subject. Who better to help me, I thought, than Geoff. So there we were, embarked on a new project together. Meanwhile, Michel had developed a cancer and it became more and more difficult for me to leave him for long. As we slowed our pace, Geoff, of course, turned up trumps and even found us a new publisher through Marc Maufort and his theatre series with Peter Lang.[19]

---

[18] Geoffrey V. Davis, *Voices of Justice and Reason: Apartheid and Beyond in South African Literature* (Cross/Cultures 61; Amsterdam & New York, 2003).

[19] *Staging New Britain: Aspects of Black and South Asian British Theatre Practice*, ed. Geoffrey V. Davis & Anne Fuchs (Dramaturgies: Texts, Cultures and Performances 19; New York: Peter Lang, 2006).

The last couple of interviews for *Staging New Britain* Geoff had to conduct alone. As his reputation grew, he became busier and busier, but found time to fly to Nice for our fortieth wedding anniversary, to say goodbye to Michel in hospital, and for his funeral. The point of telling this is to emphasize that, although Geoff may appear to be a "worldly scholar" in the sense that Edward Said uses the term, or even in the sense of "a socialite gentleman scholar" used here in the memoir of Michael Senior and Hamish Walker, he is not 'worldly' in a materialistic way. Gordon mentioned Chotro earlier. Geoff and Ganesh Devy organized with tremendous energy and efficiency the first Chotro symposium in 2006. It was a whirl of colours and vibrancy celebrating the representatives of the indigenous peoples – from American Indians to Australian Aborigines – who took part. Geoff, Alastair Niven and his wife, myself and my daughter, Shirley Chew and a few others navigated between exciting conference papers, performances, bouts of tourism, and our impoverished student residence with its hard pallets to sleep on (while others were cavorting in the grand hotels of New Delhi). He is committed to literature of many hues and genres, even more so both to his family and inner circle of friends and to the oppressed and subordinated peoples worldwide.

MARC: Those organizations and associations that we have all been tirelessly circling around, with Geoff seemingly always piggy-in-the-middle.... My own years, alongside Béné, on the boards of these associations, in which much of my time was devoted to the unrewarding tasks of fund-raising, red tape, and the penning of Newsletters for the members, were vindicated by the generosity and the progressive slant informing our policies under Geoff's gentle steering. At a time when postcolonial literary studies are fast becoming institutionalized in the academic West and are therefore at great risk of mutating into yet another bastion of economic privilege, Geoff has been able to keep alive the spirit of such pioneers as Anna Rutherford and Hena Maes–Jelinek, for whom the activity of criticism had always been less a career-making pursuit than a form of political commitment to the cause of redressing disparities – be they discursive, cultural or, indeed, economic. In view of the meagre means at our disposal, our action was necessarily modest; but we were occasionally in a position to despatch books to places where they were lacking, or to dispense scholarships to impecunious scholars wishing to attend our conferences. In what was less a membership drive than an attempt to support postcolonial studies in Eastern Europe, we also funded a mini-EACLALS conference organized by Jaroslav Kušnir at the University of Prešov, Slovakia, in 2007. With hindsight, it looks embarrassingly as if our help consisted largely in offering our own services as plenary speakers.... But what a lark! I shall never forget Geoff's comment, upon arrival, about the miraculous virtues of jet travel and its ability to extract one from the grooves of routine and mindless plodding. It is true that, in his company, even the experience of instant coffee at Košice Airport, with the kindly Norbert Platz, begins to smack of adventure – or should I say holiday?

My memories of Geoff become most real on those occasions when we were spurred into concrete action, as when Stella Borg Barthet requested the board's logistical assistance in the course of organizing her unforgettable 2005 Malta conference for EACLALS, and we became the overwhelmed recipients of her and her husband Victor's inspired hospitality; or, indeed, when we travelled to Cyprus to meet up with Stephanos Stephanides, in charge of organizing the 2010 ACLALS Triennial, whose guided introduction to the complexities of the island proved simultaneously lyrical and politicized. These journeys always reserved opportunities for Geoff and me to enter into a mood of more private confidence, which confirmed our trust in each other and the man's reserves of emotional depth, concealed behind the familiar façade of urbanity. I have sampled Geoff's many moods and modes – not least, in a gloomy graveyard on the outskirts of Liège, the elegiac intensity of his grieving for the disappearance of his dear friend Hena. It is apt that our latest shared enterprise – to date – concerned the organization, in March 2010 under the auspices of ACLALS, of a moving tribute to Hena Maes–Jelinek, which was held in the most unlikely of environments (the 'royal' Cumberland Lodge, as Béné has indicated). Not that Geoff would capitulate to melancholy, however.

GORDON: I note that, in 2008, the Cross/Cultures masthead still featured Hena, but as the ghostly memorial presence of a loved one. Along with her dear friend Anna Rutherford, Hena was part of my life and a guiding light to ethical pathways through Commonwealth and postcolonial literature from the mid-1970s onwards, and this must have been the case for Geoff, too. I would like to close my recollections – far from a tell-all exposé, though any additional tidbits would be positive confirmation of Geoff's large soul, and not a trimming of it – by evoking the image of two boys ever eager to enjoy the company of the maternal *genius loci* of Liège. For no aspect of our co-editorial work on Cross/Cultures was so rewarding (both in terms of an always ineffable lunchtime repast and in terms of tough-minded discussion and decision-making) as those meetings in Liège. Of the many memories that Geoff and I share, our memory of Hena and her shaping presence is the deepest.

BÉNÉDICTE: Geoff's tremendous work as an editor is also to be seen in the light of his altruism. As co-editor of Rodopi's Cross/Cultures series with Hena and Gordon, he has secured and helped usher into print the work of many postcolonial critics, sometimes at the expense of his own personal production. It was an honour for me to join Geoff's and Gordon's team after the death of Hena, whose presence still accompanies our editorial meetings. What a blessing to be working with such committed, jolly good fellows.

MARC: It does feel odd to think that Geoff is even now pursuing his activities at the head of EACLALS, trying to reform the Commonwealth Foundation into an anti-globalization movement, showering books and scholarships on disenfranchised intellectuals in both hemispheres, and incidentally travelling around the globe, without Béné and myself. But then, it is a proven fact that not many people can compete with his tireless energy, as his new youthful team of collaborators, to whom I extend my very best wishes, will also find with their own mixture of disbelief and delight.

ANNE: Oh, heck (as someone often says)! Is it up to me to end this? Well, *Sala khale*, Geoff, and long may you, in the company of Ingrid, keep celebrating both literature and life.

◄❖►

# AFRICA, MY AFRICA

HOLGER EHLING

# Publishing in Africa

## An Overview

A FRICA, THE POOR CONTINENT. AFRICA, THE NEGLECTED CONTINENT. The continent of diseases, civil wars, corruption, and blatant disregard for human rights.

Sounds like a lot of clichés? Yes, it certainly does. But, unfortunately, these clichés are closer to the everyday experiences of most people living in sub-Saharan Africa than most of us would like to think. Whether this is a result of home-made problems or the aftermath of the ravages of colonialism is a matter for debate – for the sake of this article, let us assume that past and present problems go hand in hand in creating a situation that continues to deprive more than half a billion human beings of existing in conditions that might be called human.

The plight of the African publishing industry may seem almost irrelevant in this context – after all, books cannot be eaten, and poems don't put next day's meal on the table. So, onward to matters more pertinent to solving the problem?

Well, don't rush it. As a conclusion to this overview, I will argue that while books are not a nourishing breakfast in terms of calories, they provide the basis for any effort to change the situation for the better – and that the lack of books is the most significant indicator of development going wrong.

## The Go(o)d Fathers of Publishing in Africa

Books as the embodiment of the written culture of the West are not historically endemic in Africa. The continent's cultures – at least, those based in Africa south of the Sahara, which is the focus of this article – have always been rooted in oral traditions. Books reached sub-Saharan Africa as part of the missionary thrust of both Christian and Muslim denominations – the earliest indigenous book production in Africa took place in Ethopia, where the bible was translated from the fourth century onwards, with copies of some religious texts in the G'eez language printed in Rome and Cologne in the 1580s.

As of the fifteenth century, European efforts to grab some of the riches of the western regions of Africa – spices, gold, ivory, slaves – became part of the everyday experiences of the continent's populace, just as it had been along the eastern shores, where trade with the Arab world and India had been thriving for centuries.

In the nineteenth century, as buccaneering forays into Africa gave way to the strategic colonial policies of Britain, France, Portugal, Belgium and bit-players such as Spain, Germany, and Denmark – which held a tiny patch of today's Ghana for a while – involving the African populace became an econo-mic necessity, which in turn triggered efforts at basic education. Missionary schools provided for this basic education, and, in the context of these mis-sions, the first elements of what might be called a publishing industry sprang to life, tightly controlled by the European powers of the day.

Catholic monks started a printing business in Eritrea in the seventeenth century, producing religious texts in Amharic. The Lovedale Press, estab-lished in the Eastern Cape province of South Africa in the 1820s, published books in African languages and encouraged the use of indigenous languages in literature. In general, however, African writers, emerging since the 1920s, did not feature prominently in the early stages of African publishing – they had to look for publishers in Paris or London to make their voices heard. Nine decades on, they still have to do this.

This model of production – European editors controlling the content of books for Africans – was  maintained well into the days of African indepen-dence, and even today, an immense share of African publishing is done by companies either owned by or closely linked to European interests, with Ger-many's Holtzbrinck, through its Macmillan subsidiary, and the UK's Pearson, with Longman, being especially active in the former British colonies. The French do not stand idly by, with the ACCT (Agence de Coopération Cul-turelle et Technique) which today goes by the moniker of 'Organisation inter-nationale de la Francophonie' acting happily as the Légion étrangère of cul-tural imperialism.

'Indigenous' African publishing companies were mainly set up in the after-math of independence, most of them in the form of state-sponsored ventures which served as symbols of national pride – and to make sure that the new-found independence did not translate too quickly into individual thinking.

## The Economics of Publishing in Africa

The first problem one encounters during the preparation of a study of the African publishing industries is the total absence of data, with the exception of South Africa. The most recent effort at collecting data was undertaken by APNET, the African Publishing Network, in 2002 – most of the data collected and presented there cannot be validated and do not prove helpful in getting a picture of what is going on.

Especially to academics, development experts, and lovers of literature, the workings of a publishing house more often than not seem to resemble a question wrapped in a riddle which is part of an enigma. This need not be so – here are the main functions of a proper publisher:

1  Selection: A proper publisher does not simply publish everything that is on offer. The selection, acquisition, and commissioning of material are the key to the editorial process that follows.

2  Finance: A proper publisher does not take payment from authors in order to publish a book, but provides the funding for these projects out of his own resources. A proper publisher is an entrepreneur who does not shy away from risk and does not shelter behind grants and subsidies.

3  Organization: A proper publisher provides the organization that turns a manuscript into the book that the reader holds in his/her hands. This process begins with the acquisition of the text, leading to editorial scrutiny, production, marketing, and distribution. Some of these processes may be outsourced to freelance professionals, but the process itself will be coordinated and controlled by the publisher at any given stage.

4  Marketing: A proper publisher will always target appropriate groups of readers, be they professional or academic or the general mass-market readership. The publisher will know the appropriate channels and instruments and will use them to serve his business interests – which are to sell as many books as possible. This also includes customer management: market intelligence cannot be found anywhere nearly so cheaply and well-targeted as by listening to existing customers.

5  Distribution: A proper publisher will make sure that his books can be found in as many sales outlets as possible. Whereas, in most of Europe and North America, the book retailing sector is highly sophisticated, thanks to intensive efforts by wholesalers and specialized distributors, the majority of African publishers cannot rely on such structures –

which leads to loss of sales and a lack of exposure of the books to their potential readers.

A publishing industry anywhere in the world is only able to thrive in economic circumstances that provide for more than the mere survival of the populace. Over the past few years, Africa has seen a significant economic upturn, with some thirty-five percent of Africans living in economies that have grown at more than four percent a year for ten years running. But this upturn is mainly statistical, created by the scramble for Africa's resources, ranging from oil – crude oil counts for over half of the continent's export earnings – to metals such as copper and aluminium. Africa has also gained substantially from debt reduction, which has freed resources for public investment and has initiated a return of private foreign investment.

But growth based on natural resources is fundamentally and notoriously volatile, endangering those two-thirds of sub-Saharan Africa's countries where one or two products are responsible for at least sixty percent of the country's total exports. And where incomes exist, they are distributed extremely unevenly: in 2005, the richest ten percent of African countries had 18.5 times the GDP per capita of the poorest ten percent. Two countries rule the roost: in combination, South Africa (which, with US$160 billion, boasts the continent's largest GDP) and Nigeria account for fifty-four percent of total sub-Saharan Africa's GDP.

This unevenness translates into rampant poverty, with all the negative effects this has: more than forty percent of all Africans live on less than one US dollar a day. Every year, nearly a million children die of malaria and more than two million children die before they are a month old.

This situation throws down unique challenges for African publishing: the small disposable private incomes severely limit publishers' ability to sell books at profitable prices. The Babylon of languages in most African countries – Nigeria claims 250 languages, and even South Africa lists eleven official languages – combined with low literacy, accounts for the very limited economies of scale that can be achieved in African book publishing. But even where linguistic fragmentation does not pose a problem, as in the case of books published in the former colonial languages, the vast discrepancies between national currencies, huge tariffs on trade between countries, high distribution costs measured against the material value of books, high VAT and tax on books in different countries – all this make publishing a difficult business.

## The Current State of African Publishing

State-sponsored publishing is especially dominant in the educational sector, a fact that has been impeding the development of an independent publishing industry in almost all countries south of the Sahara. Given the fact that some 95 percent of all books produced and distributed in Africa are textbooks, the heavy involvement of state publishing has kept back the emergence of an economic basis for independent publishing very efficiently. And where African governments, owing to financial restraints, fail to deliver, the former colonial powers and the eagerness of international donors combine to provide the kiss of death to independent African publishing, with generous gifts of books, produced mostly by the ever-obliging international publishing behemoths.

Africa imports close to seventy percent of its books and exports less than five percent of its total output. All over Africa, the emergence of independent publishing industries has been expected as a normal part of the countries' development. Therefore, the publishing sector has received scant attention from NGOs and governments alike. Support for publishing infrastructure has been negligible and incentives such as tax concessions, book-industry studies, and subsidies are practically non-existent.

As I have already stated, the African publishing industry is heavily dependent on textbook publishing and procurement by the state and NGOs. Trade publishing is often subsidized by education publishing and depends on sales to state institutions such as public and school libraries. This leads to heavy dependence on state and donor funding, both of which are commercially unsustainable. The orientation along educational curricula makes books less likely to 'travel' across national borders, thus hampering the free flow of books and the establishing of commercially sensible practices such as co-publishing and licensing.

From this, it is clear that, for African publishing to develop in a sustainable way, it has to diversify. Whether this can be done without at least initial financial support is doubtful.

So, setting up a publishing company in such an environment is not easy, and with the notable exceptions of South Africa, Nigeria, and Kenya, independent publishing remains a marginal phenomenon and, in most countries, a company with an annual output of twenty titles is considered large.

But even for those African publishers who dare set up their own companies, the struggle starts with the mere registration, which can take up to a year in some countries. Banks generally regard publishers as bad risks, and credit facilities are almost nowhere available to them. Having secured financing from whatever source for publishing projects, finding a reliable printer who has access to the tools of his trade is the next hurdle. Most governments lend a helping hand by imposing whopping tariffs on the import of paper, ink, and machinery – do we really have a reason to criticize African publishers who opt for the cheap printing facilities in China?

Their gallant efforts at making life difficult for publishers have never prevented governments from formulating one inconsequential books-and-education policy after another. Cue Robert Mugabe: the Zimbabwean strongman announced at the opening of the 1992 Zimbabwe Book Fair that "taxes on books only help to promote stupidity." I attended the ceremony and was much impressed by this statement. But, true to form, the Zimbabwean government followed up this announcement by increasing tariffs on paper, ink, and printing machinery tools, as well as import taxes on books.

The dwindling value of African currencies pushes up import prices for all goods, including books. This normally should create opportunities for indigenous publishers, who would certainly love to fill the gap. But they cannot do so, because of the prohibitive prices for the materials that have to be imported to produce books, which make book production prohibitively expensive in Africa. African publishers tend to have their books produced in China and other havens of cheap printing, which, of course, leads to the fact that African publishers' books are produced at the same prices as those of their European counterparts. World market prices for poor economies: this clearly plays havoc with local pricing and helps to keep readers away from books. Catch-22 is the name of the game.

Once a publisher has overcome all these difficulties and books have been produced and delivered, the real fun starts: distribution. For most African publishers, logistics such as warehousing or dedicated wholesalers only exist as part of the agenda of training seminars held by experts brought in from abroad. Stuffing books into the boot of a car and driving them to whichever point-of-sales is still the most common and most efficient way for many African publishers to get books to the market. Outside the larger cities, this non-system makes books a scarce commodity. One might argue that this does not really matter, as most people in rural areas could not afford to buy books anyway. But this would be cynical, and we don't do cynicism.

## How to Grow the Publishing Industries

Nowhere in Africa can one find the beginnings of a clearly defined strategy for growing the private publishing industries. The elements needed for such a strategy are not that alien: first and foremost, there needs to be a stable consumer base; people who can hardly feed themselves and their families will not be able to buy books. Providing state-produced or imported textbooks is a sure-fire way to kill off any business initiative in the sector.

Second, publishers' revenue is crucial: many Latin American countries have started well-funded book-purchasing programmes which channel public money into the private publishing sector, thus enabling these industries to invest in other segments of publishing and diversify their range. Such purchasing programmes need not be centralized: local authorities will be perfectly able to source books through local booksellers (thus helping to sustain this retail sector), and one might even attach the prerequisite that all state-purchased books should be produced locally – which would help the print industry in a great way. In countries such as Mexico, Brazil or Venezuela, rural libraries have been the main beneficiaries of these purchasing programmes, thus bringing books to people who desperately need them. I have not been able to find a law prohibiting African countries from adopting Latin American strategies.

There is also no reason why African countries should allow the importation of textbooks without levying heavy taxes: the international publishing industry has developed a highly sophisticated licensing system which would allow for stipulations that make sure that only local publishers can provide textbooks. Once again, there is no rule preventing the international behemoths from licensing their books to local partners.

With a stable stream of revenue from private consumers and state-funded purchasing schemes, the private publishing sector could flourish, attracting more entrepreneurs to set up shop, be it as producers, distributors, or retailers. More companies will also provide more employment for qualified staff – the scarcity of suitable jobs for well-trained people is one of the major problems for national development in most African countries. More jobs, of course, mean more money that people will be able to spend – which brings us back full circle to the beginning of my reflections.

Some readers may find my arguments leaning towards protectionism at a time where we all enjoy the benefits of the globalized free market. This may well be so – but in order to develop a healthy African publishing industry, this industry has to be protected until it has been able to develop a sound and sustainable infrastructure.

## Book Fairs in Africa

Book fairs are of crucial importance for the development of national and regional publishing industries, particularly in countries where a proper distribution infrastructure does not exist. And book fairs can be found in almost every African country, mainly serving as large bookshops, allowing for brisk sales to the general public as well as to retailers. Professional elements such as seminars and conferences are sometimes attached, mostly sponsored by donors from Europe and North America. None of these fairs can be called international, and most of them are not commercially sustainable, instead depending on donor and government sponsoring.

How this dependency can go wrong was shown cruelly in the case of the Zimbabwe International Book Fair, which had a brief period of glory in the 1990s, when donors poured in money which helped enable publishers from all over Africa to take part, and the setting-up of the ambitious Indaba conference programme. With the collapse of that country's civil society and economy, caused by the Mugabe regime, the Indaba became a sounding-board for partisan propaganda. Publishers stayed away from the fair, donors withdrew after being kicked out of the country, and the book fair died. Current efforts at reviving the fair have so far not resulted in a return to glory, and one remains doubtful whether the current political situation in Zimbabwe could really be conducive to such an undertaking.

Even the Cape Town Book Fair, which I helped to develop from 2003 onwards, has recently announced a hiatus in its annual rhythm; thanks to blatant mismanagement and financial overstretching, this latest addition to the African book fair calendar may well have bitten the dust.

The following is a selection of book fairs which serve as gathering-points for regional publishers:

Nairobi International Book Fair
(Nairobi; www.kenyapublishers.org)

Nigeria International Book Fair
(Lagos; www.nibf.org)

Cape Town International Book Fair
(Cape Town; www.capetownbookfair.com)

Ghana International Book Fair
(Accra; www.ghanabookfair.com)
Foire du Livre de Dakar
(Dakar; no website available)

## Electronic Publishing: The Way Forward?

In recent years, electronic publishing has developed from being a fad to becoming a vibrant business, at least in the USA, where the 'Big Six' publishing conglomerates – Hachette (Lagardère), Random House (Bertelsmann),
Penguin (Pearson), Simon & Schuster (CBS), Macmillan (Holtzbrinck), and
HarperCollins (News Corporation) – are looking to generate twenty percent
of their revenue from eBooks. Apart from North America, there is not a single
country or region in the world where eBooks have jumped over the 1–3 percent threshold, and for most non-English-speaking regions, the way towards a
significant share of publishers' revenue deriving from eBooks will be long, at
least when it comes to the non-academic, non-professional information segments of the market.

A number of projects have been trying to establish electronic publishing
structures in the academic segment of African publishing – with little or
mixed success at most. The advent of a new generation of smartphones and
electronic reading devices may accelerate the uptake in African countries,
and, at least in theory, this might result in a number of solutions for the most
urgent problems facing the publishing industry. Particularly when it comes to
distribution, electronic publishing could be a feasible way of providing reading and learning materials to consumers in regions that are hard to reach by
road. But, to be honest – these regions also tend to be 'black holes' when it
comes to mobile network capacity.

Online retailing of printed books is also heavily reliant on a working transport infrastructure: if a publisher faces difficulties in getting his books from
one place to another, so will the online retailer. There is a reason for online
behemoths such as Amazon shying away from setting up shop in Latin
America, the Arab world, Africa or Central Asia: their business model would
not work there.

## Conclusion

So, what do we do with all this? Well, the conclusion has to be that the promotion of a robust independent publishing industry in Africa has to be put
firmly on the agenda of national governments, donor agencies, and other
would-be benefactors to the continent's development. So far, funds have
mostly been poured into the setting-up of trade associations and the sponsoring of conferences, mostly on topics such as rights and licences or copy-
right. Just go to any donor's local office and ask for funding. You certainly
get it for a 'Book Policy' project, but hardly ever for anything that could
really make a difference. This, of course, is all right for the legions of (mostly
European) consultants and advisors, who can make a good living from
devising book policies. But it hardly ever trickles down to the people who actually risk their own capital to produce and sell books.

This irritating fixation on the donor's part in strategies and policies may
have to do with legal constraints which prevent them from sponsoring commercial business ventures. The underbelly of publishing – production, editorial, and especially distribution – is hardly tackled at all and desperately needs
attention. Whether investment in prestigious electronic publishing projects,
especially in the academic publishing segment, is the right way to develop a
sustainable publishing industry that one day may be able to put a book in
every child's hands is also a matter for discussion.

The current boom in commodities which has led to high growth-rates in
many African countries provides a unique opportunity: there is money in the
system. For the donors, this clearly means refocusing their attention and tack-
ling their own issues, which restrain them from helping to set up commercially viable publishing businesses that can benefit development as such.

But, despite the very clear situation that Africa's publishing industries are
in desperate need of support, government and donor funding has been dwindling over the past years. APNET, which was set up in the 1990s thanks to
generous donor funding, managed to get a couple of workshops off the
ground before – with donor funding withdrawn – it sank back into its present-
day oblivion.

Publishing has to be regarded as a key industry in the development of Africa. Without books, active literacy is impossible. Illiteracy blocks education
and lack of education stands in the way of development. True independence
can never be achieved if the basis of a country's education is still provided by
the old colonial masters. Independent nations, independent cultures need

books, just as a plant needs water. Without books, nation-building cannot succeed, and civil society cannot emerge.

## FURTHER READING

International Bank for Reconstruction and Development / The World Bank. *African Development Indicators: Spreading and Sustaining Growth in Africa* (Washington D C: World Bank, November 2007).

Altbach, Philip G. "Perspectives on Privatization in African Publishing," in *The Challenge of the Market: Privatization and Publishing in Africa*, ed. Philip G. Altbach (Bellagio Studies in Publishing 7; Chestnut Hill M A: Bellagio Publishing Network, 1996): 3–8.

——, ed. *Publishing and Development in the Third World* (Hans Zell Studies in Publishing 1; London: Hans Zell, 1992).

D A C T S. *The South African Publishing Industry Report* (Pretoria: Department of Arts, Culture, Science and Technology, November 1998).

Darko–Ampem, Kwasi Otu. "Scholarly Publishing in Africa: A Case Study of the Policies and Practices of African University Presses" (doctoral dissertation, University of Stirling, 2003).

Davies, Wendy. *The Future of Indigenous Publishing in Africa: Seminar Report* (Uppsala: Dag Hammarskjöld Foundation, 1996).

Makotsi, Ruth L. "Book Trade in Africa: Potential and Problems," *African Publishing Review* 7.4 (July–August 1998): 1–3.

Ngobeni, Solani, ed. *Scholarly Publishing in Africa: Opportunities and Developments* (Pretoria: Africa Institute of South Africa, 2010).

Wafawarowa, Brian. "The Business of Book Publishing in Africa," paper presented at the W I P O International Conference on Intellectual Property and the Creative Industries, Geneva, 29–30 October 2007 (Geneva: W I P O, 16 October 2007).

Zegeye, Abebe, & Maurice Vembe. "Knowledge Production and Publishing in Africa," *Development Southern Africa* 23.3 (September 2006): 333–49.

◄❖►

BRIAN CROW

# Charisma and Leadership in African Drama

U SED SO OFTEN AND SO INDISCRIMINATELY IN THE MEDIA, the word 'charisma' may seem to be of no real intellectual value at all. In Britain, David Cameron, it seems, has 'charisma' – that is, until the political editorialists deem that he has lost it; Gordon Brown, it seemed, couldn't lose it because he never had it. Tony Blair once had it, but it seemed to wear off rather badly as the Iraq debacle went on. Margaret Thatcher, even if you hated her (and a lot of us did), undeniably had something, and charisma is one word for it. President Nicolas Sarkozy of France apparently has it, or would like to force this impression on people, Chancellor Angela Merkel of Germany doesn't. In spite of the prestige invested in his office, George W. Bush was, for most people, including even many who once voted for him, the very antitype of the charismatic. What on earth are the political commentators on about? Is their notion of charisma really nothing more than the capacity to combine political shrewdness with a certain amount of sex appeal? When it is attached so often, so arbitrarily, and often so ephemerally to public figures – as shrewdness or physical attractiveness ebbs away – it seems fair to reject, or at best attach no more than trivial significance to, the word itself.

And yet charisma represents a central concept in the thinking of the most influential of modern political sociologists, Max Weber. Weber thought that, historically, there had been three "pure types of legitimate authority" – the traditional (resting on the sanctity of immemorial traditions), the rational (depending on normative rules), and, adapting the word from the vocabulary of early Christianity in which it signified the God-given gift of grace, the charismatic. In striking contrast to both patriarchal and bureaucratic systems – which at least have in common permanent structures fashioned to meet the demands of a normal routine – the charismatic is antipathetic to the very notion of routine, of form or ordered procedures, or even of the 'rational economic conduct' characteristic of the other two systems.[1] Weber defines it thus:

> The term "charisma" will be applied to a certain quality of an individual personality by virtue of which he is set apart from ordinary men and treated as endowed with supernatural, superhuman, or at least specifically exceptional powers or qualities. These are such as are not accessible to the ordinary person, but are regarded as of divine origin or as exemplary, and on the basis of them the individual concerned is treated as a leader. In primitive circumstances this peculiar kind of deference is paid to prophets, to people with a reputation for therapeutic or legal wisdom, to leaders in the hunt, and heroes in war. It is very often thought of as resting on magical powers. (48)

By its very nature, charismatic authority is unstable, since pure charisma does not know any legitimacy other than that flowing from personal strength:

> The charismatic hero does not deduce his authority from codes and statutes, as is the case with the jurisdiction of office; nor does he deduce his authority from traditional custom or feudal vows of faith, as is the case with patrimonial power. (22)

On the contrary, the charismatic leader has authority "solely by proving his strength in life," performing miracles or heroic deeds for the greater well-being of his followers. Psychologically, submission to the authority of the charismatic leader arises from complete personal devotion, from a belief in that leader's wholly exceptional and infallible powers. It follows that if, for some reason, the object of this devotion fails over a period of time to produce the goods for his followers, or is otherwise revealed as something less than god-like, his charismatic authority is likely to drain away. Also, even though genuine charisma and routine are by nature absolutely opposed, Weber identifies what he calls the "routinization" of charisma:

> It is the fate of charisma, whenever it comes into the permanent institutions of a community, to give way to powers of tradition or of rational socialization. This waning of charisma generally indicates the diminishing importance of individual action. And of all those powers that lessen the importance of individual action, the most irresistible is *rational discipline*. (28)

---

[1] Max Weber, *On Charisma and Institution Building: Selected Papers*, ed. & intro. S.N. Eisenstadt (Chicago & London: U of Chicago P, 1968): 21. Unless otherwise indicated, further page references are in the main text.

Charisma, in other words, is always at risk of being emasculated of its dangerously creative, heroic, individual quality and of being institutionalized – usually, Weber suggests, because of economic factors, and above all by the need of privileged followers or successors of the charismatic leader to have their position legitimized. "Routinized charisma thus continues to work in favor of all those whose power and possession is guaranteed by that sovereign power, and who thus depend upon the continued existence of such power" (40).

Weber's 'scientific' treatment of the concept of charisma is in some ways as unsatisfactory as its unscientific usage in the modern media. As Kwame Anthony Appiah points out,

> part of the difficulty with Weber's work is that, despite the wealth of historical detail in his studies of religion, law, and economics, he often mobilizes theoretical terms that are of a very high level of abstraction.[2]

Appiah notes the looseness of Weber's very definition of the term charisma, with its disjunction between qualities that are invoked as supernatural, superhuman, and "of divine origin," on the one hand, and merely "exceptional" or "exemplary," on the other. When the magico-religious aspect of charisma often seems so crucial to Weber's thinking, it is a large – and definitionally rather disastrous – concession to secularism to reduce the concept to not much more than 'out of the ordinary'. There is also a lack of clarity in Weber's account of how, precisely, charisma is generated. Weber writes as though charisma is an actual quality possessed by the charismatic person – something real that his or her followers are duly awed by. But if, as he points out, the charismatic leader fails to benefit those who hold him in such awe, then he is liable to lose his charisma – which surely means that charisma is at least as much, if not more so, in the eye of the beholder as in the one beheld.

For all its unresolved difficulties, however, the concept of charisma does seem to be an essential one. Whatever it was or is, a variety of leaders and other public figures, historically and in our own time, have projected a charismatic quality that other leaders and public figures, just as certainly, have lacked. Napoleon, Hitler, Stalin, Mao – few would claim that they did not

---

[2] Kwame Anthony Appiah, *In My Father's House: Africa in the Philosophy of Culture* (New York & Oxford: Oxford UP, 1992): 146. For Appiah's discussion of Weber's notion of charisma in the context of postcolonial and, more specifically, African modernity and postmodernism, see 144–47.

have it, whatever one thinks about the ways they used it. Martin Luther King and Nelson Mandela have been unquestionably charismatic for many of us alive today, in many different countries and cultures. And as I write, the world's most powerful nation has a leader who has already created history by achieving what many thought still impossible, and becoming the first black president of the USA. Barack Obama is unquestionably regarded, even by those who dislike him politically, as a charismatic figure. And this charismatic quality was undoubtedly a highly significant factor, first in his triumphing over the powerful, immensely well-organized Clinton machine for the Democratic nomination, and then in his presidential victory over John McCain. If, as Weber notes, charisma, as a creative power, tends to recede in the face of the dominance of permanent institutions, it nevertheless reveals its own power "in short-lived mass emotions of incalculable effects, as on elections and similar occasions" (39). How short-lived Obama's appeal will be we are yet to discover, but there is no doubt that in the run-up to the US presidential election of 2008 he succeeded in generating an extraordinary degree of emotion in large swathes of the American electorate. He also did what Weber regarded as characteristic of charismatic authority, which is to repudiate the past and to make his pitch for being the harbinger of decisive change. In the process he presented voters with the profound impression of personal revelation. Weber thought genuine charisma knows "only inner determination and inner restraint" and in general rejects "all rational economic conduct."[3] No modern politician can do such a thing, especially in the midst of a credit crunch and the onset and continuing presence of recession. But as viewers around the world watched Obama's acceptance speech, and we surveyed the faces of his audience as they were picked out by the cameras, it was evident that the appeal of this man goes well beyond routine policy into the utopian territory of spiritual hope – of something like a redemptive promise.

Only time will tell if Obama will be a charismatic figure who does not disappoint the expectations now invested in him.[4] What is certain, however, is that the continent that helped produce him, and, in the person of Nelson Mandela, fostered the most universally admired and charismatic figure of our times, has also witnessed a succession of leaders whose appeal has likewise

---

[3] Weber, *On Charisma and Institution Building*, 21.

[4] Some of the shine has been rubbed off him thanks to Republican intransigence and such constraints as have led to his retention of Guantánamo, but this has been offset by his decisiveness in the removal of bin Laden; swings and roundabouts.

been based on 'charisma', but in ways that have proved to be debased, often grotesque, and sometimes truly horrific in their destructiveness. Among the African political monsters who have either genuinely stimulated charismatic belief or cultivated a 'charismatic' personality cult to win or preserve their power are Joseph Désiré Mobutu of Zaire, Idi Amin of Uganda, Jean–Bedel Bokassa of the short-lived Central African 'Empire', and – still hanging on as I write – Robert Mugabe of Zimbabwe. Early nationalist leaders who enjoyed charismatic reputations, at least for part of their sometimes unfortunately long time in power, include Kwame Nkrumah of Ghana, Jomo Kenyatta of Kenya, Hastings Banda of Malawi, Felix Houphouët–Boigny of Ivory Coast, and Kenneth Kaunda of Zambia. And there are other leaders, too, whose political influence, for good or ill, has involved a strong element of charismatic appeal for their followers – to offer only a random selection, Jerry Rawlings in Ghana, Charles Taylor in Liberia, Steve Biko and Chief Buthelezi in South Africa, and Joseph Kony, the messianic (and psychopathic) leader of the Lord's Resistance Army in northern Uganda. I am not suggesting that there is anything uniquely African about the charismatic element in political leadership, since, evidently, charisma has exerted its power elsewhere, especially perhaps in Arab and Asian politics, whether spontaneously or in carefully constructed forms, as popular support has been cynically elicited and manipulated (though the popular uprisings in the Arab world give reason for hope, despite the knock-on danger, from Syrian intransigence, of autocratic restoration). But it is striking to what extent in post-independence Africa the destiny of the young nation has been identified with the personality and qualities of one individual, whether this has happened because of genuine popular acclaim, or because the populace has been coerced into it, or, in some cases, as a combination of the two.

◄❖►

Much African literary drama has been broadly political in its concerns, and, not surprisingly, given the continent's modern history, it has been especially preoccupied with issues of leadership. My particular interest in this essay is in trying to trace at least some of the main ways in which African playwrights have dramatized the 'problem' of leadership, and specifically in analysing the element of charisma in their characterizations. What sorts of things do they have to 'say' about the nature and function of leadership in the postcolonial African nation? How far do their representations of African leadership reflect the important role of charisma – spontaneous or constructed (or a mixture of both) – in actual politics? And to what extent do their portraits of leadership subscribe to the notion of charisma as an indispensable element in the development of modern African statehood?

As we know, a major function of the intellectual struggle against colonialism and neocolonialism has been the African revision of imperialist conceptions and interpretations of the continent's history. In the face of the prevailing Western view – that Africa had no history to speak of, or that it was, at best, a narrative of uncivilized ignorance and barbarity – African intellectuals and a few sympathetic Western historians in the period leading up to and following political independence in the late 1950s and early 1960s sought to expose the myth of African non-history and to provide a dignified historical basis for contemporary African identity and aspirations. In terms of the stage, this gave rise to one of the most popular and pervasive of African dramatic forms, the history play. In the French-speaking countries especially, literary dramatists celebrated the lives and deeds of warrior-kings largely designed to convey, as one critic puts it, "a living sense of pre-colonial African societies at their most glorious," as well as to lament, in their protagonists' defeat, "a tragic sense of lost heritage."[5] As they rewrote the imperialist narratives of such men as Shaka to translate him from barbarous tyrant to founder of a great African nation, or unearthed historical or legendary figures ignored in Western accounts of the African past, African playwrights inevitably committed themselves to identifying what history had to teach about the qualities crucial to successful nation-building in the present. A striking feature of their dramatic analyses is the central significance they attach to the presence and exercise of charisma in African leadership.

An early and thoughtful example of the francophone history play dealing with the charismatic leader is Seydou Badian's *La Mort de Chaka*,[6] published in 1962. Badian's play dramatizes two radically opposing views of Chaka, one that sees him as a destructive, bloodthirsty madman driven by his megalomanic desire for personal glory and the other as the self-sacrificing hero who cares only for his people and the Zulu nation and who is prepared to die, for their sake, at the hands of traitors. In the first of the play's five 'tableaux', the case against Chaka is forcefully put during a conclave by his generals. His fiercest critics accuse him of having built the Zulu nation only at the cost of

---

    [5] John Conteh–Morgan, *Theatre and Drama in Francophone Africa: A Critical Introduction* (Cambridge: Cambridge U P, 1994): 62.

    [6] Seydou Badian, *La Mort de Chaka* (Paris: Présence Africaine, 1962).

enormous suffering and the shedding of an enormous amount of blood, both of Zulus and of their enemies. Those who are more sympathetic to him, though troubled by his ruthless love of war, remind the others that their very existence, let alone prestige, as a nation is entirely built on Chaka's leadership. No one doubts his extraordinary and charismatic qualities. When one of the generals, Mhlangana, advocates getting rid of Chaka without delay, he tells his colleagues:

> You know what he is like. Nothing can stop him, nothing can make him change his mind. The greatness and the power of the Zulu people, the people of the sky, come first. Only Chaka, invested by Nkulunkulu, the Almighty, with the sacred mission of leading his people, may make decisions, give orders and command. Chaka alone rules.[7]

Though his words are meant to be derogatory, they articulate a truth reinforced by the entire play from which no one, including the dramatist, demurs. In the eyes of friend and foe alike, Chaka is the sole inspiration of Zulu greatness, combining the functions of father, teacher, and protector as well as superhuman warrior. Forced, after a long march, into yet another battle against a formidable coalition of enemies, Chaka's generals finally rebel. Having allowed the generals to state the case against their leader, Badian proceeds to enlist audience sympathy unequivocally with Chaka. Through Notibe and the warrior Ndlebe, we hear that Chaka's ruthlessness is more than outweighed by his achievements and extraordinary human qualities, and what appeared earlier to be the generals' valid objections to butchery and mass suffering are now presented as being motivated primarily by jealousy and self-seeking. In his tense exchanges with the dissident Mhlangana, Ndlebe is made to state what is evidently the authorial case for Chaka:

> If we are what we are, it is because we have had a leader who knew how to organize us, who knew how to guide us, who knew how to give the whole people that confidence without which there can be no victories. Cattle don't interest me. Cattle can die from sickness, cattle can be attacked and destroyed by wild animals. Beads don't interest me; they can be stolen. But the pride I bear with me today belongs to me. No one can take it from me. (111)

---

[7] Seydou Badian, *The Death of Chaka*, tr. Clive Wake, intro. Richard Bjornson (*La Mort de Chaka*, 1962; tr. in *Faces of African Independence: Three Plays*, Charlottesville: UP of Virginia, 1988): 99. Further page references are in the main text.

Chaka does not himself appear on stage until the third 'tableau'. When he does, he is not the ferocious force of nature that we have been led to expect. He tells his confidant Isanusi that he feels "strangely weary and sick at heart" (115), and Ndlebe's news of the warriors' revolt only confirms the "knowledge [that] has weighed heavily upon me" (117), that his generals aren't with him. In the course of this tableau and the next, Chaka bestirs himself from his weariness, prompted by the adulation of his followers and his own reiteration of his divine mission. Badian has his protagonist regularly speak of himself in the third person, creating a curious effect as though 'Chaka' were a persona somehow different from, and something more than, the individual person standing there, speaking with others. And this tendency in his mode of address is enhanced by what he says, which repeatedly articulates a spiritual existence and destiny that transcends his physical being. "But I know Chaka will never die," he says; a new generation of young men will "rise towards the sun with heart and mind of Chaka" (118). The Lord of the Deep Water, he tells us, has assured him that "Already you bear in you the greatness of your people," with the power to rule nature ("the rivers and the mountains") and subdue even the birds and beasts. The future of his people, even, depends on a kind of continuous spiritual reincarnation of himself: "Henceforth Chakas will be born throughout the history of our people, for no other kind of man will be able to command the Zulus" (121). But, having once again crushed his enemies and led his people to another great military victory, Chaka suffers, more than ever, from a sense of weariness and despondency. Mystically foreseeing his imminent assassination, he makes a valedictory address to his followers, telling them that the Zulus are cut out for greatness "because they know how to obey, because they know how to deprive themselves, because they have endurance" (126). But before they reach a new dawn they will have to endure a dark night of turmoil, torture, and humiliation. As he dies at the hands of his three assailants, he has the last word: "You are murdering me so as to take my place. You are too late. Unlungu, the white man, is on his way. You will be his subjects" (127).

When Badian wrote his play he was already Mali's Minister of Rural Development and Planning, committed, as so many were in that period, to an optimistic belief in the power of so-called African socialism to bring rapid progress. The official vision of socialism in Modibo Keita's Mali was only a version of an ideology held by many African intellectuals and politicians in the period immediately following independence – a conviction that a strong state, directed by a powerful leader, could plan and execute economic growth

and initiate a modernized version of the communal values thought to be traditional to precolonial African societies. The Chaka of Badian's play is presented as the historical exemplar of the Kwame Nkrumahs, Sekou Tourés, Gamal
Abdel Nassers and others of the African continent, dedicated in his lonely,
heroic way to the ennoblement of his people in the face of enemies within and
without. Charisma is crucial to this kind of African socialism. Just as Chaka is
presented by Badian as inspiring zealotry in the people and envious hatred in
the elite, so in the post-independence period did African leaders such as those
named above willingly participate in a cult of personality designed to establish beyond doubt their function as individual power-house of the revolution,
and thus their indispensability to the young state.

*The Trial of Dedan Kimathi* was written somewhat later (1974) and in a
quite different political and ideological context from Badian's *La Mort de
Chaka*. In the Kenya of Ngũgĩ wa Thiong'o and his co-dramatist Micere
Githae Mugo, the rhetoric of 'African socialism' was cynically juxtaposed
with the reality of a neocolonial order that energetically pursued capitalist
values and strategies. For its authors, the significance of the Mau Mau leader
Kimathi is his exemplary status as the champion of the Kenyan people against
not just the British colonial authorities but the African (and Indian) servants
of neocolonialism. In Ngũgĩ's and Mugo's radical nationalist view of the oppression of the Kenyan (and, by extension, other African) people, violence –
symbolized in the central device of the gun hidden in the loaf of bread – is a
necessary and legitimate weapon in the struggle against imperialism and the
African quest for justice. But while Badian's Chaka and the Kenyan playwrights' Kimathi represent very different conceptions of leadership – broadly
speaking, one 'African socialist', the other 'Marxist' – it is striking how indebted they both are to a notion of the charismatic.

In this materialist, radical-nationalist version of African history, Kimathi's
mission cannot be presented as divinely inspired, but he is like Badian's
Chaka in being god-like, with the power to work 'miracles' and to affect
Nature itself and, perhaps most strikingly of all, to engender a spiritual reproduction of himself in those who follow after him:

BOY:        … But is it true what they also say?
WOMAN:   What?
BOY:        [*becoming really excited*]: They say … they say he used to talk
            with God.
WOMAN:   Yes. The fighting god in us – the oppressed ones.

BOY:      They say … they say that he could crawl on his belly for ten
          miles or more.
WOMAN:    He had to be strong – for us – because of us Kenyan people.
BOY:      They say … they say that he could change himself into a bird, an
          aeroplane, wind, anything?
WOMAN:    Faith in a cause can work miracles.
BOY:      They say … they say that the tree under which he used to pray
          fell to the ground?
WOMAN:    There are people, my child, with blessed blood. And when some-
          thing happens to them, the wind and the rain and the sun will tell.
          Even hyenas. Their death can shake mountains and give life to
          the volcanoes long thought to be dormant.
BOY:      Maybe they only captured his shadow, his outer form … don't
          you think? … and let his spirit abroad, in arms.
WOMAN:    Your words contain wisdom, son. Kimathi was never alone …
          will never be alone. No bullet can kill him for as long as women
          continue to bear children.[8]

Although the playwrights are at pains to translate religious and magical
notions into the materialist terms of political struggle, they cannot refrain
from ascribing miraculous charisma to Kimathi and his actions: his blood is
"blessed" and Nature itself – "the wind and the rain and the sun will tell" – is
affected by it. Kimathi, in his third 'trial', resolutely rejects the Priest's Christian interpretation of Scripture as being about spiritual and not earthly struggle
for a commitment to violent struggle against oppression inspired by "the God
of my ancestors" (49). Nevertheless, the entire play is a reworking of the central Christian myth, with its protagonist as the charismatic Christ-figure who
is prepared to sacrifice himself for the salvation of his people. But the redemptive symbol of the bread, in this case, conceals the gun, while the temptation of Christ in the wilderness becomes Kimathi's "trials" as the agents of
neocolonialism try to win him over and his human kindness towards those,
like his own brother, who are prepared to betray the struggle, makes him temporarily vulnerable. Ideologically, Dedan Kimathi is the exemplary embodiment, as well as one of the leaders, of mass struggle rather than the authority
figure who alone directs the masses to achieve genuine nationhood, as in *La
Mort de Chaka*. But, ideology notwithstanding, for Ngũgĩ and Mugo as much
as for Badian the struggle for authentic national liberation and/or

---

[8] Ngugi wa Thiong'o & Micere Githae Mugo, *The Trial of Dedan Kimathi* (London:
Heinemann, 1976): 20–21.

development is presented in fundamentally charismatic terms, the political triumph of the semi-divine martyr-hero.

◄❖►

The issue of leadership has, not surprisingly, been a persistent one in African public discourse generally, and in its drama in particular. I can do no more than suggest here that the concept of charisma has been central to some of the most significant dramatic explorations of this issue. Although numerous plays and playwrights could be examined in support of this assertion, I will restrict my attention to Wole Soyinka, whose dramatic oeuvre has, more consistently and in greater depth than anyone else's, explored charismatic leadership in relation to the urgent need for drastic political change in Africa. I believe that much of Soyinka's dramatic writing over many years could be productively examined in terms of the idea of charisma – an idea that has itself been enriched through his efforts. But I will concentrate on only two plays, *Kongi's Harvest* (1967) and *Death and the King's Horseman* (1975), in my attempt to sketch what I take to be the basic tenor of Soyinka's thinking about charismatic leadership in Africa.

Soyinka wrote *Kongi's Harvest* only a few years after Badian composed *La Mort de Chaka*, but his portrayal of the supposedly benign authoritarianism of 'African Socialism' could hardly have been more different, or more unflattering. The play is a mordant satire on African leaders like Ghana's Nkrumah and Malawi's Hastings Banda whose apparently once principled direction of nation-building was already descending into self-aggrandizing despotism. Soyinka offers a portrait of a leader who, though he may once have been admirable, is now simply besotted with power for its own sake and, even though devoid of the real thing, is intent on manufacturing the illusion of charisma to legitimate his tyrannical rule. This he does through his Reformed Aweri Fraternity, a modernized version of the traditional ruler's council of elders. The hollowness of Kongi's posture of solitary charismatic rule is exposed by the cynicism and hopelessness of the so-called Fraternity, which is no more than a bunch of squabbling intellectuals on the make. Central to the play's action as well as to the empty charade of charismatic leadership is Kongi's arrogation of the traditional ceremony of the New Yam, with himself as "the Spirit of the Harvest" accepting the New Yam in an act of public submission by the traditional ruler, Oba Danlola. Although Danlola initially objects firmly to having anything to do with what he recognizes as a degrading piece of political theatre, he is persuaded by his young nephew and heir,

Daodu, to agree to it so that he and his lover Segi can subvert Kongi's out-
rageous and blasphemous project by substituting Daodu as the spirit of natural
fertility, who will give a brief "sermon on life … love …" (99) in spectacu-
larly public opposition to the tyrant.

   *Kongi's Harvest* exposes the absurdity of Kongi's (and his real life ilk's)
pretensions to charismatic leadership but, significantly, it does not offer a
critique of the notion of charisma itself. On the contrary, Daodu is presented
as the charisma-inspired progressive of the play, who owns a farm on which
he has established a "farmer's community" that has been genuinely successful
in both its productivity and its worker satisfaction, in contrast to the dismal
failure of Kongi's state farms. But the main source of Daodu's enlightened
leadership is more personal than social or political. It derives from his love
affair with the beautiful Segi, the mysterious, seductive woman who functions
as a charismatic muse, now for Daodu and once, in the past, for Kongi himself when he was genuinely "a great man."[9] As well as being Daodu's lover,
Segi is also the daughter of one of Kongi's main political opponents, who has
been detained and is now awaiting execution. She is a kind of political muse,
associated with whatever it is that makes men act in a principled way for the
well-being of their society. Although Daodu has his moments of despair, or at
least despondency, and is sceptical about how effective his and Segi's plan to
subvert Kongi's political theatre can be, he is constantly re-energized not only
by his erotic desire for her but by her dangerous but exalting aura. Soyinka
endows her with a poetic, mythic quality; she is a profoundly sensual, fertile
queen of the dark underworld (figured in the play by her nightclub). Such is
her superhuman determination and spiritual integrity that she is even presented as being able to behead her own father, after he has been shot by Kongi's
people in the abortive coup, and serve it up on a copper salver, like a latter-
day Salome, to the terrified tyrant.

   The epilogue of *Kongi's Harvest*, entitled "Hangover," is predominantly
bleak about the effect of Daodu and Segi's actions and the prospects for the
future, with a final image of the descending iron grating and its ominous clang
as it hits the ground. Segi's conviction that the only antidote to Kongi is a
gospel of love and life is certainly reinforced by the play through its depiction
of her charisma, but it seems to bear little or no tangible fruit. What seems
clear, however, is that without at least the energy and commitment inspired by

---

   [9] Wole Soyinka, *Kongi's Harvest* (New York: Oxford UP, 1967); quotation from
*Kongi's Harvest* is from *Collected Plays 2* (London: Oxford UP, 1974): 99.

her charismatic personality and its influence on others, notably Daodu, there would be no hope at all of political change. *Kongi's Harvest*, then, seems to indicate not only the importance of the idea of charisma in Soyinka's perceptions of and thinking about leadership in modern Africa but also its complex ambivalence for him. On the one hand, there is a fake charisma that is nevertheless an effective weapon in the armoury of the new African despots for oppressing their own people; on the other, there is a genuine charisma that, though apparently offering the only hope of inspiring drastic change, is less than convincing in its results.

In the many plays Soyinka has written since the mid-1960s, when he wrote *Kongi's Harvest*, his fascination with charisma and the charismatic personality has remained constant. In a succession of dramatic satires, Soyinka has continued from where he left off in *Kongi's Harvest* in pillorying Africa's military and civilian leadership for its grotesque abuses of power, among others in *Opera Wonyosi* (first performed in 1977), *A Play of Giants* (1984), *From Zia, With Love* (1992), and *King Baabu* (2001). Central to Soyinka's anatomizing of power and its abuses on the continent has been his exposure of their attempted constructions of fake or destructive charisma, often aided and abetted by corrupted members of the academic and religious elite. Sometimes, the latter, with their own pretensions to charismatic leadership, are the primary objects of Soyinka's satirical venom, notably in *Jero's Metamorphosis* (1973) and *Requiem for a Futurologist* (1983). But when he has written about power and leadership in a tragic mode he has remained no less preoccupied by the complex ambivalences of charisma, in the process creating a rich variety of flawed charismatic protagonists, including Professor (in *The Road,* 1965), the Old Man (in *Madmen and Specialists*, 1971), and Elesin Oba in what has become, internationally, Soyinka's best-known and certainly most anthologized play, *Death and the King's Horseman* (1976).

◄❖►

Nothing that I know of more powerfully and lyrically theatricalizes and celebrates the nature of the charismatic bond than the opening scene of *Death and the King's Horseman*. In writing of great dramatic brilliance, Soyinka evokes through speech, dance, and spectacle what Weber called the "peculiar kind of deference" paid by the followers of the charismatic individual to those "supernatural, superhuman, or at least specifically exceptional powers or qualities" with which he is perceived as being endowed. As the Praise-Singer celebrates Elesin in the market-place in the first scene, he tells his listeners that "there is only one world to the spirit of our race" and goes on to ask the play's most insistent question: "If that world leaves its course and smashes on boulders of the great void, whose world will give us shelter?"[10] Elesin's confident response is: "It did not in the time of my forebears, it shall not in mine." But Soyinka gradually undercuts the women's joyful celebration of Elesin's charismatic 'honour' and the assurance of a fundamental continuity his life and ritual death provides for his people. Elesin's play-acting, when he feigns angry offence at wearing the same clothes he arrived in half an hour before (315), creates the first break in the celebratory mood, to be followed by the far more serious one of his insistence on taking as his bride Iyaloja's beautiful (and already betrothed) daughter. Even though the problem is resolved it is at the cost of a definite change of mood and tone, exemplified in the final exchanges between Elesin and Iyaloja and his, according to the stage direction, "*exasperated*" response to her reminder of his imminent death (323). What the scene does, then, is to establish Elesin's charismatic presence and significance for his community, but also to hint at vulnerability. And that vulnerability derives from the communal recognition, insistently articulated by the Praise-Singer, that the preservation of their whole way of life, their whole 'world', depends on the personality and actions of this one individual. As Weber points out, it follows that if the charismatic leader "fails over a period of time to produce the goods for his followers, or is otherwise revealed as something less than god-like," then his charismatic authority can drain away or disappear at a stroke. If Soyinka evokes with beautiful lyricism the charismatic bond between the exceptional individual and his followers, he also dramatizes with great power what happens when those followers traumatically lose their faith in his charismatic infallibility. There is Iyaloja's withering contempt, and his own son's startlingly pitiless response – "I have no father, eater of left-overs." And there is Elesin's own terrible recognition of what his failure means: "The world is set adrift and its inhabitants are lost. Around them, there is nothing but emptiness" (367).

When he faces the contempt of Iyaloja, Elesin acknowledges that

> My powers deserted me. My charms, my spells, even my voice lacked strength
> when I made to summon the powers that would lead me over the last measure

---

[10] Wole Soyinka, *Death and the King's Horseman* (New York: Hill & Wang, 1975); quotations from *Death and the King's Horseman* in *Contemporary African Plays*, ed. Martin Banham & Jane Plastow (London: Methuen, 1999): 309. Further page references are in the main text.

of earth into the land of the fleshless. You saw it, Iyaloja. You saw me struggle to retrieve my will from the power of the stranger whose shadow fell across the doorway and left me floundering and blundering in a maze I had never before encountered. (372)

When she retorts that she had given him due warning of the risks he ran in renewing his attachment to worldly desires, Elesin is made to expand on what above all else immobilized him – a kind of ontological crisis beyond the pleasures of the flesh:

What were warnings beside the moist contact of living earth between my fingers? What were warnings beside the renewal of famished embers lodged eternally in the heart of man. But even that, even if it overwhelmed one with a thousandfold temptations to linger a little while, a man could overcome it. It is when the alien hand pollutes the source of will, when a stranger force of violence shatters the mind's calm resolution, this is when a man is made to commit the awful treachery of relief, commit in his thought the unspeakable blasphemy of seeing the hand of the gods in this alien rupture of his world. I know it was this thought that killed me, sapped my powers and turned me into an infant in the hands of unnameable strangers … My will was squelched in the spittle of an alien race, and all because I had committed this blasphemy of thought – that there might be the hand of the gods in a stranger's intervention. (374)

Elesin's failure, then, is not due simply to his attachment to sensual pleasure or to the physical intervention by the colonial authorities but to something more complex and elusive – a disastrous debilitation of the will whereby he loses his compelling vitality and it becomes possible to rationalize the natural temptation to choose life over death as somehow sanctioned by the ancestral spirit-world, using the colonial power as its instrument. There is more than one kind of dramatic oddness in this. One has to do with the fact that, even though Elesin, outwardly at least, did everything required of him (though admittedly a little belatedly because of his lust) and was well embarked on his dance into the ancestor-world when he was seized by Pilkings and his men, everyone – his son, Iyaloja, and the Praise-Singer, even Pilkings – seems to intuit a personal failure in him that amounts to a profound abdication of his responsibility and represents the most contemptible treachery. But even if one puts this reservation aside, one inevitably asks: where did this fatal sapping of the will come from? And why does it, at the crucial moment, afflict the man for whom the "unnameable strangers" have always been unambiguously the enemy, and with whom, in any case, he seems to have had little or no contact?

Conversely, why has the young man who had such contact – who, much more than his father, has had a foot in both traditional African and modern Western worlds – proved quite immune to the infection of this "awful treachery of relief," "this blasphemy of thought?"

Weber's writings on charisma suggest one possible answer to these questions. Although routine and charisma are in most respects incompatible, Weber identifies a process which he calls "routinization," in which charisma is institutionalized, mainly for the benefit of followers of the formerly charismatic leader who wish to legitimize their privileged position. Although this does not itself happen in *Death and the King's Horseman,* a statement Weber makes in connection with the process would seem to be pertinent:

> It is the fate of charisma, whenever it comes into the permanent institutions of a community, to give way to powers of tradition or of rational socialization. This waning of charisma generally indicates the diminishing importance of individual action. And of all those powers that lessen the importance of individual action, the most irresistible is *rational discipline.*[11]

Weber tends to see charisma, tradition, and modern bureaucratic rationalism as constituting three distinct categories. But since, in his view, charismatic authority is "specifically outside the realm of every-day routine and the profane sphere," it is " sharply opposed both to rational, and particularly bureaucratic, authority, and to traditional authority, whether in its patriarchal, patrimonial, or any other form" (51). One could argue, however, that, as in *Death and the King's Horseman,* traditional authority may be blended with charismatic authority, at least in situations where that authority is itself threatened by powerful and hostile external forces, such as colonialism. People may look to leaders who seem to exhibit exceptional powers or qualities in such contexts precisely because they are perceived as being capable, through their charisma, of preserving the established but endangered order of things. But, of course, when the preservation of the traditional order depends on the strength of mind and will of one man alone – when, as Weber puts it, the charismatic leader has authority "solely by proving his strength in life" – then that order is in a profoundly vulnerable position. When he confesses to Iyaloja that he has committed "the unspeakable blasphemy of seeing the hand of the gods in this alien rupture of his world," turning him into "an infant in the hands of unnameable strangers," is it not precisely the inevitable diminishing of charisma,

---

[11] Weber, *On Charisma and Institution Building,* 28.

and with it of individual action, at the hands of irresistible "rational discipline" that Elesin is describing?

◁❖▷

Only a much fuller examination of Soyinka's drama would do justice to the
scope and complexity of his thinking about the significance of charisma and
charismatic leadership in Nigeria and Africa more generally. And if we were
to take only Soyinka's native country, a reasonably adequate account of the
subject would need to take in the work of other major Nigerian dramatists,
particularly Ola Rotimi, who over a long career before his untimely death in
2000 explored his preoccupation with the theme of leadership in Nigeria, and
the place of charisma within it, in plays ranging from *The Gods Are Not To
Blame*, *Kurunmi*, and *Ovonramwen Nogbaisi* of the late 1960s and early
1970s through *If* and *Hopes of the Living Dead* in the 1980s to *Akassa You
Mi*, the revised version of which was published after his death. And it would
be interesting and productive, I think, to compare Soyinka's and Rotimi's
treatments with the work of a rather younger but clearly major contemporary
such as Femi Osofisan, whose work implicitly – and sometimes explicitly –
takes issue with perspectives on charisma evident in plays of the older generation. A broader survey of the topic, embracing experimental theatre, especially in francophone Africa, would involve consideration of the concern
evinced in more recent postcolonial avant-garde theatre with the need for
democratic participation in politics whose artistic analogue has been collectively devised 'alternative' performance. As Conteh–Morgan points out, it is
the "leader-as-messiah/father model of politics [...] with its almost inevitable slide into paternalism and authoritarianism, that is rejected by the postcolonial avant-garde."[12] However true this is, there is no escaping the simple
fact that, in the conditions of neocolonial and underdeveloped modernity
prevailing in Nigeria and elsewhere, the fate of society has been in the hands
of those at the top, who have generally proved conspicuously unresponsive to
the needs of those beneath them. It is sadly the case that, while there are of
course popular movements that have been instrumental in African political
struggles, the making of African history has all too often been the result of the

---

[12] John Conteh–Morgan, "The Other Avant-Garde: The Theater of Radical Aesthe-
tics and the Poetics and Politics in Contemporary Africa," in *Not the Other Avant-
Garde: The Transnational Foundations of Avant-Garde Performance*, ed. James M.
Harding & John Rouse (Ann Arbor: U of Michigan P, 2006): 114.

impact of individual figures. Just as it would be perverse to play down the enormous effect of Stalin on twentieth-century Russian history, or of Mao on Chinese history, so it would be a disfiguring of African history to underrate the quite disproportionate impact the personalities and charisma of a Nkrumah, a Mobutu, a Kenyatta, an Idi Amin or a Mandela have had on the political development of their countries and, in some cases, of the continent as a whole. Such individuals range from the genuinely heroic to the monstrously criminal, but it is not the *nature* of their qualities that is at issue so much as their impact on national and in some cases continental life, simply by virtue of their existence. If the over-determination of African history by exceptionally powerful individuals rather than, in general, by organized popular movements is a fact, then it may only be a demonstration of political realism by play-wrights that their drama has sometimes been dominated by such figures. For it to be ideology rather than realism, it would be necessary to demonstrate that the possibilities for interpreting a particular historical moment in terms of genuinely popular struggle have been ignored or discounted in favour of the charismatic 'great man' approach.

## WORKS CITED

Appiah, Kwame Anthony. *In My Father's House: Africa in the Philosophy of Culture* (New York: Oxford U P, 1992).

Badian, Seydou. *The Death of Chaka*, in *Faces of African Independence: Three Plays*, tr. Clive Wake, intro. Richard Bjornson (*La Mort de Shaka*, 1962; tr. Charlottes-ville: U P of Virginia, 1988).

Conteh–Morgan, John. "The Other Avant-Garde: The Theater of Radical Aesthetics and the Poetics and Politics of Performance in Contemporary Africa," in *Not The Other Avant-Garde: The Transnational Foundations of Avant-Garde Performance*, ed. James M. Harding & John Rouse (Ann Arbor: U of Michigan P, 2006): 92–124.

——. *Theatre and Drama in Francophone Africa: A Critical Introduction* (Cambridge: Cambridge U P, 1994).

Ngugi wa Thiong'o & Micere Githae Mugo. *The Trial of Dedan Kimathi* (London: Heinemann, 1976).

Rotimi, Ola. *The Gods are not to Blame* (Ibadan: Oxford U P, 1971).

——. *If: A Tragedy of the Ruled* (Ibadan: Heinemann, 1983).

——. *Kurunmi* (Ibadan: Oxford U P, 1971).

——. *Ovonramwen Nogbaisi* (Benin City: Ethiope, 1974).

Soyinka, Wole. *Death and the King's Horseman* (New York: Hill & Wang, 1975).

——. *From Zia with Love* (London: Methuen, 1992).

——. *Jero's Metamorphosis* (London: Eyre Methuen, 1973).

——. *King Baabu* (London: Methuen, 2002).

——. *Kongi's Harvest* (Ibadan: Oxford U P, 1967).

——. *Madmen & Specialists* (London: Methuen, 1971).

——. *Opera Wonyosi* (London: Rex Collings, 1981).

——. *A Play of Giants* (London: Methuen, 1984).

——. *Requiem for a Futurologist* (London: Rex Collings, 1985).

——. *The Road* (London & New York: Oxford U P, 1965).

Weber, Max. *On Charisma and Institution Building: Selected Papers*, ed. & intro. S.N. Eisenstadt (Chicago & London: U of Chicago P, 1968).

❮❖❯

JÜRGEN MARTINI

# The Little White Ship

T HIS IS FOR GEOFF, in fond recollection of a symposium in Erlangen decades ago. You listened to my customarily untidy thoughts and nodded your appreciation (as I have appreciated yours over all these years). Here they are, then. With a minimum of tidying up.

❖

Edgar Wallace and film: the most movie adaptations of any writer.

Highbrow literature treated the British Empire with scepticism bordering on hostility. The Empire and imperialist attitudes were judged to be hollow, repressive, hypocritical. For the population at large, the Empire continued to be important: it served as a mythic landscape for romance and adventure. To read the epic of Empire was to experience excitement and stimulation in their purest form.

That Zoltan Korda movie from 1935[1] – quintessential action, not emotion; action that concerns the Empire, not Britain. The myth of Empire serves as the vehicle for excitement, adventure, the fulfilment of longing and desire.

A world of men in which love, passion, women play a wholly subordinate role.

A *Boy's Own* yarn.

---

[1] *Sanders of the River* (dir. Zoltan Korda; starring Paul Robeson, Leslie Banks, and Nina Mae McKinney; London Film Productions, UK 1935, 98 min.).

Wallace and Korda's movie: it is no longer the claiming of Empire that's the issue, but its administration. Central themes are governance and the defence of what was conquered/acquired.

Important concepts: character, attitude.
Justification is sought for the Empire: it is morally superior; the superior British emerge as a mixture of gentlemanly behaviour and the maintenance of an ostensibly disinterested system of law, order, and justice. This generates the oft-described illusion that the Empire will never die.

Sanders as symbol: a pipe-smoker, full of good humour (towards Africans and Europeans alike). Someone to look up to. Singlehandedly, he brings peace and order, through sheer force of personality, or almost.

Simplified images, simplified situations; an excess of simplicity. The myth of the superman in its human variant: something, it would seem, attainable by anybody and everybody.

The *Sunday Times* on the film: it reveals "a sympathy with our ideals of colonial administration, giving us a grand insight into our special English difficulties in the governing of savage races, and providing us with a documentary film of East African nature in its raw state, a picture which could not be improved upon for the respect it displays to British sensibilities and ambitions."[2]

Wheeler Winston Dixon characterizes Wallace's narratives as providing a blueprint for the ideology of 'divide and rule', which, in his tales, is juxtaposed with the consolidation and observance of the law.[3]

The man on the spot, the man who knows what to do about restrictive laws that don't suit the situation, or about the interference of politicians.

---

[2] Sydney Carroll, *Sunday Times* (7 April 1935), quoted in Jeffrey Richards, "Boy's Own Empire: Feature Films and Imperialism in the 1930s," in *Imperialism and Popular Culture*, ed. John M. MacKenzie (Manchester: Manchester UP, 1986): 152; also quoted in Anthony Aldgate & Jeffrey Richards, "The Sun Never Sets: *Sanders of the River*," in Aldgate & Richards, *Best of British: Cinema and Society from 1930 to the Present* (1999; London: I.B. Tauris, 2002): 32–33.

[3] Wheeler Winston Dixon, "The Colonial Vision of Edgar Wallace," *Journal of Popular Culture* 32.1 (Summer 1998): 121–39.

Absolute faith in the superiority of the white race (despite examples to the contrary). Education for blacks – rejected. Humanitarian treatment of blacks – not an option.

Sadism: the whip, the fist, etc.

"Native folk [...] are but children of a larger growth."[4]
"'Nothing tires me quite so much as a Europeanised–Americanised native. It is as indecent a spectacle as a niggerised white man'."[5]

Connection with stereotyped images of blacks: Bosambo as Uncle Tom.

The basic scheme: the use of force, aggression, sadism.

A male world into which women only erupt destructively, whether they are white or black. If they are white, they destroy racial equilibrium; they are obscene in the way they yield to darkness. If they are black, they represent the danger of seductiveness and destructiveness; they overcome and bewitch all that is insipid, boring, rational, playing evil tricks.

"Women have an evil effect upon warriors."[6]

Wallace is no longer occupied with the penetration of darkest Africa as symbol of the feminine, but with the constant reserve and chasteness of his male heroes; an almost Catholic-celibate posture. The friendships that are struck up are male friendships with no homoerotic undertones. Only in the Bones stories is a white female Other introduced, sitting at home in the motherland and waiting for letters. But this immediately takes on a satirical cast.

Sanders as the archetypal colonial viceroy:
"I am as your father and your king, being placed here to rule you by a man who is very high in the council of kings."[7]

---

[4] Edgar Wallace, *Keepers of the King's Peace: A Sanders story* (1917; Kelly Bray, Cornwall: House of Stratus, 2001): 103 (ch. 8), borrowing from John Dryden, *All for Love* (1678) IV.i.

[5] Edgar Wallace, *Bosambo of the River* (London: Ward, Lock, 1914): 59 (Sanders, in ch. 3, "The Rise of the Emperor").

[6] Wallace, *Bosambo of the River*, 178 (ch. 11, "They").

The symbolic significance of the Maxim gun: the white technology of the white race. The requisites of power are stereotypical, simple, and reinforced by all manner of symbols. The *Zaire* will never let itself be put off course; a small number of loyal Houssas are always in attendance; modern communications technology is replaced by simpler means, particularly carrier pigeons; clairvoyance is as much a stock-in-trade as Sanders' clearsightedness.

The analogy with medieval morality plays and Shakespeare's Renaissance: the balance of the world, the cosmic order, is disturbed and must be restored, by force. At the end, a provisional state of peace has been achieved; the serial nature of the narratives, with their relentless fresh delivery of the same, demands temporary peacemaking, not final solutions.

Sanders' behaviour drives a rift through the population: there is only unconditional love, unconditional hatred, no nuances in-between. Rebellion is an attack by darkness on light, which must be protected: countless examples drive this message home.

"I am the law," said Sanders, and his voice was softer than ever. "If I say thus, it is thus."[8]

Unerring confidence in knowing the true character of the African, and the cultivation of self-control: what is the purpose of this? As proof of the need to enforce white imperial European rationality, thereby legitimizing oppression.

Sanders is represented as acting altruistically, without material interests, but at times tolerating the latter in the case of Bosambo, this mixture of trickster and Uncle Tom: as long as the trickster's self-enrichment is the positive kind endorsed by the imperial power, as long as he accepts the separate spheres, he does not need to be put in his place. But the Maxim gun is visible at all times.

What justification is there for this seeming indifference? It is a matter of meting out paternal discipline to people who are still in their infancy, are eager to grow up, but are and will remain kept hovering on the threshold of maturity.

---

[7] Edgar Wallace, *The People of the River* (London: Ward, Lock, 1912): 55 (ch. 7, "The Thinker and the Gum-Tree").

[8] Edgar Wallace, *The People of the River*, 38 (ch. 5, "Brethren of the Order").

Symbiosis between supply and demand: Sanders embodies all human virtues and is selfless enough to pass them on. The blacks are children and want to be instructed and governed.

Sanders stands apart from other colonialists, who fail to deal with the children entrusted to them with paternal discipline.

The natives of the country: these exist solely as construct and mirror, for the chief focus is on the colonial masters, who are to be identified with. The natives of the country possess no identity other than what is accorded them by their colonial masters. They are positively eager to find an existence for themselves through the agency of their colonial masters, a meaning for their lives that they themselves would never have thought to seek.

Marianna Torgovnick: the landscape is there to be entered and conquered.[9] In contrast to H. Rider Haggard, the imaginary landscape in Wallace is not psychoanalytically explicable – not on the same level, at any rate. However, it is striking that Wallace's landscapes, too, are feminized ("lush").

The colonial master treats the colonial landscape and its inhabitants with the same patriarchal attitude as he treats women: "The coloniser is to the colonised as the male is to the female, as active is to passive, white is to dark, the rational is to the intuitive."[10]

Sanders as colonial schoolmaster and instructor: alone, heroic, a bulwark, father rather than tyrant, hence educator, who will at some time or other in the future lead Africa the child into adulthood. The military brutality inflicted is the educative punishment meted out to people who are unwilling to submit, and at once the instrument applied to raise ever-new father figures.

Doug Killam: points to parallels/models in Cutliffe Hyne's novels.[11]

---

[9] See Marianna Torgovnick, "Traveling with Conrad," in Torgovnick, *Gone Primitive: Savage Intellects, Modern Lives* (Chicago: U of Chicago P, 1990): 154–57.

[10] Robert H. MacDonald, citing Marianna Torgovnick in MacDonald, *The Language of Empire: Myths and Metaphors of Popular Imperialism, 1880–1918* (Manchester: Manchester UP, 1994): 35.

[11] G.D. Killam, *Africa in English Fiction, 1874–1939* (Ibadan: Ibadan UP, 1968): 35–42 passim.

The structure of the stories: in order to keep the reader involved, the stereo-typical nature of the situations requires ever fresh inventions, distortions, ridi-culously exaggerated moments of drama. The events are travesties of actual occurrences. Just as the events are caricatures, so are the natives who populate the country and serve as the backdrop for the colonial masters. The eternal return of the same, which must needs lose its power of suggestion, as the inceptive situation of master and servant must always stay the same because no room is allowed for change, and can only be kept attractive by changing the personnel on the governing side. Here Wallace quite rightly saw that the problem couldn't be solved by introducing a Sanders Mark II, but that a con-trast had to be created (Bones as silly ass). Colonialism and its manifold bene-factions in no wise suffer thereby, as the godlike authority of Sanders can always be called upon via carrier pigeon or other devices.

With the gradually mounting number of stories (there are 102 in all), the nar-rator has to play an increasingly central role. He is an omniscient narrator who accompanies the action through commentary and manipulation, enjoys him-self at the expense of the characters, even the white ones, but would have to admit that the favours he bestows on the Africans are temporary and can always be withdrawn, and that when he makes fun of the whites (Bones), this occurs from the secure vantage point of an equality undetectable by the out-sider. The narrator does not question colonialism as such, only the clumsiness and immaturity of some of its father figures.

What we have here is a genre of popular literature that the reader experiences as a cross between the historical novel and the adventure story. The historical and its contemporary interpretation by the reader provide the matrix within which the adventure can unfold. For the reader, it is ideologically a matter of indifference whether the adventure action is historically based, is transmuted into something exotic, or takes place close to home; the main thing is that the exotic lends particular charm to the insistent presence of the ideological over-lay.

The division into serious literature and popular literature emerges for the first time in the Edwardian age, thanks to the increasing publication of stories in the penny dreadfuls. Popular literature does without psychologically subtle portraits, replacing these with episodic, cliff-hanging escapism. The lone wolf as never-questioned, never self-questioning hero. The colonial genre is constructed along lines similar to those of the ubiquitous romantic novel, but with a different readership. Popular adventure literature addresses the male reader, the settings being too brutal, too exotic, too 'illicit' for feminine taste. The characters conspicuously lack complexity – which is a positive feature, as any deflection from 'flatness' would mean the final restoration of peace and order. The themes and their treatment in popular literature constitute, at the same time, first steps towards the ideologization undertaken by the medium of film, which is much more immediately effective than the mass dissemination of the printed word.

*Chums* as penny dreadfuls in which Wallace's novels are reprinted (in serial parts).

These adventure stories can be read as popular or 'pulp' versions of the novel of personal development, the boy's growth to maturity, the European variant of the initiation narrative. At the same time, the reader is initiated into the ideological world of imperialism, an enclosing grasp that he cannot and should not escape. Although the reader is presented with many different adventures, their construction is always the same. Everything turns on revolt and rebellion, power and its implementation, self-interested engagement with Nature and the Other, the ways in which Africa's peoples 'play' with magic and myth (recalling the play of children, which can be tolerated and indulged for a time), but which 'play' is staged, something that can and must come to a sudden end. The one-dimensional nature of the characters: white innocence, immaculate, tireless, a trickster who disguises himself like Haroun al Rashid, who can change the colour of his skin; Wallace's Sanders merely feigns individuality.

Wallace's stories are male fantasies, fantasies of masculinity, of the struggle to achieve resistance to the temptations of the fair sex and of other whites who stick their noses in one's business – particularly the missionaries, towards whom the narrator is benevolently disposed but to whom Sanders is opposed.

Sanders is an autocratic ruler who runs no danger of suffering the fate that befalls Conrad's Kurtz.

Narrative style: cinematic editing, each action sequence is interrupted by a fresh one until the point is reached where the step-by-step unravelling of the riddle yields up the true chief culprit – like crime novels, this is how adventure tales are constructed.

Passage from Margaret Lane's biography: "He would outline a chain of incidents to a certain point, break off, and begin an apparently independent story; then another, and another; at the crucial point the several threads would meet and become one."[12]

Of interest in this connection is Willy Haas's analysis of the technique employed by Wallace in his crime novels:[13] "a certain number of ever-returning, unchanging types and worlds." Haas describes Wallace's cosmos as hierarchically ordered architecture, and traces the popularity of Wallace's books to what Christian Enzensberger later characterized as the search for meaning,[14] something that can also be related to the effectiveness of ideology.

Lane also writes that Wallace "made no notes, beyond a list of the characters' names, and he spun the complicated thread of his plot as he went along." When writing serials, "he rarely knew, from one instalment to the next, what was likely to happen."[15]

Popular literature creates myths and mythic figures. This makes the heroes of these myths part of a literary heritage of mythology that settles in the collective memory.

---

[12] Margaret Lane, *Edgar Wallace: The Biography of a Phenomenon* (1935; Garden City NY: Doubleday, Doran, 1939): 181.

[13] "Eine gewisse Anzahl von immer wiederkehrenden, unveränderlichen Typen, jeder ganz genau auf seiner Stelle in einer dieser vier Welten stehend"; Willy Haas, "Die Theologie im Kriminalroman: Ein paar Notizen über Edgar Wallace und die Kriminalliteratur überhaupt," *Literarische Welt* 26 (1929). Repr. in *Der Kriminalroman: Zur Theorie und Geschichte einer Gattung*, vol. 1, ed. Jochen Vogt (Munich: Wilhelm Fink, 1971): 118–19.

[14] For Enzensberger, reading 'belles lettres' "is the fictive satisfaction of a desire for meaning" ("ist fiktive Befriedigung von Sinnbedürfnis"); Enzensberger, *Literatur und Interesse: Eine politische Ästhetik mit zwei Beispielen aus der englischen Literatur*, 2 vols. (Frankfurt am Main: Suhrkamp, 1969–77), vol. 2: 61.

[15] Lane, *Edgar Wallace: The Biography of a Phenomenon*, 232.

Sanders is: superhuman, larger than life, a one-dimensional silhouette; good triumphs over evil. All this is invented, and the invention is plain to the eye yet appears to the reader as inscrutable.

The significance of John Cawelti's analysis of adventure as one of the variants of the formula story. Heroism under the sign of an uncertain world, in a construction in which the imagined world makes its escapism transparently clear yet veils it. The escapism necessarily differs according to the target audience.[16]

The analysis of colonialist literature will produce the following: the white colonial master is all-powerful yet vulnerable. He rules over the native inhabitants but also needs to have them live their own lives in order to keep on exercising mastery over them. This ideological construction repeatedly generates the urgent need to demonstrate to the implied reader of the stories that what is presented to him is his own story, his own philosophy and mind-set.

What does the black man represent? contamination, infection, bewitchment.
The colonial gaze: investigation, amused contemplation, the transfixed stare, the pseudo-ethnographic description.
Couples, passersby: male bondage. Interactive men, who exist as doubles of each other, seemingly free of any taint of the homosexual.
Quest and identity.
Seeing oneself reflected in the mirror of other whites, the doubling, the contrast. The bond (male) between reader and narrator.

Contrasts: the West as strength, self-control, rationality, mastery over Nature. In contrast to the black man: feminine, weak.
The Other. Images of things that remain nameless, masses of people that blur into uniformity, tracts of jungle that seem impassable, the sense of sinking. And over and above all this, the reassuring stability of the little white ship.

— Translated from the German by Gordon Collier

---

[16] John G. Cawelti, *Adventure, Mystery, and Romance: Formula Stories as Art and Popular Culture* (Chicago: U of Chicago P, 1977): 39–40.

## WORKS CITED

Aldgate, Anthony, & Jeffrey Richards. "The Sun Never Sets: *Sanders of the River*," in Aldgate & Richards, *Best of British: Cinema and Society from 1930 to the Present* (1999; London: I.B. Tauris, 2002): 19–36.

Cawelti, John G. *Adventure, Mystery, and Romance: Formula Stories as Art and Popular Culture* (Chicago: U of Chicago P, 1977).

Dixon, Wheeler Winston. "The Colonial Vision of Edgar Wallace," *Journal of Popular Culture* 32.1 (Summer 1998): 121–39.

Enzensberger, Christian. *Literatur und Interesse: Eine politische Ästhetik mit zwei Beispielen aus der englischen Literatur*, 2 vols. (Frankfurt am Main: Suhrkamp, 1969–77).

Haas, Willy. "Die Theologie im Kriminalroman: Ein paar Notizen über Edgar Wallace und die Kriminalliteratur überhaupt," *Literarische Welt* 26 (1929). Repr. in *Der Kriminalroman: Zur Theorie und Geschichte einer Gattung*, vol. 1, ed. Jochen Vogt (Munich: Wilhelm Fink, 1971): 116–22.

Killam, G.D. *Africa in English Fiction, 1874–1939* (Ibadan: Ibadan U P, 1968).

Lane, Margaret. *Edgar Wallace: The Biography of a Phenomenon* (1935; Garden City N Y: Doubleday, Doran, 1939).

MacDonald, Robert H. *The Language of Empire: Myths and Metaphors of Popular Imperialism, 1880–1918* (Manchester: Manchester U P, 1994).

Richards, Jeffrey. "Boy's Own Empire: Feature Films and Imperialism in the 1930s," in *Imperialism and Popular Culture*, ed. John M. MacKenzie (Manchester: Manchester U P, 1986): 140–64.

*Sanders of the River* (dir. Zoltan Korda; starring Paul Robeson, Leslie Banks, and Nina Mae McKinney; London Film Productions, U K 1935, 98 min.).

Torgovnick, Marianna. "Traveling with Conrad," in Torgovnick, *Gone Primitive: Savage Intellects, Modern Lives* (Chicago: U of Chicago P, 1990): 141–58.

Wallace, Edgar. *Bosambo of the River* (London: Ward, Lock, 1914).

——. *Keepers of the King's Peace: A Sanders story* (1917; Kelly Bray, Cornwall: House of Stratus, 2001).

——. *The People of the River* (London: Ward, Lock, 1912).

◄❖►

ELMAR LEHMANN

# "The Fateful 13"
## Sol Plaatje and the Natives' Land Act

> This appeal is [...] on behalf of five million loyal British
> subjects who shoulder "the black man's burden" every day,
> doing so without looking forward to any decoration or thanks.[1]

I N MAY 1914, A DEPUTATION WHICH INCLUDED THE REV. JOHN L. DUBE,
president of the South African Native National Congress (SANNC,
renamed ANC in 1923), and its general secretary Sol T. Plaatje, left for
England "to appeal directly to the King, to the British parliament and, if need
be, to the British public"[2] in order to secure "an imperial veto on the Land
Act."[3] Between June 1913, when the Natives' Land Act came into operation,
and the delegation's departure, Plaatje attended Congress meetings, conversed
with government officials, made arrangements for the journey to England,
and toured South Africa to investigate the consequences of the Act. He edited
*Tsala ea Batho* (*Friend of the People*), and in an "Editorial" (3 January 1914)
looked back on the year 1913, quoting Jeremiah's Lamentations (5:4) – "We
have drunken our water for money; our wood is sold unto us"[4] – and bitterly
echoing another verse from the same source – "Our inheritance is turned to

---

[1] Sol T. Plaatje, *Native Life in South Africa before and since the European War and
the Boer Rebellion*, intro. Brian Willan, preface by Bessie Head (Johannesburg: Ravan,
1982): 19.

[2] Brian Willan, *Sol Plaatje: South African Nationalist, 1876–1932* (London: Heinemann, 1984): 164.

[3] Willan, *Sol Plaatje*, 163.

[4] Sol T. Plaatje, *Selected Writings*, ed. Brian Willan (Johannesburg: Wits UP, 1996):
173.

strangers, our houses to aliens" (5:2) – when he summed up the post-Land Act situation of Africans: "we are serfs in the employ of such aliens."[5]

On board ship, Plaatje spends much of his time "compiling a little book on the Natives' Land Act and its operations,"[6] and, on further reflection, later adds chapters on the South African War and World War I as well as on the Afrikaner Rebellion of 1914.[7] These additional chapters are clearly oriented towards the British public. Plaatje reminds his readers of the unwavering African loyalty in the face of Afrikaner commandos invading the Cape Province in 1899,[8] and the wholehearted support offered by the Africans vis-à-vis the disloyalty and rebellion of large sections of the Afrikaner population in 1914.[9] Plaatje appeals for imperial protection on behalf of his African compatriots,[10] while at the same time warning the British public that for white South Africans, both of Dutch and of English descent, "the claims of South Africa come first and those of the Empire afterwards" or, worse, that for them the Empire only exists to be sucked dry and "like an orange" to be thrown away.[11]

The invocation of the imperial factor and of benign British rule as embodied in the (severely restrictive) Cape franchise for Africans is a strategy frequently employed in African political writing of the period. In the early years of the twentieth century (c.1902), Magema M. Fuze, who was educated at Bishop John W. Colenso's Natal mission station and according to Trevor Cope lived "at the forefront of the clash of cultures, values and interests,"[12] on the one hand admonishes his readers:

> When we began to be roused by foreign peoples, we then thought that we had sprung from the same source as they, ceasing to observe our own ways and respectful customs [...]. I now warn you to abandon all this pretence because it is no benefit whatever. Adhere strictly to your own.[13]

---

[5] Plaatje, *Selected Writings*, 173.

[6] "Native Congress Mission to England," in Plaatje, *Selected Writings*, 176.

[7] Plaatje, *Native Life*, 18.

[8] *Native Life*, Chapter 19.

[9] *Native Life*, Chapters 20–23.

[10] *Native Life*, Chapter 16.

[11] *Native Life*, 306.

[12] "Editor's Preface," in Magema M. Fuze, *The Black People and Whence They Came: A Zulu View*, tr. H.C. Lugg, ed. A.T. Cope (Pietermaritzburg: U of Natal P, 1998): xi.

[13] "Exhortations," in Fuze, *The Black People*, viii.

On the other hand, he almost uncritically welcomes the advent of the whites, Christianity, and 'civilization' in Africa, and emphatically quotes Bishop Colenso, who reassures Africans that

> It is well that [they] should know that the Queen [Victoria] will certainly not allow them to be treated unjustly, deprived and despised, or to be driven forcibly from the lands on which they are settled by her permission.

Still in Colenso's words, Fuze adds: "The Queen wants her black people to be taught the trades of the white people, so that they may have a stake in the country like the white people."[14] It is almost unbelievable that Fuze – and Colenso, for that matter – should not have noticed the well-nigh obscene irony of this reassurance.

Silas M. Molema, who is rather dismissive of the African past, harshly criticizes the Union of South Africa – "To the coloured peoples it was a death-knell of a long tottering identity" – and, very much like his friend Plaatje, interprets the Natives' Land Act as "reducing the Bantu people to serfdom."[15] Nevertheless, he still praises the native policy of the Cape,[16] and concludes a section headed "The Balance Sheet" thus:

> With that Imperialism, not in its narrow and selfish sense, but in so far as it presents a high political morality, with that Imperialism [Africans] identify their supreme material good.[17]

Faced with Prime Minister Hertzog's native bills of 1926, D.D.T. Jabavu celebrates the bygone days of Cape liberalism – "the ministers of Queen Victoria [...] made Britons of all civilised black men under the Union Jack in a uniform equality of citizenship with all other British subjects elsewhere in the Empire" – and calls the Cape franchise "a treasured gift of justice inherited from Queen Victoria, the Good."[18]

---

[14] Fuze, *The Black People*, 88.

[15] Silas M. Molema, *The Bantu Past and Present: An Ethnographical & Historical Study of the Native Races of South Africa* (Edinburgh: Green & Son, 1920): 246, 249. See also Wolfgang Gebhard, *Shades of Reality: Black Perceptions of South African History* (Essen: Die Blaue Eule, 1991): 38–42.

[16] *The Bantu Past and Present*, 246–47.

[17] *The Bantu Past and Present*, 321.

[18] Davidson D.T. Jabavu, "The Disfranchisement of the Cape Native" (1927), *The Segregation Fallacy and Other Papers (A Native View of Some South African Inter-Racial Problems)* (Lovedale: Lovedale Institution Press, 1928): 30, 44.

Despite his lingering belief in this imperial factor, Plaatje, with characteristic slyness, undermines the grandiloquent claims of British imperial rule
when he offers his readers a particularly apposite comparison:

> If by Home Rule to Ireland it is intended to give the franchise to a selfish,
> greedy and tyrannical few; and give *carte blanche* to these few, telling them
> thereby to do what they wish with the rest of the population of Ireland, and
> telling them further that they will be accountable to nobody for any good
> legislation that they might enact on the one hand, or any maladministration that
> they might perform on the other hand as is the case in South Africa – if that be
> what is meant by Home Rule for Ireland, then God have mercy on the Irish.[19]

Even though Molema and Plaatje squarely blame the Natives' Land Act on
the "strong racial broom" of ex-republican Afrikaners,[20] they can hardly fail
to notice that already with the Union of South Africa – with the South Africa
Act of 1909, to be precise – Britain had "unreservedly handed over the
natives to the colonists,"[21] that is, to those "selfish, greedy and tyrannical
few." His faith in the imperial government and parliament severely shaken,
Plaatje becomes aware of a problem which Fanon describes in "The Trials
and Tribulations of National Consciousness":

> History teaches us that the anticolonialist struggle is not automatically written
> from a nationalist perspective. Over a long period of time the colonized have
> devoted their energy to eliminating iniquities such as forced labour, corporal
> punishment, unequal wages, and the restriction of political rights. This fight for
> democracy against man's oppression gradually emerges from a universalist,
> neoliberal confusion to arrive, sometimes laboriously, at a demand for nation-
> hood. But the unpreparedness of the elite, the lack of practical ties between
> them and the masses, their apathy and, yes, their cowardice at the crucial
> moment in the struggle, are the cause of tragic trials and tribulations.[22]

*Native Life in South Africa* is much more than simply a brilliantly persuasive,
albeit in the end unsuccessful, appeal to the British public. It is also, and more
importantly, Plaatje's attempt to reassess his cherished ideals and to come to

---

[19] Plaatje, *Native Life*, 237.

[20] *Native Life*, 29; Molema, *The Bantu Past and Present*, 246.

[21] *Native Life*, 25; Molema, *The Bantu Past and Present*, 244–45.

[22] Frantz Fanon, *The Wretched of the Earth*, tr. Richard Philcox, foreword by Homi
K. Bhabha, preface by Jean–Paul Sartre (*Les Damnés de la terre*, 1961; New York:
Grove Weidenfeld, 2004): 97.

terms with his role as a representative of his nation.[23] In Brian Willan's words,

> [The Natives Land Act] generated in him a sense of anger and betrayal far deeper than anything hitherto, a feeling of disbelief, too, that fellow human beings could be so callous about the consequences of their actions. It was almost as though there was a sense of responsibility on his own part for having misjudged government ministers, many of whom he knew quite well by now – the men responsible for the passage of such inhuman legislation. Plaatje's response to the Land Act seems to have given him a deeper, more emotional sense of identity with the people he represented than had existed before.[24]

When, in the course of his investigation into the operations of the Land Act, Plaatje arrives at Thaba Nchu (September 1913), he interrupts his eyewitness account and inserts a brief historical sketch,[25] which is of particular interest because it covers much of the same ground to be found in *Mhudi*, the novel written shortly after the completion of *Native Life*. The sketch is no less important in other respects. Plaatje turns to an especially formative period in the history of his own nation, the Rolong under Chief Moroka in the late 1820s and 1830s.[26] The theme of the episode of the encounters between the Rolong, Mzilikazi's Ndebele, Hendrik Potgieter's Voortrekkers, and Moshoeshoe's Sotho is, significantly, the battle for land with large-scale migrations and forced removals. Finally, Plaatje recounts an historical period where the various groups, whether black or white, interact as independent agents desperately trying to survive in a time of turmoil.

"The life-story of Moroka is really the genesis of Barolong education as well as the history of their friendship with the Boers."[27] One wonders: is the obvious sarcasm confined to the "friendship with the Boers" or does it extend to "Barolong education" as well? Or does the proudly advertised achievements of Rolong education (medical men, agricultural demonstrators, authors, teachers, priests)[28] turn sour as a result of that friendship? Or are Boer

---

[23] See Laura Chrisman, "Fathering the Black Nation of South Africa: Gender and Generation in Sol Plaatje's *Native Life in South Africa* and *Mhudi*," *Social Dynamics* 23.2 (September 1997): 61.

[24] Willan, *Sol Plaatje*, 165.

[25] Plaatje, *Native Life*, 126–31.

[26] See Plaatje's article on Moroka, written in 1931, in *Selected Writings*, 406–13.

[27] Plaatje, *Selected Writings*, 413.

[28] *Selected Writings*, 409.

friendship and Rolong education inextricably and tragically interwoven? Plaatje certainly realizes that the two histories, the education process starting with the advent of missionaries, and the expropriation process characteristic of Boer friendship, are indeed closely linked: "Two Wesleyan missionaries had joined [the Rolong] as vanguards of the white population, now owning the Free State and Transvaal."[29] He realizes that, by implication, the intimate relationship between the two developments seriously affects the position of educated Africans, whose role Molema describes as "the interpreters, the demonstrators and exponents of the new and higher civilisation to their struggling brethren."[30]

Routed by the Ndebele, Moroka's branch of the Rolong, after long years of migration, finally settles at Thaba Nchu at the outskirts of Moshoeshoe's Sotho kingdom.[31] With such an experience of warfare, flight, and dislocation behind them, they immediately commiserate with, and generously support, the *voortrekkers* who seek refuge at Thaba Nchu after having been defeated and robbed of all their livestock by the Ndebele. Rolong and Boers eventually form an alliance against their common enemy and succeed in driving the Ndebele to the north. The short- and long-term consequences of this alliance and of Boer friendship are disastrous for all the African nations involved.[32] The Ndebele kingdom in the north will be brutally destroyed by Cecil Rhodes's British South Africa Company (in the 1890s). Rolong friendliness is exploited by the Boers in their land-grabbing activities against the Sotho, who are gradually driven back to what is now mountainous Lesotho and who will have to seek British protection (i.e. annexation) after Moshoeshoe's death (in the 1870s). After Moroka's death in 1880, Thaba Nchu will fall easy prey to the rapacious Orange 'Free' State – Plaatje, except when his articles are published in the white press, invariably uses inverted commas to signal his contempt for the Afrikaner republic/province, which he prefers to call the "Only Slave State."[33]

The historical sketch serves as prehistory and analogy of the post-Land Act situation. In Plaatje's view, African internecine strife (the Ndebele onslaught

---

[29] Plaatje, *Selected Writings*, 407.

[30] Molema, *The Bantu Past and Present*, 317

[31] See Molema, *Montshiwa 1815–1896: Barolong Chief and Patriot* (Cape Town: Struik, 1966): 24–32.

[32] See Plaatje, *Native Life*, 129–31; and Molema, *Montshiwa*, 35–58.

[33] Plaatje, *Native Life*, 76.

and the Sotho–Rolong disunity as well as the frequent fights for succession after a chief's death), and African virtues (their hospitality and generosity towards strangers as well as their willingness to welcome missionaries and accept a new civilization) are unscrupulously taken advantage of by the Europeans and result, first, in the loss of independence and, finally, in a "war of extermination against the blacks."[34] The collective experience of dislocation and migration of whole nations in the early-nineteenth century mirrors and intensifies the common experience of thousands of homeless and starving families victimized by the callous Natives' Land Act. This long and painful history of oppression and suffering at the hands of the whites foregrounds the burning question of African national unity, but also of a common bond between the educated elite and the masses. It is this question which Plaatje as general secretary of the S A N N C addresses in his eyewitness account of the operations of the Land Act.

Fanon offers a scathingly critical description of what Molema proudly calls "exceptional men":[35]

> The colonized intellectual has thrown himself headlong into Western culture. Like adopted children who only stop investigating their new family environment once their psyche has formed a minimum core of reassurance, the colonized intellectual will endeavor to make European culture his own. Not content with knowing Rabelais or Diderot, Shakespeare or Edgar Allen [sic] Poe, he will stretch his mind until he identifies with them completely.[36]

In what is arguably the most impressive chapter of his eyewitness account, Plaatje makes extensive use of his intimate knowledge of Shakespeare.[37] The epigraph of the chapter is a slightly, but effectively, adapted quotation from Shylock's famous "To bait fish withal" speech,[38] where Plaatje substitutes "Kaffir" for "Jew" and "white Afrikander" for "Christian."[39] In the central passage of the chapter's argument he then completely rewrites Shylock's exasperated accusations:

---

[34] Plaatje, *Native Life*, 173; and *Selected Writings*, 151.

[35] Molema, *The Bantu Past and Present*, 317.

[36] Fanon, *The Wretched of the Earth*, 156.

[37] Plaatje, *Native Life*, 136–51; this is Chapter 9: "The Fateful 13."

[38] William Shakespeare, *The Merchant of Venice*, III.i.47–66.

[39] Plaatje, *Native Life*, 136.

Have we not delved in their mines [...]? Are not thousands of us still offering
our lives and our limbs in order that South Africa should satisfy the white
man's greed [...]? Have we not quarried the stones, mixed, moulded and
carried the mortar which built the cities of South Africa? [...] Have we not
obsequiously and regularly paid taxation every year, and have we not supplied
the treasury with money to provide free education for Dutch children in the
'Free' State and Transvaal, while we had to find additional money to pay the
school fees of our own children? Are not many of us toiling in the grain fields
and fruit farms, with their wives and their children, for the white man's
benefit? [...] But see their appreciation and gratitude![40]

Ironically, in view of Fanon's dismissive gesture towards the "colonized intellectual," Plaatje has, in the recent processes of South Africa's transformation,
been canonized as an African Shakespeare. David Johnson deplores this turn
in the critical appreciation of the author, because he fears that Plaatje, like
Shakespeare, will thus be "domesticated, aestheticised, depoliticised."[41] Although Plaatje himself may have regarded Shakespeare's work as the supreme
expression of English and, indeed, universal culture, his reading of the dramatist in *Native Life* is absolutely free of depoliticizing tendencies.

Shylock's speech is already a frontal attack on Christian Venice and definitely a match for Portia's plea for mercy which easily and almost impercep-
tibly changes into legal quibbling – although, of course, she has the last word,
leaving the Jew dispossessed, dislocated, and a Christian. In the rewriting of
Shylock's speech, the dramatic character – a marginalized and isolated individual in greedy Venice, excluded from happy-go-lucky, romantically luxurious
Belmont – becomes a collective subject with specific grievances in a clearly
defined economic and political situation. In contrast to the divisive black
nationalisms of the nineteenth century, the collective subject ('we Africans')
here expresses itself in terms of an African national unity based on race and
class: black mine workers, black farm workers, black taxpayers. Moreover, it
is the Africans' endless toil that creates and guarantees South Africa's development and wealth, while the whites are mere parasitic and tyrannical depen-
dants.

---

[40] Plaatje, *Native Life*, 146–47.

[41] David Johnson, "Literature for the Rainbow Nation: The Case of Sol Plaatje's
*Mhudi*," *Journal of Literary Studies/Tydskrif vir Literatuurwetenskap* 10.3–4 (September–December 1994): 353.

Plaatje's "*voyage in*":[42] i.e. his voyage into English culture, does not fall within Fanon's verdict on the "colonized intellectual." On the contrary, Elleke Boehmer is certainly right when she points out: "As to [Plaatje's] professed 'English' principles of universal humanism, it is interesting to observe how often these constituted not so much a credo as a rhetoric of protest."[43] Plaatje's use of Shakespeare may indicate a strong belief in universal humanism and even at times border on "a universalist, neoliberal confusion," as Fanon has it,[44] but he appropriates Shakespeare from the point of view of the colonized. His intimate knowledge of the English dramatist allows him to raise an African voice in what is otherwise the white man's terrain. He speaks as a British subject, but he never for a moment forgets that his is at the same time the voice of a colonized "native workingman." Plaatje is obviously aware that this is a rather incongruous position – but the incongruity does not simply result from the contradictory coexistence of British subject and native workingman. In each of these roles Plaatje feels increasingly and deeply insecure.

In one of his early discussions of colonial discourse, "Of Mimicry and Man," Bhabha, on the authority of Said, almost apodictically declares:

> Within that conflictual economy of colonial discourse which Edward Said describes as the tension between the synchronic panoptical vision of domination – the demand for identity, stasis – and the counter-pressure of the diachrony of history – change, difference – mimicry presents an *ironic* compromise.[45]

As a British subject, Plaatje has his own vision, not of domination, but of equality and justice, of, in Molema's words, the "high political morality" of British imperialism. In more practical terms, he may even envisage a harmonious coexistence of black and white grounded in an at least economic "racial 'inseparability'."[46] His vision, however, is constantly being undermined. The pointed remarks about Home Rule in South Africa/Ireland (quoted above) highlight Plaatje's sense of disillusionment and betrayal at the hands of the imperial government, and the more and more illusory belief in equal citizenship, at least as a future prospect, if not an immediate fact. In agreement with

---

[42] Edward W. Said, *Culture and Imperialism* (New York: Vintage, 1994): 244–45.

[43] Elleke Boehmer, *Empire, the National, and the Postcolonial, 1890–1920: Resistance in Interaction* (Oxford: Oxford UP, 2002): 129.

[44] Fanon, *The Wretched of the Earth*, 97.

[45] Homi K. Bhabha, *The Location of Culture* (London: Routledge, 1994): 122.

[46] Boehmer, *Empire, the National, and the Postcolonial*, 138.

Molema, Jabavu, and many of his colleagues in the SANNC, Plaatje defines himself primarily as an educated African in contradistinction to the mass of uncivilized Africans. He is convinced that only an education based on Christianity and Western civilization will eventually lead to a significant improvement of African society, which is still very much dominated by "hereditary princes,"[47] and to the granting of equal rights to Africans in South Africa. At the same time, however, Plaatje has to realize that this is but a naive dream, that the Europeans, whether Union government or Westminster, will never cede their power in favour of the Africans or even allow their participation in the government of the country. It is in this context, where the mimicry of an ironic compromise would be pathetically out of place, that Plaatje's sarcastic pairing of black education and white friendship assumes an additional and particularly revealing meaning: the Europeans teach the Africans, as they have always done, a callous lesson of oppression and exploitation in the guise of benevolent Western civilization. It is in this context of a common educational experience that Plaatje successfully bridges the great divide between 'civilized' and 'uncivilized' Africans in an extremely moving as well as programmatic narrative.

Towards the end of Chapter 4,[48] Plaatje recounts the story of the death and burial of the Kgobadi family's little child:

> Mrs Kgobadi carried a sick baby when the eviction took place, and she had to transfer her darling from the cottage to the jolting ox-wagon in which they left the farm. Two days out the little one began to sink as the result of privation and exposure on the road, and the night before we met them its little soul was released from its earthly bonds. The death of the child added a fresh perplexity to the stricken parents. [...] The deceased child had to be buried, but where, when, and how?
>
> This young wandering family decided to dig a grave under cover of the darkness of that night, when no one was looking, and in that crude manner the dead child was interred – and interred amid fear and trembling, as well as the throbs of a torturing anguish, in a stolen grave, lest the proprietor of the spot, or any of his servants, should surprise them in the act.[49]

---

[47] Plaatje, *Selected Writings*, 141.

[48] Plaatje, *Native Life*, 78–90 ("One Night with the Fugitives").

[49] *Native Life*, 89–90.

Plaatje introduces this sad story while reminiscing about "the best and happiest days of [his] boyhood" on the banks of the Vaal River,[50] and thinking of his "own little ones in their Kimberley home of an evening after gambolling in their winter frocks with their schoolmates."[51] He ends the episode with what, in Fanon's words, would be described as "a universalist, neoliberal confusion":

> Even criminals dropping straight from the gallows have an undisputed claim to six feet of ground on which to rest their criminal remains, but under the cruel operation of the Natives' Land Act little children, whose only crime is that God did not make them white, are sometimes denied that right in their ancestral home.[52]

He reverts to the episode of the Kgobadi child in Chapter 9. A good part of that chapter is devoted to the Plaatje family's own "baptism of sorrow,"[53] when, after a long illness, their youngest son, Johannes Gutenberg, dies early in January 1914. In loving and painful detail, Plaatje describes the suffering, death, and funeral of the child, but then he suddenly interrupts himself:

> As we saw the solemn procession and heard the clank of the horses' hoofs, we were suddenly reminded of that journey in July 1913, when we met that poor wandering young family of fugitives from the Natives' Land Act. A sharp pang went through us, and caused our heart to bleed as we recalled the scene of their night funeral, forced on them by the necessity to steal a grave in the moonless night.[54]

Plaatje is the perfect eyewitness who competently demarcates his position in relation to the sufferers and his British readers in order to achieve the desired effect. On the one hand, he creates a common ground between readers and observer through the middle-class respectability (the Kimberley home, the funeral procession) and the moral code (parental love, protection of children) they share. At the same time, he distances himself from his white readers when he emphasizes his specific African experience: the death of his son as a "visitation of 1913."[55] On the other hand, the observer's "polite national dis-

---

[50] Plaatje, *Native Life*, 81.
[51] *Native Life*, 89.
[52] *Native Life*, 90.
[53] *Native Life*, 142.
[54] *Native Life*, 146.
[55] *Native Life*, 145.

course"[56] and his family's self-advertised respectability open up the deep divide between himself and the homeless fugitives. At the same time, however, the gap is closed when, in the rewriting of Shylock's speech, the subject changes from I-as-witness to we-as-victims – when, in Plaatje's own words, "the solemnity of the funeral procession [is] succeeded by the spirit of revolt,"[57] and when the "sincere narrative of a melancholy situation" turns into a fierce attack.

In his discussion of the colonized intellectual,[58] Fanon distinguishes three stages in the development of the elite. The first phase is characterized by the intellectual's "full assimilation" into the colonizers' culture.[59] In the second phase, he "has his convictions shaken and decides to cast his mind back"[60] to the "customs, traditions, and costumes [of his people], and his painful, forced search seems but a banal quest for the exotic."[61] In the third phase, he finally turns into a "galvanizer of his people" and produces truly revolutionary and national literature.[62] Instead of assuming, with Fanon, a development from "a universalist, neoliberal confusion" to a demand for nationhood, I would argue that Plaatje in *Native Life in South Africa* spans the three stages delimited by Fanon.

Despite a strong feeling of betrayal, Plaatje still believes in Western civilization as an expression of universal humanism. His appeal to the British public is not only steeped in the colonizers' national discourse (with a magnificent *captatio benevolentiae*, the learned selection of epigraphs, the quotations from, and allusions to, Shakespeare), but also asks his readers to accept the ostracized Jew's accusation and the dispossessed Africans' claims on the grounds of universal values and as a well-founded, devastating critique of Western civilization itself. However, Plaatje realizes that being a member of the African elite, although it may separate him from the mass of his compatriots, in no way prevents him from being defined as a non-European, as not quite civilized, and that, in the end, the power of definition rests exclusively with the Europeans.

---

[56] Chrisman, "Fathering the Black Nation," 60.

[57] Plaatje, *Native Life*, 146.

[58] Fanon, *The Wretched of the Earth*, 156–61.

[59] *The Wretched of the Earth*, 159.

[60] *The Wretched of the Earth*, 159.

[61] *The Wretched of the Earth*, 158.

[62] *The Wretched of the Earth*, 159.

In this contradictory situation, which he seems to be unable to resolve, but which is obviously a constant source of indignation and, indeed, outrage and inspiration, Plaatje programmatically formulates his demand for African nationhood. The civilized, competent I-as-witness claims a voice within the colonial order to document the suffering of the colonized and remind the colonizers of their responsibility. The change of subject (I/we) indicates that the colonized can do without a mediator, without someone 'civilized' enough to represent them, but can represent themselves in the sense not only of we-as-victims but also of we-as-the-South-African-nation. It is their common experience of exploitation and dispossession, and above all their long history of hospitality and generosity towards foreign and inimical intruders, and of hard physical work in the service of the country, that empowers them to speak.

## WORKS CITED

Bhabha, Homi K. *The Location of Culture* (London: Routledge, 1994).

Boehmer, Elleke. *Empire, the National, and the Postcolonial, 1890–1920: Resistance in Interaction* (Oxford: Oxford UP, 2002).

Chrisman, Laura. "Fathering the Black Nation of South Africa: Gender and Generation in Sol Plaatje's *Native Life in South Africa* and *Mhudi*," *Social Dynamics* 23.2 (September 1997): 57–73.

Fanon, Frantz. *The Wretched of the Earth*, tr. Richard Philcox, foreword by Homi K. Bhabha, preface by Jean–Paul Sartre (*Les Damnés de la terre*, 1961; New York: Grove Weidenfeld, 2004).

Fuze, Magema M. *The Black People and Whence They Came: A Zulu View*, tr. H.C. Lugg, ed. A.T. Cope (Pietermaritzburg: U of Natal P, 1998).

Gebhard, Wolfgang. *Shades of Reality: Black Perceptions of South African History* (Essen: Die Blaue Eule, 1991).

Jabavu, Davidson D.T. *The Segregation Fallacy and Other Papers (A Native View of Some South African Inter-Racial Problems)* (Lovedale: Lovedale Institution Press, 1928).

Johnson, David. "Literature for the Rainbow Nation: The Case of Sol Plaatje's *Mhudi*," *Journal of Literary Studies/Tydskrif vir Literatuurwetenskap* 10.3–4 (September–December 1994): 345–58.

Molema, Silas M. *Montshiwa 1815–1896: Barolong Chief and Patriot* (Cape Town: Struik, 1966).

——. *The Bantu Past and Present: An Ethnographical & Historical Study of the Native Races of South Africa* (1920; Cape Town: Struik, 1963).

Plaatje, Sol T. *Native Life in South Africa before and since the European War and the Boer Rebellion*, intro. Brian Willan, preface by Bessie Head (Johannesburg: Ravan, 1982).

——. *Selected Writings*, ed. Brian Willan (Johannesburg: Wits UP, 1996).

Said, Edward W. *Culture and Imperialism* (New York: Vintage, 1994).

Willan, Brian, *Sol Plaatje: South African Nationalist, 1876–1932* (London: Heinemann, 1984).

❖

ANDREW MARTIN

# Come Back, Dennis Brutus![*]
## Geoffrey Davis and the Rediscovery of
## Apartheid-Era South African Literature[1]

G EOFFREY DAVIS, AS CAN BE SEEN IN HIS EXTENSIVE WRITINGS
on South African literature, has astutely held to the view that in
order to get an informed reading of South African literature one
must go beyond the texts and look at the social, cultural, and political factors
underlying them. In an essay entitled "The Intoxicated Octopus and the
Garlic-Kissed Prawn,"[2] Davis highlights the problems he encountered in compiling a bibliography of books on South Africa. Besides commenting on the
sheer enormity of the task, he discusses the influence of censorship on South
African writing, as well as the difficulties in collecting and documenting such
books, including the literature of exiles. This essay reflects on these points,
drawing parallels with my experiences in doing bibliographic research for the
National English Literary Museum (NELM) in Grahamstown, South Africa[3]
on apartheid-era black South African literature. Using the example of the

---

[*] It is with our deep regret that, while I was in the initial stages of this essay, Dennis
Brutus died aged 85 in Cape Town on 26 December 2009.

[1] Parts of this essay and notes have previously appeared in Andrew Martin, "A Bibliography of Anglophone Creative Writing and Literary Criticism by Black South
Africans 1800–1990," *Quarterly Bulletin of the National Library of South Africa* 62.1
(2008): 48–52, and Andrew Martin, "Come Home, Dennis Brutus! The Importance of
Archiving African and South African Literature" (unpublished conference paper).

[2] Geoffrey V. Davis. "The Intoxicated Octopus and the Garlic-Kissed Prawn," in *A
Talent(ed) Digger: Creations, Cameos and Essays in Honour of Anna Rutherford*, ed.
Hena Maes–Jelinek, Gordon Collier & Geoffrey V. Davis (Cross/Cultures 20; Am-
sterdam & Atlanta GA: Rodopi, 1996): 361–70.

[3] Further information about NELM can be obtained from our website: www
.rhodes.ac.za /nelm/

works of Dennis Brutus, the importance of archives in making such literature
accessible to readers in South Africa is discussed.

In "The Intoxicated Octopus," Davis reflects on his compilation of the revised edition of the World Bibliographical Series volume, entitled *South
Africa*, published in 1994 (the first edition compiled by Ruben Musiker was
published in 1979). In this essay, he writes:

> For the bibliographer, South Africa poses a real challenge. What I hoped to
> produce was a wide-ranging bibliography which would be comprehensive in
> its coverage of material available inside the country, but which, unlike the
> earlier work, could afford to ignore the provisions of the Publications Act
> and to include banned material, work by exiles and a large selection of the
> writing about the country being produced overseas. But that is easier said
> than done. (368)

On proscription and its effects on literature, one need not look past Davis for a
thorough analysis of the often petty and ironic inner workings of apartheid-era
censorship. In "'Literature in an imperfect world': Censorship in South Africa," Davis comments on the various ways in which much of this material was
excised:

> The traces of the censor's passage were everywhere apparent, pages ripped
> out, black bands obliterating the "undesirable" verse of banned poets, writers
> silenced even into the obscurities of footnote references to their work, notes to
> the effect that "permission has been refused by the Minister of Justice."[4]

In an essay entitled "The Current State of Emergency in South Africa," Davis
describes the effect of censorship on South Africa's writers:

> Inside the country writers were struggling against the state's attempt to force
> them into silence; outside it an important body of exile literature was being
> produced which denounced apartheid before the world. But South African
> literature had been splintered; the continuity of the literary tradition had been
> seriously threatened. The banning of thousands of works – literary, political,
> sociological – was designed to render progressive works of literature from the
> rest of Africa, political theory, and above all the writings and speeches of their
> own leaders and the policy statements of their own organisations inaccessible
> to black South Africans. A whole new generation of younger writers grew up

---

[4] Geoffrey V. Davis, "'Literature in an imperfect world': Censorship in South
Africa," in Davis, *Voices of Justice and Reason: Apartheid and Beyond in South African Literature* (Cross/Cultures 61; Amsterdam & New York: Rodopi, 2003): 110.

in the 1970s with little knowledge of the works of their older banned and exiled colleagues.[5]

Under apartheid, many writers resident in the country, both black and white, were affected in various ways, but for black authors the situation was far worse, because even literature which was considered acceptable was often hampered by small print runs and limited markets. Censorship meant that sales of books were curtailed, as it became illegal to sell or possess proscribed works. As a result, a large amount of material was unfortunately destroyed. This included books, manuscripts, literary journals, and the publications of cultural groups. This was true, not only for English, but also for the literature of indigenous languages in South Africa. During the apartheid era many of the writers of other languages had no access to publishing, since the only real market was for set works for schools, translations of classics, and educational and technical materials.

Exile, too, had a huge impact on South African writing. Many writers, both black and white, left South Africa out of choice or were forced out because of political interference. The psychological effects of exile on writers and their work is well documented. The black South African writer Es'kia Mphahlele wrote: "Abroad, some of us felt cheated out of something – an audience – and had to be content to write for that vaguely defined 'world intelligence'. We would never know the reactions of those whose concerns we shared in South Africa, and who made the material for our writing...."[6]

On the broader effects of exile on South African Literature, Davis writes:

> Over the years a literature of exile came into existence. It consisted of works written by exiles before leaving, published abroad and banned in their own country, as well as – increasingly – works written while in exile. Among these were several celebrated autobiographies which first told the world of the political and socio-economic conditions their authors had fled. For many years the legislative barriers erected effectively prevented the entry of these texts into the country on any large scale.[7]

---

[5] Geoffrey V. Davis, "The Current State of Emergency in South Africa," *Awa-Finnaba* (March 1987): 19.

[6] Es'kia Mphahlele, *Africa My Music: An Autobiography* (Johannesburg: Ravan, 1984): 130; quoted in Susan VanZanten Gallagher, *Truth and Reconciliation: The Confessional Mode in South African Literature* (Portsmouth NH: Heinemann, 2002): 55.

[7] Geoffrey V. Davis, "'When it's all over, and we all return': Matsemela Manaka's play *Ekhaya-Going Home*," in *"Return" in Post-Colonial Writing: A Cultural Laby-*

Censorship and exile denied readers access to literature that was socially relevant to them. Many writers are better known outside South Africa than in it and their works are becoming distant memories. Writers such as Peter Abrahams, Lewis Nkosi, Daniel P. Kunene, and Amelia Blossom Pegram have had undeservedly little exposure in their home country. Other writers, including Can Themba, Alex La Guma, Arthur Nortje, Bessie Head, and Alfred Hutchinson, died in exile before they could receive the recognition they deserved.

My interest in apartheid-era literature, also from a bibliographic standpoint, began when I was employed to work on a collection development project for the National English Literary Museum in 1995. NELM holds the most definitive collection of Southern African English literature worldwide, consisting of manuscripts, over 30,000 published works, literary criticism, press-clippings, and audiovisual materials. All such materials are accessible on our premises to literary scholars, both local and foreign, and to the general public at large. The aim of this project, which is entitled *A Bibliography of Anglophone Literature and Literary Criticism by Black South Africans: 1800–1990*, was to bring to light black South African literature in English which had been marginalized for several decades and, wherever possible, to obtain copies that can be carefully archived and made available on our premises for research. The bibliography includes novels, poems, short stories, plays, autobiographies, articles on literature, culture and theatre, as well as reviews. One entry is made for each item in its first place of publication.

As may readily be imagined, locating this material has been a major challenge, as it includes literature published overseas by exiles. There are very few bibliographies on black South African writing. The ones that have been published have been invaluable, but they are now outdated and limited in scope. There are a number of subject and author bibliographies which have also been useful. Four of Professor Bernth Lindfors's volumes of bibliographies entitled *Black African Literature in English* are a notable example.[8] But

---

*rinth*, ed. Vera Mihailovich–Dickman (Cross/Cultures 12; Amsterdam & Atlanta GA: Rodopi, 1994): 124.

[8] Bernth Lindfors: *Black African Literature in English: A Guide to Information Sources* (Detroit MI: Gale Research 1979); *Black African Literature in English, 1977–81: Supplement* (New York: Africana, 1986); *Black African Literature in English, 1982–86* (London: Hans Zell, 1989); *Black African Literature in English, 1987–91* (London: 1995); *Black African Literature in English, 1992–1996* (London: Hans Zell, 2000); *Black African Literature in English, 1997–1999* (London: Hans Zell, 2003).

when one undertakes serious bibliographic work of this nature, one also has to rely on biographical articles, acknowledgments in books, indexes to journals, and bibliographies in the back of books and at the end of journal articles. The internet, too, has supplied several leads.

In order to gather relevant material, I have worked in most of the major libraries in South Africa. In 1998, I visited the Herskovits Library near Chicago and the Widener Library at Harvard. In 2004, I visited the University of Wisconsin–Madison. In all, I have managed to procure copies of over 300 items for the bibliography which had never before been available in South Africa. Word of mouth, too, has been very important in securing material. I have personally met over eighty authors whose works are collected at NELM, writers such as James Matthews, Gladys Thomas, Mazisi Kunene, Don Mattera, Daniel P. Kunene, Es'kia Mphahlele, and Dennis Brutus, who have all given valuable assistance, as have academics including Geoffrey Davis and Bernth Lindfors, who have also donated material for the project. With all this assistance, including that from my colleagues, over 15,000 records have been entered into our databases and tagged 'BB' for Black Bibliography.

Brutus, whom I use as an example in this essay, needs little introduction to scholars of African literature. Over a period of sixty years, he has published some seven hundred poems, fourteen published collections, and hundreds of essays, reviews, and articles. An English teacher and an activist, Brutus was banned from being quoted or published as a result of his political activities, in particular his efforts to have South Africa expelled from the Olympic Games. This was followed by imprisonment on Robben Island, house arrest, and then a move to Britain on an exit permit in 1966. Now resident in the USA, Brutus still retains his South African citizenship and visits South Africa periodically. World-renowned and forever active, Brutus remains steadfast in his fight against any form of injustice or inequality.

Despite his banning, which lasted nearly three decades, Brutus is arguably one of South Africa's best-known poets, fittingly described as "the most South African of poets."[9] As a poet, Brutus has recorded several key events in the history of South Africa – Sharpeville, Robben Island, 16 June 1976, the death of Steve Biko, etc. Brutus still continues with this, as can be seen in his more recent poetry, although much of his current work focuses on international themes and locations. Some of his poems are more personal and intro-

---

[9] Bernth Lindfors, "Dennis Brutus: A Tribute," in *The Poems of Dennis Brutus: A Checklist, 1945–2004*, comp. Andrew Martin (Madison WI: Parallel, 2005): 8.

spective, others more critical. In a number of his pieces, the poet vents his frustration that the social and economic objectives on which the struggle against apartheid was based have been cast aside unachieved.

Lindfors also points out that Brutus (at that time) had "yet to publish a volume of poetry in South Africa" and he expresses the "hope that [Brutus's] poetry will soon be repatriated to the country that inspired almost all of it, and that he will gain the recognition and respect that he deserves in the history of South African literature."[10] A poet of Brutus's calibre, who has kept his finger on the pulse of his homeland, deserves a place in any South African library, yet only recently has he even had a launch of a collection in this country. His latest collection, which also contains articles and memoirs, *Poetry and Protest: A Dennis Brutus Reader* (2006),[11] has broken this trend. Many of his other collections have never been available in South Africa. The copies that do exist were held under lock and key in select academic libraries, or were smuggled into South Africa illegally. Now unbanned, these books are on the library shelves but out of print. Brutus, in an interview with Geoffrey Davis and Holger Ehling in 1992, discusses the non-availability of his books, which at that stage would have recently been unbanned. He says:

> I have looked at the *Government Gazettes*, which announced the banning of the books, and then at the *Government Gazettes* which announced the unbanning of books, and then I went into the libraries and said: okay these books are unbanned, are they available? It turns out they are not. If you go into the bookstores and you say: These books are unbanned, are they available? No, they're not. If you ask the booksellers: Have you ordered them? No, they have not. So, the effect is, the unbanning is made known to us but the books are still unavailable. But now for different reasons. The publishers don't think they are marketable, the booksellers don't think they can sell them, and the people don't request them because they weren't even aware of their existence. They just weren't there. So it's a troubling situation.[12]

Brutus is not alone in his frustration. Many other apartheid-era writers would share this view, particularly lesser-known writers who have in many instances

---

[10] Bernth Lindfors, "Dennis Brutus: A Tribute" (2005), 8.

[11] Dennis Brutus, *Poetry & Protest: A Dennis Brutus Reader*, ed. Lee Sustar & Aisha Karim (Chicago: Haymarket, 2006).

[12] Geoffrey V. Davis & Holger Ehling, "On a Knife Edge: Interview with Dennis Brutus," in *Southern African Writing: Voyages & Explorations*, ed. Geoffrey V. Davis *Matatu* 11 (1994): 106–107.

had to distance themselves from writing in order to keep the authorities at bay or simply to make a living, being denied both recognition and royalties. It is sad that many of these writers, now several years into post-apartheid South Africa, still have limited access to publishing. This is where archiving can play a crucial role in preserving this literature.

Through its collective efforts (including my research), NELM has comprehensive holdings of both primary works by Brutus and secondary material on his work. We have a span of sixty years of writing by him, starting with a sonnet, "Rendezvous," which the young Brutus published under the pseudonym 'Le Dab' in 1945 in *The SANC*, a Fort Hare University journal. We have sixty-eight books written by him or that include discussion of his works and over fourteen hundred individual poem entries (including re-publications) indexed on computer, from journals, anthologies, and his collections.

On computer, we also have 386 indexed entries of critical material either by him or about him. We have journal and newspaper articles by him on a wide variety of subjects, including general articles on South African literature, articles on writing and exile, tributes to his pupil and friend, Arthur Nortje, articles on his prison experiences, a report on prison conditions, and articles on politics, sport, and social issues, including such topics as foreign debt relief. In addition, we have several files of press-clippings with biographical information about him, many of which are from foreign sources.

NELM's manuscript holdings on Brutus, donated by himself and others, are extensive. These include drafts of poems, correspondence with publishers, writers, and writing groups, articles about poetry readings, material related to his teaching, material and correspondence from his involvement with human rights, sports, and political groups, and a large collection of audio and audio-visual material, mostly poetry readings and interviews.

In 2005, my *Poems of Dennis Brutus: A Checklist, 1945–2004* was published by Parallel Press, an imprint of the University of Wisconsin–Madison Libraries. This checklist is a first, because it combines a listing of Brutus's earliest South African publications with his publications after he went into exile. I used material gathered from my bibliographic research (mostly from the USA and Britain) and material donated to us. Brutus himself helped me find some early pieces in South African journals and newspapers, many of which were published under pseudonyms, including B.K., Dikeni Bayi, John Bruin, and Julius Friend. The bibliography lists 605 poems in their first place of publication.

NELM's collection includes many other apartheid-era writers, black and white, such as Nadine Gordimer, J.M. Coetzee, Es'kia Mphahlele, Zakes Mda, André Brink, Mongane Serote, Sipho Sepamla, Bessie Head, and Athol Fugard, among many others.

One should not underestimate the importance of public libraries and the creation and maintenance of collections of South African literature in the task of rediscovering apartheid-era literature. Besides those at NELM, South Africa has a number of important literary collections, including those of the National Library of South Africa and the Centre for African Literary Studies at the University of KwaZulu–Natal in Pietermaritzburg. Several US university libraries have good South African collections, including Harvard, Yale, Northwestern, Wisconsin–Madison, and Texas–Austin.

This task has three vital components. First, there is a need for all libraries to have proactive collection policies. Unfortunately, library funding is often inadequate and there is greater urgency for educational and secondary material. Purchasing of older works is often not an option. This is sad, because, especially owing to the development of the internet, it has become much easier to obtain rare and out-of-print books as well as second-hand copies. Certainly, NELM has no compunction about buying used volumes: obtaining a specimen copy of the text, irrespective of its condition, is the primary consideration. It is heartening to see a recent trend of republishing of apartheid-era books. Alex La Guma's *A Walk in the Night*,[13] Ezekiel Mphahlele's *Down Second Avenue*,[14] and Mongane Wally Serote's *To Every Birth Its Blood*[15] have appeared in recent editions. Hopefully this trend will continue.

Secondly, it is important for libraries to provide maximum accessibility to research materials. Accessibility in some instances is problematical, as much of the material that still exists is very rare and becoming fragile. There are only three or four complete sets of *Drum* magazine left in the country and these and other journals are deteriorating. The scanning of documentation on the web or into electronic form is one way of circumventing accessibility issues, but for libraries this is a very costly process.

---

[13] Alex La Guma, *A Walk in the Night and Other Stories* ed. Yousaf Nahem (London: Trent, 2006).

[14] Ezekiel Mphahlele, *Down Second Avenue* (1959; Johannesburg: Picador, 2006).

[15] Mongane Wally Serote, *To Every Birth Its Blood* (1981; Johannesburg: Picador, 2004).

Thirdly, it is important to promote this writing. The creation of supplementary sources such as articles, biographical works, documentaries, lectures, and exhibitions is invaluable, especially in the classroom, to re-create the context in which this literature was written. It is also very important to promote literary scholarship. This also starts in schools. Unfortunately, only a select group of black writers, such as Mongane Wally Serote, Oswald Mtshali, Richard Rive, and Bessie Head, are part of the syllabi. The situation in universities is healthier and more theses are being written on apartheid-era literature. At the highest level, a lot of critical work has been written on apartheid literature, but there is room for more local criticism. While a large number of literary articles and reviews have been written on Brutus, there are not many books or theses on his works. Of the few studies on him, perhaps the most pivotal is Craig McLuckie and Patrick Colbert's 1995 work *Critical Perspectives on Dennis Brutus*.[16] It is also important that interest in all this literature be maintained, because the amount of literature that has been published in South Africa since 1990 is staggering and could easily eclipse interest in apartheid-era literature.

Apartheid-era literature allows the reader to gain a far deeper insight into the workings of apartheid than select chapters in history textbooks. It is important that its rediscovery should remain an ideal and that all libraries continue to play a role in this. The exiled South African writer Alex La Guma once said in an interview: "Even though I am in exile, my books have gone back home and young people are able to read them. This gives me encouragement. I think I succeeded in reflecting the national liberation struggle in our country and so made a contribution to the spirit of the people."[17]

Geoffrey Davis's role in this vital task is one of which all may be proud and for which we scholars of African literature are deeply grateful.

## WORKS CITED

Brutus, Dennis. *Poetry and Protest: A Dennis Brutus Reader*, ed. Lee Sustar & Aisha Karim (Chicago: Haymarket, 2006).

—— [as Le Dab]. "Rendezvous," *The SANC* (Summer 1945): 26.

---

[16] *Critical Perspectives on Dennis Brutus*, ed. Craig W. McLuckie & Patrick J. Colbert (Colorado Springs CO: Three Continents, 1995).

[17] Alex La Guma, "Artists in Struggle: 'My Books Have Gone Back Home'," *World Marxist Review* 27.5 (1984): 73.

Davis, Geoffrey V. "The Current State of Emergency in South Africa," *Awa-Finnaba* (9 March 1987): 15–20.

——. "The Intoxicated Octopus and the Garlic-Kissed Prawn," in *A Talent(ed) Digger: Creations, Cameos and Essays in Honour of Anna Rutherford*, ed. Hena Maes–Jelinek, Gordon Collier & Geoffrey V. Davis (Cross/Cultures 20; Amsterdam & Atlanta: Rodopi, 1996): 361–70.

——. "'Literature in an imperfect world': Censorship in South Africa," in Davis, *Voices of Justice and Reason: Apartheid and Beyond in South African Literature* (Cross/Cultures 61; Amsterdam & New York: Rodopi, 2003): 109–36.

——. "'When it's all over, and we all return': Matsemela Manaka's play *Ekhaya-Going Home*," in *Return in Post-Colonial Writing: A Cultural Labyrinth*, ed. Vera Mihailovich–Dickman (Cross/Cultures 12; Amsterdam & Atlanta GA: Rodopi, 1994): 123–38.

——, comp. *South Africa* (World Bibliographic Series 7; Oxford & Santa Barbara CA: Clio, rev. ed., 1994).

——, & Holger D. Ehling. "On a knife edge: Interview with Dennis Brutus," in *Southern African Writing: Voyages and Explorations*, ed. Geoffrey V. Davis, *Matatu* 11 (1994): 101–10.

Gallagher, Susan VanZanten. *Truth and Reconciliation: The Confessional Mode in South African Literature* (Portsmouth NH: Heinemann, 2002).

La Guma, Alex. "Artists in Struggle: 'My Books Have Gone Back Home'," *World Marxist Review* 27.5 (1984): 71–73.

——. *A Walk in the Night and Other Stories*, ed. Nahem Yousaf (London: Trent, 2006).

Lindfors, Bernth. "Dennis Brutus: A Tribute," in *The Poems of Dennis Brutus: A Checklist, 1945–2004*, comp. Andrew Martin (Madison WI: Parallel, 2005): 8–9.

——. *Black African Literature in English: A Guide to Information Sources* (Detroit MI: Gale Research, 1979).

——. *Black African literature in English, 1977–1981: Supplement* (New York: Africana, 1986).

——. *Black African Literature in English, 1982–1986* (London: Hans Zell, 1989).

——. *Black African Literature in English, 1987–1991* (London: Hans Zell, 1995).

——. *Black African Literature in English, 1992–1996* (London: Hans Zell, 2000).

——. *Black African Literature in English, 1997–1999* (London: Hans Zell, 2003).

McLuckie, Craig W., & Patrick J. Colbert, ed. *Critical Perspectives on Dennis Brutus* (Colorado Springs CO: Three Continents, 1995).

Martin, Andrew. "A Bibliography of Anglophone Creative Writing and Literary Criticism by Black South Africans, 1800–1990," *Quarterly Bulletin of the National Library of South Africa* 62 1 (2008): 48–52.

——. "Come Home, Dennis Brutus! The Importance of Archiving African and South African Literature" (unpublished conference paper).

Mphahlele, Esk'ia. *Africa My Music: An Autobiography* (Johannesburg: Ravan, 1984).

——. *Down Second Avenue* (1959; Johannesburg: Picador, 2006).

Musiker, Ruben, comp. *South Africa* (World Bibliographical Series 7; Oxford & Santa Barbara C A: Clio, 1979).

Serote, Mongane Wally. *To Every Birth Its Blood* (1981; Johannesburg: Picador 2004).

◄❖►

JAMIE S. SCOTT

# Space, Time, Solitude

## The Liberating Contradictions of Ruth First's *117 Days*

### Introduction: "An Arena of *Struggle*"[1]

R UTH FIRST WAS DETAINED IN THE MARSHALL SQUARE POLICE STATION
in Johannesburg under South Africa's Ninety-Day Detention Act, in
1963, during the time of the Rivonia Trial of Nelson Mandela and
other members of the outlawed African National Congress. This essay revisits
her prison memoir, *117 Days: An Account of Confinement and Interrogation
under the South African Ninety-Day Detention Law*,[2] originally published in
1965. Like Yvonne Vera, Werner Sedlak, Susan Nuttall, Susan VanZanten
Gallagher and others, I read *117 Days* as an instance of what Barbara Harlow
has called "the literature of resistance." As Harlow points out, such literature
presents itself as "an arena of struggle." Testifying to this struggle, autobiographical prison writings like *117 Days* at once embody and express disloca-
tions between general and particular inscriptions of loyalty and treason,
between state terror and the deeply held convictions of the political dissident.
Here, however, in an effort to understand how incarceration can so often
come to represent freedom, I want to trace more carefully the contradictory
character of *117 Days*, specifically the contradictions of space, time, and solitude.

---

[1] The phrase "arena of *struggle*" (emphasis in the original) is borrowed from Barbara Harlow, *Resistance Literature* (New York: Methuen, 1987): 2.

[2] Ruth First, *117 Days: An Account of Confinement and Interrogation under the
South African Ninety-Day Detention Law*, intro. Joe Slovo (Penguin Special; Harmondsworth: Penguin, 1965). Further references are from the reprint (London: Bloomsbury,
1988).

## Contradictions of Space

Werner Sedlak has argued that First's *117 Days* embodies what Henri Le-
febvre calls "contradictory space": i.e. "the prison becomes a 'space in-
between' – here, between domination and appropriation."[3] Political detainees
are rarely prepared for the conditions of the prison cell. The opening para-
graphs of *117 Days* convey such an impression in the starkest terms:

> Yet, not an hour after I was lodged in the cell, I found myself forced to do
> what storybook prisoners do: pace the length and breadth of the cell. The bed
> took up almost the entire length of the cell, and in the space remaining between
> it and the wall was a small protruding shelf. I could not walk round the cell, I
> could not even cross it. To measure its eight feet by six, I had to walk the
> length alongside the bed and the shelf, and then, holding my shoes in my hand,
> crawl under the bed to measure out the breadth. It seemed important to be
> accurate. (10)

Here we find a record of literal reckoning, a measuring-out and mapping of
physical restrictions, a surveying and staking of territorial claims. The clichéd
banality of what First calls the "storybook" character of this description testifies all the more acutely to the immediate unreality of incarceration.

At one point in *117 Days*, First tells us that she had been arrested before, in
1956. "But the geography of the station," she writes, "was still bewildering"
(13). And yet, the very centre of this confinement furnishes First with a kind
of sanctuary:

> Yet the bed was my privacy, my retreat, and could be my secret life. On the
> bed I felt in control of the cell. I did not need to survey it; I could ignore it, and
> concentrate on making myself comfortable. I would sleep as long as I liked,
> without fear of interruption. I would think, without diversion. I would wait to
> see what happened, from the comfort of my bed. (9)

Finding her physical bearings in this way helps First to create inner spaces
within which to formulate strategies of resistance to the interrogation which
lay ahead. In the interplay between these locations lies the contradiction of
prison space. Often, the political prisoner loses sight of the line between life
and death, which shifts and blurs under the pressures of confinement. "Isola-

---

[3] Werner Sedlak, "Ways of Appropriating Space in South African Prison Memoirs
from Ruth First to Nelson Mandela," in *Borderlands: Negotiating Boundaries in Post-
Colonial Writing*, ed. Monica Reif–Hülser (Cross/Cultures 40, ASNEL Papers 4;
Amsterdam & New York: Rodopi, 1999): 191 n6, 190.

tion in a Vacuum," the title of a chapter in *117 Days*, captures this sense of undifferentiated space, while the final chapter of First's memoir, "No Place for You," threatens to obliterate all location and includes a description of her suicide attempt (60, 131). If, as Ioan Davies has asserted in a study of writers in prison, Gaston Bachelard's "habitable spaces of the poetic image are spaces that attract, spaces that have been lived in 'with all the partiality of the imagination'," the prison writer's experience of space, "is of a different order."[4] As for other political prisoners, so for First the experience of space is contradictory; it is, "in Bachelard's sense, both familiar and hostile."

## Contradiction of Time

Moving beyond Sedlak's analysis, however, I am arguing that the prison memoir also articulates what I am calling 'contradictory time'. First finds ways of 'marking time', of performing time in between the everyday calendar of the world outside prison and the temptation to put an end to time by committing suicide in the prison cell. From the sanctuary of her bed in the Marshall Square cell, Ruth First keeps a calendar:

> From the bed I made scratches with a hairpin on the wall next to my head. Each scratch took me at the most 120 seconds to make, but I had to await the passage of 1,440 minutes, or 86,000 seconds, before I could make the next. How many marks would I have to make before I got out of this cell? (40)

True, the question with which this passage ends betrays the sort of anxiety which will haunt First on and off throughout her time in prison. Later, for instance, in the cell in the Women's Central Prison, she writes:

> Ninety days. I calculated the date repeatedly, did not trust my calculation, and did it again. Every day I repeated that little rhyme "Thirty days hath September" and I counted days from 9 August, the date of my arrest. (74)

But First's ability to transform the formless flow of prison time into a familiar children's rhyme reveals a deeper degree of psychological stability, just as the scratches on the wall inscribe First's determination to resist the tedium of life in her cell, literally to pin down prison time.

   In the most striking strategy of resistance, First marks the passage of prison time with stitches behind the fold of her dressing-gown lapel:

---

[4] Ioan Davies, *Writers in Prison* (Toronto: Between the Lines, 1990): 59.

Here, with my needle and thread, I stitched one stroke for each day passed. I
sewed seven upright strokes, then a horizontal stitch through them to make a
week. Every now and then I would examine the stitching and decide that the
sewing was not neat enough and the strokes could be more deadly exact in
size; I'd pull the thread out and re-make the calendar from the beginning. This
gave me a feeling that I was pushing time on, creating days, weeks, and even
months. Sometimes I surprised myself and did not sew a stitch at the end of the
day. I would wait three days and then give myself a wonderful thrill knocking
three days off the ninety. (74)

As Yvonne Vera has noted, she re-creates

the conventional public calendar, which has been appropriated by the apartheid
regime, which is able to abstract from it repressive portions such as the ninety-
day detention. [...] First sees herself as an initiator and creator, able to conjure
days and months, to weave them into being.[5]

This sewing ritualizes the meaninglessness of prison time. The careful
stitching and unstitching of days, the play of delay and catch-up, lend identity
to, and enable First to transcend, the tedium of prison time imposed by her
jailers and the political powers whose bidding they do. In her cell, "[time] had
lost its momentum," but, ironically, ninety days' detention becomes an opportunity to remake time "from the beginning," to domesticate the power of the
totalitarian state (74). If at one point interrogation brings First to the brink of
suicide, a confrontation with meaninglessness expressed as losing track of
time, of losing interest in "sewing stitches behind my dressing-gown lapel"
(75, 131–32), the ritualizing of prison time transforms First's stitches into
"certificates of endurance" (75). Ironically, First's tormentors also understand
the importance of ritualized time; towards the end of *117 Days*, they try to
bribe a confession from her with promises of release for the birthday of her
daughter Robyn (143).

## Contradiction of Solitude

As we have seen, contradictions of space and time represent First's efforts to
resist institutionalized state oppression by finding meaning in her spatial and
temporal isolation. In-between space and in-between time, I am now suggesting, come to constitute the contradiction of solitude. For First, the spatial and

---

[5] Yvonne Vera, "The Prison of Colonial Space: Narratives of Resistance" (doctoral
dissertation, York University, 1995): 198.

temporal isolation of imprisonment eventuate in communities of solidarity with family and friends, as well as with other detainees, and, most ironically, with her oppressors.[6]

In the chapter "Isolation in a Vacuum," First reveals concern about her parents, on the one hand, and, on the other, about her fellow conspirators:

> Even now I cannot write how it happened but shortly after this I was given two pieces of information that froze my limbs. First leak: a delegate present at a meeting I had attended at Rivonia with Mandela, Sisulu, and others had blurted information to the police. Second leak: the Security Branch was investigating my father and my mother. (61)

Almost immediately, she discloses a further, important family worry. "My parents, and through them the children," she writes, "were being pulled into the line of fire" (62). And later: "I had to stop thinking about the children. I needed all my concentration to handle my own situation […] but of course I couldn't stop thinking about them" (63). These contrasts between First's isolation and the safety and security of family and fellow conspirators define the contours of solidarity within which her confrontation with the forces of oppression must be conducted. The South African Security Branch is well aware of the dangers of such solidarity. As Barbara Harlow has noted,

> The calculated use by the Security Branch of information against First is, by contrast, directed in malicious design, and its experience with interrogation informs that design, on at two ideological fronts: First's organizational allegiances and her filial loyalties.[7]

---

[6] Writing of South Africa under apartheid, Sarah Nuttall identifies such contradictions of solidarity specifically with the prison:

> While race has been a vector of segregation, especially in terms of macro spatial arrangements and judicial dispositions, it is also clear that in everyday life there have been spaces – some public, others private, domestic – in which if not intimacy, at least a close proximity of 'oppressor' and 'oppressed' developed. This was true not only of the house but also of the prison, for instance.

— Nuttall, "Ways of Seeing: Beyond the New Nativism," *African Studies Review* 44.2 (September 2001): 119.

[7] Barbara Harlow, *Barred: Women, Writing and Political Detention* (Hanover NH & London: Wesleyan UP, 1992): 151.

Visits from her mother provide the most obvious solidarity between First
and her family, while *117 Days* incorporates the dissident community in two
ways. In detailing her own prison experience, First often alludes to other
figures in the struggle against oppression. Allies include all those internees
who, in acts of resistance, have scratched their identities in "the blistering
green paint of the yard door," or the sixteen other detainees, scattered among
jails in Kliptown, Fordsburg, Jeppe, Rosebank, Brixton, and Rosetteville, for
whom the government magistrate responsible for First's well-being is also ac-
countable (43, 45).

More concretely, however, the fact that First enjoyed a period of freedom
in exile between her release from prison and her assassination enabled her to
weave into her own narrative accounts of the incarceration of other detainees,
some written by the detainees themselves. Italicized to stress their effect as
commentary on as well as solidarity with First's own carceral experience,
these passages embrace Arthur Goldreich, Dennis Brutus, "W," Looksmart
Solwandle Ngudle, James April, and John Marinus Ferus within the community of resistance. Particularly poignant, the account of Looksmart catalogues
the principal figures detained under the nationalist government's Suppression
of Communism Act, including Nelson Mandela and First's husband, Joe
Slovo. But further, in carefully crafted fictional dialogue, we are exposed
here to the conditions of persecution which culminated in Looksmart's death,
ostensibly a suicidal hanging in his prison cell, and of officialdom's efforts at
the judicial inquest to cover up police involvement in this murder by the
cynical manipulation of legal technicalities.

This interweaving of historical and fictionalized prison writings simultaneously recapitulates and reinforces the communal nature of dissident resistance to the South African nationalist regime. Blurring the boundaries between fiction and history constitutes a written refusal to acknowledge official
versions of events, and in so doing invites anyone under the official aegis to
participate in the resistance struggle. In Vera's words, "*117 Days* is not simply
a personal diary, but a social document that seeks its legitimacy from the history of the collectivity."[8] Indeed, on occasion, the circle of resistance expands

---

[8] Yvonne Vera, *The Prison of Colonial Space* (1995), 207. Similarly, Sedlak notes:
"In this manner, her prison memoirs achieve the form of a more generalized counter-
discourse intended to mobilize the international public against the General Law
Amendment Act of 1963" ("Ways of Appropriating Space in South African Prison
Memoirs," 193).

to include figures either remote from First's own politicized incarceration or responsible for it. African women imprisoned for petty crimes and even the prison authorities themselves are implicated in the struggle against apartheid. Sometimes, First catches glimpses of African prisoners exercising through the bars of her cell, and she and her fellow internees "would make gestures to one another across the yard" (67). Once, the prison matron seems "even sympathetic," and when First is returned from Pretoria Central Prison to Marshall Square Police Station, a warder suggests she take the cell previously occupied by the recently released Mrs Goldreich, since "it's the lucky cell" (69, 89). In First's words, "jail spells had not broken us; they had helped to make us" (134).

## Conclusion: "Contrascriptions" of Resistance

Writing of writers in prison in 1990, Ioan Davies remarks:

> their writing connects the reality of violence and the attempt to rearticulate humanity, re-establishing a bond between our sense of finitude and the infinity of our experiences.[9]

Such are the conditions under which First, though not first and foremost a writer, found herself. For First, a culture of violence subverts, dissolves, and confuses individual and collective identities and the principles of equity by which we would hope to conduct everyday life. As a white woman, First herself recognized that, even in prison, she enjoyed a position of privilege, as Susan Nuttall and others have noted: "as First attempts to erase her whiteness, she marks herself as white even more strongly." Ultimately, though, "in Ruth First's case [...] white identity is defined in terms of a watching and a splitting."[10] As we have seen, in *117 Days* contradictions of space, time, and solidarity at once reveal and reflect this ethos of surveillance and fractured identity.[11]

---

[9] Ioan Davies, *Writers in Prison* (Oxford: Basil Blackwell, 1990): 18.

[10] Sarah Nuttall, "Ways of Seeing," 121, 123.

[11] Nuttall contrasts Judith Butler's invocation of performativity "not as the act by which the subject brings into being what she/he names but, rather, as the reiterative power of discourse to produce the phenomena that it regulates and constrains" (Butler, *Bodies that Matter: On the Discursive Limits of Sex* [London: Routledge, 1993]: 2). Butler's point, Nuttall asserts, draws on Michel Foucault's theory of relations between discourse and power, and associates the trope of "watching" in First's *117 Days* with

At the same time, however, these contradictions afford some political dissidents one last, ironic form of resistance: writing. As H. Bruce Franklin and
others have argued, an intimate link has always existed between prison and
writing in modern Western cultures.[12] The oppressor knows that writing *per
se* enacts resistance. "Writing is more serious than killing," a guard tells
Nawal el Sa'adawi in the Women's Prison in Cairo in the 1980s.[13] For this
reason, oppressive regimes censor the writing that leaves a prison, and even
forbid writing in prison altogether. Conversely, political prisoners search out
any and all means to write. "Writing becomes for me a means, a way of survival," reveals Breyten Breytenbach, another member of the South African
community of prison writers.[14] In the case of *117 Days* and other prison texts,
political dissidents use times and spaces of respite from the apparatus of state
oppression to pen testimony to the conditions of incarceration.

As will be remembered, on 17 August 1982 a parcel bomb from the South
African Bureau of State Security silenced First herself, who was working as
Director of the Centre for African Studies, Eduardo Mondlane University,
Maputo, Mozambique. According to her husband, Joe Slovo, "it was espe-
cially hard for Ruth to write *117 Days*," but

> she was moved to go ahead in the hope that the narrative would help focus
> world attention on the plight of the growing number of victims of the [South
> African apartheid] regime's physical and mental torture-machine.[15]

My title speaks of 'the liberating contradictions' – literally, the 'speakings-
against' – of space, time, and solitude. It might therefore be better to speak of

---

Franz Fanon's "use of the tropes of seeing and watching to disclose the workings of
racialized identity," as well as Jacques Lacan's "more universalized elucidation of the
split subject, in the phrase 'I am unable to see myself from the place where the other is
looking at me'" (Nuttall, "Ways of Seeing," 121). In a related vein, Gallagher notes
that First was "unmade" by her prison experience, "her self-identity shaken to its
foundations" (Gallagher, *Truth and Reconciliation: The Confessional Mode in South
African Literature*, 98).

[12] H. Bruce Franklin, *The Victim as Criminal and Artist: Literature from the American Prison* (New York: Oxford U P, 1978).

[13] Nawal el Sa'adawi, *Memoirs from the Women's Prison* (London: Women's Press,
1986): 73.

[14] Breyten Breytenbach, *True Confessions of an Albino Terrorist* (London: Faber &
Faber, 1984): 155.

[15] Joe Slovo," "Introduction" to Ruth First, *117 Days*, 5.

the 'liberating contrascriptions' – literally, 'writings-against' – simultaneously embodied and expressed in *117 Days*. This notion of contrascription appears in *Writing and the Experience of Limits*[16] by Philippe Sollers, co-founder in 1960 of the celebrated French avant-garde journal *Tel Quel*. As an understanding of reading and writing, contrascription seems not to have caught on with English-language literary and cultural commentators. But here is Charles Lock in the introduction to Anne Blonstein's collection of poems *worked on screen* (2005):

> Contrascription instructs its readers in the complexities of writing, alerts us to the presence of unexpected messages and unbidden guests: to signals at odds with each other, criss-crossing, zigzagging, resisting the semantic seductions of the straight line. Contrascription teaches us to look askance and aslant, aft and fore, to treat the page as a screen on which nothing is, as it appears to be, fixed: eye and ear must continue to work on screen.[17]

"… must continue to work on screen," as the incarcerated Ruth First worked freedom writing of the sewing and undoing of stitches on the folded lapel of her dressing-gown, and as we must continue to work on the contradictions of space, time, and solitude in the "arena of struggle" to which literature of resistance like *117 Days* testifies.

## WORKS CITED

Breytenbach, Breyten. *True Confessions of an Albino Terrorist* (London: Faber & Faber, 1984).

Butler, Judith. *Bodies that Matter: On the Discursive Limits of Sex* (London: Routledge, 1993).

Davies, Ioan. *Writers in Prison* (Oxford: Basil Blackwell, 1990).

El Sa'adawi, Nawal. *Memoirs from the Women's Prison* (London: Women's Press, 1986).

First, Ruth. *117 Days: An Account of Confinement and Interrogation under the South African Ninety-Day Detention Law*, intro. Joe Slovo (Penguin Special; Harmondsworth: Penguin, 1965; repr. London: Bloomsbury, 1988).

---

[16] Philippe Sollers, *Writing and the Experience of Limits*, ed. David Hayman, tr. Philip Barnard with David Hayman (*L'Écriture et l'expérience des limites*, 1968; New York: Columbia UP, 1983).

[17] Charles Lock, "Introduction" to Anne Blonstein, *worked on screen* (Salzburg: Poetry Salzburg, 2005): i.

Franklin, H. Bruce. *The Victim as Criminal and Artist: Literature from the American Prison* (New York: Oxford UP, 1978).

Gallagher, Susan VanZanten. *Truth and Reconciliation: The Confessional Mode in South African Literature* (Portsmouth NH: Heinemann, 2002).

Harlow, Barbara. *Barred: Women, Writing and Political Detention* (Hanover NH & London: Wesleyan UP, 1992).

——. *Resistance Literature* (New York: Methuen, 1987).

Lock, Charles. "Introduction" to Anne Blonstein, *worked on screen* (Salzburg: Poetry Salzburg, 2005).

Nuttall, Sarah. "Ways of Seeing: Beyond the New Nativism," *African Studies Review* 44.2 (September 2001): 115–40.

Sedlak, Werner. "Ways of Appropriating Space in South African Prison Memoirs from Ruth First to Nelson Mandela," in *Borderlands: Negotiating Boundaries in Post-Colonial Writing*, ed. Monica Reif–Hülser (Cross/Cultures 40, ASNEL Papers 4; Amsterdam & Atlanta GA: Rodopi, (1999): 189–204.

Sollers, Philippe. *Writing and the Experience of Limits*, ed. David Hayman; tr. Philip Barnard with David Hayman (*L'Écriture et l'experience des limites*, 1968; New York: Columbia UP, 1983).

Vera, Yvonne. "The Prison of Colonial Space: Narratives of Resistance" (doctoral dissertation, Graduate Programme in English, York University, North York, Canada, 1995).

## Supplementary Readings

Camus, Albert. *The Rebel: An Essay on Man in Revolt*. tr. Anthony Bower (*L'Homme révolté*, 1951; tr. New York: Alfred A. Knopf, 1967).

Gelfand, Elissa D. *Imagination in Confinement: Women's Writing from French Prisons* (Ithaca NY: Cornell UP/Methuen, 1983).

Lifton, Robert Jay. *Thought Reform and the Psychology of Totalism: A Study of 'Brainwashing' in China* (New York: W.W. Norton, 1961).

Saro–Wiwa, Ken. "Keep Out of Prison," *The Independent* (London; 8 September 1994): 7.

Scott, James C. *Domination and the Arts of Resistance: Hidden Transcripts* (New Haven CT: Yale UP, 1990).

Scott, Jamie S. *Christians and Tyrants: The Prison Testimonies of Boethius, Thomas More and Dietrich Bonhoeffer* (New York: Peter Lang, 1995).

◄❖►

ANNE FUCHS

# Njabulo Ndebele: From Rediscovering the 'Ordinary' to Redefining South African 'Renaissance'

N JABULO NDEBELE WAS ONE OF THE FEW black South African writers renowned worldwide as an intellectual before the end of apartheid; he continues today to write and reflect upon culture, in particular on the relationship between literature and politics. Each generation in the twentieth century had its intellectuals. This began with critics such as R.R.R. Dhlomo and Sol Plaatje, through the *Drum* generation with the Nkosis and Mphahleles. Black Consciousness took over in the 1970s with the influence of Steve Biko and Pascal Gwala. Ndebele himself was of a slightly later generation and a slightly different category; he was very much involved in the magazine *Staffrider* and in 1987 became President of the Congress of South African Writers. Parallel with his creative and literary career, Ndebele also pursued a prestigious academic path. Pro-Vice-Chancellor of the National University of Lesotho, Head of the African Literature Department at the University of the Witwatersrand, Vice-Chancellor of the University of the North, Vice-Chancellor of the University of Cape Town, he had an 'extraordinary' knowledge of South African academia, which is evident in his essays.

It was Ndebele himself who referred to the term 'ordinary' as far back as 1984 when he presented a keynote address at the conference on "New Writing in Africa: Continuity and Change," held at the Commonwealth Institute in London. The address, "The Rediscovery of the Ordinary: Some New Writings in South Africa," was, in 1991, included in a Congress of South African Writers' publication entitled *Rediscovery of the Ordinary: Essays on South African Literature and Culture.*[1] In eight essays and an appendix, Ndebele here explores the present and the future of black South African writing and culture; these essays and the call for writers to explore the everyday lives of black

---

[1] Njabulo Simakhale Ndebele, *Rediscovery of the Ordinary: Essays on South African Literature and Culture* (Fordsburg: C O S A W, 1991).

South Africans were, at the time, a revelation and were discussed at length by
many prominent intellectuals and critics.[2] What, in fact, does Ndebele say
about the 'ordinary' in his earlier work but also in his latest collection of
essays, entitled *Fine Lines from the Box* (2007)?[3] How, if at all, has he interpreted this notion through his own fiction, in particular in *The Cry of Winnie
Mandela* (2003)? Writing a novel about Winnie Mandela is in itself emblematic of his confrontation of the ordinary with the extraordinary, of the public
with the private, and of his effort to explain private failures in the light of a
South African renaissance.

Published in 1991, after the release of Nelson Mandela and the negotiation
between the ANC and De Klerk, but before the 1994 elections which gave
power to the black majority, the individual essays in *Rediscovery of the Ordinary* date mainly from the 1980s. Judging from the preface, but also from
other pieces, the main concern of Ndebele at this point in history is how to
counter the "manipulation" of the black community by the whites. The preface, indeed, is quite surprising, in that Ndebele openly questions the good
faith of the nationalist government in liberating Mandela:

> Suddenly the nationalist government also proclaims 'human rights,' and
> 'non-racialism.' It now expresses concern about 'all our people'; declares its
> intention to 'redress imbalances,' and is determined to 'turn away from the
> past.' (8)

Given the disastrous situation of the "vast masses" of the population, Ndebele
considers that the nationalist government is just manufacturing "the illusion of
freedom" in order to hold on to their own power. He also underlines the complexity of a situation in which the blacks have effectively been denied "the
resounding defeat of an enemy. The Bastille has not been stormed" (9).

The confusion caused in 1991 by the Afrikaner government's concessions
can be linked with another even more insidious "manipulation" dealt with in
"Turkish Tales," a piece written in 1983. In this text Ndebele points out that
the reception of information in South Africa by blacks under apartheid was
necessarily skewed in one of two ways depending on whether it was furnished

---

[2] See Geoffrey V. Davis, *Voices of Justice and Reason: Apartheid and Beyond in
South African Literature* (Cross/Cultures 61; Amsterdam & New York: Rodopi,
2003): 287.

[3] Njabulelo Simakhale Ndebele, *Fine Lines from the Box: Further Thoughts about
our Country*, comp. Sam Raditlhalo (Roggebaai, SA: Umuzi & Houghton: Random
House, 2007).

by the regime – in which case it was more than suspect – or by the white liberal press or institutions – when it was acceptable. The second case is, for Ndebele, highly significant, in that it created a form of dependence as far as the African resistance movement was concerned, since the latter were never "in control of the information gathering, interpretation, and dissemination process."[4] He cites the influence in the townships of the *Daily Mail*, linked to the mining group Anglo-American, in turn linked to the University of the Witwatersrand and the Institute of Race Relations. Through the eyes of the white liberals' "essentially anthropological approach," Africans perceived their society under apartheid as debased: on the one side, there were the 'tsotsis', the mine compounds and the witch-doctors, and, on the other, an elite who were "caricatures" of the white man. This superficial way of thinking, induced by an all-powerful if liberal form of modern capitalism, led to intellectual powerlessness and a reliance on sensationalism and sloganeering (the very opposite of analysing the 'ordinary') denouncing the atrocities and wrongs of apartheid. Ndebele, in this same essay, goes on to talk about writing based on these premises, which never creates a process of transformation in the reader but only a sense of recognition confirming what they already know.

Before explaining how Ndebele suggests trying to counter this "manipulation" by the whites and the effect it has on the literary scene, it is worth mentioning what he calls the "popular culture" of music, theatre, and the visual arts, which, unlike black fiction and poetry during apartheid, seemingly escaped the white-liberal syndrome. In an essay analysing the music of Hugh Masekela and other internationally known musicians, Ndebele concludes that they succeeded in developing and promoting popular South African "location" music.[5] What Ndebele does not discuss is the extent to which this international promotion was helped by the white-liberal American and European anti-apartheid movements. As far as theatre is concerned, the author makes an important point about the work of the township dramatist Gibson Kente. Even the latter, it could be argued, started his career under the auspices of a white-liberal arts organization, Dorkay House. However, Ndebele is right to point out the "popular" (in its best sense) success of Kente in the townships, thanks

---

[4] Njabulelo Simakhale Ndebele, "Turkish Tales and Some Thoughts on South African Fiction" (1984), in *Rediscovery of the Ordinary*, 25.

[5] Njabulelo Simakhale Ndebele, "Actors and Interpreters: Popular Culture and Progressive Formalism" (1984), in *Rediscovery of the Ordinary*, 69–91.

to his exploration and intimate knowledge of the lives of the black inhabitants, together with his use of popular music and dance in his township community-centre performances. In 1980, it must be remembered, he had only a partial success at Johannesburg's Market Theatre when he came up against the in-comprehension of most white theatre critics with his play *Mama and the Load.*[6]

Ndebele does tend to a manichaean approach when contrasting the afore-mentioned arts with fiction.[7] This, however, is not the case in his actual anal-yses of the black works of fiction under scrutiny. In "The Rediscovery of the Ordinary: Some New Writings in South Africa," starting with the stories of R.R.R. Dhlomo, where "people and situations are either very good or very bad," he treats what he calls "spectacular representations."[8] This may take many forms, from the beginnings of *Drum* magazine, where fiction was separate from societal issues written about by other journalists and aimed at producing "entertaining stories"[9] about the new urban life-style, to the new protest literature of the late 1950s. Ndebele examines at length a story by Alex La Guma, who, with Ezekiel Mphahlele, Can Themba, James Matthews and others, was responsible for a new political dramatization. He sums up these remarks thus:

> We can now summarise the characteristics of the spectacular in this context. The spectacular documents; it indicts implicitly; it is demonstrative, preferring exteriority to interiority; it keeps the larger issues of society in our minds, ob-literating the details; it provokes identification through recognition and feeling rather than through observation and analytical thought; [...]. It is the literature of the powerless identifying the key factor responsible for their powerlessness. Nothing beyond this can be expected of it.[10]

In "The Rediscovery of the Ordinary," Ndebele seems to ignore the changes brought about by the Black Consciousness movement as such, and

---

[6] See Anne Fuchs, *Playing the Market: The Market Theatre, Johannesburg* (1990; Cross/Cultures 50; Amsterdam & New York: Rodopi, rev. ed. 2002): 140.

[7] This statement concerns the white liberal influence only. When analysing the "spectacular," he admits that this is also present in the popular visual arts, music, and dancing.

[8] Ndebele, "The Rediscovery of the Ordinary: Some New Writings in South Africa," in *Rediscovery of the Ordinary*, 39.

[9] Ndebele, "The Rediscovery of the Ordinary," 40.

[10] "The Rediscovery of the Ordinary," 46.

refers, rather, to "new trends,"[11] using as an illustration three short stories, by Joel Matlou, Michael Siluma, and Bheki Maseko, all of which had been published in the journal *Staffrider*. This in itself is an indication of Ndebele's own political contradictions, in that *Staffrider* started out as a pro-ANC publication but with, once again, some white-liberal support (notably that of Nadine Gordimer). Ndebele only discusses, and rather briefly, Black Consciousness work in the following essay, "Redefining Relevance." It is quite evident that, for him, the notion of the consciousness of being black, as far as culture was concerned at that time, was not entirely the same as that of the movement inspired by Steve Biko. In discussing the three stories from *Staffrider*, he shows how Siluma in "The Conversion," for example, has moved on from "protest" literature:

> from merely reflecting the situation of oppression, from merely documenting it, to offering methods for its redemptive transformation [...]. He de-romanticises [sic] the spectacular notion of struggle by adopting an analytical approach to the reality before him.[12]

Ndebele also partly approves of *To Every Birth Its Blood* by a well-known member of the ANC in exile, Mongane Wally Serote. The latter, however, while exploring "the ordinary concerns of people," allows the spectacle to take over "and the novel throws away the vitality of the tension generated by the dialectic between the personal and public."[13]

This "direct concern with the way people actually live" means that fiction must explore "a range of complex ethical issues involving man–man, man–woman, woman–woman, man–nature, man–society relationships";[14] Black Consciousness fiction, on the other hand, is just making a spectacular statement, but, this time, passing "from the exterior manifestation of oppression, to the interior psychology of that oppression,"[15] hence the predominance of poetry emanating from the Movement. From a postcolonial perspective, it is significant that, even at this point in time (i.e. before the 1994 elections), Ndebele is advocating not only freedom from political oppression but also

---

[11] Ndebele, "The Rediscovery of the Ordinary," 47.

[12] Ndebele, "Redefining Relevance," in *Rediscovery of the Ordinary*, 49.

[13] "Redefining Relevance," 55.

[14] "Redefining Relevance," 55.

[15] "Redefining Relevance," 65.

to free the entire social imagination of the oppressed from the laws of perception that have characterised apartheid society. For writers this means freeing the creative process itself from those laws. It means extending the writer's
perception of what can be written about, and the means and methods of
writing.[16]

The need for this new "perception" will constitute one of the major concerns
of *Fine Lines from the Box* (2007), as will the notion that underlies white
hegemony in Africa and contributes to white dominance through "accul-
turation": "art civilises natives by exposing them to western culture and thus
reducing their capacity to resist that culture in its totality" (128).

This form of resistance to white hegemony, which (as I have tried to explain) has a strong connection with the awareness of being black rather than
with Black Consciousness, is foregrounded and becomes the major articu-
lation of the first collection of essays. Ndebele also underlines what he calls
"the literary manifestation of the principle of contradiction"[17] as "irony,"[18]
confounding (in the sense of 'mixing') "irony" with "dialectic" or even Bakh-
tinian "dialogism": "the dialectic between appearance and reality" and "the
dialectic" between politics and art.[19]

The first essay in *Fine Lines from the Box*,[20] written in 1987, constitutes an
obvious link with the previous volume; "manipulation" by the whites once
more comes to the fore, this time at the university. Ndebele poses the question
of how universities should develop a post-apartheid society and how excellence may be achieved (or maintained), emphasizing that efficiency in universities does not necessarily depend on state ideology. Is the maintenance of
European culture in South Africa an absolute necessity? "While apartheid insisted that the oppressed would develop better alone, liberals insisted they
would develop better within the prescriptions of European standards."[21]

---

[16] Ndebele, "Redefining Relevance," 65.

[17] "Redefining Relevance," 67.

[18] Cf. Johan Geertsema, "Ndebele, Fanon, Agency, and Irony," *Journal of Southern African Studies* 30.4 (December 2004): 749–63.

[19] Ndebele, "Redefining Relevance," 67, 68.

[20] Njabulelo S. Ndebele, "Good Morning, South Africa: Whose Universities, Whose Standards?" (1987), in Ndebele, *Fine Lines from the Box: Further Thoughts about our Country*, comp. Raditlhalo, 13–18.

[21] Ndebele, "Good Morning, South Africa," 15.

Getting away from this paradox, Ndebele sees the future as belonging to the masses:

> Recognising the rise of the masses, the universities must try to find ways of consulting with the mass-based democratic movement on policy issues. This is premised on the recognition that the oppressed will steadfastly refuse to be turned into consumers of the pre-packed activity of knowledge production.[22]

This passage can be related to certain articles in the same collection that are of later date: the first in 1994, the text of a public address given as vice-chancellor at the University of the North, the second in 2002 entitled "The 'Black' Agenda and South Africa's Universities" and subtitled "Some Sobering Thoughts." Sobering, indeed, in that these two essays recognize the failure of 'black' universities in post-apartheid South Africa to achieve excellence or even efficiency. Ndebele catalogues his own frustrations as vice-chancellor and points to the "infrastructural decay and unrelenting student and worker activism on many campuses,"[23] the heritage of institutions both 'black' and 'white' set up by the whites. The implication is that, in 2002, the prospective elite students of a 'black' regime will automatically choose a traditionally white institution rather than "historically disadvantaged institutions." If there is a certain irony to be found in the situation in 2002 compared with Ndebele's hopes and certainties in 1994, a third article reflects on the global situation of higher education:

> The reflective capacity of higher education has given way to marshalling the human intelligence towards economic productivity. [...] reflection has significantly given way to instrumentality, and [...] this has potentially disastrous effects on the evolution of contemporary civilisation towards more humane forms of global awareness.[24]

Here Ndebele is speaking of South Africa but also of the USA, from where he has just returned; he writes in other essays in this collection of the situation in Lesotho, and in Africa generally; nevertheless, his most telling remarks concern the new dispensation in South Africa. Two themes recur throughout, that of the new leadership and that of the written word.

---

[22] Ndebele, "Good Morning, South Africa," 17.

[23] Ndebele, "The 'Black' Agenda and South Africa's Universities: Some Sobering Thoughts," in *Fine Lines from the Box*, 167.

[24] Ndebele, "Higher Education and a New World Order" (2003), in *Fine Lines from the Box*, 195.

Leadership as such cannot here be reduced to members of the government but includes such figures of the elite as Brenda Fassie and Winnie Mandela. The concept might also be said to include Ndebele himself. A particularly telling, ironical, and psychologically revealing piece is devoted to his own experiences of holidaying at a game lodge. Near the beginning it is stated that "this particular lodge, raised up on its wooden posts, allowed you to enjoy the illusion of being lifted protectively above all the 'creeping things' of the earth."[25] And Ndebele puts behind him the idea that these "things" might still come creeping up the stilts. But is it really behind him? The interpretation of the game lodge as a form of colonial leisure and all its various advantages is followed by the "most damning ambiguities" for Ndebele himself and the new black tourist in general:

> Living somewhere 'out there', beyond the neatly clipped frontier, the black workers come into the clearing to serve. And then they disappear again. In their comings and goings, they are as inscrutable as the dense bush from which they emerge and to which they return.[26]

Analyses of difficult relationships in the game lodge – black tourist/black worker; black/white tourist – give way to another possible metaphor, that of South Africa seen as "one big game lodge where all its black citizens are struggling to make sense of their lives."[27] And Ndebele concludes: "How is it that a simple quest for peace and restoration turned into an unexpectedly painful journey into the self? We think: there is no peace for those caught in the process of becoming."[28]

It may be assumed that it is to some extent the personal experience of Ndebele that drove him to ponder at length the problems of leadership in the new state and in Africa in general. Leaving aside his essays full of admiration for such figures as Desmond Tutu, Brenda Fassie, and Moshoeshoe, his most innovative texts are those dealing with "the process of becoming" for South Africa's new political leaders. Two outstanding figures, Thabo Mbeki and Jacob Zuma, are foregrounded in all their postcolonial complexity. Each is a well-known and controversial public leader, and each is shown by Ndebele to be conditioned by apartheid, the struggle and the present, or by what, in a

---

[25] Ndebele, "Game Lodges and Leisure Colonialists Caught in the Process of Becoming" (1998), in *Fine Lines from the Box*, 99.

[26] "Game Lodges and Leisure Colonialists," 101.

[27] "Game Lodges and Leisure Colonialists," 104.

[28] "Game Lodges and Leisure Colonialists," 105.

1997 paper on English in South Africa, he calls "a constantly transforming environment."[29] He states:

> Anyone familiar with the so-called science of complexity and related theories of chaos will be able to appreciate all at once the strengths of our historic transformation towards democracy, as well as our distressing vulnerability.[30]

"Vulnerability" is perhaps the quality that predominates in Ndebele's reflections on the personalities in question. Winnie Mandela, even more vulnerable, appears briefly in essays devoted to Archbishop Desmond Tutu[31] and to a documentary by John Pilger entitled *Apartheid Did Not Die* in the essay entitled "Innocence Lost, Opportunity Gained."[32] Writing in 1998, Ndebele questions himself and Tutu about whether Winnie is to be believed when she apologizes to the Truth and Reconciliation Commission. The complexity of her situation was to be explored later in Ndebele's novel *The Cry of Winnie Mandela*. The collection of essays rationalizes the postcolonial situation of the two leaders, Mbeki and Zuma, the former as far as his attitude to AIDS goes, and the latter under trial for corruption. Mbeki, Ndebele claims, has been misrepresented by the world press over the HIV/AIDS controversy. Mbeki never said he did not believe in the West's solution to the health problem, but, having been severely let down once by a "breakthrough" in the form of a cure invented by white South African scientists in 1997, he eventually set up an AIDS advisory panel to investigate all possible aspects of the pandemic and to recommend new initiatives. Ndebele's own conclusions do not really throw much light on the controversy, but the interest lies in the associations he makes between what he terms "ecological consciousness" and AIDS:

> It is a disease that forces post-modernity to confront the phenomenon of species mortality. And because fighting it calls for far more than the administering of drugs, it compels us to define health in terms of the global condition. Mbeki's comprehensive view of the pandemic demonstrates the workings of an ecological mind. Responding to the AIDS pandemic potentially places

---

[29] Ndebele, "Whither English in the 21st Century? Sharing a Common Language" (1997), in *Fine Lines from the Box*, 71.

[30] "Whither English in the 21st Century?" 71.

[31] Ndebele, "Moral Anchor: An Interview with the Arch" (1998), in *Fine Lines from the Box*, 77–83.

[32] Ndebele, "Innocence Lost, Opportunity Gained: A Path towards Renaissance" (1998), in *Fine Lines from the Box*, 92.

South Africa, where wealth and poverty exist side-by-side, at the cutting edge of global awareness.[33]

To a large degree, Ndebele seems to be defending the position of Mbeki against, in particular, the attacks of "global media." This is less evident in another short essay on Thabo Mbeki which was written a year earlier (2001) and concerned only South Africa's internal politics. It deals with Ndebele's disappointment over the ANC leadership squabbles and a recognition that South Africa has, indeed, become 'more ordinary'; "our own brand of ordinariness ought to work at a higher level [...] known for our resourcefulness, are we running out of creative options?"[34] A definite shift in the meaning of the term 'ordinary' can be noted, and, far from defending President Mbeki, he appears to have definite doubts: "is it possible that the issue may not only be that some people want to be president of South Africa but also that some people want to be the only president of South Africa within living memory?"[35]

Here there seems to be a link with what Ndebele had hoped would be an "African Renaissance." In this collection of essays he drifts between the notion that South Africa has great possibilities because of the strength it has gained through its struggle against apartheid and an explanation of present difficulties as stemming from this same apartheid situation. The case of Jacob Zuma is used as an illustration of this paradox. Rightly or wrongly brought to trial in 2003 for the offence of rape, Zuma resented his fall from grace with the ANC, or his "family," as Ndebele puts it. The ANC had survived in exile thanks to the extraordinary solidarity of its members, the "family"; this form of solidarity was not always appropriate to a governing body: "The family ethos must transform in the direction of a robust public and professional culture. Where the ANC has called on everyone and every institution to transform, it is time it, too, did so."[36]

Throughout Ndebele's essays, at the heart of his reasoning is the notion he terms "counter-intuitive." This is thoroughly discussed in an essay in which

---

[33] Ndebele, "AIDS and the Making of Modern South Africa: Responding to a Pandemic in a Time of Complexity" (2002), in *Fine Lines from the Box*, 188.

[34] Ndebele, "Thabo Mbeki: Comradeship, Intrigue and Betrayal: A Vital Leadership Endgame" (2001), in *Fine Lines from the Box*, 162.

[35] "Thabo Mbeki: Comradeship, Intrigue and Betrayal," 163.

[36] Ndebele, "Jacob Zuma and the Family: How Zuma's Bravado Brutalized the Public" (2003), in *Fine Lines from the Box*, 232.

he envisages the ANC as being able to accept what seems contrary to the "common intuition" imposed from on high.[37]

> This is the formidable challenge of a popular post-apartheid political movement. Can it conceptually anticipate a future when it is no longer overwhelmingly in control, in the form in which it currently is, and resist, counter-intuitively, the temptation to prevent such an eventuality?[38]

A 'counter-intuitive' approach is always the questioning of the obvious, Socratic or dialectical in form. Two animal tales, one traditional and the other modern, present the 'counter-intuitive' interpretation of the animals' roles and characters. "The Lion and the Rabbit" bears the subtitle "Freeing the Oppressor" and presents what Ndebele terms "two frames of interpretation" whereby we can sympathize in the first instance with the seemingly heroic Rabbit and, secondly, if we ask further questions, with the Lion – and "someone may be Lion today and Rabbit tomorrow."[39] "The Year of the Dog: A Journey of the Imagination" was written in 2006, the year of Zuma's conviction for rape when Zizi Kodwa of the ANC Youth League called for "the dogs to be beaten until their owners and handlers emerge."[40] One of the dogs so designated was Ndebele himself. What is a dog? What is his role?[41] During apartheid there were the underdogs, beaten and oppressed, but for Ndebele there is also the image of the dog as "this remarkable friend of humans: intelligence, empathy, loyalty, dependability, friendship, courage, protectiveness, sensitivity and caring." And at the same time he questions whether the dog might not become a national symbol for the humanity of South Africans, and 2008 be declared 'The Year of the Dog'.

If the prevailing optimism of Ndebele is still apparent even in this essay dated 2006, he had openly opposed in 1998 what he terms "slogans of optimism" relating to Africa. These slogans, which originated in the colonial era

---

[37] Ndebele, "Leadership Challenges: Truth and Integrity in an Act of Salesmanship" (2006), in *Fine Lines from the Box*, 233.

[38] "Leadership Challenges," 243.

[39] Ndebele, "The Lion and the Rabbit: Freeing the Oppressor" (1999), in *Fine Lines from the Box*, 109.

[40] Ndebele, "The Year of the Dog: A Journey of the Imagination" (2006), in *Fine Lines from the Box*, 251–56.

[41] One cannot help thinking of J.M. Coetzee's obsession with dogs. See *Disgrace* (London: Secker & Warburg, 1999) and *The Lives of Animals*, ed. & intro. Amy Gutmann (Princeton NJ: Princeton UP, 1999).

and for Africans served as a counter to the exploitative world-view of Africa, are essentialist in nature: "Negritude, the African Personality, African Social-ism, African Philosophy, African Humanism, and Authenticity" (96). But, says Ndebele, there is "a new kid on the block":[42] "African Renaissance," proclaimed by Thabo Mbeki. The latter cites four developments as the reason for optimism:

> the successful transition to majority rule in South Africa;
> the cessation of lengthy and debilitating conflicts in various parts of the (Afri-can) region;
> a significant upturn in the region's economic performance; and
> a growing reliance on elections and democratic governance.[43]

Ndebele himself states that African Renaissance is

> not coincident with African authenticity. Rather, it is a life to be lived in which emergent forms of successful social practice are recognised and helped along through innovative, purposeful and relevant means that are political, scientific, artistic and professional.[44]

In these essays, as we have shown, most of the "relevant means" have been analysed. What are Ndebele's own artistic means? He has, in fact, produced relatively little fiction as such. His most significant works are the collection of stories *Fools* (1983) and the novel *The Cry of Winnie Mandela*. The twenty years which separate these texts are years of immense change, for South Afri-ca but also for Ndebele's own development and artistic means. *Fools* is com-posed of four stories narrated from the point of view of children with two first-person and two third-person narratives; the fifth story, an adult first-per-son narrative, relates the transformation of a school-teacher from a state of moral and political unconsciousness or "fool" to a state of moral awareness, consciousness of ignorance, knowing which questions to ask. In all the stories, the narration is 'ordinary', with the seeming simplicity of nineteenth-century critical realism. From the young boy, who eventually realizes that the water from the street tap has the same miraculous effect on his sick mother as the water he was supposed to obtain from the prophetess in the eponymous

---

[42] See Ndebele, "African Renaissance: A New Kid on the Block" (2002), in *Fine Lines from the Box*, 96–98.

[43] "African Renaissance: A New Kid on the Block," 97.

[44] "African Renaissance: A New Kid on the Block," 98.

story, to the school-teacher in "Fools,"[45] there is a form of apprenticeship. Life is learnt, however, from an exceedingly complex reality, with ethical issues involving relationships between men, women, and children and between black South Africans in general in their own ordinary but 'apart' society. Within each story are numerous characters and episodes not necessarily vital or at first sight relevant to the narrator's progress but which create a richness and vibrancy, the atmosphere of a small town, district or township lived in by 'ordinary' people.

*Fools* partakes of the language[46] used by South African writers in their work from Ezekiel Mphahlele's *Down Second Avenue* (1959) to Mbulelo Mzamane's *My Cousin Comes to Jo'burg* (1980) and Mongane Serote's *To Every Birth Its Blood* (1981). Although far from transcribing literally the English that would have been used by their African characters (and it must be remembered that, contrary to the fictional persona, the average urban black South African would have mainly used one or several indigenous languages), these English-language writers all maintain one of the principles Ndebele himself was to invoke in "The English Language and Social Change in South Africa":

> South African English must be open to the possibility of its becoming a new language. This may happen not only at the level of vocabulary [...] but also with regard to grammatical adjustments that may result from the proximity of English to indigenous African languages.[47]

In *The Cry of Winnie Mandela*, Ndebele is still using English in much the same way. In "An Encounter with my Roots" (2000), he has meanwhile envisaged the possibility of multilingual fiction for himself: English, Sesotho, and isiZulu.[48] Conscious, however, of finding (or not finding) a reading public for any particular three out of the eleven official languages, in *The Cry of*

---

[45] Njabulo Ndebele, "Fools," in *Fools and Other Stories* (Johannesburg: Ravan, 1983): 152–280.

[46] It has been pointed out numerous times that black South Africans, for fear of censorship in their own country, had to write in English to be published in England. Ndebele himself also gives the explanation that before the Bantu Education Act they had learned to read and write in English. Ndebele, "Actors and Interpreters: Popular Culture and Progressive Formalism" (1986), in *Rediscovery of the Ordinary*, 90.

[47] Ndebele, "The English Language and Social Change in South Africa" (1986), in *Rediscovery of the Ordinary*, 114.

[48] Ndebele, "An Encounter with my Roots" (2000), in *Fine Lines from the Box*, 151.

*Winnie Mandela* he makes only slight adjustments: a marginally greater increase in the use of indigenous expressions, for which he now sees the necessity of a glossary at the end of the volume and, of more weight, the introduction of occasional metalinguistic elements. For example, he comments on the
isiZulu expression for 'a gathering of waiting women', asking whether it
shouldn't be "mourning women,"[49] then several times explains in English not
only the literal meaning but also the significance of an indigenous term:
"*Botekatse*," lechery (52), or "*Mkhaya*," home-girl or boy (81). The really
new development in Ndebele's fiction, however, is the postmodernist mode
he adopts in this novel. A work of fiction which has to be preceded by "A
Note to the Reader" specifying "This is a work of fiction, with quotations
from some non-fiction texts listed at the end of the book" (np) not only an-
nounces its intertextuality, but also warns the reader before the incipit that
s/he should be aware of this feature (and it can be noted that this division in
the diegesis is not always obvious). This intertextuality assumes another
aspect with two figures from the past, the fictional Penelope and the historical
Sarah Baartman; the first appearing as Homer's character at the beginning of
Part One and on the same level as Ndebele's fictional characters at the end of
Part Two; the second, inscribed as the dedicatee, emblematic of South African
womanhood "who endured the horrors of European eyes" (np).

The incipit goes beyond an introductory address to the reader: "Let's begin
with the blurb of an imaginary book about a South African woman during the
long years of struggle against apartheid. It reads: […]" (1) and we are told
what the book is about and what we should think of it. There follows the story
of Penelope and the connection of her story with that of four South African
women, "her descendants." Is this a way of being 'ordinary', of introducing
the reader in a manner s/he understands to a complex construction of tales and
narrators? But is this a necessity or a postmodernist ploy? Part One continues
and ends with one first-person and three third-person narratives of the contemporary waiting and suffering of four 'ordinary' South African women.
Part Two opens with a gathering of the women and another incipit in the same
vein: the narrator tells of his relationship with the four women, who talk to
each other and discuss their own situations and that of Winnie Mandela. In
turn they "play a game" and "enter into a conversation" (46) with Winnie

---

[49] Njabulelo Simakhale Ndebele, *The Cry of Winnie Mandela* (Cape Town: David
Philip, 2003; Banbury: Ayebia Clarke, 2004): 48. Further page references are in the
main text.

Mandela. Then she herself replies and analyses her own situation. In the last chapter, "The Stranger," the four women and Winnie have a fleeting encounter with Penelope; they have hired a minibus and driver and set off on a holiday trip together or, as the last sentence in the book affirms, "their pilgrimage to eternal companionship" (139). The narrator maintains throughout the metafictional relationship with his reader: "We read about other people, reflect on them and never think that we ourselves, the readers, could be our own book to read and reflect upon" (65) and "We've all been profiled in the book that created us. Don't expect me to go over what you know" (95). However, it could seem that this artifice is paradoxical. The text is no 'ordinary' text and, contrarily to *Fools*, necessitates re-reading again and again to appreciate the complexity of the South African reality for black women.

Ndebele has transcended the 'ordinary' in this fiction by exploring the relationship between the mundane and the extraordinary, between private and public concerns, between the conversational or confessional mode of writing and public discourse. The questioning without the giving of easy solutions reveals the rich irony of "successful social practice," not only through the major problem presented by the life of Winnie Mandela, beloved and hated, faithful to the cause and source of evil, but also through the lives of ordinary people. That of Penelope's third descendant, Mamello, is the story which renders insane. It is a case in point: the only story in Part One written as a first-person confession, it induces an ironic distancing not only from Mamello herself and her suffering but also, paradoxically, from the new South Africa. The latter is represented by the public discourse used in the letter sent to her by her unfaithful ex-husband, an ANC official who has subsequently remarried a white woman and had a 'Coloured' child. His arguments are forceful and politically correct; with the new dispensation, Coloureds are no longer to be manipulated by the whites and his child will throw in his lot with the blacks. The political correctness and public discourse mode are deconstructed by the fact that, as a consequence of his "private" actions, Mamello has been rendered insane. Winnie Mandela had twenty-seven years of "waiting," Penelope had only nineteen, other women no end.

One question remains. All of Ndebele's work, both essays and fiction, is based on what he himself terms "counter-intuition" or the faculty of probing beneath the surface, revealing the irony of a situation or mode of behaviour. The title of his latest collection of essays, *Fine Lines from the Box*, describes his method of exploring not only the main lines of an issue but also the "fine lines" that are not always apparent.[50] The "art of the fine line," originally defined as the two sides of "writing and reading" (10), became in the essays "the attempt to capture the essence of issues through a thoughtful engagement with them" (11). As readers, we certainly partake of the fine line in Ndebele's prose, and insights so acquired most certainly lead us to a consciousness of "some common recognizable patterns of socio-historical behaviour."[51] A slight disappointment, however, on reading the ending of *The Cry of Winnie Mandela*: the author's "fine lines" have made it clear that no palliative exists to the waiting women's suffering other than societal reform or the "tangibles" of African Renaissance. Was it really necessary to hold out as a solution "a pilgrimage to eternal companionship" of which the irony is not apparent? But, once again, "fine lines" are meant for understanding issues, not resolving them.

This mode of writing echoes a new consciousness of richness and complexity in South Africa's art and politics, which can no longer be confined to Peter Horn's central notion of aesthetics and revolution.[52] Indeed, in "The 'War on Terror' and the African Renaissance," Ndebele not only calls for an African Renaissance but, reasoning from his past experience of apartheid South Africa, launches into a call for "global leadership":

> The millions of people around the world who have stood up against war do not want us to go back there. This desire takes us beyond the notion of the African Renaissance towards a more compelling and global one: global renaissance. [...] The greatest question is: can the United States conceptualise and commit to an overarching global interest which in some vital ways may override its own national interest, in the service of that very same national interest? What we need is global sustainability beyond the notion of empire. Which country or countries will take us there?[53]

---

[50] The "box," as he explains in his preface (9–11), is the box of banned books he, as an adolescent, found in his father's garage.

[51] Ndebele, "African Renaissance: A New Kid on the Block," in *Fine Lines from the Block*, 97.

[52] Peter Horn, "Aesthetics and the Revolutionary Struggle: Peter Weiss's Novel *The Aesthetics of Resistance*," *Critical Arts* 3.4 (1985): 7–54.

[53] Ndebele, "The 'War on Terror' and the 'African Renaissance': On Identity and Citizenship Today" (2003), in *Fine Lines from the Box*, 206.

## Works Cited

Coetzee, J.M. *Disgrace* (London: Secker & Warburg, 1999).

——. *The Lives of Animals*, intro. Amy Gutmann (Princeton NJ: Princeton UP, 1999).

Davis, Geoffrey V. *Voices of Justice and Reason: Apartheid and Beyond in South African Literature* (Cross/Cultures 61; Amsterdam & New York: Rodopi, 2003).

Fuchs, Anne. *Playing the Market: The Market Theatre, Johannesburg* (1990; Cross/Cultures 50; Amsterdam & New York: Rodopi, rev. ed. 2002).

Geertsema, Johan. "Ndebele, Fanon, Agency, and Irony," *Journal of Southern African Studies* 30.4 (December 2004): 749–63.

——. "Passages into the World: South African Literature after Apartheid," in *After Apartheid: The Second Decade*, conference at the MacMillan Center, Yale University, 27–28 April 2007, www.yale.edu/macmillan/apartheid/geertsmap2.pdf (accessed 22 July 2009).

Horn, Peter. "Aesthetics and the Revolutionary Struggle: Peter Weiss's Novel *The Aesthetics of Resistance*," *Critical Arts* 3.4 (1985): 7–54.

Mphahlele, Ezekiel. *Down Second Avenue* (London: Faber & Faber, 1959).

Mzamane, Mbulelo. *My Cousin Comes to Jo'burg* (Johannesburg: Ravan, 1980).

Ndebele, Njabulo Simakhale. "Actors and Interpreters: Popular Culture and Progressive Formalism," in *Rediscovery of the Ordinary*, 69–89. Repr. in *South African Literature and Culture*, 75–97. Sol Plaatje Memorial Lecture, University of Bophuthatswana, 14 September 1984.

——. "African Renaissance: A New Kid on the Block," in *Fine Lines from the Box*, 96–98. First published as "African Renaissance: A Social Quest," *Siyaya* 2 (Winter 1998): 58.

——. "AIDS and the Making of Modern South Africa: Responding to a Pandemic in a Time of Complexity," in *Fine Lines from the Box,* 170–89. Oliver Tambo Memorial Lecture (21 October 2002).

——. "The 'Black' Agenda and South Africa's Universities: Some Sobering Thoughts," in *Fine Lines from the Box*, 165–69. First published as "The 'Black' Agenda and the Restructuring of Higher Education" (2002).

——. *The Cry of Winnie Mandela* (Cape Town: David Philip, 2003, repr. Banbury: Ayebia Clarke, 2004).

——. "An Encounter with my Roots," in *Fine Lines from the Box*, 146–52. First published as "Multilingual Fiction: Writing, Language and Identity" in *Connect: Art, Politics, Theory, Practice* (Fall 2000): 191–96.

——. "The English Language and Social Change in South Africa," in *Rediscovery of the Ordinary*, 90–114. Repr. in *South African Literature and Culture*, 98–116. Keynote address at the Jubilee Conference of the English Academy of South Africa, 1986. First published in *TriQuarterly* 69 (Spring–Summer 1987): 217–35.

——. *Fine Lines from the Box: Further Thoughts About Our Country,* compilation & appreciation by Sam Raditlhalo (Roggebaai, SA: Umuzi & Houghton: Random House, 2007).

——. *Fools and Other Stories* (Johannesburg: Ravan, 1983).

——. "Game Lodges and Leisure Colonialists Caught in the Process of Becoming," in *Fine Lines from the Box*, 99–105. First published in *Blank: Architecture, Apartheid and After*, ed. Hilton Judin & Ivan Vladislavic (Rotterdam: NAI & Cape Town: David Philip, 1998): 119–23.

——. "Good Morning, South Africa: Whose Universities, Whose Standards?" in *Fine Lines from the Box*, 13–18. First delivered in Senate Lecture Series, University of the Witwatersrand (1987).

——. "Innocence Lost, Opportunity Gained: A Path towards Renaissance," in *Fine Lines from the Box*, 92–95. First published in *Cape Times* (27 April 1998).

——. "Jacob Zuma and the Family: How Zuma's Bravado Brutalized the Public," in *Fine Lines from the Box*, 230–32. First published as "Jacob Zuma and the Transformation of the ANC" in *Sunday Times* (S.A.; 6 March 2003).

——. "Leadership Challenges: Truth and Integrity in an Act of Salesmanship," in *Fine Lines from the Box*, 233–44. Inaugural King Moshoeshoe Memorial Lecture, University of the Free State (25 May 2006). Edited version first published as "Perspectives on Leadership Challenges in South Africa" in *City Press* (28 May 2006); then as "True Leadership May Mean Admitting Disunity" in *Sunday Times* (S.A.; 4 June 2006).

——. "The Lion and the Rabbit: Freeing the Oppressor," in *Fine Lines from the Box*, 106–109. First delivered as "The 'Languages' of Lions and Rabbits: Thoughts on Democracy and Reconciliation" at the After the TRC: Reconciliation in the New Millennium Conference, University of Cape Town (August 1999). First published as "Of Lions and Rabbits: Thoughts on Democracy and Reconciliation" in *Pretexts: Literary & Cultural Studies* 8.2 (1999): 147–58.

——. "Moral Anchor: An Interview with the Archbishop," in *Fine Lines from the Box*, 77–83. First published in *Siyaya* 3 (Spring 1998): 13–17.

——. "Redefining Relevance," in *Rediscovery of the Ordinary*, 49–68. Repr. in *South African Literature and Culture*, 60–74. Revision of "Beyond 'Protest': New Directions in South African Literature," *High Plains Literary Review* 1.1 (Winter 1986): 19–36.

——. "The Rediscovery of the Ordinary: Some New Writings in South Africa," in *Rediscovery of the Ordinary*, 37–48. Repr. in *South African Literature and Culture*, 41–59. Originally published in *Journal of Southern African Studies* 12.2 (April 1986): 144–57.

——. *Rediscovery of the Ordinary: Essays on South African Literature and Culture* (Fordsburg S.A.: COSAW, 1991). Enlarged edition as *South African Literature and*

*Culture: Rediscovery of the Ordinary*, intro. Graham Pechey, preface by Ndebele (Manchester: Manchester UP, 1994).

——. "Thabo Mbeki: Comradeship, Intrigue and Betrayal: A Vital Leadership Endgame," in *Fine Lines from the Box,* 161–64. First published as "Thabo Mbeki: New Opportunities for Leadership" in *Cape Argus* (3 May 2001).

——. "Turkish Tales and Some Thoughts on South African Fiction," in *Rediscovery of the Ordinary*, 11–36. Repr. in *South African Literature and Culture*, 17–40. Originally published in *Staffrider* 6.1 (1984): 40–48.

——. "The Year of the Dog: A Journey of the Imagination," in *Fine Lines from the Box*, 251–56. First published in *Mail & Guardian* (1–7 September 2006).

——. "The 'War on Terror' and the African Renaissance': On Identity and Citizenship Today," in *Fine Lines from the Box,* 200–206. Inaugural UKUZA Lecture, British Council, Spier, Stellenbosch (4 April 2003).

——. "Whither English in the 21st Century? Sharing a Common Language," in *Fine Lines from the Box*, 67–76. First delivered at AUETSA Conference, University of the North (30 June 1997). First published in *Current Writing: Text and Reception in Southern Africa* 10.1 (1998): 86–96.

Serote, Mongane. *To Every Birth Its Blood* (Johannesburg: Ravan, 1981).

◄❖►

BRIAN WORSFOLD

# To Every Miracle Its Gods

## Mongane Wally Serote's *Gods of Our Time* as a Post-Apartheid Perception of Black Experience

G ODS OF OUR TIME,[1] PUBLISHED IN 1999, is Mongane Wally
Serote's second novel. His first novel, *To Every Birth Its Blood*,
published in 1981, was one of a plethora of novels by black South
African writers[2] who recorded the events of June 1976 which are known as
the Soweto schoolchildren's uprising. These novels document the formation
of schoolchildren's cells in the South African townships to protest against the
imposition of Afrikaans as a medium of instruction in their secondary schools
and the evolution of these cells into units of underground resistance against
the oppression of the apartheid regime. Many of the children were killed during 'the Struggle',[3] many were imprisoned and tortured by the South African
Police, but many crossed the border into the neighbouring states of Botswana,
Zambia, Mozambique, Angola, and Swaziland to be trained in the arts of
guerrilla warfare. Mongane Wally Serote's third novel to date, *Scatter the
Ashes and Go*,[4] narrates the circumstances of those same schoolchildren who,
after the demise of apartheid, have returned to a South Africa that cannot be
compared with the one that years earlier they were forced to leave behind.

---

[1] Mongane Wally Serote, *Gods of Our Time* (Johannesburg: Ravan, 1999).

[2] Mongane Wally Serote, *To Every Birth Its Blood* (Johannesburg: Ravan, 1981).
Among other novels were Miriam Tlali's *Amandla* (Johannesburg: Ravan, 1980),
Sipho Sepamla's *A Ride on the Whirlwind* (Johannesburg: Ad. Donker, 1981) and
*Third Generation* (Johannesburg: Skotaville, 1986), Mbulelo Vizikhungo Mzamane's
*The Children of Soweto* (London: Longman, 1982), and Mothobi Mutloatse's *Mama
Ndiyalila* (Johannesburg: Ravan, 1982).

[3] The term 'the Struggle' is widely used by black South Africans to refer to their
long fight against the apartheid authorities.

[4] Mongane Wally Serote, *Scatter the Ashes and Go* (Johannesburg: Ravan, 2002).

The Soweto schoolchildren's uprising of June 1976 is perceived in retrospect as a major watershed in South African history and the beginning of the
end of apartheid. Yet fourteen years were to pass before Nelson Mandela
walked from Victor Verster prison in February 1990, a free man, and only in
1994 did the African National Congress win South Africa's first democratic
general election. What happened on the ground in the meantime, however,
has not received the same degree of attention by creative writers as did the
events of the second half of the 1970s. This is due possibly to the intensified
oppression of the apartheid authorities during the 1980s and the subsequent
increased strictures of censorship. Also, writers like Sipho Sepamla, in novels
such as *A Scattered Survival* (1989),[5] turned to look at the effects of apartheid
on the daily existence of black townspeople, rather than focusing on 'the
Struggle' per se. From the vantage point of the early post-apartheid dispensation and with the benefit of hindsight, Mongane Wally Serote has filled in
glaring gaps in the record. *Gods of Our Time* is set in Alexandra, Tembisa,
Atteridgeville, Sebokeng, and other parts of rural and urban South Africa
during the mid-1980s.

In many ways, Serote's representation of different periods in the recent history of apartheid South Africa are not reflected in the content or even the style
of the novel. Like *To Every Birth Its Blood*, *Gods of Our Time* is a complex
novel whose narrative threads are intricate and difficult to trace. The entran-
ces and exits of the numerous characters seem random and almost coinci-
dental. This gives the novel a sense of spontaneity and moments of intensity,
but the overall impression that remains with the reader is a blur of characters
and events, a morass of experiences, feelings, and ideas in which it is difficult
to discern any dynamic or direction. This clearly is the author's intention; the
spontaneity of the character's behaviour is symptomatic of the madness and
chaos of the moment. Serote describes the relationships between the young
people in the townships as they are forced further and further underground by
members of the South African Police, the South African Defence Force, their
agents, and black informers. Ultimately, most young people find themselves
asking to be assisted to cross the border into the African National Congress
(ANC) training camps in the front-line states.

However, similar activities have already been narrated in novels about the
June '76 Soweto uprising. Indeed, Serote leaves his reader in no doubt that
the "gods" in the title of the novel are the young people and the women of

---

[5] Sipho Sepamla, *A Scattered Survival* (Johannesburg: Skotaville, 1989).

South African townships, with 'freedom fighters' like Steve, Sizakhele and the narrator himself, Moses Motsamayi, in supporting roles. This was not new at the time. Sipho Sepamla's *Third Generation* (1986) lauds the commitment and bravery of black South African young people and women, and is dedicated to "Emma Sathekge, 15 year old, and Thabo Sibeko, 6 year old, undying victims of apartheid."[6] Yet Serote goes further in *Gods of Our Time*. The novel touches on numerous themes, but one theme that is dealt with in greater depth is the psychology of mass action undertaken by children under the duress of long-term oppression.

For many adults, including black South African parents at the time, it seemed impossible that their children's actions could have such a profound effect on their entire social order. Adults tend to underestimate the power of the collective action of their offspring. This generational blindness is causing errors in political decision-making on a global basis. Even today, one has to look no further than the West Bank and Gaza where intifadas have taken place to have evidence for this contention. In *Gods of Our Time*, Serote applies his political experience and his poetic sensibility to ascertaining the nature and development of the power of collective attitudes among young people in the context of continued and prolonged oppression: i.e. among people who have never experienced true freedom in all their short lives.

◄❖►

Mongane Wally Serote became an ANC sympathizer when he was a secondary-school student at the Morris Isaacson High School in Soweto. In 1969, at the age of twenty-three, he was arrested and detained without trial for nine months. In 1974, he left South Africa to take up a Fulbright Scholarship at Columbia University, New York and he returned in 1977. This meant that he was outside South Africa during the June '76 schoolchildren's uprising of which his former secondary school was an epicentre of the student action. Even when he returned to Southern Africa in 1977, it was to Gaborone, Botswana, and not to South Africa. It was during the six-year period from about 1974 to 1980 that he wrote *To Every Birth Its Blood*, which was published in 1981. This means that the novel was conceived and written in its entirety outside South Africa. Yet, as one commentator on Serote's work has pointed out, *To Every Birth Its Blood* "provides, self-consciously, a vivid insight not

---

[6] See dedication in Sipho Sepamla, *Third Generation* (Johannesburg: Skotaville, 1986).

only into life in a revolutionary society but into the very processes through which personal and political commitments develop."[7] Perhaps it was the fact that Serote was absent from Soweto when the uprising took place, unlike other writers who witnessed the violence at first-hand, that prompted him to look at the psychology of the process of revolt in greater depth. Moreover, following a three-year period in the USA and from beyond the boundary of South African apartheid in Botswana, Serote was in a position to give robust expression to his political commitment.

On arriving in Botswana in 1977, Serote resumed political activities in the exiled ANC and its military wing, Umkhonto we Sizwe (MK). In 1986, he went to London, becoming the ANC Cultural Attaché in the UK, returning to South Africa in 1990 to direct the Department of Arts and Culture of the newly unbanned ANC. He had been outside South Africa for sixteen years and, as with the June 1976 Soweto uprising, had observed the disturbances of the mid-1980s from a distance. Like *To Every Birth Its Blood*, therefore, *Gods of Our Time* is an extrapolation of the events rather than a witness's first-hand account, a fact that gives both novels universalized significance.

In the first all-race elections held in April 1994, Serote stood as an ANC candidate and was elected to a seat in the South African parliament. He has since chaired the Portfolio Committee on Arts, Culture and Language, Science and Technology and also the Steering Committee of the Indigenous Knowledge Systems.[8] These responsibilities have enabled him to stay in close contact with "students from historically disadvantaged universities"[9] and, in a roundtable paper, he confirmed his faith in the youth of South Africa:

> The youth who emerge from this institution [of initiation] emerge with knowledge to build the basic structure of society – the family, and roles of men and women are put in place, as also the roles of the girl and boy child are defined.[10]

---

[7] See entry "Serote, Mongane Wally" in Douglas Killam & Ruth Rowe, *The Companion to African Literatures* (Oxford: James Currey, 2002): 263.

[8] Currently, Mongane Wally Serote is the Chief Executive Officer of Freedom Park, a 52-hectare memorial site where all South Africans can commemorate the pain of the past and celebrate the renewal of the human spirit that was opened at Salvokop on the outskirts of Pretoria in 2009.

[9] See "Column in the Year of Science and Technology by Mongane Wally Serote," *Indigenous Knowledge and Development Monitor* (December 1998).

[10] "One Fundamental Threshold," paper delivered at a roundtable organized by the World Intellectual Property Organization (Geneva, 23–24 July 1998).

Serote's deep-rooted confidence in the maturity and ability of young indigenous South Africans underpins his intention in *Gods of Our Time*. The novel is based on events in the South African townships around Johannesburg and Pretoria in the 1980s, tragic events which came to a head with the Sebokeng massacre of July 1990. However, the underlying meaning of the novel is to be found not in characterization, plot or descriptive accounts of these events but, rather, in the interrelation of highly effective but seemingly unconnected, chaotic occurrences. But is this controlled chaos or uncontrolled chaos? What is the nature of this chaos, that it can cause miracles to happen, like the end of apartheid or the fall of the Berlin Wall?

*Gods of Our Time* would appear to be set in the period 1984–85. This was the time of P.W. Botha, Ronald Reagan, and Margaret Thatcher. It was also the era of the United Democratic Front (UDF), the increasing power of black trade unions, to the extent that comparisons were drawn between South Africa's black unions and the Solidarity movement in Gdańsk, Poland, and a period when the army was brought in to help the police keep the lid on township violence. The "stayaway"[11] referred to in Chapter 28 of the novel, therefore, could be an explicit reference to the major strike which took place on the Witwatersrand on 6 and 7 November 1984. The Federation of South African Trade Unions (FOSATU), the Council of Mining Unions, and the Metal and Allied Workers' Union backed the strike to protest against the government treatment of township residents. *The Economist* wrote of the event at the time:

> As many as 90% stayed away in the black townships of Sebokeng, Sharpeville and Biopatong, where a combined force of 7,000 police and troops had carried out house-to-house searches affecting nearly a quarter of a million inhabitants last month. [...] Instead of cowing the township residents, the raids seem to have made them braver.[12]

Furthermore, there are parallels between the deaths of the characters Eddy Monnakgotla and James Mlambo and the death in police custody of Andreas Raditsela, a FOSATU shop steward, who died of head injuries on 6 May 1985. In the novel, the trade-union leaders Eddy Monnakgotla and James Mlambo are arrested by the police officer Derek van Niekerk and his three black assistants and both are tortured to death, the former by the 'helicopter ride' and the latter by a bullet to the head and 'necklacing'. The death of Mr

---

[11] A 'stayaway' or *Azikhwelwa* was an institutionalized form of protest by which a day was set for all black workers to remain in the townships and not go to work.

[12] Anon., *The Economist* (10–16 November 1984): 45.

Raditsela was followed by acts of sabotage by the ANC, including the bomb-ing of the police station in the township where the funeral was taking place, a funeral attended by more than 25,000 workers.[13]

These events took place when Mongane Wally Serote was in Botswana and just prior to his move to England in 1986. For this reason, he would have experienced the happenings from a distance. Indeed, much of Serote's back-ground material for the novel would have probably come to him in the form of personal accounts of the young black men and women as they moved through Gaborone on their way to ANC training camps in other front-line states. This may account for the kaleidoscopic nature of the presentation of the characters and their activities, aptly described by Anthony Egan as "a col-lage of characters and incidents."[14] On the other hand, it gave Serote a chance to analyse the tactics and strategies of the young people and to try and pene-trate their mind-set.

◄❖►

*Gods of Our Time* is the story of Lindi, a well-known black night-club singer who agrees to conceal a group of young children in her Alexandra house dur-ing the township violence of the mid-1980s. Her story is told by the journalist Moses Motsamayi, who is also an ANC 'freedom fighter'. Through Lindi's account, the narrator learns of the behaviour and activities of the young child-ren under her protection. For the narrator, "there is a silence here,"[15] but it is a silence which "is now too loud" and can no longer be concealed (9). Though difficult to obtain, this information is important because it fills a gap in the history of 'the Struggle'. But the tale is about the deaths of countless children and is difficult to tell – "It was deep, deep in us; its heat was intense [...]. This present [...] had [...] burnt into our tongues a language which Lindi and I [...] were consciously trying to articulate" (97).

As a leitmotif which runs through the whole novel, the deafening silence is picked up again in Chapter 4. At a mass burial of numberless young people in Tembisa,

---

[13] See *The Economist* (18–24 May 1985): 51; (15–21 June 1985): 51.

[14] See Anthony Egan, "*The Spilling of Blood* by Thabo Shenge Luthuli (Gariep); *Gods of Our Time* by Mongane Wally Serote (Ravan)," *Mail & Guardian* (29 October 1999).

[15] Mongane Wally Serote, *Gods of Our Time* (1999): 9. Further page references are in the main text.

> Someone had decided that children take too much space. They decided that
> they should be buried in a mass grave. There were many of these mass graves.
> I wondered how many coffins each mass grave takes. Many of these graves
> still had fresh flowers on them, and toys which looked brand-new. (28)

The Reverend Mokone's voice breaks the silence which "was as large as the
world and the sky"(28). Speaking of the children's ultimate sacrifice, he says:

> We have come to bury our warriors […]. They faced [death] with absolute
> contempt, they hurled their lives so we can be free men and women. We must
> not, we must never forget them. (30)

Rather than stifle rebellion, the slaughter and mass burials cause increasing
numbers of young people in the townships to commit themselves to 'the
Struggle'. The image of the whirlwind had been used as a metaphor to symbolize the schoolchildren's fervour in the June 1976 uprising,[16] and in *Gods of
Our Time*, the affiliation of young people to the Movement becomes a roller-
coaster ride. Their behaviour spontaneous and instinctive, the young people of
the townships queue up to be sent beyond South Africa's borders for training.
James Mlambo indicates the power of the children when he says:

> The children who burn shops and delivery vans are our children, we can talk to
> them, we can tell them what we [their parents] can do and what we can't, we
> can come to agreements with them. (62)

The narrator tries to comprehend the intensity of the oppression they are
reacting to and the psychology of collective revolt:

> Who is the Movement? […] This crowd? People who are drowning must
> feel like this: space and space, substance and substance all around, but no-
> where to hold – life then thrusts, thrashes out, becomes alive like life itself.
> We rise as a people, we rise slowly, as slow as rain clouds. We rise, and rise,
> and rise. (74)

Serote's image of the claustrophobia of oppression is extended as the children
hide beneath a tree on the outskirts of the township. Serote globalizes the
metaphor:

> The West […] would never come to know that hate of oppression had become
> so ripe, it was hateless; suffering had been lived to its fathomless depth, and so
> had become non-existent […]. Life had stopped being lived in Tembisa, the

---

[16] Cf. Sipho Sepamla's title for his novel on the Soweto uprising, *A Ride on the
Whirlwind* (Johannesburg: Ad. Donker, 1981).

Vaal, Uitenhage. In every single space of South Africa [...] life was no longer
being lived. (85)

Ridding oneself of such oppression is a long-term task:

> "[...] no longer measured in terms of life." [...]
> "It is measured in terms of cutting, link for link, the chain of oppression,
> whatever the cost."
> "[...] can singing do that, can hiding children do that, can throwing a stone
> or a petrol bomb do that [...]?"
> "That's the point, you see – not a single act, but a combination of all those
> can do it." (98)

For the narrator, the Western mind-set is not aware of the power of this combination, a fusion of seemingly unrelated actions which constitutes an all-
powerful force:

> "I see; I feel a force stronger than any steel or diamond. It is unleashed, and I
> hear America, Britain and France, and I think, how come they don't know that
> this force exists, that this force is strong? Why do these countries talk as if this
> force is not in motion, as if they do not know that it will crush everything
> before it? Why?" (99)

The township children operate from within a fully integrated sub-culture –
"a world underneath the world" (109) – whose activities, propelled by a
psychosis of oppression, rise suddenly to the surface of township life and
then, just as suddenly, sink out of sight, the children disappearing into hiding
places offered by the maze of streets, two-roomed houses, and back yards.
Not only have parents lost all authority over their children, but "the old people
are being controlled by children" (111). The oppressor perceives the children
as pawns manipulated by their elders and metes out a stereotypical, heavy-
handed response to the children's action:

> The police and the army came, searching, swearing, beating, raping. [...] They
> had, in their search for criminals and hooligans, left behind a few corpses of
> school children. (113)

There is no attempt on the part of Derek van Niekerk to understand why the
children behave as they do. When the Tembisa businessman, Lucas Ngubeni,
comments to van Niekerk that there was no reason to kill the children, the
white police officer retorts: "If that is what you think, you hold very dangerous and naïve thoughts" (113). On the other hand, the narrator does understand how, after living cheek-by-jowl with one's oppressor over a long period
of time,

you listened to the sound of the gun, and as your mind and your flesh listened, got frightened, became taut, snapped and became numb, to find you were alive the next day was to stand up immediately and do what had to be done. Drive a car. Throw a stone. Talk with comrades. Stop cars. Make someone drink cooking oil. Whatever had to be done, you went out to do. To stop and think; to miss someone; to look closely, to examine – this came when one was alone, when time seemed plentiful, and then you realised, change is as tough as steel. (181)

Although *Gods of Our Time* is based on events which preceded the dismantling of apartheid, towards the end of the novel Serote states that "the townships and rural areas held power in their hands" and "everywhere a new energy and restlessness began" (195). The beginning of the end was in sight, and Serote knew as he wrote this that the children – "in their blindness and deafness to danger, because a future is not real until it is lived – the young with their strong legs and arms and curious minds, [who] were thrust into the present to judge it" (152) – had won, making them the "gods" of their time. But Serote is also aware that generations are unique because they live through unique periods in the history of the world. Cynthia, one of the "gods," grows impatient with adults who say "all youth is like that. It is impatient. It thinks it knows everything. It is always critical of its time" (238), and, in the last paragraph of the novel, the narrator sees the new generation of youth of the new South Africa:

I see the youth, black and white, young men and young women, in haircuts I have never seen, in dress, which I am tempted to say is mad, they are laughing and giggling and throwing their heads and their shoulders and talk at the top of their voices. (281)

The image depresses the narrator – "I must go now, this apparent twilight weighs heavily on my heart" (281). He is depressed because the new, younger generation makes him think of the young men and women of the previous generation who gave their lives to rid South Africa of apartheid, and also because he feels that this new generation would not lay down their lives for 'the Struggle' in the same way. The values of youth have changed. But then, as Mapule Sechele, the old woman from Marquard, said at the Women's Day meeting in Regina Mundi, "When we fight so we can walk, we are also fighting so that we can have a new way of talking!" (67). In *Gods of Our Time*, Serote suggests that today's leaders in the post-apartheid, post-Cold War, and, we can now add, post-9/11 world must also develop a "new way of talking."

In our struggle for the attainment of peace and democracy in a globalizing world, vote-winning slogans must adapt. To paraphrase the former US president Bill Clinton, "It's the children, stupid!"

## WORKS CITED

Anon. "South Africa: Black Solidarity," *Economist* (18–24 May 1985).

——. "South Africa: Solidarity is Black," *Economist* (10–16 November 1984).

——. "South Africa: The Underground is Shifting," *Economist* (15–21 June 1985).

Egan, Anthony. "*The Spilling of Blood* by Thabo Shenge Luthuli (Gariep); *Gods of Our Time* by Mongane Wally Serote (Ravan)," *Mail & Guardian* (29 October 1999).

Killam, Douglas, & Ruth Rowe. *The Companion to African Literatures* (Oxford: James Currey, 2000).

Sepamla, Sipho. *A Ride on the Whirlwind* (Johannesburg: Ad. Donker, 1981).

——. *A Scattered Survival* (Johannesburg: Skotaville, 1989).

——. *Third Generation* (Johannesburg: Skotaville, 1986).

Serote, Mongane Wally. "Column in the Year of Science and Technology by Mongane Wally Serote," *Indigenous Knowledge and Development Monitor* (December 1998): online.

——. *Gods of Our Time* (Johannesburg: Ravan, 1999).

——. "One Fundamental Threshold," paper delivered at the roundtable on Intellectual Property and Indigenous Peoples (Geneva: World Intellectual Property Organisation, August 1998).

——. *Scatter the Ashes and Go* (Johannesburg: Ravan, 2002).

——. *To Every Birth Its Blood* (Johannesburg: Ravan, 1981; London: Heinemann, 1983).

◄❖►

CHRISTINE MATZKE

## Girls with Guts
Writing a South African Thriller
—Angela Makholwa in Conversation

I N A RECENT ARTICLE ON THE CRIME WRITER WESSEL EBERSOHN, Geoff Davis writes that detective fiction "has rarely been considered a major genre in South African literature," with regard neither to its critical reception nor to its place in the nation's literary history.[1] However, crime fiction has always existed at the edges of literary production in South Africa, waiting to be read, enjoyed, and 'investigated'; from the early stories of Arthur Maimane in *Drum Magazine* in the 1950s to crime writers 'proper' during the apartheid years, Ebersohn and James McClure; from South Africa's best-selling 'export', the Afrikaans-writing Deon Meyer, to countless texts that borrow elements from the genre.[2] Indeed, when informally enquiring about contemporary crime novels in South Africa in 2003, the short-story writer and novelist Ivan Vladislavic replied: "Come to think of it, most South African literature is about crime."[3]

---

[1] Geoffrey V. Davis, "Political Loyalites and the Intricacies of the Criminal Mind: The Detective Fiction of Wessel Ebersohn," in *Postcolonial Postmortems: Crime Fiction from a Transcultural Perspective*, ed. Christine Matzke & Susanne Mühleisen (Amsterdam: Rodopi, 2006): 182.

[2] For a brief overview of South African crime fiction, see Mike Nicol, "South African News from Mike Nicol," http://www.thrillerwriters.org/2008/09/south-african-news-from-mike-nicol.html, and Mike Nicol, "Guest Blogger Mike Nicol of Crime Beat (South Africa), Saturday, November 22, 2008," http://detectivesbeyondborders .blogspot.com/2008/11 /guest-blogger-mike-nicol-of-crime-beat.html; see also "Who's Who of South African Crime Writing," http://crimebeat.book.co.za/whos-who-of-south-african-crime-writing/ (all accessed 3 December 2008).

[3] Personal conversation with the author at Johann Wolfgang von Goethe University, Frankfurt am Main, 2003.

There is no doubt that crime fiction has been burgeoning in the 'new' South Africa, but particularly so in recent years. The reasons given are various, but all are equally compelling. In a 2006 radio interview, Deon Meyer reasoned that

> it would have been totally impossible to write a book about policemen or former policemen in the old South Africa under the apartheid regime. What Nelson Mandela and F.W. de Klerk did for me personally was they freed up police detective heroes and private eyes so that one can write about them. I don't think it is possible to have a protagonist in a police state as a hero.[4]

Others elsewhere have argued in a similar vein, considering crime novels a particularly "democratic" genre, "produced on any large scale only in democracies; dramatizing, under the bright cloak of entertainment, many of the precious rights and privileges that have set the dwellers in constitutional lands apart from the less fortunate."[5] But there are also other viewpoints coming from contemporary South Africa. Barbara Erasmus, for example, a journalist and co-founder of the Cape-based Crime Beat blog, an exciting new online forum for South African crime-fiction aficionados, notes that "Crime has overtaken colour as a headline-grabber in South African newspapers – and the same trend can be detected in local literature."[6] She also expresses a certain tiredness of "apartheid and transformation literature," which explains her own interest in the genre.

Whatever reasons individual readers or writers might put forward, the fact is that crime fiction in all its multi-dimensionality has brought many new South African voices to the fore, one of whom is Angela Makholwa. A young professional with her own PR agency in Johannesburg, Makholwa published her first novel, *Red Ink*, in 2007 and is currently working on her third. *Red*

---

[4] NPR Radio, "Deon Meyer: Probing South Africa in Crime Fiction," *Weekend Edition* (Saturday, 27 May 2006), http://www.npr.org/templates/player/mediaPlayer .html?action =1&t=1&islist=false&id=5435833&m=5435834 (accessed 4 November 2008).

[5] Howard Haycraft, *Murder for Pleasure: The Life and Times of the Detective Story* (1941; New York: Biblo & Tannen, new enlarged ed. 1968): 313. For a more detailed discussion of how Haycraft's argument has been taken up, see Katja Meintel, *Im Auge des Gesetzes: Kriminalromane aus dem frankophonen Afrika südlich der Sahara – Gattungskonventionen und Gewaltlegitimation* (Aachen: Shaker, 2008): 3–7.

[6] Barbara Erasmus, "Greetings and welcome to the Crime Beat blog!" (4 August 2007), http://book.co.za/bookchat/topic.php?id=1461 (accessed 4 November 2008).

*Ink* is a racy thriller featuring the Jo'burg PR consultant Lucy Khambule, who receives an unusual request from a convicted serial killer in C-Max prison – to write his story. When she agrees, sinister events begin to unfold which draw her deeper and deeper into the murky waters of crime and begin to threaten her world of professional and private successes. The novel has been hailed as a page-turning, gripping thriller and was praised for its "distinct urban dialogue"; it has also made its mark on the literary map as the first crime novel by a black South African woman.[7]

In January 2008, Angela Makholwa attended the 9th Jahnheinz Jahn Symposium, "Beyond Murder by Magic: Investigating African Crime Fiction," at Gutenberg University, Mainz, Germany, which had brought together writers and critics from all over the world to discuss crime fiction from a dozen African countries written in nine different languages. Between panels, readings, and guided tour, she kindly agreed to talk to me about her novel *Red Ink*, her experience of writing it, and about the South African crime-fiction community.

CHRISTINE MATZKE: *Thanks for coming to Mainz, Angela. I would like to know what got you interested in crime fiction, and what made you write this particular story.*

ANGELA MAKHOLWA: When I was younger, I used to read adventure stories. I have always been drawn to strong characters that are about unravelling something, that are involved in a mystery. I think it started out with the *Secret Seven*, these young kids trying to discover things. Then, as I grew older, I started reading a lot of crime fiction, thrillers, and the like. For example, I was drawn to Mary Higgins Clark, John Grisham, and other legal thrillers. That's where it comes from. It's just a genre that I have always really loved and really, really relished. My book was inspired by the fact that I have always been reading in that genre. It's easier to write what you like to read.

CM: *When I researched you on the internet I discovered that you had taken a creative writing course. Was that the decisive moment when you decided you were going to write this book?*

---

[7] Kate Fuller, "A Brave New Voice," *The Citizen* (19 July 2007), http://www.citizen.co.za/index/article.aspx?pDesc=43667,1,22 (accessed 2 January 2009); Mike Nicol, "Red Ink: Angela Makholwa's Page-Turning Debut Reviewed" (25 July 2007), http://crimebeat.book.co.za/blog/2007/07/25/red-ink-angela-makholwas -page-turning-debut-reviewed/ (accessed 4 November 2008).

AM: I started writing the novel, and I think, quarter way, I thought: 'This doesn't sound like a proper novel'. I wasn't convinced. I was not confident that I had the right structure, that I used the right technique, and so on. The course says it teaches you how to write a novel, including all the structural elements. So I signed up and wrote for the course. Most of the book was written while I was taking it. It was a really short course. I think it was about eight weeks long. The good thing about the course was that it really forced you. It said: "Write a chapter per day. Just do it. Don't make excuses." It was very motivational.

CM: *So it was eight weeks full-time?*
AM: No, no. It was a really a short course in a short time. It was an hour per week, but you had to submit assignments. There was also a very good manual that told you the kind of excuses that writers make, writer's block and the like. And it said, don't make excuses, just do it. It was really excellent, it really was. And for the manuscript to get published, I sent it to the person who administered the course, Amanda Patterson. She knows the publishers and decided to send it to Pan Macmillan. And Pan Macmillan liked it and I got published. That's the whole story.

CM: *I had the feeling that* Red Ink *appeals particularly to a young urban audience. It catches this fast-paced, racy spirit of a city, what you might want to call a 'particular Jo'burg pulse'.*
AM: Yes, the book is always bubbling. It was deliberate. When I look at South African fiction, it tends to be very heavy. It's not a criticism because of where we come from. I think as a young person as well – I've always wanted to look for something that captures the spirit of Johannesburg and what happens, whatever the sub-context of it is. I was particularly interested in the current mind-set of young professional urban South Africans; it is not so heavy. I wanted to show that there is life beyond apartheid – there is life beyond all the heavy history we come from. And the way those characters in the book are portrayed – that's how most people, young urban South Africans, live now. So it was important for me to capture that spirit.[8]

---

[8] In an interview conducted two months after the Mainz conference, Makholwa somewhat modified her stance. Referring to the recent violence against migrant workers from other African countries, she said: "The absence of apartheid rhetoric was deliberate because I thought South Africa had reached the political maturity to enjoy the kind of literature that is unburdened by our past. However, events of the past few months make me feel a bit like a school teacher who prescribes a 12th grade textbook

CM: *As a reader, I could really feel it and that's what I liked about the book. Take Fundi, for example, the protagonist's best friend. The only place where you can creatively imagine her is in a fast and edgy environment like Johannesburg; her flamboyant style, her ambitions to become an actress combined with the economic necessity to make a living which results in her doing telephone sex and all that. She is such a wonderfully quirky character….*

AM: Yes, I like her too. She's crazy; one of my favourite characters.

CM: *What I also liked is this almost deliberate mixing of genres.* Red Ink *is very much steeped in a thriller tradition, but it is also connected to other forms of popular writing, such as romance. I have noticed this quite a bit in more recent African women's crime fiction. I am just thinking of Monica Genya's* Links of a Chain *(1996) or Amma Kyerewaa's* Kimberlite Flame *(2002), which were mentioned in some of the papers given at the conference. But, then again, your novel differs dramatically from these two. In Kyerewaa, for example, the romance element is much stronger than in your book, and more in the vein of mass-marketed romantic fiction; and Genya, of course, is very hyperbolic, in the sense that she creates this female James Bond, supersecret agent Susan Juma, who has a very heart-throbbing love affair with her male counterpart, Chain. Lucy Khambule, your protagonist, also has a romantic streak, but she is more rooted in an urban life that to me as a reader feels 'contemporary South African' and much more 'realistic' than the other two novels. You also seem to contrast the 'thriller' and the 'romance' elements starkly, the love lives of your characters to all the bloodcurdling elements. On the one hand, you have these very carefree moments, women meeting in cafés and talking about their lovers, and then …*

AM: … then you have all that gory stuff and details, the bloodbath and all that. Yes, there is juxtaposition in my book. This is what I was trying to achieve. I wanted to make the characters real. I wanted them to be fun as well. They must be just normal people that you meet, but are now confronted with these extraordinarily violent circumstances which, in fact, do happen in South Africa. However, it does not mean that if you find yourself in that kind of situation, you are suddenly going to lose your essential self. I mean, that's

---

to a group of third grade pupils. I'm no longer as certain of our ability to think outside of the racial boxes that we've been allocated. Perhaps we are not so ready after all, which would be profoundly sad." "Angela Makholwa in Conversation with Mike Nicol," http://crimebeat.book.co.za/blog/2008/03/12/angela-makholwa-in-conversation-with-mike-nicol (accessed 11 November 2008).

who they are. They are very carefree women who have lives beyond the serial killer and what happens. And obviously they are there for each other. It's about their camaraderie and their friendship and how they pull each other out of the darkness. Every time there is a dark episode, of course they discuss it, they become worried, they are trying to troubleshoot their way out of it, but they still remain a shoulder for each other to lean on and to say, 'Look, this is happening but I am still there for you. Let's see how we can try to get you out of the situation'.

CM: *What I also enjoyed was the detail. Coming from a PR background yourself, you obviously know how to run a PR agency, and that is clearly well portrayed in the book. But other scenes also seem extremely thoroughly researched. I am thinking of Lucy going to C-Max prison to meet the convicted serial killer, for example. She passes all these security checks, but it's not the way you would imagine a C-Max prison to be like. There are no heavy doors and grilles, and the area inside the prison seems very tranquil, almost like a garden.*

AM: Yes, a bit like the University of Mainz [*laughs*]. Yes, of course, I had to do some research. I had to go to Pretoria C-Max because I had never been in a prison complex before. I worried that I had to give the book as much authenticity as possible; it was essential I did it. I also got to interview one or two inmates in the prison section of C-Max. Again, I wanted to ensure that I don't give the serial killer a one-dimensional character that is just evil. Within those layers of evil is somebody who was able to lure his victims, charm them, make them feel very comfortable in his company. According to the book, they were all strangers to him. So you have to bring out that aspect of his personality that was able to charm a Johannesburg girl. I mean, Johannesburg women don't go round accepting lifts from strangers. But if someone has that kind of personality and presents himself in a way that lets your own guard down, and maybe he promises you something.... If you look at the opening chapter, you have this helpful stranger. This woman is in the middle of a busy street and her things are falling apart, her shopping is all over the road, and there comes this stranger saying, 'Look, sorry for that, let me help you with this'. He is a very gentle, very handsome young man. It was important for me to be able to paint that portrait of a killer who has many layers to him – like any other person, of course. All of us are multi-faceted.

CM: *The ending of your novel suggests that there might be a sequel; it's relatively open-ended. As a reader you wonder whether there isn't more danger coming from the serial killer. Would you like to tell me what your second novel is going to be about?*

AM: Ah, you are worried about the main character, Lucy? Well, a lot of people have asked me that question, whether I am going to kill her off. I am very ruthless, you know; that's what the critics say. You see, to be quite honest, that ending I added after the book had already been approved – it was already going into print. And then I just decided that I wasn't going to let it end like that. You know, when she finishes the book, she is so happy that her dream has come true – that's how it was going to end before. Then they sent it back to me for final proof, and when I'd gone through it I thought, 'No way, I think I need a bit of a twist'. Because I like books that end with a bit of a twist. So that was my twist.

CM: *It really leaves the reader on tenterhooks, because you imagine the protagonist to be in danger again.*

AM: Yes, you want to know what happened afterwards, don't you? There could be a sequel, but it won't … well, now I am on my third novel in terms of planning and all of that, but it's still not Lucy's story. It will be further down the line. It is still too fresh in my mind. I had to read that book a hundred times, for editing, rewriting, so I don't want to touch it yet, but there might be a sequel in the future.

CM: *Now that you are telling me you are already onto your third novel – do you have any time left to do your 'regular' work as a PR consultant?*

AM: Well, I have a son and a dog and a busy professional life, so I do it when people are sleeping. Or when they watch TV, that's when I write my books. I do the homework with my son. We relax a bit, and then when everybody goes to sleep I start writing. Or if I am really getting into the book, I wake up very early the next morning. I'll sleep at twelve, wake up at six, because I am so thrilled by where the story is going that I want to continue. So I am thinking, 'This is what happens, this is what happens!' As a result I wake up before the thought goes away.

CM: *A final question. Where do you place yourself in terms of South African literature, especially crime fiction? It seems to be really booming.*

AM: It's a very fresh market and it's very exciting. There are a lot of possibilities. I am intrigued by what is happening and the potential of developing it as a genre. I definitely want to be in that space. The third novel, that I am currently working on, is very much in that space. And it's very different to the other. And I think it has your 'girls' that are empowered, but there is still so much else going on. Well, all I can say is that I am very excited about it. I think readers of crime fiction will love it, even more so than *Red Ink*.

CM: *Thank you very much for talking to me, Angela.*

Angela Makholwa, picture courtesy of the author

❖

# Marcia Blumberg

# The Politics of Hope

## Engaging Lara Foot Newton's
## *Tshepang: The Third Testament**

L ARA FOOT NEWTON'S POWERFUL PLAY *TSHEPANG* (2001) invokes
      "hope" in its eponymous character, the nine-month-old baby, who is
      raped and miraculously survives. The epigraph, "Based on twenty
thousand true stories," reminds us that the play portrays just one of twenty
thousand stories per year about child rape in South Africa. The play has two
characters onstage – Ruth the mother of the baby and Simon a friend who has
loved her since childhood – and takes place three years after the rape of baby
Siesie, who is later named Tshepang (hope). Ruth was expelled from the
village and they manage to survive in a new locale, where they eke out a
meagre existence. We learn about the village from Simon, the narrator, who
speaks to us throughout the play, moving between the past and present, and
between stories and enactments; as a storyteller par excellence, he evokes the
lives of diverse villagers and provides a context for the horrifying details of
the rape of baby Tshepang. In contrast, Ruth, the mother of Tshepang, remains verbally silent throughout the play except for the final word, the quiet
uttering of her baby's name, which signifies hope on different levels. Strapped to Ruth's back is a small version of the big bed in which Tshepang was
raped, signifying the way that African women carry their babies and, in this
instance, foregrounding the indelible memory of her baby and the burden she
always carries. Ruth's gestural communication is masterful; not only does she
respond physically to Simon's stories, her facial expressions and postures
convey her grief, despair, regret, and guilt. Throughout the play, Ruth sits on
a pile of salt, which she rubs into animal hides to cure them. No small reminder of how black women in South Africa were foremost menial labourers,

* My sincere thanks to Jeanne Colleran for her constructive reading of this essay and
to Thom Bryce and Darren Gobert for their input.

"(*her manic and obsessive rubbing of the salt*)" produces an incessant scraping sound that reminds us of how she traumatically revisits the event, "rubbing salt into her wound," and also relating to Simon's response to the ambulance driver who came to deal with the raped baby: "We stood, bags of salt."[1]

Even as it evokes a context of abject poverty, unemployment, and hopelessness in a village in the Cape Province, a place where "nothing ever happens," *Tshepang* is, I believe, a watershed play in post-apartheid South African theatre. It is a cultural expression of the on-going work of restorative justice in South Africa, through its attempt to transform violence, refuse modes of vengeance, and promote an essential societal process of healing. Situating this work in the stark reality of a post-apartheid South Africa, I explore the ways in which the play innovatively contributes to the disruption of the cycle of vengeance and engages the politics of hope. In the South African context the play embodies small glimmers of hope unlike the much-vaunted expressions of hope and change that formed the basis of Barack Obama's Presidential election campaign and his book *The Audacity of Hope*.[2] Despite inheriting a dire national scenario linked to a global downturn, in 2008 President Obama promised changes, like national healthcare, aimed at the basic needs of the working class and the poorest members of American society. In contrast, the South African Government has unfortunately fallen far short of its goals of uplifting and improving the lives of millions of its poverty-stricken people. The crime-rate rises daily; statistics about violence, especially against women, have reached devastating proportions. Yet this powerful play, *Tshepang [hope] The Third Testament* provokes spectators to remember the bold promises and dreams of South Africa's first non-racial government and refuses to allow them to ignore urgent societal issues, so that the future may offer a little more hope than the present and past.

At the outset, it is necessary to clarify the term 'post-apartheid', which I define as a stage following apartheid (from 1948 to 1993) not in the sense of completion but, rather, as another phase that continues after the watershed democratic election of 1994. While marked juridical changes and a new constitution promised greater equity for all and prohibited discrimination on the

---

[1] Lara Foot Newton, *Tshepang: The Third Testament*, foreword by Adrienne Sichel, intro. Tony Hamburger (Johannesburg: Witswatersrand U P, 2001): 23, 36. Further page references are in the main text.

[2] Barack Obama, *The Audacity of Hope* (New York: Three Rivers, 2006).

grounds of race, gender, religion, and sexual orientation, material conditions have become more onerous for millions of South Africans. Archbishop Emeritus Desmond Tutu drew attention to this problem in 1999:

> The huge gap between the haves and the have-nots, which was largely created and maintained by racism and apartheid, poses the greatest threat to reconciliation and stability in our country.[3]

While apartheid has left indelible physical and emotional scars and financial problems for millions of people, a decade after Tutu's pronouncement it is no longer simply a question of racism, since the majority of the cabinet and many of the wealthy new entrepreneurs are from the very racial group who were disadvantaged under the apartheid regime. It appears as if there has been forgetfulness about the economic inequity experienced by many of their brothers and sisters, since cronyism, corruption, crime, and class differentials spell exclusion for millions. The setting for *Tshepang* exemplifies a village where poverty, abjection, unemployment, violence, drunkenness, and hopelessness represent the norm of the villagers' existence; while in this post-apartheid era they can all, irrespective of race, vote, nothing much has changed and there seems little potential for the hope of prosperity.

At the core of the play is the act of rape, which, according to Charlene Smith, is "the most silent of four letter words"[4] and, for some, is too horrific to contemplate. That sense is exacerbated when the rape involves a child or, worse still, a baby. Forced sex involves violence, often physical injury, and certainly psychological harm. While rape is an international problem, it is rampant in South Africa. With his characteristically dark but spot-on humour, Pieter Dirk Uys's 2003 play, *Auditioning Angels,* features a character who calls rape "the new national sport"[5] of South Africa. Accurate statistics are difficult to find, because social taboos and threats keep many victims silent. South African statistics vary – one rape every thirty-seven seconds, or every twenty-six seconds – but it is one of the highest incidences in the world. Many instances of rape are not reported, because of stigma and inadequate

---

[3] Desmond Tutu, *No Future Without Forgiveness* (Garden City NY: Doubleday, 1999): 273.

[4] Charlene Smith, "The Relation between HIV Prevalence and Virgin Rape," *News from the Nordic Africa Institute 2003*, http://www.nai.uu.se/publications/news /archives/032smith/ (accessed 23 July 2010).

[5] Pieter Dirk Uys, *Auditioning Angels*, http://www.pdu.co.za/Text/Auditioning%20 Angels.pdf:20 (accessed 23 July 2010).

police and medical/health services; moreover, the reporting and investigation present additional trauma and victimization. Women are often raped in places in which they should be safe and by men they know and should be able to rely on and trust.

An article on child rape in South Africa cites the former deputy president Jacob Zuma saying: "As we all know the apartheid history of this country left behind a legacy of a serious breakdown of the moral infrastructure of our society."[6] How ironic, when the same Jacob Zuma, who was elected President in 2009, was accused of rape in 2005 by a family friend, and was found not guilty after a court trial the following year. In South Africa about one-third of child rapes occur between teachers and students. In this culture of violence, many men have been left with a sense of powerlessness, a perceived emasculation. Men of all races may feel able to assert their power and dominance against the perceived 'weaker' individuals in society – women and children. Rape is then an assertion of power and aggression in an attempt to reassert the rapist's masculinity.

The notion of rape also varies somewhat according to cultural difference. In the black and Coloured communities, refusing sex with a spouse or a partner is not tolerated. In a traditionally patriarchal society where gender structures have imposed a hierarchy that positions men as more powerful than women, the notion of rape becomes problematical. In some black cultures, a girl is told that having sex with an older relative such as an uncle is acceptable. In South Africa, the virgin-rape myth, disseminated by unscrupulous witchdoctors, promises a cure for men living with HIV/AIDS who have sex with a virgin. This makes every little girl vulnerable and, at the same time, perpetrators try to shift responsibility for their actions. Moreover, rape is often gang rape with one or more of the perpetrators HIV+. The latter scenarios, however, did not apply to baby Tshepang.

In the actual case on which the play is based, the rape of baby Tshepang took place when the rapist was angry with the baby's mother, a former girlfriend, who refused to have sex with him and instead went to the tavern to drink. He found the infant sleeping on the bed and raped her. Child rape is often considered punishment for the mother and this is applicable in the case of baby Tshepang. After the hasty arrest and jailing of six men, DNA evidence proved their innocence and they were released from jail. Yet they have

---

[6] Quoted in Sam Francis, "Diversity Versus Safety – Child Rape in the New South Africa," http://www.rense.com/general20/diversityAL.htm (accessed 23 July 2010).

continued to suffer from the stigma of the charge and the consequences of putative involvement in this well-publicized case. The rapist was found when his common-law wife, who witnessed the event but was frightened into silence by previous beatings, eventually told the police the truth. After the trial, the rapist was given a life sentence plus eighteen years. The real baby Tshepang, whose story inspired the play, has fully recovered from her many surgeries for anatomical reconstruction. She is an intelligent and apparently happy child who lives with her foster parents and has started school. She has yet to face the knowledge of the events that transpired, but that will be revealed when she is older; psychological support has been available and will continue to help her.

The place where the actual event happened is Louisvaleweg in the Northern Cape, which is a village inhabited by a Coloured (mixed-race) community. The author transformed this story into one about black people. In 2007, an Afrikaans version of the play was commissioned and directed by Maurice Podbrey, and translated by Gerhard Marx, who was also the designer; they worked on the assumption that the people who had been most affected should have the opportunity to see the play. It even played in Louisvaleweg, although the villagers were quite ambivalent about attending the production and Tshepang's birth mother decided not to see the play. It then moved from town to town for Afrikaans speakers – either whites or Coloureds. Podbrey has since commissioned and directed a production in Zulu that toured KwaZulu–Natal.

In the introduction, I mentioned that I apply the term 'restorative theatre' to this watershed play. I have taken this phrase from the set of terms applicable to justice and reconciliation in South Africa. First, retributive justice, *lex talionis*, proffers an eye for an eye and a tooth for a tooth. Mahatma Gandhi has responded to this concept: "An eye for an eye and a tooth for a tooth and the whole world will soon be blind and toothless."[7] The Truth and Reconciliation Commission (TRC), a central concept in the construction of a democratic South Africa, began hearings in 1996 to address gross violations of human rights that had been committed from 1960. They particularly sought to avoid retributive justice and worked instead towards restorative justice, which, Charles Villa–Vicencio argues, is "a theory of justice that needs to pervade all

---

[7] http://www.newworldencyclopedia.org/entry/Lex_talionis (accessed 23 July 2010).

of society rather than a specific act in and of itself."[8] Howard Zehr has eloquently explained the concept in *The Little Book of Restorative Justice*. He
contrasts the different perspectives of criminal justice versus restorative justice thus:

> Crime is a violation of the law and the state of people and relationships. [...]
> Whereas the criminal justice system focuses upon offenders getting their just
> deserts, restorative justice focuses upon the needs of victims and the respon-
> sibility for offenders to repair harm. "Putting things right" implies reparation,
> restoration or recovery – yet there are scenarios that can never fully be re-
> stored. At least harms must be addressed and their causes in an inclusive col-
> laborative process that involves victim, offender, communities.[9]

Similarly, Daniel Herwitz reminds us that the term reconciliation implies that
beings were once one, came apart, and are now back together again. This is
hardly the case from the historical point of view:

> There has been constant conflict. Through the Xhosa wars, the Zulu empire,
> the great Trek and the Boer war, to the apartheid state there has been little
> oneness between peoples. [...] Reconciliation in South Africa is not simply
> between agents and the social world, which has been a world of deprivation,
> indignation, and horror for so many. It is also between agents and other agents,
> between perpetrators and victims of human-rights abuses.[10]

The question of reconciliation is therefore much more complicated and relates
to my sense of restorative theatre, that cannot restore an original scenario but
operates, rather, according to a *modus vivendi* that works to restore victim and
perpetrator to a society whose structures are carefully interrogated so that all
involved may face a more productive and hopeful future.

Zehr emphasizes that in restorative justice "crime has a societal dimension,
as well as a more local and personal dimension"; a vital aspect is that the vic-

---

[8] "Restorative Justice: Dealing with the Past Differently," in *Looking Back, Reaching Forward: Reflections on the Truth & Reconciliation Commission of South Africa*,
ed. Charles Villa–Vicencio & William Verwoerd (Cape Town: U of Cape Town P,
2000): 70.

[9] Howard Zehr, *The Little Book of Restorative Justice* (Intercourse PA: Good
Books, 2002): 29.

[10] Daniel Herwitz, *Race and Reconciliation: Essays from the New South Africa*
(Minneapolis: U of Minnesota P, 2003): 41, 43.

tims "tell their stories in significant settings – in other words that they re-story their lives."[11] For Dirk Louw,

> there is no single restorative justice model but, rather, restorative approaches to justice. He also links these approaches with the African concept of Ubuntu – that people are people through other people.[12]

This respect for other human beings, which in turn defines our own humanity, is a principle for which we must strive. Louw cautions: "Ubuntu is a given but clearly also a task. [...] It needs to be revitalized."[13] There is undoubtedly a huge dichotomy between the philosophical notion of Ubuntu that is often referenced, the ethical imperative that this implies, and the putatively unending violence that is perpetrated in many different forms.

Utilizing these concepts and applying them to the play, we find different approaches that refuse to work as a violent unforgivable series of actions which perpetuate greater brutality; instead, the focus veers away from vengeance and centres on understanding and doing things differently, not in taking revenge. I interpret Tshepang this way because the *terrible* act of baby rape is not perpetrated by a monster but by a man, Alfred Sorrows, who was brutally beaten and broken in pieces as a young boy by his father's *houvrou* (literally, a kept woman). Simon, the narrator, tells the story and enacts the atrocious violence of the *houvrou* by beating the straw broom on the ground so hard that it breaks into pieces. He describes how Alfred was saved: "It was my mother who took him to the hospital, and it was my mother who nursed his broken body for many months" (29). As he tells us the story, Simon carries the broken pieces of broom and places them on the bed, which will later be the site where Alfred Sorrows, the man, rapes baby Siesie. At first Simon narrates the powerful story about the rape, then he takes one of the same pieces of broken broom, signifying Alfred, to penetrate a loaf of bread. This powerful representation builds on resonance of the pieces of broom (Alfred) and the fact that only minutes before the baby's mother Ruth was cradling the bread. As shocking as is the mother's lack of response when she hears that her baby has been raped and continues drinking, so is the sense of the town's

---

[11] Zehr, *The Little Book of Restorative Justice*, 12, 15.

[12] Dirk Louw, "The African Concept of *ubuntu* and Restorative Justice," in *Handbook of Restorative Justice: A Global Perspective*, ed. Dennis Sullivan & Larry Tifft (New York: Routledge, 2006): 161.

[13] Louw, "The African Concept of *ubuntu* and Restorative Justice," 170.

being gang-raped many times by apartheid; the 'dop system', where payment
for work on the vineyards takes the form of cheap wine, fostering rampant al-
coholism. Carol M. Kaplan notes the deliberate choices made by the playwright to avoid perpetuating the cycle of violence and vengeance and to refuse the sensationalism demonstrated by the media:

> Newton rejects the easy route of resorting to our customary notions of crime,
> punishment and justice. There is no criminal, no prosecutor, no cathartic act,
> and no trial, jury, or judgment [...] the implications of the crime flow well be-
> yond the village itself. It is here that Newton achieves the play's purpose:
> turning responsibility and culpability for the crime into a collective experi-
> ence.[14]

The amazing loyalty and concern and love for the mother that are demonstrated by Simon constitute another aspect of the restorative nature of the
play. We know that she feels remorse – she tries to cut off both her breasts –
and hasn't said a word in three years, until the final moment of the play.
Simon has cared for her for three years and does everything in his power to
encourage her to live. Khuthala Nandipha, who wrote about the play and
interviewed the cast, emphasizes their appreciation that the playwright has
offered

> a male narrator [who] speaks from a male perspective presenting a new dimen-
> sion in the struggle against child abuse. [...] Men still need to address their
> own issues related to violent abuse. "We need to converse man to man, and
> realise just how big a part of the problem we are."[15]

In the play, we are situated in a particular locale – a village in the Northern
Cape – yet the socio-political ramifications apply to many communities. The
mantra "nothing happens here" or "nobody does anything here" (mentioned
twelve times from the first page of the play onwards) is all-pervasive and
speaks to the lack of motivation, the vacuum in their lives, that is known and
ignored by the larger body politic. Yet many awful incidents have occurred:
Alfred Sorrows being beaten to a pulp by his father's *houvrou*; the disappearance of Dewaal's child; the forced removal of Mary, Simon's daughter,
"the first and last thing that ever made sense to me" (33); the attempted sui-

---

[14] Carol M. Kaplan, "Voices Rising: An Essay on Gender, Justice, and Theater in
South Africa," *Seattle Journal of Social Justice* 3.2 (2004–2005): 730.

[15] Kuthala Nandipha, "Fighting Child Rape Through Theatre," *Drum* (14 April
2005): 25.

cide of Trompie; the self-mutilation of Ruth; the devastating effects of *vaal-wyn* (rotten wine); the stabbing of Sarah and her prostitution as a young adolescent by her brother; and baby Siesie's rape, which is referred to as "it happened" on six occasions. Violence has thus occurred on many levels as well as self-imposed silence, a culture including evasion, concealment, denial, hopelessness, the hell of nothingness, or, as Simon puts it, "because fokkol happens here" ( 25).

After Lara Foot Newton wrote the play, she devised the production as a cooperative theatre piece with Gerhard Marx, the designer, and the two actors, Mncedisi Shabangu and Kholeka Qwabe, whose role has been recently taken over by Nonceba Constance Didi. The stage is arranged with three areas, three beds, and Simon's Nativities – Joseph, Mary, and the baby sister of Jesus. The three areas form a triangle. First, there is the old iron single bed where the boy with the broken bones, Alfred, was laid to heal and, later on, where the rape was committed by Alfred, the man; the dirty mattress and tattered pink blanket still mark the place where they sleep, since there is no money to replace the bed or its covers to help erase the haunting memories. Two more beds are smaller versions of the biggest bed. The small bed, about the size of a baby, is carefully strapped to Ruth's back and powerfully evokes the absent presence of baby Tshepang, and the tiniest version of the bed Simon lifts out of Ruth's house in the village, when he finds her self-mutilated, and carries her on the bed to seek medical help. Secondly, there is the pile of salt which is Ruth's space (which I have discussed above), and, last, the model of the town, consisting of seven buildings that resemble a stark grid of government housing. These miniature buildings house the community and include the church and Ruth's former home, from which she was expelled.

The only time that the tone changes in the play, when Simon expresses real fury, is directed against the journalists who come to the town to get more information on a sensational story. They call the place the town of shame. This scene is understated but powerful: Simon takes pages of newspapers and pushes them onto the branches of trees standing upright on stage left near the village. Each tree has pairs of spectacles hanging from it representing journalists; the trees remind us that if the journalists have faulty sight that may require corrective glasses to improve their vision, they also lack insight and hurl blame at the villagers, especially the mother, Ruth, and the rapist(s). Simon says "shame on you!" (40) to the journalist, Maureen Witt, and points to the audience during this powerful speech:

> Get out of here! Take your cameras and get out! This town was raped long
> ago. This town was fucking gang-raped a long, long, long, long time ago!
> Shame on us? Shame on you, shame on all of us. (40–41)

Gershen Kaufmann calls shame "a sickness of the soul" (5):

> It is the most poignant experience of the self by the self, whether felt in humi-
> liation or cowardice, or in a sense of failure to cope successfully with a chal-
> lenge. Shame is a wound felt from the inside, dividing us both from ourselves
> and from one another. (16)

Simon's words poignantly address the depth of damage to his world. For
Antjie Krog,

> Guilt is linked to violation; shame is linked to failure. Shame requires an
> audience. Guilt does not. And shame is more overwhelming and more isolating
> than guilt.[16]

Ruth is devastated by guilt and tries unsuccessfully to end her life. All the
villagers, including the participants in this crime, are tarnished to different
degrees by shame. As Simon points to the audience, I feel complicitous as a
spectator, since, although I had nothing to do with the rape, I also did nothing
to facilitate societal change. So the focus alters from killing the "monster" to
analysing the monstrous action and asking what kind of lives and opportunities the villagers had and can have in the future. This exemplifies the Ibsen-
esque 'villain-shift', when society rather than individuals becomes the root of
evil; in this case, the villain-shift works specifically to focus on apartheid
social structures, their legacies, and the lack of substantial change for millions
of people. Consciousness-raising, not least with regard to the wellnigh incom-
prehensible rape statistics, is vital on many different levels. Our task is to
interact with a theatre piece and see how it touches us as readers and spectators. A well-known South African critic, Adrienne Sichel, comments on the
role of the audience: "On leaving the theatre there is no way anyone can say
'We didn't know'. *Tshepang* is part of that canon of conscientising drama."[17]

The subtitle of the play, *The Third Testament*, offers a range of religious
symbolism. We know the First Testament, which starts with paradise in the
garden of Eden, and the Second Testament, which ends with revelation and
the new Jerusalem. In this play, the place that forms the context is a hell –

---

[16] Antjie Krog, *Country of My Skull* (Johannesburg: Random House, 1998): 262.

[17] Adrienne Sichel, "Foreword" to *Tshepang: The Third Testament*, xv.

blazing heat, stench, no money, just the illness-inducing *vaalwyn*, no food, no jobs, and no prospects. The names of characters are evocative: Simon, the Greek version of Hebrew Shimon, means 'to hear' or 'to be heard', also 'hearkening' and 'listening'. Simon, as the narrator, listens to the stories and struggles of those in the community and gives them voice through his humorous and serious accounts of their daily lives and modes of survival. In the New Testament, Jesus calls Simon "Peter," the most important of the twelve apostles. The biblical Ruth is the Hebrew name for 'friend' or 'friendship' and exemplifies compassion and a love for which she is prepared to make sacrifice. In the play, Ruth, the mother, is ironically the recipient of Simon's love and compassion. He has sacrificed his own needs and wishes during the three years he has cared for her. Ruth's sitting on the pile of salt also reminds us of Lot's wife, who turned into a pillar of salt.

Biblical imagery is present not only in the names but also in the holy family that Simon creates. His wire sculptures occasionally bring in money when DeWaal tries to sell them in Kimberley and also become interlocutors on stage. Most importantly, the holy family, an idealized unit that stands in stark contrast to the family and dynamics that involve baby Tshepang, which means 'hope' or 'saviour', provides a source of inspiration when Simon uses his ingenuity as a storyteller to respond to the boy, Alfred, who suggests that "Jesus has forgotten us" (30). Simon, acknowledging that Jesus has failed to take upon himself the pain and sins of the world, creatively invents the possibility of his sister's performing that role at the end of the twentieth century:

> Jesus's sister was going to ride through the streets of our village on a donkey, and give the children plenty of sweets, and everyone would be happy. Every child would have sweets and a mother and father. (30)

This idyllic vision represents a powerful sense of what is absent and the limitations of their lives. However, since baby Siesie miraculously survives the extensive injuries from the rape and is renamed Tshepang, she offers hope as Jesus's sister, the possible saviour: "She has taken on the sins of the world, just like Jesus – and from now on all children would be saved. Tshepang, Tshepang – saviour, hope. That's what it means. The girl Christ had come" (39).

The play as a whole is not a tirade against the rapist, whose own abused childhood is carefully represented in a powerful scene. We see neither court proceedings, nor a trial and conviction, nor does the play place blame on any single person, but it does remind us very strongly through Simon's words that the community as a whole has been raped, ganged-raped, for many years. In the metaphorization of rape, we must be careful, since we can dilute and sanitize the horror of the specific act by describing other scenarios metaphorically. The hope through all of this comes from knowing that, despite her harrowing experience, Tshepang survived and thrives, that Ruth, although expelled from the village, has Simon as a loyal friend and supporter – a man who exemplifies the notion of *ubuntu* – there is still humanity and decency in a world that seems to be like hell. Thus so much violence is exposed, yet we feel empathy and unease about what has happened and the seemingly inevitable status quo. The scene with Simon addressing Maureen Witt begins to sow seeds of our own complicity, our own silence. By the end of the play spectators feel part of the collective experience. Russell Vanderbroucke notes:

> 'Tshepang' is Sotho for 'have hope.' Where does hope lie in a threnody about an infant's rape? In the eloquence of art that speaks the truth as fathomed by its creator.[18]

The ending points to hope in the utterance of Ruth's only word in the play and in the past three years, when she speaks the name of her child, Tshepang. Yet hope is mostly exemplified through the words and actions of Simon, the narrator, an artist who carves figures, a man who cared for his daughter until she was suddenly removed, and who looked after Ruth when the village expelled her and she had nobody to support and care for her. Tony Hamburger, a clinical psychologist, argues that Simon is

> the character equated with hope [...]. He is the one character who seems to be able to think, reflect and feel [...]. He has words and he has memory [...]. Now, perhaps we can see where hope is located, namely in relationships.[19]

Simon confirms this early in the play when he says: "What you see is what I have. Me and Ruth" (21). For Hamburger, "the capacity to hope requires the capacity to experience pain [...] Hope, not solution. Perhaps hope that the next generation will be in less pain."[20] Awareness and empathy for others rather than the evasion and denial that occur through the numbing effects of alcohol, the demotivation of unemployment, poverty, and other consequences

---

[18] Russell Vanderbroucke, "From the Ashes, a New South Africa," *American Theatre* (October 2005): 115.

[19] Tony Hamburger, "Introduction, Tshepang – A Morality Play?" in Lara Foot Newton, *Tshepang: The Third Testament*, 12–15 passim.

[20] Tony Hamburger, "Introduction, Tshepang – A Morality Play?" 16.

of the oppressive apartheid system, which has been followed by slow changes during the years of the new democracy, offer a glimmer of hope to create a better environment and future. The play is framed by recorded sounds of children at play laughing and shouting with joy. Perhaps this, too, offers the prospect that there can be happy, vivacious children in South Africa who can live their lives without trauma and with the possibility of hope.

## Works Cited

Foot Newton, Lara. *Tshepang: The Third Testament*, foreword by Adrienne Sichel, intro. Tony Hamburger (Johannesburg: Wits UP, 2001).

Hamburger, Tony. "Introduction, Tshepang – A Morality Play?" in Lara Foot Newton, *Tshepang: The Third Testament*, 1–17.

Kaplan, Carol M. "Voices Rising: An Essay on Gender, Justice, and Theater in South Africa," *Seattle Journal of Social Justice* 3.2 (2004–2005): 711–48.

Kaufman, Gershen. *The Psychology of Shame* (New York: Springer, 2nd ed. 1996).

Krog, Antjie. *Country of My Skull* (Johannesburg: Random House, 1998).

Louw, Dirk. "The African Concept of *ubuntu* and restorative justice," in *Handbook of Restorative Justice: A Global Perspective*, ed. Dennis Sullivan & Larry Tifft (New York: Routledge, 2006): 161–73.

Nandipha, Kuthala. "Fighting Child Rape Through Theatre," *Drum* (14 April 2005): 24–25.

Sichel, Adrienne. "Foreword" to Foot Newton, *Tshepang: The Third Testament*, xiii–xvi.

Smith, Charlene. "The Relation between HIV Prevalence and Virgin Rape," *News from the Nordic Africa Institute* (2003), http://www.nai.uu.se/publications/news/archives/032smith/ (accessed 23 July 2010).

Tutu, Desmond. *No Future Without Forgiveness* (Garden City NY: Doubleday, 1999).

Uys, Pieter Dirk. *Auditioning Angels*, http://www.pdu.co.za/Text/Auditioning%20Angels.pdf (1–67) (accessed 23 July 2010).

Vanderbroucke, Russell. "From the Ashes, a New South Africa," *American Theatre* (October 2005): 109–15.

Villa–Vicencio, Charles. "Restorative Justice: Dealing with the Past Differently," in *Looking Back, Reaching Forward: Reflections on the Truth and Reconciliation Commission of South Africa*, ed Charles Villa–Vicencio & Wilhelm Verwoerd (Cape Town: U of Cape Town P, 2000): 68–76.

Zehr, Howard. *The Little Book of Restorative Justice* (Intercourse PA: Good Books, 2002).

◄❖►

JOHN A STOTESBURY

# Rayda Jacobs's *Confessions of a Gambler* as Post-Apartheid Cinema

T HE YEAR 2007 SAW THE PUBLICATION OF THE FIRST MAJOR
edited anthology of academic writing on the South African cinema
since the end of apartheid: Martin Botha's *Marginal Lives and
Painful Pasts*.[1] The publishing company has since gone bust, but the volume
survives and bears witness to the impressive range of cinematic enterprise that
the liberation of the South African political process has given rise to. Writing
in 1989, immediately prior to Ferdinand de Klerk's decision to open up the
South African political process to democratization, Keyan Tomaselli was able
to disparage the South African film world at that moment in history thus:

> While white South Africans continue with their heads in the cinematic sand,
> foreign producers are cashing in on South Africa's international visibility and
> making the kind of films that South Africans should be making.[2]

In the brave new post-apartheid cinematic world, Tomaselli's observation
is no longer completely valid. There continue to be South African movies
made with at least one eye on the prospect of international distribution, most
of them employing at least one major international 'star' in a key role to add
glamour and appeal, but their directors are now local South Africans. A case
in point is the South African re-make of that "paternalistic"[3] novel by Alan
Paton, *Cry, The Beloved Country* (1995, dir. Darrell Roodt), starring the African-American actor James Earl Jones in the role of the Reverend Kumalo, and

---

[1] *Marginal Lives and Painful Pasts: South African Cinema after Apartheid*, ed.
Martin Botha (Parklands: Genugtig!, 2007).

[2] Keyan Tomaselli, *The Cinema of Apartheid: Race and Class in South African Film*
(London: Routledge, 1989): 222.

[3] Luc Renders, "Redemption Movies," in *Marginal Lives and Painful Pasts*, ed.
Botha, 232.

the Irish actor Richard Harris in the role of the conservative white South African farmer whose son is murdered. A similar observation could be made of other recent films targeting the international market, two in particular based on books depicting the work of the Truth and Reconciliation Commission: *Red Dust* (2004, dir. Tom Hooper), and *In My Country* (2004, dir. John Boorman), all of these films featuring actors of non-South African origin.

These all can be regarded as, more or less, effective cinema aimed at narrating to the wider world an 'insider' view of political and social change in the 'New' South Africa. Inevitably, however, there also exist numerous films that speak mainly to a domestic South African audience and which, for a variety of reasons, have not been released internationally: films, some again inspired by the TRC, such as *Forgiveness* (2004, dir. Ian Gabriel), with its totally indigenous South African cast, which works through a visual medium that at first sight appears drab, lifeless: washed-out colours that symbolize the bleakness of memory, guilt, and the desire for amnesia vis-à-vis the apartheid past. *Forgiveness* is concerned with the conciliatory rapprochement attempted by a former white policeman and the 'Coloured' family of one of his apartheid victims. The perpetrator visits them, desiring to confess in order to find forgiveness and a form of personal and historical closure, but the past returns in the shape of three of his victim's co-fighters, and the former policeman's personal fate is sealed. Jason Xenopoulos's *Promised Land* (2002), which draws heavily on Karel Schoeman's apartheid-era and differently nuanced novel *Na die geliefde land* (1972), also explores – again in washed-out cinematic colours – the connection between past and present, depicting a lack of desire on the part of a marginalized, patriarchal, incestuous white Afrikaner *Bittereinder* community for either reconciliation or redemption; their sole recourse is communal annihilation, which, at its melodramatic climax, the movie achieves graphically and bloodily.

Thus, if a major part of recent South African cinema can be summarized, very crudely, in terms of an attempt to explore the often convoluted personal and communal relationships engendered by colonialism and apartheid, Rayda Jacobs's first feature film, *Confessions of a Gambler* (2007, co-directed with Amanda Lane), is distinctive for its sheer difference from the mainstream. In consequence, this brief article will consist largely of a discussion of what the film achieves and how it does what it does. At the same time, I would emphasize that, despite its winning the major South African *Sunday Times* Literary Award in 2004, I will pay no attention here to Jacobs's original novel bearing the same name, which she published in 2003, not least to avoid any unnecessary confusion arising from comparisons of verbal and visual texts. It may, however, be worth recalling that, in addition to several SABC documentaries devoted to aspects of contemporary South African Muslim life, her main cultural production consists of a volume of short stories published in Canada immediately prior to her return to Cape Town from an exile-turned-absence that lasted from 1968 to 1995, several novels, all published initially in South Africa in the years since 1995, a memoir, and an account of her participation in the *hajj*; she has recently published another novel under the title *Joonie* (2011).

A reading of any and all of Jacobs's narratives insists, first, on roots, origins – a significant topic for a South African woman whose apartheid classification as 'Coloured' led her, perhaps naively to begin with, into a life-time of absence from her homeland, the land of her home, South Africa. Her endeavour since returning in 1995 has evidently been to reconstruct her personal share of those missing decades. Speaking in interview in 2001 of her Canadian-written collection of short stories, published as *The Middle Children*, she says that writing and publishing them then, a year prior to her return migration to Cape Town, was "cathartic":

> RAYDA: [...] Even though a lot of people didn't pick up what it was about. A lot of them thought they were just local South African stories. They didn't pick up the thing about the displacement of identity. Or maybe they did, and they wrote a lot about the book but not about that. My whole life is wrapped up with identity, and I didn't realise it until somebody pointed it out to me.
>
> JOHN: That's certainly a South African thing, but also a worldwide phenomenon.
>
> RAYDA: Yes, it's huge. But I feel more displaced than they are.[4]

Her work is nevertheless not backward-looking. As narratives including that of the movie version of *Confessions of a Gambler* demonstrate, her ongoing ambition is to re-define an identity – a woman's identity – that overcomes the traumas of displacement and extended exile.

In remaking the *Confessions of a Gambler* novel as a screenplay, and by producing the film locally, *in situ*, at the Cape and under her own direction, Jacobs appears to reach for a new filmic image in a doubly imposing sense. In the film version of the story, rather than concealing her womanly identity con-

---

[4] John A Stotesbury, "Remembering: An Interview with Rayda Jacobs," *The Atlantic Literary Review* 3.2 (2002): 226.

tinuously behind the modesty of a textual veil, the Muslim woman protagonist – powerfully performed by Jacobs herself – visibly gains 'flesh and blood'. Her strengths and weaknesses are visually 'there', in-yer-face, unsecret, flirting even with the, in some quarters, perception of 'womanly immodesty' inherent in the notion of removing the veil. This spiritual and cultural 'striptease' is accompanied throughout the movie by (largely English) dialogue that is unmistakably South African, demotic, earthy: but the film's dialogue is in fact a striking mélange of language that shifts constantly between the loud, brassy, sexual profanity of the protagonist and her female cronies and the mellifluous Arabic certainties and consolations of the Qur'an.

Jacobs's largest challenge to the audience of the movie, however, consists in forging the identification of 'author' with 'character' through her own performance as actor in the lead role of Abeeda, whose secrets, deceptions, and confessions make up the story of a modern South African Muslim woman.[5] The screenplay itself opens with two strikingly different utterances made by Abeeda in quick succession: "The first thing I have to confess is that I am a Muslim woman," closely followed (after the film titles) by: "The second thing I have to confess is that I like risk." Confession functions autobiographically, but its origins may be readily associated with both a faith-related revelation of personal sin, and then also, of course, with the confession of the commission of crime: in Abeeda's story, the spiritual and the secular become closely interwoven and assume a strongly gendered identity.

Abeeda's filmic persona, as enacted by Jacobs, is forceful, centred in the independence of a divorced forty-nine-year-old woman whose life swiftly threatens to unravel as her story proceeds. She brings home one of her sons, a homosexual, to die of AIDS, in the aftermath of which Abeeda seeks solace in a taboo activity: gambling on the fruit machines at "the devil's playground," a local casino. Her life becomes marked by her obsessive addiction, and, as her money disappears, she coaxes more from friends and another son, and, in order to continue gambling, she humiliates herself by borrowing 500 Rand from Margaret, her (poorly paid) African maid. In an attempt at staging an insurance scam, she sets up the hoax theft of her car, the voice-over in-

---

[5] For an informal account of Rayda Jacobs's experience, as a novice, of acting in *Confessions of a Gambler*, see her article "Confessions of an Actress," *Mail & Guardian* (4 April 2008), http://mg.co.za/article/2008-04-04-confessions-of-an-actress (accessed 17 April 2008). Repr. in her autobiographical *Masquerade: The Story of My Life* (Roggebaai: Umuzi, 2008): 305–10.

forming us that "I forgot all about my promise to God." The ploy fails, and she loses her car.

Finally, however, at her lowest ebb, Abeeda dons her *nijab* and turns to an imam at her mosque for advice and guidance. From this point on, she undergoes a personal reconstruction. Her sister falls terminally ill with cancer, and Abeeda promises to assume responsibility for the care of her sister's child. Eventually, with the aid of a friend's gift of money, also won at the casino, Abeeda is able to cast out her gambling "demons" by feeding all of the "dirty money" back into the casino and having herself permanently and conclusively banned by the casino from ever entering its premises again; in a renewed sense of the expression, Abeeda is, quite literally, banned "for life."

*Confessions of a Gambler* can, then, be seen to differ considerably from most other post-apartheid cinematic productions. Ungenerously, perhaps, we could dismiss it as soap-like: a succession of focuses on the emotional minutiae of the 'particular' in an ordinary middle-class, middle-aged woman's daily existence. Abeeda, after all, is a very conventional human being: as a Muslim, she prays five times daily and dresses with due modesty. But she resists the conventional Muslim abhorrence of homosexuality – although her son's lover, Patrick, is a non-Muslim, he is not rejected by Abeeda, and Abeeda plays the maternal role of nursing her son through the final stages of his illness. Her common humanity is also displayed in her weakness as her Muslim resolve falters and she succumbs to her addiction to gambling. In sum, her identity is not only that of a Muslim woman and a risk-taker but also that of a survivor who, in surmounting the spiritual and social displacement caused by her addiction to gambling, returns to a new sense of personal equilibrium within her community.

Cinematically, *Confessions of a Gambler* works in terms of the local and the locality, and in doing so takes on many of the features of a traditional 'soapie', with its domestic and marital melodramas and its conventional female gossiping and squabbling. The film's credits refer to the city localities of Athlone, Rylands, and Bo Kaap, but Jacobs's awareness of a wider legacy of the cinematic effect of the local appears in her visual indebtedness to another, very different movie, *The French Lieutenant's Woman* (1981). At two points in *Confessions of a Gambler*, Abeeda, in striving to regain control over her gambling addiction, walks on the jetty wall at Kalk Bay close to its small harbour lighthouse. On the first occasion, she is penitent, but still in the grip of her material dilemma, and she fails; but on the second occasion, in the closing scene of the film, she stands firm, informing her audience that she has established "a contract with God – the details are between us": she will survive. The visual echo is, naturally, an echo of the opening of *The French Lieutenant's Woman*, a borrowing that Jacobs has readily acknowledged:

> It is exactly as you say. When I saw the movie all those years ago I was so struck by Meryl Streep's mournful expression when she stood on the pier with the waves crashing all about her, that I was inspired by it and decided to have my character stand on a pier and think back on her life as she starts to tell her story. So, yes, it is not coincidence. I wanted a mournful Abeeda as a soulful figure against the vast ocean to set both the tone of the film and also to show that she is remorseful and wants to turn a new page. I very much love the whole deal with the black cloak – although I didn't get all the shots we wanted when I filmed. A bit of vanity on my part too, I must agree, doing the Meryl Streep thing.[6]

Curiously, in the final cut, the scene concludes rather than opens the movie, but its import underlines the extent to which Jacobs has been able to re-shape her original novelistic insight to realize an effective cinematic vision.

Finally, it must be emphasized that *Confessions of a Gambler* presents no "dialogue between cultures" in the sense suggested by Asade Seyhan.[7] Cultures, in Jacobs's movie, do not "collide, unite, and are reconciled in real and virtual space in unprecedented ways,"[8] although this is certainly the case in Jacobs' earlier novel *Sachs Street* (2001), where Cape Town Muslim divorcee meets South African fundamentalist Christian white man, to hugely comic effect. Abeeda's world, as we see it in the film, is, instead, self-contained and self-sufficient, its working rules laid down in the directives of the Qur'an rather than in the post-apartheid pluri-cultural terms of a wider Cape Town society or of the world at large.

## WORKS CITED

### Filmography

*Confessions of a Gambler* (dir. Rayda Jacobs & Amanda Lane; screenplay by Rayda Jacobs from her novel; starring Rayda Jacobs, Tauriq Jenkins, and Aqeel Khan; Riempie Productions, Rogue Star Films, S A B C 2, South Africa 2007; 87 min.).

---

[6] Jacobs, personal communication, 16 August 2010.

[7] Asade Seyhan, *Writing Outside the Nation* (Princeton N J : Princeton U P , 2001): 7.

[8] Seyhan, *Writing Outside the Nation*, 7.

*Cry, The Beloved Country* (dir. Zoltan Korda; screenplay by Alan Paton from his novel; starring Canada Lee, Sidney Poitier, and Charles Carson; London Film Productions, UK 1951; 103 min.).

*Cry, The Beloved Country* (dir. Darrell Roodt; screenplay by Ronald Harwood, from the novel by Alan Paton; starring Richard Harris, James Earl Jones, and Tsholofelo Wechoemang; Alpine Pty Limited, Distant Horizons, Miramax Films, South Africa | USA 1995; 106 min.).

*Forgiveness* (dir. Ian Gabriel; screenplay by Greg Latter; starring Quanita Adams, Christo Davids, and Zane Meas; Giant Films, Dv8, South Africa 2004; 112 min.).

*In My Country* (dir. John Boorman; screenplay by Ann Peacock from the novel *Country of My Skull* by Antjie Krog; starring Juliette Binoche, Samuel L. Jackson, and Brendan Gleeson; Chartoff Productions, Film Afrika Worldwide, Film Consortium, UK | Ireland | South Africa 2004; 105 min.).

*Promised Land* (dir. Jason Xenopoulos; screenplay by Jason Xenopoulos from the novel by Karel Schoeman; starring Nick Boraine, Lida Botha, and Daniel Browde; Film Afrika Worldwide, Khulisa Productions, South Africa 2002; 100 min.).

*Red Dust* (dir. Tom Hooper; screenplay by Troy Kennedy–Martin, from the novel by Gillian Slovo; starring Jamie Bartlett, Hilary Swank, and Ian Roberts; BBC, Distant Horizon, Videovision Entertainment, UK | South Africa 2004; 110 min.).

*The French Lieutenant's Woman* (dir. Karel Reisz; screenplay by Harold Pinter, from the novel by John Fowles; starring Meryl Streep, Jeremy Irons, and Hilton McRae; Jupiter Films, UK 1981; 124 min.).

## General

Botha, Martin, ed. *Marginal Lives and Painful Pasts: South African Cinema after Apartheid* (Parklands: Genugtig!, 2007).

Jacobs, Rayda. "Confessions of an Actress," *Mail & Guardian* (4 April 2008), http://mg.co.za/article/2008-04-04-confessions-of-an-actress (accessed 17 April 2008). Repr. in Jacobs, *Masquerade: The Story of My Life* (Roggebaai: Umuzi, 2008): 305–10.

——. *Confessions of a Gambler* (Cape Town: Kwela, 2004).

——. *Joonie* (Cape Town: Jacana, 2011).

——. *The Middle Children* (Toronto: Second Story, 1994).

——. *Sachs Street* (Cape Town: Kwela, 2001).

——. Personal communication with the author, Facebook, 16 August 2010.

Paton, Alan. *Cry, the Beloved Country: a story of comfort in desolation* (London: Jonathan Cape, 1948).

Renders, Luc. "Redemption Movies," in *Marginal Lives and Painful Pasts*, ed. Martin Botha (Parklands: Genugtig!, 2007): 221–53.

Schoeman, Karel. *Na die geliefde land* (Cape Town & Pretoria: Human & Rousseau, 1972). Tr. by Marion V. Friedmann as *Promised Land: a novel* (London: Friedmann, 1978).

Seyhan, Azade. *Writing Outside the Nation* (Princeton NJ: Princeton UP, 2001).

Stotesbury, John A. "Remembering: An Interview with Rayda Jacobs," *The Atlantic Literary Review* 3.2 (2002): 220–31.

Tomaselli, Keyan. *The Cinema of Apartheid: Race and Class in South African Film* (London: Routledge, 1989).

❖

# Mbongeni Malaba

## Exile and Return in Kavevangua Kahengua's *Dreams*

T HE THEME OF EXILE AND RETURN IS A RECURRENT ONE in Kavevangua Kahengua's anthology *Dreams* (2002). He is a descendant of
the Ovaherero who fled Namibia during the Herero–German war in
1907.[1] Some Ovaherero managed to escape to Botswana, including Kahengua's grandmother, Taureondja Kamutenja, who is presented as a heroic
figure in the poem "For Grandma, Who Crossed the Thirstland (1907)." In this
poem, the funereal imagery vividly captures the anguish of the Ovaherero during this tragic phase in the history of South West Africa, as Namibia was
known during the German and the Afrikaner colonial eras:

> Yellow on-shore winds raged
> And ravaged
> In agony of death
> Eighty thousand voices howled
> Forever they faded like a burial dirge
> With luck of an elusive prey
> Grandma escaped the massacre
> Like a desert lizard
> She took cover behind the scorching
> Namib desert
> On the way, from the same thirsty nipple
> Father, son, and daughter suckled
> A belief in immortality of human life

---

[1] For an incisive commentary on the contested historiography of the Herero–German
war 1904–1907, see Andreas Eckl, "The Herero genocide of 1904: Source-critical and
methodological considerations," *Journal of Namibian Studies* 3 (2008): 31–61.

Its invaluable being
Waded through the *Kgalagadi* sand dunes
As winds start to change colours
From yellow to ebony
Grandma whose hair refuses to grey with age
Perceives the freedom flame.[2]

The poem pays eloquent tribute to the resilience of the Ovaherero who, "Like a desert lizard," survived the twin scourges of the ruthless German colonial forces and "the scorching / Namib desert." The strength of the poet's grandmother is captured powerfully in the image of suckling the "Father, son and daughter" from "the same thirsty nipple." Significantly, despite the horrors of war, dispossession, and suffering, the poem ends on an optimistic, prophetic note, which suggests that the poet has come to terms with the painful past. The poem is visually striking, as a photograph of the matriarch, in traditional dress, sitting cross-legged, features prominently in the right-hand corner of the page, superimposed on a photograph of sand dunes. It is not surprising, therefore, to find that identity is another major theme in *Dreams*, as Kahengua pays tribute to his Namibian and Tswana heritage.

"Ongua Jandje," sub-titled "My Birthplace," reflects the poet's pride in his roots in "Mosu, Botswana" and his sensitivity to his environment, a characteristic feature of his verse:

Mba kwaterwa komiti
Omire otjomborora
Mbi kuha kutwa ondu no ndana
Mosu, ko Tjauana t ovikori

Every birthplace has a song
For in birth we are anchored in nature
I was born in a place of tall breasted trees
Around which no sheep
Nor calf is tethered
Mosu, Botswana. (43)

---

[2] Kavevangua Kahengua, *Dreams* (Windhoek: Gamsberg Macmillan, 2002): 32. Further page references are in the main text.

In an explanatory note, the poet states that "The verse in English is not a direct translation of the Otjiherero verse but expresses similar emotions associated with the importance of a birthplace" (43).

Like other exiles, his community has to ponder which land is 'home'. In the poem "Lost Companion,"

> Ground wet from rain
> Inspired we went hunting
> The hunting climax all in vain
> Sun at zenith, shadows under feet,
> Thirsty, restless and changed
> Into the power of ignorance.
>
> He pointed westwards
> I advised west is darkness and death
> A hungry lion, *Kgalagadi* awaits its prey
> We engaged in a tug of war
> Each savouring the power of being in the light.
>
> I countered. Let us not follow
> The conventional patterns of the lost ones,
> When the Herero perished
> In the Kgalagadi [sic] sands,
> The callous German guns in pursuit
> Let's retrack and retrace
> Our footprints eastwards
> Where refuge is. (65)

Kahengua states that Botswana is the land "Where refuge is"; the land of his birth offers comfort and security. One notes the imagistic parallels with "For Grandma, Who Crossed the Thirstland." The *Kgalagadi* symbolizes "darkness and death," the memory of the community's flight to freedom has been passed down from generation to generation. *Dreams*, to some extent, reflects the "tug of war" in the poet's heart, in terms of where 'home' is.

In a poem published in another anthology, Kahengua foregrounds the tensions faced by exiled communities in terms of linguistic identity. The generational conflict is pithily captured in "Woman breastfeeds," where the mother uses an adopted tongue, Setswana, in a vain attempt to quieten her child, who only responds positively when addressed in the ancestral language:

> The baby cries
> She rocks her
> The baby cries
> She lulls her
> She vainly breastfeeds her
> The baby cries
> She kisses her
> The baby purses her lips
> She says *didimala* – be quiet, in Setswana
> The baby cries
> Grandma intervenes:
> Why don't you say *mwina*? – be quiet, in Otjiherero
> Are you possessed by foreign spirits?
> Why do you breastfeed her on a foreign language?
> Even your milk has turned foreign!
> Should we mourn the death of our language?
> Is this the commemoration of the death of our language?
> She says *mwina*
> The baby breastfeeds.[3]

Composed on 30 January 2004, this poem shows how the grandmother is the custodian of her culture and fiercely fights to preserve the community's linguistic heritage, to ensure cultural survival.

A quest for belonging runs through Kahengua's poetry. In exile, it makes sense to immerse oneself in the culture of the host community. Mastery of the local language(s) is a positive sign of a willingness to accommodate others, in line with the proverbial wisdom "If [s]he speaks like us, [s]he is one of us." It is also a sign of respect for one's hosts. Bearing in mind that the flight of the Ovaherero to Botswana was not a voluntary migration but a response to

---

[3] *In search of questions: a new collection of Namibian poems*, ed. Keamogetsi J. Molapong, Christi Warner & Volker Winterfeldt (Basel: Basler Afrika Bibliographien, 2005): 50. The title in the table of contents is listed as "Woman breastfeeding," which differs slightly from the title on the page itself.

military aggression, it is not surprising that a yearning to discover one's ancestral land features prominently in *Dreams*. "Coming Home" captures the persona's yearning to rediscover his lost heritage and lay claim to his birthright:

> A Namibian child in 'diaspora',
> I am coming home
> Call me not a returnee
> For I am no Omukwendata
> Who has returned from the graves
> Call me he who comes home
> I have come to be nourished
> On the breast of my culture
>
> Bear with me, when I spear
> The Namibian languages
> For I wish to straighten my stammer
> Nurture me into a songbird, for I aspire
> To sing the melodies of the holy fire,
> Across the deserts, over the mountains
> And along the shores
>
> I have come home for a sense of origin
> When time has come to rest,
> I want to rest in your arms, mother Namibia. (38)

It is striking that "diaspora" is rendered in inverted commas; the poem captures both the secular and the religious overtones of the word. The Ovaherero were 'scattered' during the Herero–German war of 1904–07, in line with the Greek origin of the word, *diaspeirō*.[4] The lines "Nurture me into a songbird, for I aspire / To sing the melodies of the holy fire" reflect the spiritual dimension that "the holy fire" symbolizes among the Ovaherero.

Kahengua begins "Ongua Jandje" ("My Birthplace") in Otjiherero, thus acknowledging the reality of a Otjiherero-speaking community in Botswana that found "refuge" there. One notes the poet's ambivalent handling of his linguis-

---

[4] *Reader's Digest Oxford Complete Wordfinder*, ed. Sara Tulloch (1993; London, New York, Montreal, Sydney & Cape Town: Reader's Digest, 1994): 401.

tic heritage, captured in the enigmatic poem "Languages," which implies a prevailing sense of rootlessness. The linguistic tension with the home language, Setswana or Otjiherero, is also captured in "Woman breastfeeds." In this poem, Grandma castigates her daughter for trying to quieten her child in a foreign language, suggesting a loss of cultural identity. "Coming Home" foregrounds the poet's stammer, which can be read symbolically as reflecting his hesitant appropriation of his ancestral identity as a Namibian, although he was born in exile:

> I would like to learn
> Languages
> But I abhor them
> Because none
> Is mine. (7)

The poem suggests a sense of linguistic alienation, which might shed light, in part, on why the author writes predominantly in English. As noted earlier, "Ongua Jandje" celebrates his "Birthplace," Mosu, in Botswana, in Otjiherero. The second and third stanzas of "Dedication" reveal his family's Tswana roots, as his "elder brother / Nguaepe 'alias' Morolong Kahengua" had a Tswana[5] nickname and the poet's son's first name "Thabiso" is also Tswana. Kahengua's multilingual background is revealed in the poem, as his son calls him "papa" and "Taté" (49) (a Namibian and Kalanga term for 'Father').

The collection ends with a short story, "They dreamed of home." I believe that Kahengua's strength lies in his poetry; his short stories lack the conciseness of his verse and, curiously, tend to be overwritten. Nevertheless, "They dreamed of home" is fascinating, as it highlights the harsh experiences of some 'returnees', whose 'welcome' fell short of their expectations.

While Botswana did provide "refuge" for Namibian refugees, xenophobic feelings were also expressed. The Namibian protagonist of "They dreamed of home," Rihongee Ndovazu's great-uncle, was the heroic "leader of the Ova-

---

[5] "All Tswana ruling lineages are traced to one of the three founding ancestors, namely Morolong, Masilo and Mokgatla." Neil Parsons, cited in Paul Maylam, *A History of the African People of South Africa from the Early Iron Age to the 1970s* (London: Croom Helm, 1986): 31.

herero" (68), Samuel Maharero, who died in Mahalapye, in central Botswana. Despite his pedigree, Rihongee is dismissed as "a Motlamma" (79) – a derogatory term for Ovaherero – by his neighbour Dipuo, who disapproves of the fact that Rihongee married Tshenolo, a Tswana princess.

Tshenolo suggests that the family should settle in Namibia, after it gains independence, where her husband will be respected. Ironically, she encounters prejudice at the border, and is warned that her legal status is unclear. Job- and house-hunting are ordeals; it takes Rihongee seven months to secure a post as a senior bank clerk and Tshenolo struggles for four years to find work. The immigration officers are openly hostile to her desire to earn a living:

> "If you are so impatient, you might as well pay the two thousand five hundred for permanent residence."
>
> "But last week I was told that permanent residence is free."
>
> "The law just changed this week, madam. The laws of the country are changing in line with the influx of immigrants. The government wants to keep folenas outside the borders of the country as much as possible."
>
> "Foreigners? You were refugees in other countries weren't you? And you got hospitality, didn't you?"
>
> "The rainbow is in the hands of the people and they now control its destiny," the immigration officer answered cryptically. (75)

The coded message challenges notions of pan-Africanism that lie at the heart of the nationalist struggles. The tensions found in the relationship between Namibians and the Batswana are reflected in those between Namibians and Angolans. It took over two decades for the founding President of Namibia, Sam Nujoma, to visit Angola, despite the fact that SWAPO's armed struggle was waged from Angola.

Once she is employed, Tshenolo is frustrated by entrenched racism, corruption, and sloth; she chooses to return home with her daughter, leaving the son with his father. Faced with the break-up of his family, Rihongee commits suicide – which is distressingly common in Namibia. Tshenolo abandons her plans to migrate and decides to beat the system at its own game, *onyune*, a Namibian tactic which highlights cheating and deception:

> As the aim is to win and to outwit the rival, each competitor must try to predict
> the opponent's moves. Experienced players, like corrupt members of a society,
> cheat their rivals and break the rules of the game. (74)

This bleak environment raises questions of belonging and implies that the promised freedom is stillborn. Furthermore, the crime endemic among the black residents of Katutura township casts a pall over the nation's future prospects.[6]

Kahengua's poetry is acutely conscious of "boundaries" and argues that these should be transcended. The poem "Travelling" challenges the insularity of Namibians. It urges them to accept "the other," to welcome difference, to go beyond a fixation with the "strange" and acknowledge people's common humanity. "Eye of the Beholder" eloquently praises the visual beauty of Norway and Namibia. The poem is printed on striking photographs representing northern and southern landscapes:

> Your land is beautiful
> Those stone-age volcanic hills
> With baby faces
> As if they were born yesterday
> Those brown mountains
> Whose ridges are exposed
> Like ribs of a cow
> Dying a slow death
> Those sand dunes
> Such a vast lap on which the young
> And old play
> Pacifies the mind
> Namibia
>
> Your land is beautiful
> Those pools of tranquil waters
> Pacify the mind
> Those lush, snowy mountains

---

[6] For a detailed analysis of Kahengua's critique of the societal ills bedeviling Namibia, see also Mbongeni Z. Malaba, "Kavevangua Kahengua's *Dreams,*" *Englishes: Contemporary Literatures in English* 29.10 (2006): 83–95, and "Namibia in the Poetry of Kavevangua Kahengua," *African Journal of New Poetry* 4 (2007): 175–84.

On which the young
And old ski
Are spectacular
Norway. (57)

The poem seems to suggest a union between north and south, founded on mutual respect, in a globalized world. The incorporation of photographs enhances the appeal of this wonderful collection, as they complement the atmosphere generated by the poems.

Migration is presented as part of modernity, in "The Drifter," and its positive aspects are foregrounded, since the absent elder sister and elder son have attained professional recognition, respectively, as a "great teacher" "Beyond the borders" and "a famous doctor / Overseas [...]" (48). In other contexts, the relocation might be involuntary, as with the African Americans whose ancestors were transported as slaves, as in "Travelogue":

What turned my spinal cord cold
Was not being airborne
Like a bird which visits the skies
Nor democracy
For democracy is a virtue I cherish
I have seen the ebony face
As dark as the African night sky
I have heard the ebony voice
From the shelters
I have seen the offspring
Whose ancestors' scattered bones
Nourish the Americas
I have heard the whispers of the ebony face
In alienation craving for education
I have heard the ebony voice
Lead the singing of the national anthem
Of hope in which every child will flourish
This experience boomerangs me home. (51)

The spine-chilling recognition of the suffering and yearning of 'the other' challenges the persona to ponder the situation in his 'home' country. The legacy of the degradation of black people in America implies the globalization of apartheid. For many Africans, the underlying racial tensions in America raise questions about multiculturalism. However, the historic election of Barack Obama as the forty-fourth President of the USA is a vindication of the democratic process and an affirmation of the inclusive nature of the American Dream. It is also a reminder of the stark reality that not all dreams are easily realized, for, as Obama himself proclaimed, his success was only achievable in America.[7]

Nevertheless, the anthology attests to the importance of "Dreams," as seen in the title poem:

> My conscious being has travelled
> Beyond the frontiers
> Like the South-Western winds
> My unconscious spirit revisits the playhouse
> Where we set our dreams beyond the horizon
> Kavee aspired to be the novelist
> I aspired to be a poet
> Nocturnally I visit the far streets
> Of the Old Location
> Where dreams have roots. (2)

The "South-Western winds" are not bound by geographical or man-made "frontiers." Writing unites the poet-persona's "conscious being" and his "unconscious spirit." The transcending of horizons and the realization of "dreams" are central to Kahengua's vision. "Dreams" are classically associated with the night, and linked to the "Old Location" (which the poet "Nocturnally" visits) from which the black South-West Africans were forcibly relocated, to make way for the "white" residential suburb of Hochland Park, where the poet now resides, in an independent Namibia.

In conclusion, this essay has demonstrated that the historical experience of Kahengua's people is an important element in his poems; it influences his

---

[7] See Stryker McGuire, "The first world election," *Newsweek* (10 November 2008): 20–23; Pieter van Zyl, "Obama: Era of Hope," *YOU Magazine* (29 January 2009): 10–20.

vision, which celebrates the strength and resilience of Ovaherero communities, both those that remained in Namibia, during the German and Afrikaner colonial periods; and those that found refuge in Botswana. Kahengua is justly proud of his "roots," of his dual Tswana and Namibian heritage. The legacy of dispossession and the efforts to reclaim what is rightfully his and his people's emerges in the celebration of hybridity found in *Dreams* and captured succinctly in "Handshake," which reveals that he feels "at home" in both countries:

> I had been away
> Like the African sun
> On my return, the young ones
> Who could still identify my face
> Shook my hands joyously
> Nearly dislodging them
>
> The journey to the land
> Of matriarchs and patriarchs
> Was not in vain
> I brought images of culture
>
> Suddenly it rained in hails
> Of diamonds, here in Orapa
> Though the machine works
> And the man waits,
> I wished it were drizzling
> On the Swakop dunes. (45)

## WORKS CITED

Eckl, Andreas. "The Herero genocide of 1904: Source-critical and methodological considerations," *Journal of Namibian Studies* 3 (2008): 31–51.

Kahengua, Kavevangua. *Dreams* (Windhoek: Gamsberg Macmillan, 2002).

Malaba, Mbongeni Z. "Kavevangua Kahengua's *Dreams*," *Englishes: Contemporary Literatures in English* 29.10 (2006): 83–95.

——. "Namibia in the Poetry of Kavevangua Kahengua," *African Journal of New Poetry* 4 (2007): 175–84.

Maylam, Paul. *A History of the African People of South Africa from the Early Iron Age to the 1970s* (London: Croom Helm, 1986).

McGuire, Stryker. "The first world election," *Newsweek* (10 November 2008): 20–23.

Molapong, Keamogetsi J., Christi Warner & Volker Winterfeldt, ed. *In search of questions: a new collection of Namibian poems* (Basel: Basler Afrika Bibliographien, 2005).

Tulloch, Sara, *Reader's Digest Oxford Complete Wordfinder* (1993; London, New York, Montreal, Sydney & Cape Town: Reader's Digest, 1994).

van Zyl, Pieter. "Obama: Era of Hope," *YOU Magazine* (29 January 2009): 10–20.

◄❖►

M.J. DAYMOND

# Making a 'Home' Elsewhere
## The Letters of Bessie Head, 1963–1974

S
IX YEARS AFTER LEAVING SOUTH AFRICA ON AN EXIT PERMIT IN
1964 and entering Botswana, Bessie Head was able to build a small
house for herself and her child on the outskirts of the village of
Serowe. To do this she used the proceeds from the American paperback rights
for her novel *When Rain Clouds Gather*, which was first published in 1968.[1]
She called her house 'Rain Clouds'. Her choice of name is personal, regional,
and literary, indicating the interwoven needs which she wanted her home to
satisfy: a place in which she could write, a location that would give her
harmony, a place to which she could feel that she belonged, and a protective
space for her and her child. As with many of the changes that her move to
Botswana brought, however, 'Rain Clouds' afforded her both less and more
than the fulfilment she might have expected from having a 'home' of her
own.[2] Head's accounts of this experience in her letters speak to a matter which
has become central to postcolonial studies – a rethinking of the ideology of
'home' as both an intimate, personal space and as one that promises member-

---

[1] Gillian Stead Eilersen, *Bessie Head: Thunder Behind Her Ears: Her Life and
Writing* (1995; Johannesburg: Wits UP, rev. ed. 2007): 142, and Bessie Head, *When
Rain Clouds Gather* (New York: Simon & Schuster, 1968; London: Gollancz, 1969).

[2] The name 'Rain Clouds' is a reminder that this teasing combination is also a characteristic of the Serowe climate. In a later book, Head describes the clouds that usually
gather in November heralding rain, and observes that their promise is often not ful-
filled: "That's about all you get in Serowe most summers – the rain-wind but not the
rain." *Serowe: Village of the Rain Wind* (Cape Town: David Phillip, 1981): x.

ship of a larger collectivity such as a nation. This rethinking has been demanded by the growing phenomenon of migrant, diasporic, and otherwise marginalized lives in the contemporary world.

As a lonely exile, Bessie Head conducted an extensive correspondence, and as more of it is published, it becomes clear that she was one of the region's finest letter writers. Two collections of her letters have so far come out: those to Randolph Vigne and those to Patrick and Wendy Cullinan.[3] The editing of what will be a two-volume set of her collected letters is currently being undertaken by Linda–Susan Beard.[4]

Bessie Head's letters indicate that her move to Botswana had results that, from the first, she herself found somewhat contradictory. After just a year in Serowe, she wrote to Patrick Cullinan: "Here where so little or nothing was given me I was in some inexplicable way able to get at the source of strength and creativeness inside me,"[5] leading him to comment in retrospect that "Botswana – Serowe – gave her nothing except all that she had, all that she was creating" and to see "this paradox" as "central to Bessie's work."[6] Again the all-yet-nothing paradox appears. I will pursue it in Head's comments to her friends about building her own house, and the meaning that it accrued. 'Rain Clouds' seems to have become both a place that anchored her as a writer and a space that allowed her to rise free of a context in which she often felt herself to be a "social outcast"[7] and yet found too constraining. It was a home that would remain an 'elsewhere'.

---

[3] *A Gesture of Belonging: Letters from Bessie Head, 1965–1979*, ed. Randolph Vigne (London: SA Writers & Portsmouth NH: Heinemann, 1991), and Patrick Cullinan, *Imaginative Trespasser: Letters between Bessie Head, Patrick and Wendy Cullinan 1963–1977* (Johannesburg: Wits UP, 2005).

[4] Linda–Susan Beard, "Bessie Head's Epistolary Art," in *The Life and Work of Bessie Head: A Celebration of the Seventieth Anniversary of Her Birth*, ed. Mary S. Lederer, Seatholo M. Tumedi, Leloba S. Molema & M.J. Daymond (Gaborone: Pentagon, 2008): 183–203.

[5] Cullinan, *Imaginative Trespasser*, 87.

[6] *Imaginative Trespasser*, 90.

[7] Desiree Lewis, *Living on a Horizon: The Writings of Bessie Head* (Trenton NJ & Asmara, Eritrea: Africa World Press, 2007): 20.

It is tempting to suggest that the larger, perhaps compensatory, community to which Bessie Head could feel that she belonged was one that she created for herself in her letters, but as letters set up a complex web of fragile and unpredictable connections, creating a 'home' in them might not secure equilibrium. As will be shown later, Head herself saw her letter-writing as a form of speculation. Her sense of letters and their fragile connections is wonderfully expressed in Franz Kafka's trenchant comment that letters are "a traffic with ghosts."[8] If 'selves' do circulate in letters, then the presenting self (the writer) is a ghostly being that is born afresh in each act of writing, and the receiving self (the letter's first reader) is equally ghostly, called into being by the letter itself. This is a condition of epistolary interaction which Head found useful, for it enabled her to try out her ideas from a variety of angles as she adapted each utterance to her sense of her correspondent, and it is one that must inform any idea of the larger home that her letters may be thought to have afforded her.

Besides her sense of her recipient and her wish to try out ideas, Head's letters are inflected by her inner volatility. The letters to Vigne and the Cullinans are among the earliest that have survived, and from the beginning they show that the writer's persona could change radically with each letter, and not necessarily only in response to her idea of her correspondent. Far from being merely capricious, these changes were usually imposed on Head by her circumstances, but they also indicate that at times Head relished an opportunity

---

[8] I am indebted to Anthony O'Brien, *Against Normalisation: Writing Radical Democracy in South Africa* (Durham NC & London: Duke UP, 2001) for his stimulating exploration of some of Bessie Head's letters and for the phrase from Kafka, which he first encountered in Janet Gurkin Altman's *Epistolarity: Approaches to a Form* (Columbus: Ohio State UP, 1982). Bessie Head's letters have received critical attention as a distinct genre only in the last decade, but were extensively consulted by Gillian Stead Eilersen for the biography, *Bessie Head: Thunder Behind Her Ears*. Besides O'Brien, Lewis, in *Living on a Horizon*, has explored the generic features of letters in her discussion of Bessie Head's correspondence. A simpler sense of letters as documenting a life is used in Annie Gagiano, "Writing a Life in Epistolic Form: Bessie Head's Letters," *Journal of Literary Studies/Tydskrif vir Literatuurwetenskap* 25.1 (2009): 8–33. See also Beard, "Bessie Head's Epistolary Art."

to try out another way of presenting herself. Cullinan records that he first met Bessie Head in Cape Town in July 1962, when her infant son, Howard, was just three months old. The first letter he received from Head, a month after their meeting, was an act of ventriloquism in that it purported to come from the baby and to thank him "for the pretty toy that you sent me."[9] Head's charming ploy illustrates the scope that letter-writing offered her for constructing a voice suited to an occasion, and her intuitive sense of this liberty. The next letter was sent a year later and in it Head writes from a very different subject-position. She presents herself as an abandoned wife (she uses the past tense about her marriage), who is "at the edge of despair and terror"[10] because her application for a passport has been refused without explanation, but probably, she thinks, because she was "once a member of the banned PAC."[11] She writes of her desire to leave South Africa to find "a free Africa [...] that [...] would be an impetus and inspiration to my writing" but, as that now seems impossible, says that her immediate need is "just [... to find] five years of peace in what has been a life of pain, frustration and disillusionment."[12] It was this sudden, anguished cry that led the Cullinans to consult a lawyer and to obtain an exit permit for her a few weeks later so that she could leave for Serowe, where she had been offered a teaching job.

Besides the selves of various circumstances that Head presents in her letters, her desire to explore her ideas is evident from the beginning, as is the care with which she established the position from which she would do so. In the earliest letters to Cullinan from Serowe, Head is quite formal, suggesting that she wanted consciously to explain herself to a man whom she hardly knew but who had been concerned enough to help her leave South Africa, and who, himself a poet, had faith in her determination to be a writer: "I am writing to you for a number of reasons – the most important being writer's vanity

---

[9] Cullinan, *Imaginative Trespasser*, 9.

[10] *Imaginative Trespasser*, 11.

[11] Like other political parties radically opposed to apartheid, the Pan African Congress was banned in 1960 following the massacre at Sharpeville.

[12] Cullinan, *Imaginative Trespasser*, 14.

– I have to direct my ideas somewhere and have an audience."[13] She does not limit herself to polite or impersonal topics, but the full speculative utterance that she would gradually create for herself is embarked on with care, as if she felt that her words had first to create a connection on which she could rely. The published letters to Randolph Vigne, on the other hand, suggest that Head began from a stronger, more confident sense of how the man to whom she writes would receive her. Their friendship had begun when they were members of a radical political circle in Cape Town. The first published letter is dated October 1965 and seems to resume an earlier correspondence, and perhaps a conversation as well. Again her letter appeals for help in what is a desperate situation – she has been dismissed from her Serowe teaching job and accused by the school authorities of insanity – but, perhaps because she can rely on their having attitudes in common, Head's wording is relatively relaxed even in this crisis.

As with her letters to Cullinan, those to Vigne are also marked by her inner volatility. For two months after losing her job, Head regularly reports that people in Serowe want to "destroy"[14] her, and that she has been in "an absolute panic,"[15] but then, in a letter written just a day later, she is full of jaunty plans for her writing and assures Vigne that she and Howard are doing well. Her precarious circumstances might be enough to account for such mood swings, but their suddenness might also suggest an inner disturbance. What is indicative of Head's sense of her correspondent, and of the resilience she had to develop, is that she does not undertake to explain this abrupt mood swing to Vigne – what, if anything, has changed and why she now feels so differently. Instead, she chooses to deflect attention onto an analogy, referring to a story that she wrote while "intensely unhappy" and claiming that it consequently possesses "a swing and flow of its own"[16] that is quite contrary to the present bleakness of her life. It would seem that her jaunty letter to Vigne is not just designed to hide from him how troubled she is, but comes from a belief that

---

[13] Cullinan, *Imaginative Trespasser*, 23.

[14] Vigne, *A Gesture of Belonging*, 12.

[15] *A Gesture of Belonging*, 16.

[16] *A Gesture of Belonging*, 18.

her writing could bring into being another self that is able to gainsay her troubled circumstances.

After the publication of Head's first novel, the circle of her correspondents grew rapidly. These letters remain mostly unpublished except for quotations from them in Eilersen's biography.[17] They are held in the Bessie Head Papers in the Khama III Memorial Museum in Serowe. Eilersen explains that there are "over 2000 letters in the collection [...]. Bessie Head [...] kept up sustained correspondences lasting three or more years with over 30 people – keeping carbon copies of almost everything she wrote."[18] All of her letters were written at night, by candlelight, and, after 1967, on her typewriter. One of their striking features as a collection is the extraordinary capacity that Head had by now developed to move swiftly into intimate, profound, and confident communication with persons she had never met and, as far as she knew, would never meet. In this Head was making a full and steady use of the capacity of letters to connect selves that are "invented by the dialogic of the letter."[19]

Reading across the range of Head's published and unpublished letters, it becomes more evident that she did not simply repeat her views but preferred to explore ideas that were important to her from the various angles that her range of correspondents made possible. She writes very carefully *for* each of the readers she invokes in her letters, and at the same time she avoids sustaining a single subject-position, preferring to be creative in her standpoint, too. But her strategies did not always bring her the results she desired; epistolary connections can be unreliable. To the American poet Nikki Giovanni, she explained her strategy:

> I pace [...] [my letters] very sensitively against the person to whom I am communicating because it is something outside of what you can buy and sell. And it is intended to give happiness to the recipient. It is something for free.[20]

---

[17] For further information about the Head collection and its catalogue, see www.bessiehead.org (accessed 23 May 2010).

[18] Eilersen, *Bessie Head*, 61.

[19] O'Brien, *Against Normalisation*, 226.

[20] Quoted in Eilersen, *Bessie Head*, 210–11.

But she also did not hesitate to rebuke her correspondent when she seemed un-responsive to this care, telling Giovanni:

> It is hard for me to write a full and coherent letter to someone who only sends short scrawls because I don't know if you cared about all my latest specula-tions.[21]

Head was seeking an exchange of ideas: she was an intellectual. Her use of "speculation" indicates that she wanted her ideas, which might be couched as indisputable fact or conviction, to be received as exploratory and even experi-mental. Head put her trust in the viability and validity of her own ideas but, because her letters were a substitute for conversations, she also depended on her readers to be responsive, endorsing or challenging what she said.

Desiree Lewis has indicated that Head was aware of this tension. Lewis's conclusion is that "Head's interest in the interactive role of the letter does not contradict an assertive autobiographical impulse" and that the over-riding need to transmit an "authoritative autobiographical message"[22] – in which a novel such as *A Question of Power* played its part[23] – would account for some of the dramatic ruptures between Head and her correspondents. Read in the limbo of an archive,[24] or even in their published form, the letters might not convey how

---

[21] Quoted in Eilersen, *Bessie Head*, 210. Giovanni excused herself on the grounds that in her culture friendships were conducted by telephone, not letter (Eilersen, *Bessie Head*, 211). This exchange is also discussed in O'Brien, *Against Normalisation*, and Lewis, *Living on a Horizon*.

[22] Lewis, *Living on a Horizon*, 69.

[23] Bessie Head, *A Question of Power* (London: Davis–Poynter & New York: Pan-theon, 1973).

[24] Tom Holzinger writes of his initial surprise on reading the excerpts from Bessie Head's letters in Eilersen's biography: "The same sturdy woman who swung into varied projects by day was at the edge of despair and collapse by night [when she wrote her letters] and not only during her truly awful periods. Her correspondents were made to suffer the desolation of B. Head [...] as surely as her daily colleagues enjoyed her cheer and her exasperations. Another B. Head contradiction"; Holzinger, "Conversa-tions and Consternations with B. Head," in *Writing Bessie Head in Botswana*, ed. Mary S. Lederer & Seatholo M. Tumedi (Gaborone: Pentagon, 2007): 45. This indication

tenuous was the connection between correspondents, or even the tension between provisionality and authority of utterance, but Head's account of what
seems to have happened with one friend suggests that she was, at least at
times, aware of how difficult some of her correspondents might find the epistolary relationship that she desired. In a letter to Vigne, she begins by mentioning her break with Naomi Mitchison and then, continuing her account of
losses, she says that after reading *A Question of Power* and her letters about
her novel, her American friend Tom Carvlin "became too emotionally involved in my affairs. It frightened him and he pulled out of the correspondence
but what a man he is! I never cared to bother him. Friends come and go for
strange reasons."[25]

◄❖►

Bearing in mind the variety and fragility of the connections that Head's letters
established, and the ghostliness of correspondents, I now return to another
seemingly strong but significantly troubled set of connections in her life: those
which, as an exile in Serowe, she created when she built her house there. Like
her letters, her house had to meet many, and sometimes contradictory, needs.
Her quest for somewhere where she might find herself 'at home' expands in
the letters from the personal, intimate space of the house to the larger context
of a society, or a culture, or even a nation.

  Bessie Head said that she went to Botswana filled with the hope of finding
"a free Africa [… that] would be an impetus and inspiration to my writing."[26]
Her dream of freedom suggests that during her life in South Africa she had
had to construct an alternative 'Africa' that would sustain her spirit in the face
of the racist policies to which she was subjected, and so it is not surprising that
she should have imagined a place that was the polar opposite of the apartheid
world she knew – one that was tranquil, hospitable, and generous. But from

---

that multiple selves, and truths, inhabit Bessie Head has to be considered in relation to
the possibility that the impact of the letters changes when they are not received and read
piecemeal but contemplated as a body of archived or published writing.

[25] Vigne, *A Gesture of Belonging*, 174.

[26] Cullinan, *Imaginative Trespasser*, 14.

the first she had misgivings about finding such a world in Serowe. Soon after arriving she wrote to Cullinan about a mis-match between her new surroundings and her pan-African ideal: "it's just not possible to assert my kind of Africanness which is a wide, all-encompassing feeling of great intensity."[27] Besides her sense of a stifling rigidity in Tswana village culture, Head seems to have found that as a refugee she was at the mercy of Botswana's inevitable subservience to South Africa's economic power in the region, and to the impact of local varieties of racism on her own and her child's lives. She was also hostage to the in-fighting among refugees of various political allegiances,[28] and her letters claim considerable sexual harassment by local and refugee men.

When speaking of the insecurity that she felt in her new context as well as about her earlier condition in South Africa, Head often used the word 'homeless'. A year after her arrival in Serowe, she explained how she had been shaped by the lack of a home:

> I've always had to live in someone's house – the unwanted stranger. You get to have an odd, unpredictable view of everything that way. You just gravitate naturally to the outer bounds of any environment.[29]

In what should have been her homeland, South Africa, the state had questioned her right to exist for two sets of reasons: she was illegitimate and she was designated 'Coloured'.[30] It was as a counter to this double emptying of her identity that she believed ardently in the pan-African vision of Robert Sobukwe – hers was a socio-political as well as an aesthetic concept of 'Africa'. Now, as she and her husband had separated, leaving her a single

---

[27] Cullinan, *Imaginative Trespasser*, 24.

[28] Vigne, *A Gesture of Belonging*, 39.

[29] Cullinan, *Imaginative Trespasser*, 81. A month before writing this letter, Head sent a gift to Wendy and Patrick Cullinan which is a short, meditative piece called "This is the House that We Built" (Cullinan, *Imaginative Trespasser*: 69–74). The 'house' Head imagines represents a way of life untrammeled by the contemporary prejudices that she and her "mythical man" (Cullinan, *Imaginative Trespasser*, 47) have left behind them.

[30] 'Coloured' was the term for someone of mixed race, and it was a catch-all category for those (such as people originally from the East Indies) who did not fit apartheid's racial categories.

mother of a two-year-old boy and alone, she needed security. But, rising above all the domestic responsibility and anxiety which shaped her desire for a stable home, she felt herself destined to be a writer, and for this she also required a home – although one with a difference. It had to allow her freedom of mind and soul. These somewhat incompatible predisposing factors mean that, besides the specific difficulties of living in a strongly hierarchical community and in generally hostile conditions, she would probably have felt herself an alien, 'homeless', in any and all circumstances.

The misgivings that Head felt about her prospects of settling in Serowe could have been dispelled by her delight when it became possible to build a house on the outskirts of the village, on land that was secured for her by Patrick van Rensburg, the founder of Swaneng Hill School and of the Brigades movement in Serowe. She certainly delighted both in the material reality of the building – "The house is minute but the pride is overwhelming. It is the first brick thing I shall ever own"[31] – and in the processes of its construction. These she described to an American friend, expressing her pleasure in its young builders, and the Brigade system to which they belonged:

> The builders are young primary school leavers who before had no future and much hardship. They build while they learn a trade. To add to the gaiety, once I saw the house going up I recovered from my mental blackout and added two of my own architectural inventions in the yard – one a seed-storage shed and two, a seedling nursery.[32]

To another friend she wrote of "the serious, intense, concentrated expressions of the students for whom a whole new life of dignity has been created."[33] The house meant that her physical conditions for writing were vastly improved.

---

[31] Vigne, *A Gesture of Belonging*, 98.

[32] KMM 38 BHP 17. The archival reference is to Khama Memorial Museum (KMM), the Bessie Head Papers (BHP), the numbering of the files and the page. Permission to quote from the unpublished letters has kindly been given by the Khama III Memorial Museum, Serowe. For an account of the Brigades system, see Head, *Serowe: Village of the Rain Wind*, Eilersen, *Bessie Head* and Patrick Van Rensburg, *Looking Forward from Serowe* (Gaborone: FEP, 1985).

[33] KMM 74 BHP 7.

*When Rain Clouds Gather* had been written in an isolated shack on a bleak stretch of land between the African and the expatriate areas of Francistown, a designated centre for refugees in Botswana.[34] Her next novel, *Maru*, was written in a small, circular mud hut in Serowe where she had "to cook, wash and eat"[35] in the same room, and she described with some amusement the practical problems that her cramped quarters posed for her writing:

> There is no space to spread out my files, notes and working materials without their becoming covered with layers and layers of dust. Many insects also make their abode in the grass thatching and calmly submit their droppings all over the place.[36]

When she was about to move into her house, she told Randolph Vigne about its naming which sealed a reciprocity between the building and her writing:

> The thing is, the house and the book go together and I would very much like to call the house *Rain Clouds*. I wanted [… a] name [plate] done by someone who would do it out of affection. Indeed, there are some artistic types at Swaneng but I really have no friends there or anyone I could call [on] for some gesture of affection.[37]

To Paddy Kitchen, an English novelist friend whom she knew only through letters, she wrote both more joyfully about her house and more obliquely about her isolation:

> I impulsively ordered a name plate from a friend who wanted to give me a gift for the new house – part of the title of my book – RAIN CLOUDS, but all the time I feel it should be HEAVEN. It is not so much a resting place for me as for some treasures I've carried around through years of a battered existence, number one being a collection of most of D.H. Lawrence who is the one great love of my life […]. A house is someplace to put things you love intensely.[38]

---

[34] Eilersen, *Bessie Head*, 88–89.

[35] Eilersen, *Bessie Head*, 133.

[36] KMM 60 BHP 18.

[37] Vigne, *A Gesture of Belonging*, 91.

[38] KMM 74 BHP 7.

She did not have much:

> two beds, a table and two chairs for the kitchen, and a writing desk and book-case for [… her] room. There was no electricity. She continued to write by candlelight, but now she had gas rings fed by a portable cylinder installed in the kitchen. This was a luxury, as was the running water.[39]

But Head valued the prospect of having friends in her house too. The letter to Paddy Kitchen goes on to express the hope that 'Rain Clouds' will become "that kind of house where [… people who] simply believ[e] in goodness [will] enter."[40]

Building and then working in her own haven did not, however, dispel Head's sense of exclusion from the ambient culture or protect the inner freedom that was necessary to her writing. Head had arrived in Serowe hoping for a wide and generous life of the mind. While she continued to hope for this 'Africa', her letters also testify to the anger caused by her cultural exclusion as well as revealing her knowledge that she could not always counter it by attempting to live from day to day in a free-floating, boundless condition. Nor, she sometimes admitted, could she write that way. Angered by the daily social rejection she experienced, she said:

> To a certain extent, even wholly[,] I had made some kind of identification with [… Africa]. How else can I have a shred of dignity? I am alive. That means I must live somewhere on this earth.[41]

And about a year later she asked:

> How do you write about nothing. You must make yourself a part of the life of the country, even if it's painful and confused and people struggle for their own expression in a maybe brutal and cruel manner.[42]

As with the early story which she said countered the dreariness of her life, writing the antithesis of what was "brutal and cruel" was a stratagem that Head

---

[39] Eilersen, *Bessie Head*, 143.

[40] KMM 74 BHP 7.

[41] Cullinan, *Imaginative Trespasser*, 61.

[42] Vigne, *A Gesture of Belonging*, 38.

sometimes used in her fiction, saying that writing for her "is a healing thing in the sense that all the things I cannot create in life I can create when I put words down."[43] But the strain of such visionary writing was great: referring to *Maru*, she told Randolph Vigne:

> You know the torture and conflict in my heart will never end. I tell you I hate everything here, but when you read the stuff I have produced in this country, the contradiction is so obvious. [...] most of my dreams were so long distance, the reality being the opposite.[44]

In a postscript to her anger, she makes a specific link between her condition and her writing: "I think, like Pat [van Rensburg], we have no home or anything solid to get a grip on. [...] the children and me live with no love, no hope; but we work all the same, you are forced to be generous."[45]

Despite her sense of rejection, by 1974 and shortly after the publication of *A Question of Power*, Head's letters begin to indicate her conviction that she could not leave Botswana. This was not because she felt that she had been accepted; it was, rather, that she had not the energy to cope with dislocation again. Her attitude does, however, also have positive sources. One lies in her frequent listing of what she has come to love in the village: "goats, solitude, old women, small village boys, my home, the panoramic landscape and so on."[46] Foremost in her list is her house:

> I decided to stay here, because I love my little house and everything around it. I mean I built my house myself and where would I get it again – it *looks* like me and I cannot part with it as it may be the only home I ever own in my life. (Head's emphasis)

This letter also suggests that she was sometimes able to find an affinity between her writing and her domestic life:

> Someone asked me: "What's your next masterpiece?" And I replied: "At pres-ent I am baking cakes for a lot of hungry little boys, weeding my garden and

---

[43] Cullinan, *Imaginative Trespasser*, 45.

[44] Vigne, *A Gesture of Belonging*, 124–25.

[45] *A Gesture of Belonging*, 124–25.

[46] KMM 48 BHP 2.

cleaning my house – it's all of one thing like writing a book!" He looked very disappointed and replied: "I see nothing creative in that." So I just thought that the ability to do all that is the extension of my typewriter and didn't bother to explain that all that made me happy.[47]

But, in view of the exploratory nature of her declarations, it is not surprising that this affinity is sometimes undermined by another aspect of her sense of 'home'. For example, in order to convey to Nikki Giovanni her affection for aspects of Serowe and for her house in particular, she depicts herself as standing at the gate, seeing it as an outsider would. She writes of

> My home at night with its candle light, the hours I spent at the gate watching the candle light through the yellow glow of the curtains, the long solitary hours of thought.[48]

These sentences read as notes for further exploration, but Head's brief indication that she confirms the inner warmth of her house by stepping outside it may mean that she did not know how to receive, as her right, the emotional and spiritual comfort it provided. Perhaps this is one writer communicating to another how she manages to stand alongside her daily self in order to contemplate (and so write about) it, but her recorded position at the gate also suggests that she needed to remind herself of what her house excluded so that what it included might give her joy. Her positioning indicates that the complex states of being 'at home' and 'homeless' could not be kept apart, for to confirm one condition Head had to entertain the other.

Ultimately, Head's published writing did provide her with the sense of belonging in Serowe that she had needed, but by this stage acceptance seems not to have been a fulfilment of her early hopes. In producing *Serowe: Village of the Rain Wind* and its offshoot collection of short stories, *The Collector of Treasures*,[49] she felt that she had written her way into a legitimate place in her

---

[47] K M M 5 B H P 20.

[48] Quoted in O'Brien, *Against Normalisation*, 228.

[49] *The Collector* was sent to publishers in 1975 and published in 1977; *Serowe* was sent in 1974 but not published until 1981. Bessie Head, *The Collector of Treasures* (London: Heinemann, 1977) and *Serowe: Village of the Rain Wind* (Cape Town: David Philip, 1981).

adopted country and village, even if official recognition had not yet been granted to her. In 1977, the year her short stories were published, her application for citizenship was turned down. Then, it was the sudden, definite, and ironically timed offer of a way to leave Botswana that consolidated Head's gathering reluctance to go. A doctor friend who was a Norwegian citizen, Marit Kromberg, had secured a formal offer of citizenship for Head and her son, and so Head had the difficult task of explaining to her why, although she was still stateless, she would not take up the offer. She writes to Kromberg:

> I was so troubled in heart after posting it [*Serowe*] that I sat up a whole night wondering what I should do. Towards morning, I simply decided I would stay. It was like choosing death, deliberately. I don't think I should live for so long, five years more would be a miracle. Then I'd prefer to die in the little house I built for myself. [ … ] my life is almost over and I cannot make any other effort than what I have made already.

And she concedes: "Nothing is logical about my decision. There is not much hope for me here but I'd rather stay."[50] Head's phrasing, especially her calling her choice "death" and saying that she expected to live for only five more years (she was thirty-seven at the time and seemed to be in good physical health), is possibly shaped by her sense of having let down a friend who had done so much to help secure her and her child's future. To Randolph Vigne she wrote with a different sense of "death":

> I had to read the book through before posting it and that finally finished me up. It is a damn beautiful book and I simply thought: 'After work like that with so much humour, value and information, this is my home, and only death will take me out of it.' So I set my focus straight a bit, if one can call my reasoning straight. There's nothing but death for me so I might as well get busy on a few more books.[51]

And she wrote to another Swaneng friend:

> I'd been crying all the time. It's a damn beautiful thing. Then I just stopped crying and thought: 'After work like that I belong here. This is my home. Why

---

[50] KMM 52 BHP 6.

[51] Vigne, *A Gesture of Belonging*, 185.

the hell should I go anywhere else?' This logic holds good until I die and I
don't care much else about anything.[52]

Her refusal to move has been used to establish a reassuring trajectory for
Head's life – the self-exiled refugee who gradually puts down roots and finds
acceptance in her new setting. But what disturbs this reading are her references
to death. Given her age, these are chilling; they are not protest or lamentation,
but her earlier determination to do battle has gone, leaving an acceptance of
nothingness ahead. Identifying the place she now loves as the one where she
wants to die is not utterly strange, but it disturbs any idea that she had found
the fulfilling, "felicitous space"[53] that a 'home' might be expected to offer.

What is salient in these letters is that Head's house did not function for her
as 'home' does in the ideology of domestic life that was developed in the
nation-states of the West during the nineteenth and twentieth centuries. In this
thinking, 'home' was the locus of identity, one in which its inhabitants learned
to identify and relate to their own kind, thereby earning themselves the place
in a larger, homogeneous society to which they in turn felt entitled. 'Home' is
the innermost of a concentric set of circles radiating out from self-and-home to
family-and-home, to community, to state. 'Rain Clouds' and the presence of
Howard did anchor Bessie Head in Serowe, but it was always as an outsider,[54]
and her house did become the base from which she could produce first *A
Question of Power* and then the Serowe books which gave her a substitute
sense of entitlement to live there. But it remained an 'elsewhere' which did
not, in her life-time, provide her with integration into Serowe, let alone Botswana. In a brief memoir of Bessie Head as she was in the early 1970s, her
friend Tom Holzinger says: "All in all, then, she enjoyed a generous measure

---

[52] KMM 48 BHP 7.

[53] Gaston Bachelard, *The Poetics of Space*, tr. Maria Jolas (*La Poétique de l'espace*,
1957; tr. 1964; Boston MA: Beacon, 1969): xxxi.

[54] I have omitted discussion of Head's participation in the Boiteko garden project and
her friendships with Bosele Sianana and staff members at Swaneng. This school and its
staff were situated on the outskirts of the village, as was Head's own house, and were
thus not necessarily an integral part of Serowe.

of power over her own demesne – just as surely as she suffered powerlessness on the larger scale."[55]

◄❖►

The split between home and its surroundings, evident in different ways throughout Head's letters, is also a key feature of 'home' that is explored in much other writing about dislocation in our times. When Rosemary Marangoly George suggests that migrant people do not necessarily "yearn for assimilation into the mainstream," that "'feeling at home' may or may not require assimilation," that "the process of making oneself at home is a project that may not be completed even by several successive generations," and that for many migrant peoples "the wandering never stops,"[56] it is clear that new understandings of the experience of 'migrant', 'refugee', 'exile', and 'diaspora' are emerging, and inviting a reconsideration of 'home'.

It is to the rethinking of 'home' and 'exile' that Bessie Head's letters contribute most particularly. The valence most familiar in 'exile,' that of someone who has been forced to leave and live beyond a beloved country, is not what she ever reports. Shaped by denial, she refused ever to claim an ancestral or a personal 'homeland'.[57] In deciding to leave her non-homeland, Head, like many migrant workers or refugees, had little choice about where she could go and where she would live when she reached her 'elsewhere'. Although this double denial of locatedness seems eventually to have sapped Head's own energies, she did imagine a positive re-location for her child, despite the early racist attacks he suffered in Botswana. She herself never learned Setswana, but

---

[55] Holzinger, "Conversations and Consternations," 39.

[56] Rosemary Marangoly George, *The Politics of Home: Postcolonial Relocations and Twentieth-Century Fiction* (Cambridge: Cambridge UP, 1996): 184. George takes the example of Vassanji's novel *The Gunny Sack* (1989) for her argument.

[57] In a late letter to a young woman whom she calls "Niece Wally," Head recalls her life in Pietermaritzburg and then comments on how meaningless the name of the town where she was born has seemed whenever she has had to supply biographical information to publishers. But she offers her foster-family member some place in her life, saying: "Your letters begin to make that small town not so meaningless now" (KMM 373 BHP 3).

Howard spoke it fluently from childhood. Head encouraged her son to feel that he was a Motswana, suggesting that she saw assimilation into the local culture as a viable objective for her offspring. In herself though, Head did not settle.

Postcolonial migration and the new racism it brings have produced two broad responses among oppressed peoples, the poles of which are an essentialist wish to recover the ancestral home or homeland, on the one hand, and, on the other, the idea that a country might have "a diverse, multiracial population of many different peoples."[58] Bessie Head's letters traffic with both possibilities, and they raise the personal and writerly question of an individual person's relationship with either kind of larger home. When she first realized that she would not find her 'Africa' in Serowe, Head wrote that perhaps it "meant that I [am to] become a sort of universal [person] [...] that I am not meant to make any identification with any place."[59] For the autobiography she began to plan in 1984 (and was apparently working on when she died unexpectedly two years later), Head wanted to use the title "Living on an Horizon" because, as she said in a letter to its prospective publisher, Heinemann, the phrase described someone who "lives outside all possible social contacts, free, independent, unshaped by any particular environment, but shaped by internal growth and living experience."[60] Her words suggest that Head continued, alongside

---

[58] Edward W. Said, *Freud and the Non-European* (London & New York: Verso, 2003): 41. This is Edward Said's account of what Palestine once offered. In his essay considering Sigmund Freud's account of Jewishness, he says that currently "Israeli legislation countervenes, represses, and even cancels Freud's carefully maintained opening out of Jewish identity towards its non-Jewish background" (44).

[59] Cullinan, *Imaginative Trespasser*, 61.

[60] Quoted in Eilersen, *Bessie Head*, 327. Lewis, echoing Head's title in her study, makes a general claim for Head's fiction:

> Although this global perspective [and Head's use of "universal patterns"] suggests an abstract vision, it is firmly grounded in relationships and subjects that the writer knew intimately. Head developed philosophies about oppression, resistance and social and creative freedoms in ways that were intensely personal and rooted in everyday experiences. (Lewis, *Living on a Horizon*, 2)

My focus is somewhat different – the moment-to-moment tensions in the letters between Head's desire for a personal life in a community and her need for a larger,

her choice of Botswana as her 'home', to think of herself as profoundly unconnected, a free spirit. But hers was always a conflicted view. In the sentence
preceding her imagining herself as a "universal" person in the letter to Patrick
Cullinan, she protests angrily: "I am alive. That means I must live somewhere
on this earth. There are some things one must take from an environment."[61]
This is the anger of the rejected, and is a reminder that as a person and as a
writer she often yearned to enjoy her 'home' as the locus of her identity and
the foundation for all wider relationships.

## WORKS CITED

Altman, Janet Gurkin. *Epistolarity: Approaches to a Form* (Columbus: Ohio State UP,
    1982).

Bachelard, Gaston. *The Poetics of Space*, tr. Maria Jolas (*La Poétique de l'espace*,
    1957; tr. 1964; Boston MA: Beacon, 1969).

Beard, Linda–Susan. "Bessie Head's Epistolary Art," in *The Life and Work of Bessie
    Head: A Celebration of the Seventieth Anniversary of Her Birth*, ed. Mary S.
    Lederer, Seatholo M. Tumedi, Leloba S. Molema & M.J. Daymond (Gaborone:
    Pentagon, 2008): 183–203.

Cullinan, Patrick. *Imaginative Trespasser: Letters between Bessie Head, Patrick and
    Wendy Cullinan 1963–1977* (Johannesburg: Wits UP, 2005).

Eilersen, Gillian Stead. *Bessie Head: Thunder Behind Her Ears: Her Life and Writing*
    (1995; Johannesburg: Wits UP, rev. ed. 2007).

——. "Serowe, Bessie Head's 'Bits of Ancient Africa,'" *Lekgapho, The Khama III
    Memorial Museum Review 1988–89* 1 (1990): 61–66.

Gagiano, Annie. "Writing a Life in Epistolic Form: Bessie Head's Letters," *Journal of
    Literary Studies/Tydskrif vir Literatuurwetenskap* 25.1 (2009): 8–33.

---

perhaps universal, selfhood. Nixon has commented that Head's projecting "social
acceptance" in her novels was a product of a "determined optimism [which] quietened
in her fiction the cadences of desolation that distinguished her letters." Rob Nixon,
"Rural Transnationalism: Bessie Head's Southern Spaces," in *Text, Theory, Space:
Land Literature and History in South Africa and Australia*, ed. Kate Darian–Smith, Liz
Gunner & Sarah Nuttall (London & New York: Routledge, 1996): 252.

[61] Cullinan, *Imaginative Trespasser*, 61.

George, Rosemary Marangoly. *The Politics of Home: Postcolonial Relocations and Twentieth-Century Fiction* (Cambridge: Cambridge UP, 1996).

Head, Bessie. *The Collector of Treasures and Other Botswana Village Tales* (London: Heinemann; Cape Town: David Philip, 1977).

——. *Maru* (London: Gollancz; New York: McCall, 1971).

——. *A Question of Power* (London: Davis–Poynter & New York: Pantheon, 1973).

——. *Serowe: Village of the Rain Wind* (Cape Town: David Phillip, 1981).

——. *When Rain Clouds Gather* (New York: Simon & Schuster, 1968 & London: Gollancz, 1969).

Holzinger, Tom. "Conversations and Consternations with B. Head," in *Writing Bessie Head in Botswana*, ed. Lederer & Tumedi, 35–57.

——. "A Warrior Alone," in *Writing Bessie Head in Botswana: An Anthology of Remembrance and Criticism*, ed. Mary S. Lederer & Seatholo M. Tumedi (Gaborone: Pentagon, 2007): 30–34.

Lewis, Desiree. *Living on a Horizon: The Writings of Bessie Head* (Trenton NJ & Asmara, Eritrea: Africa World Press, 2007).

Nixon, Rob. "Rural Transnationalism: Bessie Head's Southern Spaces," in *Text, Theory, Space: Land Literature and History in South Africa and Australia*, ed. Kate Darian–Smith, Liz Gunner & Sarah Nuttall (London & New York: Routledge, 1996): 243–54.

O'Brien, Anthony. *Against Normalisation: Writing Radical Democracy in South Africa* (Durham NC & London: Duke UP, 2001).

Said, Edward W. *Freud and the Non-European* (London & New York: Verso, 2003).

Van Rensburg, Patrick. *Looking Forward from Serowe* (Gaborone: FEP, 1985).

Vassanji, M.G. *The Gunny Sack* (London: Heinemann, 1989).

Vigne, Randolph, ed. *A Gesture of Belonging: Letters from Bessie Head, 1965–1979* (London: SA Writers & Portsmouth NH: Heinemann, 1991).

‹❖›

JAMES GIBBS

# The Portrait of the Artist as a Younger Traveller

A Reader's Response to Wole Soyinka's
*You Must Set Forth at Dawn*

W OLE SOYINKA'S *YOU MUST SET FORTH AT DAWN*[1] takes its title from a line of his poem "Death in the Dawn."[2] The first word of that line, "Traveller," has been omitted, but I find it easy to put it in, to fill in the addressee and then to take this volume as partly about Soyinka the Traveller. The journeys are described with immense vitality and contribute significantly to making the book a page-turner. On publication in the USA in April 2006, it was well-received, and it came out later the same year in London from "Methuen in association with Bookcraft." With apologies to Bookcraft (Ibadan), I will refer to this simply as 'the U K edition'. I will draw attention to some alterations that were made in the journey across the Atlantic, and to elements that make the U K edition more substantial than that published in New York. In the pages that follow, I will refer to the tone of the book, its attitude to detail, and its presentation of selected episodes. I start off by drawing attention to the way Soyinka refers to individuals and groups ("Titles, Names, Acronyms and a Quotation") and then move through a series of events that can be looked at from different points of view. These are arranged in chronological sequence and involve moments during the Rockefeller years (1960–62), the radio-station hold-up and trial (1965), and the search for

---

[1] Wole Soyinka, *You Must Set Forth at Dawn: A Memoir* (New York: Random House, London: Methuen & Ibadan: Bookcraft, 2006).

[2] Wole Soyinka, "Death in the Dawn," in Soyinka, *Idanre and Other Poems* (London: Methuen, 1967): 10–11.

the Ori Olokun (1978–79). I suggest that Soyinka sometimes makes mistakes and sometimes makes broad generalizations, that the narratives are clarified or balanced by comparison with other sources, and that the author is concerned to present himself in particular ways. My intention is to try to determine what sort of a book this is, and what sort of a portrait of a younger traveller Soyinka has presented.

While entertaining those who have picked up his book, Soyinka does not encourage close attention. In both editions of *You Must* there is a page of acknowledgments – placed at the end of the US edition, and at the beginning of the UK edition. In this Soyinka thanks his editors and takes responsibility for any "flaws." He thanks data-checkers and academic institutions; he refers to "the mental gadget that sometimes pretends to the function of memory" and to the loss of "useful documentation." The final paragraph of these acknowledgements, that can be read as a 'Keep Off' notice, includes the following:

> it would be churlish not to acknowledge the industry of those assiduous scribblers whose monographs, conference papers, etc, on the life of this subject finally goaded me into abandoning a rational decision: not to pursue the task of recollection and reflection beyond the age of innocence – calculated at roughly eleven and a bit. While, unlike those authoritative voices, I still hesitate to claim definitive knowledge of the subject, I can at least flaunt the advantage of having lived with him all his life, without even a day off, which is far longer than has any other being on the literary planet.

While admiring the deftness of these sentences, I think readers should be prepared to engage in critical reading of the memoir. Everyone should ponder the position Soyinka adopts. The resources of libraries and websites allow curious readers – who may also be "assiduous scribblers" – to check names and to compare accounts. Autobiographers and biographers are not omniscient narrators of lives, and one group can learn from the other in the never-ending attempt to get closer to the always elusive 'truth'. I hope that the points I make below shed light on the complexity of the process Soyinka engaged in when writing *You Must*.

Aspects of Soyinka's conduct and of the way he writes about himself have been discussed before, but we get a much fuller self-portrait here in *You Must*, one that shows darker sides. Often a gracious guest with a princely manner,

Soyinka is also capable of being off-hand or angry. One of the most extraordinary moments in *You Must Set Forth* is found in the account Soyinka provides of his intervention in a quarrel between a couple on a New York side-walk. In that, he describes how a woman he had chivalrously moved in to help turned on him. At that moment his chivalry was transformed and he advised her partner to "take her home, please" and to "beat her shitless." He clarified this wholly unacceptable advice by adding: "I mean, beat her to a shitty pulp" (US 433; UK 513).[3] This eruption of brutal rage provides a glimpse of part of Soyinka that has to be taken along with his grace, charm, and wit, his industry, self-sacrifice, and commitment.

## Titles, Names, Acronyms, and a Quotation

In drawing attention to examples of Soyinka's attitude to selected titles, names, and acronyms, I will begin with an example from England. In recording his efforts to help the Nigerian politician Anthony Enahoro, Soyinka describes contacting friends with political clout in London. He writes of "profiting from [his] friendship with […] Lord Kenneth of the House of Lords, whom [he] had known in his plebeian days as Wayland Young" (US 60; UK 69). In fact, Wayland Young was the son of a (plebeian) journalist who had been elevated to the peerage; the title he inherited was 'Lord Kennet'.

In describing how members of his family were able to join him in the USA during, I think, the mid-1990s, Soyinka writes that they were "aided and abetted by the French ambassador in Lagos Garrigue–Guyounaud" (US 396). This is later rendered as 'Pierre Garriguere–Guyonnaud' (UK 467). The difference between the editions here is marked by the introduction of a first name, good, and the correction of the last name, also good. However, I think an error is introduced into the first part of the double-barrelled name. The man referred to is, I think, Pierre Garrigue–Guyonnaud, whose postings have included Luxemburg.[4]

---

[3] For convenience, page references are given to two of the editions in the body of the text.

[4] See direct.bl.uk/research/10/3A/RN138288479.html (accessed 1 October 2008).

Among Nigerians who have maligned Soyinka, one is described by the latter in the Random House edition as "the police boss, Comassie" (US 376) and there is a reference in the same edition to "Alhaji Ibrahim Commassie," "the brother of the inspector general of police" (US 406). In the Methuen edition, the first reference becomes "Coomasie" (UK 444) and the second is abbreviated to "Alhaji Commassie" (UK 480). From comparison of various sources, I think that the family name should be rendered 'Coomassie', that the I-G of Police was Alhaji Ibrahim Coomassie, and his brother, sometime editor of the mischievous *Today* newspaper, was Alhaji Dahiru Coomassie. It may be that different sources use different spellings, or that different branches of the family favour a particular version. However, I suspect that the matter could have been clarified. Asked to indicate a recent, hopefully reliable source for the spelling of the names, I would point to Lawal Saidu's article that appeared in *Leadership* on 18 September 2008. In that, Saidu reported that the former I-G of Police had been hurt and was headed: "Nigeria: Coomassie Critically Injured in Accident."

On pages referred to above (US 406; UK 479), there are references to "Jude Uzowanne," described as "an ambitious youth from Swarthmore College" who provided a "confession" to a Northern-based newspaper. Searching the web, I found a reference that linked "Jude Uzonwanne" to Swarthmore College.[5] Since Uzonwanne ran a website with the title *The Coalition Against Dictatorship in Nigeria*,[6] it seems likely that this is the person Soyinka was referring to. Incidentally, my experience of the Northern-based *To-day* newspaper, linked to the Ibrahim Coomassie just mentioned, suggests that it was an utterly unscrupulous publication. It was adept at manipulating material in order to malign Soyinka.

Writing of "a well-known Abacha crony of Yoruba stock" (US 445; UK 528), Soyinka refers to him as "Triple A" and explains this as "Alhaji Alao Arisekola" (US 446; UK 529). A web search reveals that this may be 'undercounting' the number of As scored by the Aare Musulumi of Yorubaland.

---

[5] http://www.iasfbo.inaf.it/extras/Services/Local/WhatsNew/whats-new-9602.html (accessed 1 October 2008).

[6] http://www.sccs.–swarthmore.edu/org/nigeria/index.html (accessed 1 October 2008).

There are online references to "Alhaji Azeez Alao Arisekola," who scores a "Triple A" on his names alone, and the title he earned from making the Hajj could give him a fourth. An article in the *Compass* newspaper discussed his proximity to Sani Abacha, suggesting that this is indeed the man Soyinka was referring to.[7]

The sixth excursion I am going to make in this preliminary section in relation to the names posed particular problems for the web check. In the closing pages of *You Must*, Soyinka describes the opposition movement's "dependable base in Benin." He recalls addressing Nigerian groups in Porto-Novo when on "a visit that was sponsored by Professor Albert Tedjevore," who is described by Soyinka as his "elder collaborator in more than a few African causes" (US 488; UK 579). Having drawn a blank with that name in that form, I found my way to sites relating to an "Albert Tévoedjrè," notable for his membership of the Commission on Human Security and this, I think, produced a match.[8] Despite the lapse of time between the two editions, Methuen did not pick up what seems to have been an error in the Random House volume. What surprises me most about this misspelling, for that is what I think it is, is that Soyinka can't have stopped to check. He moved on, perhaps typing at speed, the creative drive carrying him forward. When he read it through, he didn't say 'Better check that'. He sent it off.

Fallible checking is not new where the laureate's writing is concerned. On pages 4 and 145 of *Open Sore of a Continent* (1996),[9] he refers to the "Movement for the Salvation of the Ogoni People." In fact, the 'S' in MOSOP stands for 'Survival'. In other words, in 1996, despite having travelled far and wide campaigning on behalf of Ken Saro–Wiwa, Soyinka was under the misapprehension that the 'S' in MOSOP stood for 'Salvation' (421). Ten years later, during which time profiles of both Saro–Wiwa and MOSOP remained high, Soyinka persisted with the religious explanation: in writing *You Must*, he

---

[7] http://compassnewspaper.com/news.php?extend.1267 (accessed 1 October 2008).

[8] http://www.humansecurity-chs.org/about/profile/tevoedjre.html (accessed 1 October 2008).

[9] Wole Soyinka, *Open Sore of a Continent: A Personal Narrative of the Nigerian Crisis* (Oxford: Oxford UP, 1996).

reflected his conviction that MOSOP was concerned with Salvation. It comes as a relief to see that 'Survival' was correctly inserted in the UK edition (498). I like to think that the correction was made after an 'assiduous' reader 'scribbled' something, and, naturally, I ponder the significance of the 'Freudian slip'.

The reference to MOSOP is, incidentally, in the context of a brief account of the trial and execution of Ken Saro–Wiwa, or 'Saro–wiwa' as it is rendered in the US-edition version. This form was corrected in the UK edition (UK 17, 18, 265, 346, 497–505.). I note that the chapter about Saro–Wiwa, headed "Requiem for an Ecowarrior" in the US edition, becomes the more teasing "Requiem for an 'Eco' Warrior" in the UK edition. I suspect that change may have been because of the intervention of the Methuen 'house stylist', of whom more below.

Finally in this section of what some may regard as 'typos', and as a bridge to the next section that includes a quotation, I want to look at a couple of lines from *As You Like It*. When recalling cold, student days in Leeds, Soyinka incorporates the lines "Blow, blow, thou winter wind … thy tooth is not so keen."[10] He then, apparently from the same source, quotes "Freeze, freeze thou winter sky" (US 395; UK 466). While at first glance that might pass for a line by Shakespeare, it is, in fact, a misquotation: the Shakespearean text actually reads: 'Freeze, freeze, thou *bitter* sky."[11] In a sense, there is not much significance in this slip. No one is hurt, no one is misrepresented, no hidden feelings are exposed, no sensitive preoccupations glimpsed. It is just a mistake, such as we are all capable of making. It is nonetheless disconcerting to find Shakespeare misquoted, not least because the lines could so easily have been looked up. Particularly in the UK format, *You Must* has the appearance of an academic publication – indeed, at over one kilo it is a tome! Misquotations of Shakespeare should have been eliminated.

---

[10] William Shakespeare, *As You Like It* II.vii.173–76.

[11] *As You Like It* II.vii.183.

## The Rockefeller Years 1960–62

In writing of his days as a researcher at the beginning of the 1960s, Soyinka suggested the "undeserved courtesies" he received from rural Nigerians had "much to do" with the "University of Ibadan" logo on the side of the Land Rover he drove (US 48; UK 53). I am sure the institution was held in high esteem and generated positive responses. It is worth noting, however, that the University of Ibadan as such did not exist when he was driving the Rockefeller Land Rover. We might have expected the vehicle to have had "University College, Ibadan" on the side. Many Nigerian readers, particularly those over a certain age and with an interest in educational development in the country, will be aware of this mistake and it is surprising that none of the data checkers listed in the Acknowledgements drew attention to it either when the book was in typescript or after the publication of the US edition.

Incidentally, a comparison of the presentation of the US and UK editions reveals that the text has been completely reset and that different 'house rules' have been followed. Those employed for the Methuen edition result in capitals and the insertion of tone marks for UNIVERSITY OF ÌBÀDÀN. The UK house rules also prefer the form 'early sixties' to 'early 1960s'. It should be noted, however, that the text remains fundamentally the same. Although the Methuen volume includes (welcome) illustrations, an appendix of documents and an index, and while it impresses with this 'apparatus', it remains fundamentally the same as the US book – and it is "A Memoir."

My next point concerns the way Soyinka describes how he used the Land Rover just referred to. He writes that, at that period (1960–62) and in the course of his research, he "toured the entire West African coast" (US 46; UK 53). He then adjusts the impression created by this very broad gesture by adding: "My forays outside Nigeria were infrequent" (US 47; UK 53). My understanding is that they were infrequent indeed, and, one might add, limited in range. Soyinka certainly made two trips along the coast, and 'assiduous scribblers' have already reconstructed these from the records held in the Rockefeller Archives. In 2008, Bernth Lindfors brought together several relevant essays he had written in a volume entitled *Early Soyinka* and I have also stumbled into the same territory.[12] From the information Soyinka provided the Rockefeller Foundation for the period of his research fellowship (1960–62), I think he travelled only as far west as the Ivory Coast, and he made only a few stops or detours on the way. The claim to have "toured the entire West African coast" gives a distorted impression and the vagueness of this expansive assertion prepares us for the fact that loose generalizations rather than precise descriptions will be found elsewhere in the book.

## Learning Lasky's Lesson 1961

The Land Rover just referred to featured in an episode from 1961 that might be dubbed "Confrontation with a Strip of Film." For this episode we have not only Soyinka's 2006 account, but also one published in 1961 by the 'other man' in the story, Melvin J. Lasky.[13] The basic situation was that Soyinka gave Lasky, the editor of *Encounter* who was visiting Nigeria, a lift back to his hotel in the Land Rover already mentioned. Lasky's description, which occupies a brief paragraph in a sixteen-page article, began: "Wolé driving on the longest, darkest short-cut ever taken, [...] suddenly brakes, reverses, lunges the (vehicle) forward and backward a half-dozen times, criss-crossing the same patch of road."[14] I want to set those lines beside the version of the same event that appears in Soyinka's book. The account in *You Must* reads:

> One evening, as I drove [Lasky] in my Land Rover back to his hotel, close by Ibadan's pioneer television station – W N T V: First in Africa – I swerved suddenly to ensure I did not miss a large, shiny snake attempting to cross the road. I appeared to have succeeded. I reversed the car, and there it was, stopped in its tracks but still writhing in the light of the headlamps. I ran over it two more

---

[12] See Bernth Lindfors, "The Rockefeller Ride" and "The First Field Trip" in *Early Soyinka* (Trenton NJ: Africa World Press, 2008), and James Gibbs, "'Marshall Ky of African Culture' or 'Heir to the Tradition?': Wole Soyinka's position on his return to Nigeria in 1960," in *"Return" in Post-Colonial Writing: A Cultural Labyrinth*, ed. Vera Mihailovich–Dickman (Cross/Cultures 12; Amsterdam & Atlanta G A: Rodopi, 1994): 85–99.

[13] Melvin J. Lasky, "Africa for Beginners," *Encounter* 94 (July 1961): 32–48.

[14] Lasky, "Africa for Beginners," 39.

times to make sure it was quite dead; still it continued to writhe. (US 73–74 UK 85)

Thus far the two accounts have been similar. Lasky wrote that Soyinka then shouted "Snake!" and got out of the vehicle while he himself "tip-toed out behind" him and "peered out at an enormous elongation glistening in the moonlight." He continued: "It was still quivering slightly; and well it should. Wole's tyres had twisted a derelict piece of 35 mm celluloid into an agitated wriggling strip." Lasky concluded the paragraph – on the seventh page of his sixteen-page article – with the following: "Tonight's lesson of the jungle: one looks for the beast and finds only a film."

Returning to *You Must*, we find Soyinka continues *his* account by saying that, having stopped, he took the "engine crank" and "descended [from the Land Rover] ready to apply the coup de grace." He went on that "Melvin wisely [declined] my invitation to join in the fray," adding: "It turned out to be no snake at all but a discarded filmstrip – very likely thrown out by the television station!" He then observes that Lasky

> used the incident to end the narrative of his African excursion, published in *Encounter* – his concluding words continued to ring in my head for some time afterward: "In Africa, you confront a serpent, and it turns out to be a filmstrip!" (US 74 UK 85)

Let us pause here and note that Soyinka thought he knew Lasky's essay well enough to refer to its structure, but, equally clearly, he recalled it inaccurately – the incident does not *end* Lasky's article. Having established this error, one wonders about the other variations, and, inevitably, one ponders the factors affecting recall.

When he sat down to write his account of the episode for *You Must*, Soyinka produced a narrative that differed in important respects from Lasky's. For example, he made his own role marginally more decisive and even mildly heroic, with a pleasant touch of the mock-heroic. We read that he "armed himself" and got down from the vehicle alone while Lasky "declined" the invitation to "join the fray." In Soyinka's version, he alone (the isolated hero?) descended from the safety of the vehicle to face the danger. In Lasky's version, we have a nervous "second" hovering in the rear.

A comparison of key words shows that, while Lasky's "lesson" may, as Soyinka writes, have "rung" in his head for some time, it did not 'ring true'; his memory let him down. Soyinka did not remember it in 2006 in the way Lasky had recorded it in 1961. In order to see where Soyinka's memory has taken him, I want to focus on the words in two versions. Paired up, very slightly altered, they emerge, as follows:

> Lasky:     Tonight's lesson of the jungle: one looks for the beast and finds only a film.
>
> Soyinka:  (*'quoting' Lasky*) In Africa, you confront a serpent, and it turns out to be a filmstrip!

The usages and resonances are significantly different, and could profitably be the subject of extended analysis. One might, for example, note that Lasky opts for a setting that stresses the vegetation and uses a cliché, "the jungle." Soyinka, by contrast, saddles his guest visitor with a geographical reference, an allusion to a continent, making him, perhaps, the narrator of a Conradian tale.

We then notice that Lasky's verbs suggesting cautious, impersonal enquiry and discovery, "one looks for and finds," are replaced by Soyinka, who introduces a martial dimension and the second person, "you confront." This builds on the mood already established by the use of "coup de grace" and "fray," confirming a (mock-) heroic, combative swagger.

Lasky's "beast" has several layers of meaning. It could, for example, have emerged from the Book of Revelations, from folk memory, or from the awareness that infected William Golding's schoolboys on their "coral island." Soyinka's vocabulary remains closer to the creature the two men feared on that dark night, a snake, but, very significantly, he transforms the snake into – or, perhaps, it transforms itself ("turns out to be") – a "serpent." With this fascinating reference to a metamorphosis and that weighty word "serpent," Soyinka introduces a plethora of religious and mythical associations. He locks the lesson-drawer into perceiving an epic struggle with evil forces, one that begins near the very beginning, the Judaeo-Christian, and involves the Prince of Darkness in the shape of a serpent.

Whereas Lasky concludes with "a film," standing for the "derelict length of 35 mm celluloid" he has already referred to, Soyinka has a "filmstrip." This usage may remind the reader of the distance between the Nigerian writer and the English language, for a filmstrip is not the same as a strip of film.

From the comparison of the versions much may be extracted, but one thing is clear: in writing his book Soyinka did not consider it necessary to go back to Lasky's article and remind himself of what Lasky had written. Soyinka can't have tracked down a copy of *Encounter* for July 1961. He must have relied on his memory, the faculty that he knew to be faulty. Based on his recollections, he took it upon himself to write not only about an episode, but also about a visitor's account of that episode. He rashly relied on his memory for a quotation, assuming, perhaps, a capacity for total recall. Not surprisingly, given the passage of the years, we don't get an accurate quotation. Instead, we get a variation on the Lesson, a message 'mediated' by Soyinka, self-dramatist, raconteur, mythopoet.

## The Radio Station Hold-Up and Trial, 1965

Moving through the 1960s, we come to one of the most (in)famous episodes in which Soyinka has been involved: the Radio Station Hold-Up at Ibadan (October 1965). It may be recalled that Soyinka pleaded 'Not Guilty' to the charges levelled against him relating to the hold-up, and for many years he maintained a studied coyness about what happened. This coyness can be seen in *The Man Died*[15] where he blocked off enquiry about his role in the armed raid by drawing attention to the fact that he had been tried and acquitted. Twenty-two years later, in *Ibadan: The Penkelemes Years*,[16] he adopted a different approach, taking his readers through the hold-up while maintaining that the protagonist was not Wole Soyinka but "Maren." Six years into the new millennium, the last veil was cast aside and Soyinka at last confirmed what many had long suspected: he 'came out' as the armed intruder with all that that implies. In the course of providing a first-person account of his role, it emerges that his alibi was fraudulent, his defence based on lies, his plea perjury, and that his action caused distress to individuals caught up in events. The

---

[15] Wole Soyinka, *The Man Died: Prison Notes* (London: Rex Collings, 1972): 156.

[16] Wole Soyinka, *Ibadan: The Penkelemes Years: A Memoir: 1946–1965* (London: Methuen, 1994): 359–62.

account in *You Must* also shows that his recollection of important elements in the case is seriously flawed, and reveals how he 'tidied up' the muddle he created.

There are various accounts of the trial available: these include newspaper reports from the time and a 1996 book that Soyinka mentions (US 95; UK 111), *The Mystery Gunman* by Kayode Eso.[17] Given Soyinka's footnote directing attention to Eso's book, we might have expected him to have refreshed his memory by engaging with it. He does not seem to have done this and, as a result, there are discrepancies, some minor, some major, between Soyinka's 2006 account and that provided by Eso. Given that he knew his memory to be faulty, it is surprising that, in a work funded by academic institutions, Soyinka did not consult the source that he knew existed.

The 're-presentation' of events begins with a minor change: Soyinka records that the charges against him involved the theft of "one magnetic tape. Cost: two pounds, seven shillings" (US 88; UK 103). From the newspaper reports of the time, it is clear that the items he, with Engineer Oshin at one stage, was accused of stealing were two tapes and the price put on them was £2. 12s 6d.[18] While of no great moment in itself, this rewriting reveals a cavalier attitude to the past: while including detail, that detail is not checked.

Of much greater moment than this tiny detail is the fact that Soyinka misrepresents his defence counsels' strategy. According to *You Must*, Soyinka's lawyers argued that their client had no case to answer and he maintains that this plea was upheld. Soyinka summarizes Eso's ruling in the following terms:

> [Justice Kayode] Eso upheld the submission of our defense: no prima facie case to answer. The prosecution had undone itself. We had secured a verdict through a pure technicality that came from a crucial contradiction within the prosecution's elaborately presented case. The defense strategy had worked, and I had not even been placed in the witness stand. (US 95–96; UK 112)[19]

---

[17] Kayode Eso, *The Mystery Gunman* (Ibadan: Spectrum, 1996).

[18] Anon., "Soyinka's trial begins today," *Daily Times* (Lagos; 10 November 1965). See also the British observer John Mortimer, "Nigeria – land of law and disorder," *Sunday Times* (London; 28 November 1965): 5. Note: figures in these sources vary by 6d!

[19] The editorial changes in the Methuen edition have led to UK spelling and the use of dashes instead of colons. All quotations here are from the first edition of the book.

In fact, Eso's book contains no reference to the grand statement that there was "no prima facie case to answer." Quite the contrary. Eso points out that, with Soyinka's alibi "completely shattered by the evidence of the head of department of the accused party, Professor Geoffrey Axworthy," it was impossible for "a reasonable tribunal [to] discharge [Soyinka] on a no-case submission."[20] From this it seems that Soyinka has misremembered, and so misrepresented, the very basis of his defence. He has, I suggest, 'tidied up' a muddle, and introduced a colourful Latin phrase that was often on the lips of bright lawyers.

Incidentally, it is difficult not to smile when reading the lines quoted above about "the defense strategy" having worked without Soyinka "even" having to enter the witness box because Eso's recollection is that Odesanya "submitted that [...] he had no intention of putting his client into the witness-box."[21] One can understand why Odesanya made this decision: given that his alibi had been blown out of the water and that his statement to the police had been discredited, Soyinka would not have been a credible witness. At this point the gap between Soyinka's picture of himself, in this instance as master-speaker kept in reserve, and that held by others, such as Odesanya, who might have thought "Wole will blow it if he gets to speak," yawns cavernously.

When it comes to the reasons why he was let off, Soyinka's account and Eso's overlap: the prosecution witnesses were certainly at variance and the case turned on this. Eso quotes his ruling as including the following statement:

> With this sharp contradiction in the evidence of the prosecution, I am bound to give the accused person the benefit of the doubt. I therefore find him not guilty and he is, accordingly, acquitted and discharged. (240)

Rather than seeing this as a triumph for Soyinka and justice, I see it as Eso, who had been placed in a difficult position, finding a loophole and letting Soyinka slip through it. In doing this, Eso bravely defied powerful politicians, including S.L. Akintola, and saved Soyinka's skin. However, the whole sequence raises numerous questions about justice and the law, for, after all, here

---

[20] Eso, *The Mystery Gunman*, 234.

[21] *The Mystery Gunman*, 233.

was a case in which a man who had held up a radio station and lied about it went free. Justice was neither done, nor seen to be done. I suspect that Soyinka realized that his action, more rag stunt than revolutionary deed, made a mockery of the justice system and, for that reason, he deflected enquiries about the case for many years.

With this as background, I want to glance back over the Hold-Up and The Trial for what they show about Soyinka. I suggest that Soyinka wanted the reader of *You Must* to see him in a particular light and so cast himself in a starring role as The Man Who Held Up the Radio Station at Ibadan. Despite Soyinka's bland "It all proceeded according to plan…" (US 84; UK 98), there seems to have been considerable confusion about the venture. For example, a crisis was created for staff at the broadcasting station, who were asked to identify Soyinka at parades, and particular distress must have been endured by one of them, Akinwande Oshin, who was initially charged along with Soyinka with the theft of the tapes.

When it came to the alibi, Soyinka's head of department, Geoffrey Axworthy, was interviewed by the police and his testimony put Soyinka on the University campus on the day of the hold-up. Though crucial in the "was the intruder bearded or beardless?" dimension of the case, this demolished Soyinka's claim that he had travelled from Ibadan on the day in question.

In The Trial, Soyinka had an extraordinary platform for a performance. The meta-theatrical elements in the court were many and were articulated by Prosecutor Gomez, who, at one point, opposed the defence lawyer's application that Soyinka should be granted bail:

> Whatever happens here, the accused should always be considered in the light of his profession. As a playwright and a dramatist he could feign sickness now and the next minute he could feign another character. *There is no limit to what dramatists can do.* It is perfectly obvious that the hold-up was nothing more nor less than a rehearsal for a coup d'etat.[22]

---

[22] "Ruling Today on Bail for Soyinka," *Daily Times* (Lagos; 4 November 1965): 16. My emphasis.

Those lines were reported in the *Daily Times*, which, we might note, transcribed the drama as it unfolded.[23] Indeed, the press devoted considerable space to the trial, often running the story on the front page and sometimes producing text that pointed up awareness of the theatrical dimension. For example, on 26 November, the *Daily Times* unscrolled a headline which recalled a prince who had detected "something rotten" in the state. It read: "To reply or not to reply?" The Trial ended happily, and theatrically, for Soyinka, who, thanks to Eso's giving him "the benefit of the doubt," was acquitted. His supporters carried him shoulder-high from the court.

From the language used by Gomez and in the newspapers, it was apparent that participants and observers were aware of Soyinka's 'trial as theatre'. Readers of *You Must*, at least those who also read Eso, can perceive elements of reinterpretation of the original drama: the 'rewriting' is most obvious in the case that Soyinka says his lawyers made.

## The Brazilian Job, 1978–79

One of the most extraordinary tales told in *You Must* might be referred to as "The Brazilian Job" and sub-titled "The Search for the Ori Olokun." Much of this narrative is mock-heroic in tone, infused with an amused awareness of the high drama that followed what Soyinka takes to have been a "missed wink." This "missed wink" was the failure to register the fact that the anthropologist, photographer, and scholar of the transatlantic world Pierre Verger was joking when he confessed to having smuggled the bronze head of a Nigerian deity across the Atlantic to the collection of his friend, Hector Julio Páride Bernabó–Carybé. "The Brazilian Job" is a rattling good yarn about a mission to recover a cultural artefact; it is related with self-deprecating humour and with nods in the direction of *Indiana Jones and the Temple of Doom*. The most remarkable of the carefully orchestrated let-downs comes when the clay head that Soyinka has stolen from Carybé's house in Brazil is subjected to examination in Dakar and the initials 'B M' are found on the base. This indicates that the Brazilian

---

[23] See "Ruling Today on Bail for Soyinka," *Daily Times* (Lagos; 4 November 1965): 1, 16, and other coverage.

heist left Soyinka holding an item purchased in the British Museum gift shop –
with mud on his face and a hole in his bank account.

The *You Must* version is self-fashioning of himself as Indiana Jones with
both a vengeance and a sense of humour, and it might be considered churlish
to carp too much about this very obvious self-representation. However, there is
a disconcerting dimension to the whole episode. This is because this is not a
Spielberg fiction; it is 'real life', human beings were involved, and human
beings were hurt. Interestingly, the fundamental problems with the Brazilian
Job will not surprise those who have read thus far: it was lack of basic research
mixed with eagerness for dramatic action. When Indiana Jones sets off on a
quest, we 'accept' that the character played by Harrison Ford has done his
homework – and then we enjoy the acting, the twists, the turns, the special
effects, the fiction. Soyinka acts precipitately, setting off on a wild goose chase
in the course of which good people are hurt simply because an 'action hero'
has not done the necessary research.

In his writing about the Ori Olokun Episode, we can see traces of the inadequate 'research' Soyinka undertook. For example, in the US edition, he writes
of the historical background to the looting of the Benin treasures, and he refers
to an important encounter between "a Captain Phillips and King Overawhen"
(US 188). The latter spelling is changed ('corrected') in the UK edition to
Ovoramwen (222). Even that alteration does not bring it into line with the
widely employed ('correct') form. In fact, what seems to be the most widely
accepted form is very familiar to all those, like Soyinka, concerned with Nigerian theatre from the title of a play by Ola Rotimi, *Ovonramwen Nogbaisi*.
This is a sensitive area, and, I suspect, some are hurt by what they see as lack
of consideration for their naming conventions.

Phillips, spelled with two 'l's, is also, I think, an error. A web search indicates that the name of the Captain involved in the typically brutal punitive raid
on Benin is generally spelled 'Philips'. This is a minor lapse, since it is hard to
imagine anyone feeling personally slighted or offended by it. However, it confirms the somewhat off-hand approach to names that seems to surface again in
the reference to "Oba Akenzua Iku Akpolopkolo," whose funeral rites were
being performed when Soyinka returned from the Brazil trip (US 207; UK
244). I think the reference is to the man I have found recognized as Oba

Akenzua II, whose name appears as "Uku Akpolokpolo."[24] There are various Edo nation groups that might well take exception to the 'disrespect' indicated by Soyinka's lapse.

The approach to the spelling of names may be conveniently linked with the cavalier attitude to people that is reflected in the whole Brazilian adventure. At the risk of sounding narrowly moralistic, I would suggest, once again, that Soyinka's deed of derring-do had its victims. One old man, Pierre Verger, was kept under house arrest and subsequently found he couldn't travel freely; another, Carybé, who opened his home to visitors, was robbed. Soyinka recognizes Verger's sufferings and, to his credit, expresses regret that he did not manage to 'stage' a reconciliation (US 219–21; UK 258–61). This failure was, indeed, very regrettable. It should be kept in mind that Verger and Carybé were men of good will and distinction, scholarly collaborators on a major study of the Yorùbá use of medical plants. One was cruelly inconvenienced and the other's home was violated in the course of a poorly researched, hastily embarked upon, swashbuckling ego-trip to Latin America.

In an interview, Soyinka referred to the Brazilian adventure as a "mad cap episode" and added that it "embarrasses me until this moment."[25] The mock-heroic, Spielbergian treatment of the episode should not distract readers from recognizing the deeply embarrassing, regrettable – indeed, shameful – role played by the younger traveller. Soyinka was right to feel embarrassed, and readers should not feel they have to excuse him because in a certain mood he wrote about his headstrong (mis)behaviour with verve and wit. The episode can't be 'laughed off'.

## Conclusion

At the beginning, I quoted the final paragraph of the acknowledgements and I now refer back to it, insisting that the 'Keep Off' injunction should not be

---

[24] See Osadola Edomwonyi, *A Short Biography of Uku Akpolokpolo, Omo N'oba N'edo Akenzua II, C.M.G., C.F.R., J.P. LL.D, Oba of Benin* (Benin City: Bendel Newspapers, 1981).

[25] See "Conversation with Wole Soyinka," http://www.thenewgong.com/Soyinka Conversation.html (accessed 21 October 2008).

allowed to silence those who are not Wole Soyinka and will never be Soyinka from engaging with the accounts of his life that he has put in the public domain. Close attention should be paid to the way he writes about others and about himself. Cutting free from checking spellings and from looking up the texts of Eso and Lasky may have allowed him to write with fluency and gusto. But with freedom from restraint came danger. In this essay, I have suggested that there are points when close readers will reflect critically on the portrait of the artist as a young traveller presented in *You Must Set Forth*. It is appropriate for such 'close readers', if they are also "assiduous scribblers," to break into print; indeed, doing so is part of an important dialogue. It goes without saying that the dialogue should be marked by courtesy and an awareness of the complexity of the processes of both self-presentation and the examination of self-presentation.

## WORKS CITED

Anon. "Albert Tevoedjre," Commission of Human Security, http://www.human security-chs.org/about/profile/tevoedjre.html (accessed 1 October 2008).

Anon. "Conversation with Wole Soyinka," http://www.thenewgong.com/Soyinka Conversation.html (accessed 21 October 2008).

Anon. "Why Abacha gave me N100m – Arisekola," in *Nigerian Compass*, http://compassnewspaper.com/news.php?extend.1267 (accessed 1 October 2009).

Ajao, Adewole. "On the road with Prof. Wole Soyinka" (14 September 2008), http://odili .net/news/source/2008/sep/14/208.html (accessed 14 September 2009).

Akingbade, Tunde, & Flora Onwudiwe. "Wole Soyinka and mystery gunman at radio station, by German journalist," *Vanguard* (14 September 2008), http://www .vanguardngr.com/index.php?option=com_content&task=view&id=16894&Itemid= 42 (accessed 14 September 2008).

Edomwonyi, Osadola. *A Short Biography of Uku Akpolokpolo, Omo N'oba N'edo Akenzua II, C.M.G., C.F.R., J.P. LL.D, Oba of Benin* (Benin City: Bendel Newspapers, 1981).

Eso, Kayode. *The Mystery Gunman* (Ibadan: Spectrum, 1996).

Gibbs, James. "'Eshu Confuser of men!' Questions Prompted by Wole Soyinka's *Ibadan: The Penkelemes Years*," in *The Contact and the Culmination: Essays in*

*Honour of Hena Maes–Jelinek*, ed. Marc Delrez & Bénédicte Ledent (Liège: L3, 1997): 119–30.

——. "'Marshall Ky of African Culture' or 'Heir to the Tradition?' Wole Soyinka's position on his return to Nigeria in 1960," in *"Return" in Post-Colonial Writing: A Cultural Labyrinth*, ed. Vera Mihailovich–Dickman (Cross/Cultures 12; Amsterdam & Atlanta GA: Rodopi, 1994): 85–99.

Lasky, Melvin. "Africa for Beginners," *Encounter* 94 (July 1961): 32–48.

Lindfors, Bernth. "The Rockefeller Ride" and "The First Field Trip," in *Early Soyinka* (Trenton NJ: Africa World Press, 2008).

Meuer, Gerd. *Journeys around and with Kongi – half a century of the road with Wole Soyinka* (Neumarkt: Thomas Reche, 2008).

Mortimer, John. "Nigeria – land of law and disorder," *Sunday Times* (London; 28 November 1965): 5.

Saidu, Lawal. "Nigeria: Coomassie Critically Injured in Accident," *Leadership* (Abuja; 18 September 2008), http://allafrica.com/stories/200809180709.html (accessed 1 October 2009).

Soyinka, Wole. *Ibadan: The Penkelemes Years: A Memoir: 1946–1965* (London: Methuen, 1994).

——. *Idanre and other poems* (London: Methuen, 1967).

——. *The Man Died, Prison Notes* (London: Rex Collings, 1972).

——. *Open Sore of a Continent: A Personal Narrative of the Nigerian Crisis* (Oxford: Oxford UP, 1996).

——. *You Must Set Forth At Dawn, A Memoir* (New York: Random House, London: Methuen & Ibadan: Bookcraft, 2006).

*The Daily Times* (Lagos) for October, November, December 1965 covered the arrest, detention and trial of Wole Soyinka. Details of specific articles referred to can be found in footnotes.

◄❖►

SHIRLEY CHEW

# Putting Freedom to the Test
## Wole Soyinka's *You Must Set Forth at Dawn*[*]

A CCORDING TO WOLE SOYINKA, one of his mother's favourite aphorisms, "with her comic yorubization of the key English word 'trying', [was] '*Itirayi ni gbogbo nkan*' – 'The trying is all'."[1] Wild Christian, Soyinka's mother, applied the saying to

> a full gamut of incompatible situations – from the shrug of resignation that followed a failed attempt to charge exorbitantly for her goods to falling with full relish on the dubious results of an exotic recipe that she was attempting for the first time. (18)

In this reading of *You Must Set Forth at Dawn: A Memoir*, the third of a trilogy with *Aké* and *Ìsarà*, I see *itirayi* as impelling, shaping, and structuring the narrative. What is 'tried' here – in two of the possible senses of the word – is freedom. First, in Wild Christian's sense of 'to put to the test', in order to determine the feasibility of an action or the quality of a thing; and, second, in the sense of 'to examine and determine issues' – for example, of guilt or innocence – in a court of law.

What does Soyinka mean by 'freedom'? Obviously, political freedom, with Nigerian independence on 1 October 1960 given here as the beginning date of a new era in the country's history. Then there is freedom which, political self-

---

[*] A version of this essay was given at the EACLALS triennial conference at Venice on 25–29 March 2008. Geoff was then Chair of EACLALS.

[1] Wole Soyinka, *You Must Set Forth at Dawn: A Memoir* (New York: Random House, 2006): 18. Further page references are in the main text.

determination having been achieved, must surely mean for the nation's citizens "the right to exercise the choice to move or not to move" (490) – in other words, the right to one's own space and place. This is a key concern in the memoir, one that accrues emotional weight as the occasions continue to multiply in which Soyinka's national passport is seized by Immigration officers at Lagos airport. Finally, there is freedom as a concept and a condition of humanity, which, for Soyinka, is inseparably linked to "justice as the basis of society" (105).[2] The truth of this becomes markedly evident when he is framed and imprisoned without trial during the Civil War (July 1967–January 1970). From that pivotal moment onwards in *You Must Set Forth at Dawn*, the very idea of 'freedom', particularly in its several guises in Nigeria, is itself to be scrupulously examined and tried. After two years and four months in Kaduna prison, Soyinka emerges in January 1969 to find civic institutions, such as the judiciary, severely eroded within a militarized Nigeria. With brutal displays of power being all part of the everyday scene – humiliations, beatings, kidnappings[3] – there is a pervasive sense of rottenness in the state.

> Thus, somewhere within the nation called Nigeria, some feeling of a suspension – at the very least – of the expectation of justice had to exist [...]. There had to be innocent victims, both individual and community. The Biafrans, major actors in this war, assuredly nursed a feeling of injustice. The Midwest Ogbo, first compromised by their kin from across the Niger, then "liberated" by federal forces and slaughtered in batches for "collaborating" with the Biafrans, must feel engulfed in blood founts of injustice. The minorities of the delta region, forced into an unwanted entity called Biafra and brutalized, had surely undergone at the hands of Biafrans a monumental injustice. The very process of their liberation must have caused some undeserved suffering, thus breeding a

---

[2] Furthermore, freedom is directly opposed to power, positioned as they are "at either end of a living axis" (80).

[3] Consider the case of Ola Rotimi, the playwright and director, who was horsewhipped in public on the motorway; furthermore, during a "routine blackout," the manager of the local station would be sent for and his head shaved with a piece of broken glass; and a participant in a private quarrel could find himself taken hostage to make him agree to the terms of settlement (150–51).

sense of double injustice. Justice denied, injustice unmerited, even as expressions of the barest possibilities, surely existed beyond dispute. (144)

I explore in this essay two interconnected strands in *You Must Set Forth at Dawn* which together body forth for Soyinka "the palpable essence of freedom" (490): first, the compulsion to establish on the personal level the right of 'movement' which goes hand in hand with the right to "an accustomed space, a sanctuary [...] of one's own choice and designation" (152); and, second, the compulsion to redeem on the national level that "commodity called justice" (144) which, badly crushed and betrayed though it has been in the thirty and more years covered by the narrative, continues to be upheld by Soyinka as "central to my self-apprehension and ordering of the human community" (144).

To turn to the first narrative strand noted above. The powerful opening section of the memoir – "IBA – For Those Who Went Before" – recounts the author's journey back to Nigeria in 1998 after "five years of a restless exile" (3). For, with the death of the dictator Sani Abacha, the "long-craved homecoming" (4) is finally possible. How, then, should one explain Soyinka's psychological state as the plane moves towards Lagos? How to account for his experience of near emotional void during the flight and the seemingly "featureless flatness" (5) of his mind? Behind the shifts of memory and mood registered in the narrative, a number of possible reasons for his "deflation" (487) can be identified.

It is likely, for example, that the abrupt and unexpected end to the tyrant's rule,[4] and at a point when the opposition groups, Soyinka among them, were gearing up for "confrontation [...] with violence" (497), has induced a sense of anticlimax, even of the futility, so to speak, of the lost years in exile. Then any anticipation of return on Soyinka's part can only be undercut by the realization that certain family members and friends will be irrevocably missing from among the crowd gathered to welcome him back to Nigeria. "IBA" – Yorùbá for 'homage' – remembers and names these personages who are intimately part of his human and political landscape. His parents, Essay and Wild

---

[4] Abacha died "in the arms of Asian prostitutes flown into Abuja for one of his periodic orgies" (487).

Christian; his young cousin, Fela Anikulapo Kuti, the "Afro-beat king" (21);
Bashorun M.K.O. Abiola, president-elect of the June 1993 polls;[5] and two
altogether special friends – Femi Johnson (OBJ) with his unstinting generosity, loyalty, and infectious love of life; and Ojetunji Aboyade (Oje), vice-
chancellor of the University of Ifẹ, an "intellectual sparring partner" (9) and an
enthusiastic if inept hunting companion in the bush. Finally, the mental
journey homewards must be attended with the very real though suppressed
fear "that my house is gone anyway, that I am returning to a conspicuous gap
in the landscape at which I had hacked and quarried, years before my departure, to give expression to my appetite for space" (8). Just a small cottage on a
piece of land to begin with, home at Abeokuta, an hour by road from Lagos, is
where, echoing the classical literature he knows so well, Soyinka could expect
to indulge his fantasies of "a life of interdependency between the arts and the
farm" (19). Later, with the money from the Nobel Prize, 'home' is to grow in
size to incorporate the Essay Foundation for the Humanities, a "periodic retreat for writers and artists" (8). Over and above all else, 'home' is the site of
"the cactus patch, a bristling phalanx of thorned markers to which I had as-
signed the role of covering my remains" (20).

A passing episode – curious yet telling – underlines the singularity of Abeokuta and Soyinka's attachment to the retreat he has carved out for himself. In
1990, in the district of Westmoreland in Jamaica, he had come by chance upon
a slave settlement founded by "a group of slave descendants" fleeing the low-
land plantations for "a hilly terrain that would prove nearly impenetrable for
their pursuing owners but would also remind them of home" (21). Presided
over by an ancient survivor of the original settlers, Bekuta – the name being a
corruption of Abeokuta – had entertained the visitor with cultural traces of the
distant homeland, "dishes whose recipes had been carefully preserved" and
dances which mimed the "sedate ceremonial steps of the Egba" (23). If, sus-

---

[5] Abiola, it seems to Soyinka, was also "a dogged disciple of the doctrine of *itirayí*"
(18). After a foiled first attempt to be the president of Nigeria, he won the elections in
June 1993, was imprisoned, and was about to be released after the death of Abacha
when he died suddenly – the alleged cause being years of slow poisoning while in
prison.

pended in time and space, Bekuta was a source of interest to Soyinka on that first visit, it becomes, during the Abacha years, a seriously viable option as a substitute home:

> I announced openly that, if ever the worst happened, I did not want Abacha's triumphant feet galumphing over my body and would settle for the surrogate earth of Jamaica. And I began to make preparations to buy a patch of land in Bekuta. (23)

By the second visit in 1995, the old lady, guardian of the settlement, is dead. Furthermore, repeated floods in the area have resulted in the exodus of the small community, thereby leaving Bekuta to return to the jungle. Perhaps the death of the place can be deemed inevitable, and for the following reasons. Within the broader context of diaspora, the settlement is little more than a pale reflection of a faraway homeland. Isolated among the rockhills and mountain cul-de-sacs, and cut off from the regenerating forces of change, it has in the course of time become atrophied.[6] In the specific context of Soyinka's exile and search for a home, Bekuta, the duplicate, has to be set aside in order that the return and repossession of Abeokuta, the original home space, can ultimately be achieved.

Whether 'home' for Soyinka is the nation territory that is Nigeria or Abeokuta with the cactus patch at its heart, it has in fact never been absent from his consciousness even when he is directly confronted with Abacha's threats. The narrative dynamic of "IBA – For Those Who Went Before" makes this plain when 'home' as absence is continually sounded against 'home' as felt presence. Desire and memory conjure up, even in the artificial space and air of the plane's interior, the "smells, muted sounds, textures and often impenetrable silence" of the bush; the oppressive noises and odours of the streets and markets of Lagos; the delicate scent of the wild mints in his garden; Fela's blaring music; Wild Christian's acerbic tones; the face of Femi, "black as the cooking pots, supervising the kitchen in a frenzy of anticipation" (4). The recurrent

---

[6] As Stuart Hall has remarked, "Cultural identity [...] is a matter of 'becoming' as well as of 'being'. It belongs to the future as much as to the past." Hall, "Cultural Identity and Diaspora" (1990), in *Colonial Discourse and Post-Colonial Theory: A Reader*, ed. Patrick Williams & Laura Chrisman (London: Prentice Hall, 1993): 394.

play of these sensuous recalls – visual, tactile, olfactive, auditory – serves to look ahead in the memoir to the upsurge of joy that will overtake Soyinka when he finally lands in Lagos: "No, there is no question about it this time – at long last, my viscera yield and concede: *I am back in the place I never should have left*" (499).

Before moving on to the second narrative strand in *You Must Set Forth at Dawn*: i.e. the compulsion to redeem on the national level the "commodity called justice" (144), I wish to pause for a moment at *The Climate of Fear: The Reith Lectures, 2004*.[7] An adherent of the tenet "Dialogue [...] involves exchange," as opposed to monologue and harangue, Soyinka puts forward in the *Lectures* a number of structures for action in the face of crimes against humanity. They are:

(a)   galvanizing international communities and organizations, such as the UN, to take action not merely on moral but on agreed legal principles;

(b)   negotiating, formally or informally, with the powerful and the in-fluential, whether state or personage, for resolution to crisis situations. This could involve, as he notes in the memoir, supping on occasions with the devil himself, albeit with a long spoon and making sure that one does not to let go of the handle;

(c)   submitting oneself to self-interrogation, so that, "if certain acts against humanity appear to place their perpetrators beyond dia-logue," then the question must be asked, "in what way, in turn, have we contributed to the making of such a moment?"[8]

(d)   resorting, when other strategies have failed, to violence, and in *You Must Set Forth at Dawn* Soyinka does not rule this out even though it is "a stage to be avoided for as long as and whenever possible" (80).

---

[7] Wole Soyinka, *The Climate of Fear: The Reith Lectures, 2004* (London: Profile, 2004): 60.

[8] Soyinka, *The Climate of Fear*, xiv–xv, 87, 133.

Published two years after the *Lectures*, the memoir is, first, a chronicle of Soyinka's unflagging attempts, stoutly supported by friends and activist groups, to put these strategies of intervention into operation at critical moments in the nation's history. These moments include, within the time frame of 1960 to 1998, the already compromised freedom from the start,[9] ethnic rivalry, the rigged elections of 1964–65 followed by civil war, a spiral of coups and counter-coups, and successive military dictatorships. Accumulatively, the episodes determine in the main the formal structure of the memoir; and the strands of activism and self-questioning, interwoven as they are throughout, stage in unmistakable ways Soyinka's interrogation both of the nation-state and of the nature of his own participation in the struggle for freedom and justice.

To take an example from the early years – the attempt in 1962 to lobby the British parliament against the extradition of Tony Enahoro. Political intrigues among the different political parties, as well as in-fighting among the Yorùbás of the Western region, lead to charges of treason against some of the main figures in the Yorùbá-dominated Action Group, among them Tony Enahoro. Accused of being one of the masterminds of what would have amounted to a civilian coup d'état, Enahoro flees to Britain, and is wanted back in Nigeria to stand trial. So it happens that the youthful Soyinka – who "*found it intolerable* that all the progressives were being netted and incapacitated," who "*held that political sanctuary was a universal given*," especially in "a thriving democracy" such as Britain, and who is "restless with *the knowledge that I was fortuitously placed to lend a hand*" (60, my emphases) – decides to fly to London to enlist the support of "one or two figures in the British establishment" whom he knows from his days at the Royal Court Theatre. But, to his astonishment, "the battle was lost" (60). Despite his intervention and his recourse to influential friends and the British government, the extradition takes

---

[9] "Ours was no more than a 'flag independence', a situation where economic control remained in London, while the local leaders left behind were stooges"; Femi Osofisan, "'The Revolution as Muse': Drama as surreptitious insurrection in a post-colonial, military state," in *Theatre Matters: Performance and Culture on the World Stage*, ed. Richard Boon & Jane Plastow, foreword by Wole Soyinka (Cambridge: Cambridge UP, 1998): 12.

place. Enahoro stands trial and is imprisoned along with Chief Awolowa and other party leaders. What has to be noted here is the then wide-eyed and youthful confidence that Soyinka brings to his own reading of events and to his own ability to make a difference.

Take, as another example, the plan to halt the deepening crisis of Biafra in 1967 which is fabricated out of discussions with Dennis Duerden and others at the Transcription Centre for African Arts and Culture in London. The un-impeded and lofty conclusion is that "someone would have to go to the East and have a talk with Ojukwu, head of the secessionist state, and meet with Chinua Achebe and other leading writers and intellectuals in Biafra" (113). The aim being

> a revocation of the declaration of secession and the calling off of all hostilities. Then, using our international connections to invoke the aid of neutral countries such as Sweden, with her sound credentials of assistance to African liberation, we would facilitate a return to the conference table. (113)

Needless to say, Soyinka volunteers to be the messenger, thereby entangling himself in a web of intrigue, half-truths, and lies, largely spun by Olusegun Obasanjo, then Officer Commanding of the Western Zone. The outcome is the imprisonment without trial already referred to at the start of this essay.

Ato Quayson has noted that in auto/biography "the individual's growing awareness of selfhood emerges," not only at "the conjuncture of relations be-tween the self and others" but in the relationships – adversarial and/or non-contradictory – which the self enters into with social and other institutions. In the context of African literature and auto/biography, "the most significant in-stitution is that of the nation-state in all its dispersed expression."[10] Quayson's essay appeared in 1995 and its concern was restricted to *Aké* and *Ìsarà*. A similar engagement between self and other, 'private' and 'public' history, fact and fiction is clearly to be seen in *You Must Set Forth at Dawn* and figures as the dynamic of Soyinka's narrative.

---

[10] Ato Quayson, "Memory, history and 'faction' in Wole Soyinka's *Aké* and *Ìsarà*," in *The Uses of Autobiography*, ed. Julia Swindells (London: Taylor & Francis, 1995): 81, 85.

With the "I" centred in *You Must Set Forth at Dawn* (whereas pseudonyms are used in *Ìsarà* and *Ibadan*), Soyinka is keenly observant of the people he meets – his studies of people in power are usually captured in a couple of sentences. Examples are Colonel Ojukwu; Gorbachov; a faceless member of a foreign embassy; personal friends, among them the delightful Femi Johnson; and people on the street, such as the unfortunate taxi driver who is coerced into giving Soyinka a ride and breaking every one of the road barriers between Cotonou in the Republic of Benin and Lagos. The sketches attest to the skill of a dramatist. At the same time, Soyinka role-plays in self-conscious manner – the many parts including statesman, politician, conspirator, trickster – only to remark wryly in hindsight upon some of his less laudable traits of character: "my overclever self" (39), "an interventionist tendency had begun to manifest itself in my temperament, though I was yet to become fully conscious of it" (60), and "Given half a chance, in a nation like Nigeria, I sometimes feel I would betray [...] the dictatorial devil in me. One's social and moral responsibility, however, is to curb such a propensity, especially its abuses, not only in oneself but in others" (181).

Furthermore, in chronicling the public history of post-independent Nigeria, Soyinka's insider account can be expected to be managed, at the very least in its emphases. Writing on the Civil War, for example, partly because it has been recorded by others, partly because of a sharp desire to put the record straight concerning his actual involvement, he lays considerable stress on his secret meeting with Obasanjo, and on what is actually said and not said. The Nigeria we are shown in the memoir leaves little room for what else is going on outside the periphery of Soyinka's own activities. For one thing, while the narrative is punctuated with recollections of his political statements as a dramatist – *A Dance of the Forests*, *Kongi's Harvest*, *The Beatification of Area Boy* – little else from the cultural scene enters the narrative. So that simply to read an article by Femi Osofisan[11] is to be reminded that other

---

[11] "The nation yearned for freedom, for the impulse to liberate its enormous potential for creativity, and put its muscles behind the wheel of modernisation. But the soldiers were everywhere with their guns and bayonets, haughtily feathering their own nests alone, stifling initiative with their decrees. [...] Incredible wealth was flowing into the nation's coffers from the discovery of oil and the prodigious revenue it brought. Yet for

Nigerian writers and intellectuals are also speaking out against the injustices and brutalities, and the "myriad paradoxes"[12] in the nation-state. Soyinka does not deny other contributions to the struggle. He has also acknowledged the place of "faction" in his writing. But it is as if, in his compelling desire to re-possess his space and place – both his human and his political landscape – he must be less scrupulous and leave others to speak for themselves. The contest, in other words, is strictly between the antagonists who are the 'I' narrator and the nation-state as represented by its men of power.

The prose in *You Must Set Forth at Dawn* is well-paced, the tensions netting conspiracy nicely registered, and the heady excitement at the prospect of danger and possible violence conveyed with verve. At the same time, there is no denying that, within the overall pattern of the narrative, each episode, as if echoing the opening section, "IBA – For Those Who Went Before," results in a sense of "deflation" (487). Indeed, there is a strong and persistent suggestion of Soyinka's own hubris, and the governing movement and mood of the memoir lead inexorably from the self-pleased irony of "my overclever self" to the dark despair when faced finally with a "monster" like Abacha and the futility of dialogue. As in the case of Enahoro, Soyinka is astonished on each subsequent occasion to find the battle lost: the night meeting with Obasanjo ends disastrously; the joint appeal made with Chinua Achebe and J.P. Clark to General Babangida to stay the execution of General Mammon Vatsas proves futile; the support for Abiola, and the strategies for trying to reinstate him as the rightfully elected leader of the elections of 1993, lead to Soyinka's flight and his indictment by Abacha for treason. I have remarked on the ebullient

---

the majority of the people misery and squalor formed the dough of their daily life. The more money the nation earned, the more the official corruption pullulated, and the worse grew the impoverishment of the common folk. [...] Now and then public anger over these accumulated grievances [...] exploded into violence, but these protests were always scattered and random [...] and never anything at all like 'the great revolution' expected. Indeed, each outburst only helped the soldiers, for in its wake would come another *coup d'état*; a more brazen sector of the military would replace the previous one, and business would be resumed again as usual." Osofisan, "'The Revolution as Muse'," 13.

[12] Osofisan, "'The Revolution as Muse'," 13.

voice of the early passages. We need only compare the shifts in tone between the youthful, self-satisfied activist who, by holding up the radio station, foils the state's attempt to falsify the electoral results in 1965 and the apprehensive, reluctant, exhausted diplomat who speaks below:

> The average human composition – the range in which I group myself – has ensured that there is a limit to how many heads of state the body is built to encounter; how many ignorant – willfully or genuinely so – foreign affairs ministers it can educate; how many cause-famished pressure groups it can co-opt; under how much solidarity by human rights organizations it can bask; how many meetings of EU/UNESCO/UNO/OAU caucuses it can attend, into how many diplomatic gatherings it can be escorted like Dresden china or else gatecrash; how many "working" lunches, dinners, and so on, it can absorb; how many congressmen and – women and parliamentarians – feisty, outraged, or impotently sympathetic – it can lobby; how many bureaucracies it can infiltrate; how much mealy-mouthing it can stand; how many compromises it can withstand; how many promises are left for it to believe in; how many immigration officers it can morally eviscerate; how much debt – both moral and material – it can accumulate; how many slanderous countercampaigns it can endure; how many safety measures it can tolerate; how many distractions it can overcome; how many betrayals it must anticipate.... Every day, it seemed as if I had reached the end of my tether, yet I *dared not give up.* (399–400, my emphasis)

But whatever the cost, the case of Nigeria has to be placed before the world, the brutal regime drawn to the attention of the international community. It is a lengthy process of diplomatic representations to the leaders of African countries, including President Yoweri Museveni of Uganda and Paul Kagame, the vice-president of Rwanda, "the nation that had undergone a near-unspeakable horror" (410); to Britain after the ascendancy of the Labour Party; Canada; a sometimes ambiguous France; the European Union; the USA. Ultimately, it is the execution of Ken Saro–Wiwa and eight Ogoni colleagues on 10 November 1995 – the appallingly dark climactic moment of *You Must Set Forth at Dawn* – that provides irrefutable proof of the unconscionable tyranny of Abacha. A last-ditch attempt to galvanize the concerted action of Commonwealth leaders at their meeting in Auckland is made. But, given Soyinka's knowledge of the Abacha type – "Power had mounted the head of the dictator; it needed its periodic nourishment in blood" (420) – he has little hope that the tragedy can be averted. In addition, Soyinka has far fewer illusions by now of the efficacy of international diplomacy. The Commonwealth leaders and their retinue are bland, ineffectual, or "potential clones of the Abacha breed and simply wondered what the fuss was all about" (422). The uselessness – indeed, the death – of dialogue has long been accepted, and the recourse to organized violence as opposition to tyranny becomes a daily possibility. Abacha, as noted above, eludes the war of attrition that Soyinka with others have planned for him. What remains true incontestably and for all times are Ken Saro–Wiwa's final words before he is hanged: "Lord, receive my soul [...] but the struggle continues" (427).

According to Jacques Derrida in "Force of Law: The 'Mystical Foundation of Authority'," "Justice remains, is yet, to come, *à venir*, it has an [sic], it is *à-venir*, the very dimension of events irreducibly to come."[13] It is, in short, the experience of the impossible. At the same time, Derrida goes on to say, "incalculable justice requires us to calculate":

> [And] not only *must* we calculate, negotiate the relation between the calculable and the incalculable [...] but we must take it as far as possible, beyond the place we find ourselves and beyond the already identifiable zones of morality or politics or law, beyond the distinction between national and international, public and private and so on.[14]

The compelling artistry of *You Must Set Forth at Dawn* can be said to lie in the Derridean paradox which informs and galvanizes the narrative – the ideal continually deferred at the same time as the actual struggles for justice have to be undertaken, and are undertaken, ceaselessly. Above all, it is a paradox that is embodied in the Yorùbá god who is Soyinka's "companion deity" (6). I began this essay with a Yorùbá saying. Let me conclude by returning to the cultural context in which Soyinka's imagination has its deepest roots, and out

---

[13] Jacques Derrida, "Force of Law: The 'Mystical Foundation of Authority'" ("Force de loi: le 'Fondement mystique de l'autorité'," 1989; tr. 1990), tr. Mary Quaintance, in *Deconstruction and the Possibility of Justice*, ed. Drucilla Cornell, Michel Rosenfeld & David Gray Carlson (New York & London: Routledge, 1994): 27.

[14] Derrida, "Force of Law," 28.

of which he speaks most powerfully, by invoking the god of "the restless road and creative solitude, the call of the lyric and the battle cry" (427) – Ògún.

## Works Cited

Derrida, Jacques. "Force of Law: The 'Mystical Foundation of Authority' " ("Force de loi: le 'Fondement mystique de l'autorité'," 1989), tr. Mary Quaintance, in *Deconstruction and the Possibility of Justice*, ed. Drucilla Cornell, Michel Rosenfeld & David Gray Carlson (New York & London: Routledge, 1994): 4–67. English version originally in the *Cardozo Law Review* 11 (July–August 1990): 920–1046.

Hall, Stuart. "Cultural Identity and Diaspora" (1990), in *Colonial Discourse and Post-Colonial Theory: A Reader*, ed. Patrick Williams & Laura Chrisman (Hemel Hempstead: Harvester Wheatsheaf, 1993): 392–401.

Osofisan, Femi. " 'The Revolution as Muse': Drama as surreptitious insurrection in a post-colonial, military state," in *Theatre Matters: Performance and Culture on the World Stage*, ed. Richard Boon & Jane Plastow, foreword by Wole Soyinka (Cambridge: Cambridge UP, 1998): 11–35.

Quayson, Ato. "Memory, history and 'faction' in Wole Soyinka's *Aké* and *Ìsarà*," in *The Uses of Autobiography*, ed. Julia Swindells (London: Taylor & Francis, 1995): 81–88.

Soyinka, Wole. *Aké: The Years of Childhood* (London: Rex Collings, 1981).

——. *The Beatification of Area Boy: A Lagosian Kaleidoscope* (London: Methuen Drama, 1995).

——. *The Climate of Fear: The Reith Lectures, 2004* (London: Profile, 2004).

——. *A Dance of the Forests*, in *Collected Plays 1* (Oxford: Oxford UP, 1973).

——. *Ibadan: The Penkelemes Years: A Memoir: 1946–1965* (London: Methuen, 1994).

——. *Ìsarà: A Voyage Around "Essay"* (London: Methuen, 1990).

——. *Kongi's Harvest*, in *Collected Plays 2* (Oxford: Oxford UP, 1974).

——. *You Must Set Forth at Dawn: A Memoir* (New York: Random House, 2006).

◄❖►

BERNTH LINDFORS

## *The Lion and the Jewel* on BBC Radio

An Audience Survey

P LAYS BY AFRICAN PLAYWRIGHTS HAVE BEEN STAGED in many parts
of the world, but it is hard to find reliable surveys of how non-African
audiences have responded to them. Reviewers may have remarked on
whether a particular theatrical production was received well or poorly by those
who saw it, but such reports often were impressionistic, lacking any direct input from the scores of eyewitnesses present at a performance who may have
viewed the play differently. Missing from discussions of the international reception of African drama have been adequate samples of the diverse reactions
of theatregoers outside Africa.[1] We need a larger body of data on which to
draw our conclusions.

One example of a good audience survey may suffice. On 19 May and 5
June 1966, the Drama Department of the British Broadcasting Corporation's
Third Programme aired a dramatic reading of Wole Soyinka's *The Lion and
the Jewel* to radio listeners in the UK. The BBC's Audience Research Department then sent out a questionnaire to more than 1,300 members of their Third
Programme Listening Panel asking for reactions to the play. They received
120 responses, roughly nine percent of the total number solicited, from those
who reported having heard all or most of the broadcast. Before examining the
range and variety of these responses, however, it may be well to review Soyin-

---

[1] An exception is Awo Asiedu, "West African Theatre Audiences: A Study of
Ghanaian and Nigerian Audiences of Literary Theatre in English" (doctoral dissertation, University of Birmingham, UK, 2003). I am grateful to James Gibbs for this
reference.

ka's activities in the UK and elsewhere before May 1966 in order to assess
whether his name is likely to have been known to the British public before this
radio transmission.[2]

Soyinka had studied at the University of Leeds between 1954 and 1957,
earning a B.A. with an Upper Second in English Honours and beginning work
toward an M.A. that he never completed. Upon leaving Leeds, he moved to
London, where he worked as a substitute teacher, a broadcaster for the BBC's
"Calling West Africa" programme, and a script reader for the Royal Court
Theatre. During this time he produced one of his earliest plays, "The Swamp
Dwellers," for the Annual Drama Festival of the National Union of Students
held at the University of London in September 1958, and fourteen months
later he wrote, produced, and acted in an evening programme at the Royal
Court Theatre that included performances of two other early plays, "The Invention" and excerpts from "A Dance of the African Forest" (which he later
amplified and published as *A Dance of the Forests*), as well as readings of
some of his poems. He also published a few short stories in university literary
magazines. However, these accomplishments would not have been widely
noticed in Britain. He was still a young, unknown writer lacking a discernible
public profile.

In 1960 he returned to Nigeria on a two-year Rockefeller fellowship that
afforded him freedom to travel widely and to write, act, broadcast, and form
his own theatre company, the 1960 Masks. In 1962 he began teaching at the
University of Ifẹ campus in Ibadan and the following year moved to the University of Lagos, but he continued to devote much of his time and energy to
theatrical activities and other creative pursuits. In 1963, he published his first
three books: *Three Plays*, *A Dance of the Forests*, and *The Lion and the Jewel*,
the latter two under the joint imprint of Oxford University Press in London
and Ibadan. He also organized a guerrilla drama troupe, Orisun Theatre, which
specialized in partly improvised performances of political and social satire. In
September 1965 he was back in the UK recording his radio play "The De-

---

[2] A reliable summary of his activities during these years can be found in the first
chapter of James Gibbs, *Wole Soyinka* (Houndmills & Basingstoke: Macmillan, 1986):
1–8.

tainee" for the B B C, participating in a Commonwealth Arts Festival by taking part in a Poetry Conference in Cardiff and a Festival of Poetry at the Royal Court Theatre, and serving as an adviser on a production of his new play, *The Road*, at the Theatre Royal, Stratford East. Later that year, in the midst of an election campaign in Nigeria, he was arrested and charged with holding up an Ibadan radio station at gunpoint to prevent the airing of a victory speech by Samuel Ladoke Akintola, the Premier of the Western Region, but the judge who presided over the case in court acquitted him on a technicality. News reports of his arrest, detention, and trial were carried in the international press, prompting writers' groups abroad to send letters of concern to the Nigerian Government. During these months, Soyinka may have gained more visibility in the U K as a prisoner than as a playwright.

This is not to say that he was still unknown there as a rising dramatist. Friends in London had been working to advance his career by arranging to stage, film, and broadcast some of his plays. Chief among these helpers was Dennis Duerden, a former British Education Officer in Nigeria and producer for the B B C's African Service who, in January 1962, had founded a Transcription Centre in London to promote African artists and writers by creating radio and television programmes based on their work and distributing them internationally. Early in January 1963, Duerden had written to Soyinka asking him to direct a dozen modern African plays, including three of his own, for British television, using actors from the West Indies, black America, and West, East, and South Africa.[3] Soyinka, however, objected to the concept of a theatre company unified only by pigmentation, saying he had no use for theatre of the dispossessed.[4] When Duerden wrote again in April offering to arrange a filming of "The Swamp Dwellers" with an all-African cast, Soyinka quickly

---

[3] Letter from Duerden to Soyinka, 2 January 1964. This information, as well as much that follows, was gleaned from folders in the twenty-five boxes of Transcription Centre Records (hereafter cited as T C R) held at the Harry Ransom Humanities Research Centre at the University of Texas at Austin. The details recorded here were found in T C R 11.10 and 18.1. For an account of the history of the Transcription Centre, see Gerald Moore, "The Transcription Centre in the Sixties: Navigating in Narrow Seas," *Research in African Literatures* 33.3 (Autumn 2002): 167–81.

[4] Letter from Soyinka to Duerden, 20 January 1964. T C R 18.1.

agreed.[5] After the film was shot, Duerden set up a Theatre Workshop at the Transcription Centre, calling it the Ijinle Theatre Company, the purpose of which was to work collaboratively with Soyinka's Orisun Theatre Company in Nigeria to stage and film more African plays in Britain.[6] Soyinka and Duerden were named as co-Directors of the Ijinle Theatre Company, and a group of talented, experienced African actors and actresses based in London were recruited to get projects started.[7] One of their first initiatives was to rehearse two of Soyinka's short plays, *The Trials of Brother Jero* and *The Strong Breed*, as well as one by the South African playwright Athol Fugard, *The Blood Knot*, for presentation at the Hampstead Theatre Club from 28 June to 16 July 1966. Fugard, who was in London at that time, was brought in to direct all three plays with a cast hailing from South Africa, Nigeria, Sierra Leone, Ghana, and Uganda.[8] Subsequently, the Ijinle Theatre Company, with the South African filmmaker Lionel Ngakane as manager, was invited to perform Soyinka's *The Lion and the Jewel* at the Royal Court Theatre in December 1966 and to reprise it at the Leicester University Arts Festival in February 1967.[9] All these productions were quite successful.

However, we are getting ahead of our story of the BBC's radio premiere of *The Lion and the Jewel*, which had taken place half a year before the production at the Royal Court Theatre and may, indeed, have led to the invitation to the Ijinle Theatre Company to perform the play there with some of the same actors and actresses.[10] The BBC's radio version was produced by Douglas Cleverdon, who, the year before, on behalf of the Poetry Book Society, had

---

[5] Letter from Duerden to Soyinka, 27 April 1964 and telegram from Soyinka to Duerden, ca. early May 1964. TCR 18.1. See also TCR 11.10.

[6] TCR 11.12. According to a document in TCR 11.11, Ijinle is a Yorùbá word meaning 'the root, the essential, the deep'.

[7] TCR 11.11 and 11.15.

[8] TCR 11.11, 11.14 and 12.7.

[9] TCR 11.11, 11.12 and 11.15.

[10] This information, as well as much that follows, is taken from materials in the Douglas Cleverdon Collection (hereafter cited as DCC) at the Lilly Library, Indiana University, Bloomington.

arranged for Soyinka to read his poem *Idanre*, with musical accompaniment by Akin Euba, at the Festival of Poetry held at the Royal Court Theatre.[11] It was then that Cleverdon had proposed to Soyinka a radio broadcast of *The Lion and the Jewel* with authentic Yorùbá drumming and other music recorded in London or Lagos to enhance the production.[12] In January 1966, a month after Soyinka had been acquitted in court and released from prison, Cleverdon reminded him of this project, informing him that *The Lion and the Jewel* was scheduled for radio transmission the following May and asking if he could come to London to supervise the musical part of the production.[13] Soyinka, who at that time was involved in rehearsals of his play *Kongi's Harvest* for staging at the First World Festival of Negro Arts in Senegal in April, replied that he could not come to London but could have the necessary media work done by the Radio Station in Lagos.[14] Accordingly, in March he arranged to send Cleverdon a recording of the Arithmetic Times chant at the beginning of the play, the prisoners' chant (on page 24 of the published text),[15] the victory song of Baroka's impotence (54 and 57), the song of blessing (64), the final song "Tolani" (64), and a bull-roarer sound. Some of this material proved to be unsatisfactory technically, so Cleverdon borrowed a Yorùbá talking drum from the Horniman Museum and employed two Nigerian musicians in London, Femi Fatoba and Sanya Dosunmu, to redub the scenes requiring drumming.[16]

Cleverdon, in the meantime, had consulted Duerden for advice on casting the play and had received from a member of staff at the Transcription Centre an annotated list of seven African actors and actresses and one musician

---

[11] T C R 12.8 and 18.1.

[12] Mentioned in a letter from Cleverdon to Soyinka, 25 January 1966. D C C.

[13] Letters from Cleverdon to Soyinka, 25 January and 14 February 1966. D C C.

[14] Undated letter in March from Soyinka to Cleverdon. D C C. See also T R C 3.1 for a programme of the production of *Kongi's Harvest* in Dakar.

[15] Wole Soyinka, *The Lion and the Jewel* (London & Ibadan: Oxford U P, 1963).

[16] In-house memo from G.M. Cooke to Douglas Cleverdon, 2 May 1966, and letter from Cleverdon to Soyinka, 23 May 1966. D C C.

(Fatoba), emphasizing their professional credentials.[17] The BBC tried out these and other performers before selecting for the principal parts two Nigerians (Sam Iyamu as Lakunle, Jumoke Debayo as Sadiku), a South African (Lionel Ngakane as Baroka), and a Sierra Leonean (Tonie Tucker as Sidi). Another South African, Cosmo Pieterse, was chosen to play a Storyteller who narrated many of the stage directions. Five other performers from Nigeria and elsewhere played minor supporting roles.[18]

The play opened with a brief summary of the plot:

> For this delicious comedy of African village life, Wole Soyinka has used verse-rhythms for the dialogue and drums for the mimed dances. It is the story of Sidi, beloved by the Europeanized school teacher. When a full-length photograph of her appears as a two-page spread in a glossy magazine, her status soars far above that of Baroka, the elderly chieftain of Ilujinle, who reflects that it is five full months since last he took a wife. (BBCDCC)

In the survey conducted afterwards by the BBC's Audience Research Department, it was estimated that the broadcast had reached 0.1 percent of the population of the UK. Reactions to the play, gleaned from the 120 questionnaires returned by members of the Third Programme Listening Panel, ranged from A+ to C-, with a large majority at the high end of the scale: A+ (23), A (39), B (27), C (10), C- (1). This sample gave "a REACTION INDEX of 68, close to the average (66) for Third Programme features during 1965. In Week 18, Nokhwezi (a Zulu folk tale) by Alexius Buthelezi had an index of 71."[19] So *The Lion and the Jewel* was one of the better features aired on the Third Programme in the first half of 1966, ranking two points above the average and only three points below the leading broadcast.

The full report of the Audience Research Department then followed:

> References to *The Lion and the Jewel* as a "delicious" and "enchanting" piece cropped up freely in the comment of the largest proportion of listeners in the

---

[17] Undated letter from Maxine Lautre to Douglas Cleverdon. TCR 15.7.

[18] Letter from Cleverdon to Soyinka, 27 April 1966. DCC. See also in DCC the transcript of the survey issued on 8 June 1966 by the BBC's Audience Research Department (hereafter cited as BBCDCC).

[19] BBCDCC.

sample audience who certainly seem to have found much that was charming in this comedy of Nigerian village life. However, in this group (not far short of two-thirds of the reporting sample) some listeners came less easily than others to recognise and respond to the qualities of the writing. As was said, interest in the earlier part of the play was held in check by an unaccustomed and, indeed, distinctly exotic setting and only gradually grew to thoroughpaced [sic] enjoyment, or, as a Housewife put it, "just a little difficult to get into this piece, but once well launched it became more and more acceptable as it went along." On a more critical tack, several listeners took the attitude that, fascinating as this was as an insight into African ways of seeing life, it failed in rapport with a Western audience because as a Cartographer's Draughtsman observed, "one could not naturally identify oneself with any of the characters, be in sympathy with them or understand people living under the sway of emotion, custom and so on." He continued. "there was a gulf; it was slightly too un-British for one to feel at ease in it."

From a distinctly unenthusiastic minority came complaints that Wole Soyinka had laboured his piece out of proportion to its theme. There was a certain amount of boring repetition, listeners said here, regarding the crux of the plot – the virility of the elderly and much-wived Chief in whose village the action is set. In addition, there was some feeling that *The Lion and the Jewel* was not best suited to radio treatment, as containing a number of situations that called for visual representation, it was said[;] none was [more] so, perhaps, than the mimed dances (with characterisations and action described by a Storyteller) which did not come over very effectively, it was held.

For all this, the play was far more commonly assessed as having an unusually strong appeal and a many-sided one at that, incorporating, as the enthusiasts made clear, special felicities of style and language as well as memorable character-drawing, much humour in the telling of the story and a most attractive freshness of flavour overall. To begin with, many listeners reflected that they had rarely heard a play (or feature) with so much atmosphere ("it portrayed very vividly and colourfully personal and village life in Nigeria. I was there in 1958–59 and could easily recapture this"). In addition (said a Lecturer, who had also lived in Western Nigeria), "the characters were portrayed with that essential (but in so many modern plays, apparently outmoded) attitude – love of the artist for this extraordinary, marvelous and funny creature, man. Moreover, the locale, characterisation and mixture of social attitudes *rang true*. Soyinka does communicate the spirit of his people living *now*: not a dead culture." In addition to plenty of inventive human interest, other listeners pointed out, the writing (both in the storytelling and dialogue) had a richness and lusty turn of phrase that resembled the Elizabethan style ("very Shaksperian, but not just an imitation," said a Farming Student), with "lively imagery" and easy-flowing transitions from speech to verse – rhythms and songs – "altogether energetic and eloquent writing, and very amusing withal." In particular, however, listeners who relished "this vital and entertaining play" reflected most on the insight it gave into the stresses occasioned by the impact of Western ideas upon the unsophisticated but nonetheless subtle patterns of African village life. The character of Lakunle, the Europeanised schoolteacher, wooing Sidi, the local beauty, whose status soars when her photograph appears in a Lagos magazine, was very shrewdly observed, by all accounts, and, as a Chemical Engineer remarked, his reactions to Sidi's involvement with Baroka (the Bale, or chieftain) "rightly portrayed attitudes of mind derived from the superficial things in Western culture."

Although not all found it easy to accustom themselves to African accents, most listeners in the sample who mentioned this aspect of the performance liked the voices of the cast very much (one recognising from personal recollection the "lilt" of the Western area). The parts of Baroka, Sidi and Lakunle (taken by Lionel Ngakane, Tonie Tucker and Sam Iyamu) were frequently said to have been memorably played, with action that could always be understood, according to comment. In regard to the production, the commonest feeling was that the "put over" matched the matter to perfection, especially suggesting that high-flown exuberance of Nigerian life and theatre. Plenty of its sparkle and verve came across, said a Lecturer, and he was [among] many who also enjoyed "the varied effects" and the music, particularly the Yoruba singing and drumming – "every bit as thrilling as the 'High Life' I can remember so well," said a General Practitioner in retirement. (BBCDCC)

What is most striking in this report is the contrast between the unenthusiastic and uneasy reactions of listeners with no experience of African life and the overwhelmingly positive responses of those who had lived and worked in Nigeria or other parts of West Africa. Indeed, it appears that much of the sample audience had tuned in because they were eager to hear an African play, particularly one by a playwright whose name they may have recognized and a few of whose extant works they perhaps may even have read. In this sense, the majority of the audience surveyed may have been predisposed or readily inclined to applaud a work that reminded them of the "spirit" or "atmosphere" of a colonial or postcolonial African culture they had once experienced. They could recall the situations, social attitudes, and sounds of indigenous village life as authentic and amusing, whereas listeners like the Cartographer's Draughtsman, who evidently felt excluded from such intimacy with anything African, found only a gulf of understanding because the world the play evoked was "slightly too un-British," too alien, for him to feel at ease in it.

Nonetheless, even some of those initially put off by the exotic setting – someone like the Housewife, for example – were gradually drawn into the play as it went along, charmed perhaps by the voices of the cast and the "high-flown exuberance," "sparkle and verve" of their acting. Despite a few complaints about the "boring" overemphasis on the elderly Chief's virility and the inadequate treatment on radio of scenes requiring visual representation, the production evidently did not fail to entertain its listeners. The respectable score the play achieved on the BBC's Reaction Index testifies to its success.

One wonders if the same broadcast would have done so well in the USA, where audiences would have been composed of far fewer individuals with direct experience of African life. Soyinka has sometimes had difficulty in mounting his plays in American cities. A case in point is his production of *The Road* at Chicago's Goodman Theater in 1984, which, he admitted, was "a traumatic experience," "a harrowing, painful experience," partly because he was working with an African-American cast, the leading actor of which did not understand the role he was called upon to play as Professor.[20] Soyinka felt compelled to keep cutting his lines until the play was "totally unbalanced [and] lopsided," leading to "general bafflement" among the audience.[21] Chicago's *Sunday Times* called *The Road* "a long, bumpy ride."[22] Of course, *The Road*, even in a masterful production, would still bewilder most American theatre-

---

[20] Chuck Mike, *Soyinka as Director* (Ifẹ Monographs on Literature and Criticism, 4th Series, No. 4; Ilé-Ifẹ: Department of Literature in English, University of Ifẹ, 1986): 25, 49.

[21] Mike, *Soyinka as Director*, 50–51.

[22] Dick Saunders, "*The Road* Provides a Long, Bumpy Ride," *Sunday Times* (Chicago; 1 May 1984): 47.

goers because it is far more deeply invested in Yorùbá metaphysics than are his comedies and satires. *The Lion and the Jewel* would stand a better chance of being understood and enjoyed in America, but it is perhaps significant that, like most of his other plays, it has seldom been performed in any of the fifty states. The British colonial experience may have guaranteed Soyinka an audience in the UK and regular opportunities for producing his plays there – advantages that he has been denied in much of the rest of the English-speaking world outside Africa.

This situation is not unique to Soyinka. Many other talented African playwrights have suffered the same neglect abroad. Their national and ethnic cultures may be regarded as too foreign or unfamiliar to be readily understood and appreciated by non-Africans, and their writings may be totally unknown in distant lands. However, what the BBC's survey seems to suggest is that a good performance of a well-made African play dealing with a universal theme – in this case, a humorous love triangle – and written in comprehensible English or translated into a local language would very likely appeal to international audiences. One proof of this is that, not long after *The Lion and the Jewel* was broadcast in the UK, the BBC heard from a Danish radio station that wanted to borrow the BBC's tapes of the singing and drumming to use in their own production of the play.[23] Perhaps radio transmission is one very effective way of extending the global reach of African drama. Hearing a play may lead some listeners outside Africa or the UK to desire to read it, see it, or even stage it. Like the Jewel's picture in a pop magazine or the Lion's stamp-making machine, the ability to project and disseminate a positive image of Africa and Africans by harnessing the power of far-reaching media technology can be both seductive and productive of better human relations.

---

[23] Letter from Douglas Cleverdon to Wole Soyinka, 28 October 1966, and memo from Douglas Cleverdon to Miss E. Jury, 28 October 1966. DCC.

## Works Cited

Asiedu, Awo. "West African Theatre Audiences: A Study of Ghanaian and Nigerian Audiences of Literary Theatre in English" (doctoral dissertation, University of Birmingham, UK, 2003).

Fugard, Athol. *The Blood Knot* (Johannesburg: Simondium, 1963).

Gibbs, James. *Wole Soyinka* (Houndmills & Basingstoke: Macmillan, 1986).

Mike, Chuck. *Soyinka as Director* (Ifẹ Monographs on Literature and Criticism, 4th Series, No. 4; Ilé-Ifẹ: Department of Literature in English, University of Ifẹ, 1986).

Moore, Gerald. "The Transcription Centre in the Sixties: Navigating in Narrow Seas," *Research in African Literatures* 33.3 (Autumn 2002): 167–81.

Soyinka, Wole. *A Dance of the Forests* (London & Ibadan: Oxford UP, 1963).

——. *Idanre & Other Poems* (London: Methuen, 1967).

——. *The Invention; & The Detainee* (Pretoria: Unisa P, [2005]).

——. *Kongi's Harvest* (London, Ibadan & Nairobi: Oxford UP, 1967).

——. *The Lion and the Jewel* (London & Ibadan: Oxford UP, 1963).

——. *The Road* (London & Ibadan: Oxford UP, 1965).

——. "The Strong Breed," in *Three Plays*: 79–118; repr. in *The Trials of Brother Jero, and The Strong Breed*, 35–67.

——. "The Swamp Dwellers," in *Three Plays*, 3–42.

——. "The Trials of Brother Jero," in *Three Plays*, 43–77; repr. in *The Trials of Brother Jero, and The Strong Breed*, 5–34.

——. *Three Plays* (Ibadan: Mbari, 1963); repr. as *Three Short Plays* (London: Oxford UP, 1969).

——. *The Trials of Brother Jero, and The Strong Breed: Two Plays* (New York: Dramatists Play Service, 1969).

Saunders, Dick. "*The Road* Provides a Long, Bumpy Ride," *Sunday Times* (Chicago; 1 May 1984): 47.

I am grateful to the Harry Ransom Humanities Research Center, University of Texas at Austin, and the Lilly Library, Indiana University, for permission to quote and cite documents from their collections.

◄❖►

STELLA BORG BARTHET

# The Politics of Myth in Ayi Kwei Armah's *Fragments*

I N AN ESSAY ON THE POSTCOLONIAL AFRICAN NOVEL, WOLE OGUNDELE makes some very thoughtful remarks about the dearth of "narratives of the factual precolonial past, which should complement and give reality to the fictions." The main thrust of Ogundele's essay is that novelists and critics have simply not given enough attention to the recuperation of Africa's precolonial past despite early professions of this need by some of Africa's most influential writers. I agree with Ogundele about the fundamental importance of retrieving as much as possible of the historical reality of the African past. I disagree, however, with Ogundele's assumption that myth is a "device of evasion" in literature, used by writers to deflect attention from historical realities and national priorities. Ogundele's concern about the "homogenizing ideology of nation-statism" and its "substitution of myths and folklore for actual events"[1] may be justified, but while I agree that there is a need to record particular histories in Africa, I do not think that the representation of myth precludes an historical thrust in literary writing. Moreover, Ogundele's call for "narratives of the factual precolonial past" to "complement and give reality to the fictions" fails to indicate how "narratives" are to be distinguished from "fictions."[2]

---

[1] Wole Ogundele, "Devices of Evasion: The Mythic versus the Historical Imagination in the Postcolonial African Novel," *Research in African Literatures* 33.3 (Autumn 2002): 136.

[2] Ogundele, "Devices of Evasion," 137.

The opposition of myth to history and to realism goes back a long way. 'Myth' implies falsehood, although it also suggests a higher truth. Richard Priebe defines myth thus:

> a narrative that explains, explores or attempts to resolve the primary onto-logical, psychological and physical contradictions that man has recurrently faced. The essential characteristic of any myth is that in one or more ways we are led outside of a time referent.[3]

Priebe uses this definition to create a binary distinction between two kinds of African writers, those "encompassed by the idea of a mythic consciousness" such as Ayi Kwei Armah, Kofi Awoonor, Wole Soyinka and Amos Tutuola, and others, like Chinua Achebe, whose "ethical consciousness" he defines "in contradistinction," or in opposition to the previous group whose sensibility is "mythic."[4] Interestingly, while Priebe selects Achebe for his study of an "ethical consciousness," and explores *Things Fall Apart* as a novel in which Igbo life "proceeds in a realistic, linear and historical manner,"[5] Ogundele dis-cusses the same novel as an example of how "the African novelist wishing to recover moments in the distant precolonial past has been substituting myth, folklore, etc. for what really happened."[6]

I think a re-examination of myth and history in the West African novel has become important because readings built on the assumption of a dichotomy between myth and history, or myth and reality, such as we find in Priebe and in Ogundele, preclude the possibility of a writer's re-construction of traditional myth for the purpose of social direction. Studies of myth from the late 1960s have shown that myth does not necessarily lead beyond a temporal referent but can serve actual and current socio-political purposes. In their study of the genealogies of the Tiv and Gonja of West Africa, Jack Goody and Ian Watt show that the tales "serve the same function that Malinowski claimed for myth; they act as 'charters' of present social institutions rather than as faith-

---

[3] Richard Priebe, *Myth, Realism, and the West African Writer* (Trenton NJ: Africa World Press, 1988): 5.

[4] Priebe, *Myth, Realism, and the West African Writer*, 12.

[5] *Myth, Realism, and the West African Writer*, 48.

[6] Ogundele, "Devices of Evasion," 133.

fully historical records of times past."[7] Myth, therefore, can be concerned with the here and now, used to validate contemporary culture and to promote social cohesion. Although Ayi Kwei Armah's handling of myth is more complex than Achebe's, both writers aim to retrieve the past of their communities from the debris left by colonialism. This is not nostalgic retrospection or a romantic hunting-out of an idyllic past to flaunt before non-African readers but a search through history for the retrieval of modes of thought and action that would take the continent into the future.

My focus here is on Armah's second novel, *Fragments* (1969), and I would like to show that Armah's use of myth in this novel is politically structured to combat neocolonialism in contemporary Ghana. Armah here explores Akan myth to discover a thread running from the past through the present to the future – a linearity of time and its forward-moving image embodying the community's destiny as it seeks to escape the nightmare of the colonizer's exploitation and continuing neocolonial oppression towards freedom and real independence. Armah uses myth in his construction of characters and events in order to call attention to a traumatic break with the past and its traditions; and to help bring about healing through remembrance and through action, based on the achievement of a new understanding of present conditions.

Armah's awareness of the need to re-connect with the past in a politically effective way reflects historical realities and owes much to the work of Frantz Fanon, who writes in his essay "On National Culture":

> But it has been remarked several times that this passionate search for a national culture which existed before the colonial era finds its legitimate reason in the anxiety shared by native intellectuals to shrink away from that Western culture in which they all risk being swamped. Because they realize they are in danger of losing their lives and thus becoming lost to their people, these men, hot-headed and with anger in their hearts, relentlessly determine to renew contact once more with the oldest and most pre-colonial springs of life of their people.[8]

---

[7] Jack Goody & Ian Watt, "The Consequences of Literacy," in *Literacy in Traditional Societies*, ed. Jack Goody (Cambridge: Cambridge U P, 1975): 33.

[8] Frantz Fanon, *The Wretched of the Earth*, tr. Constance Farrington, preface by Jean–Paul Sartre (*Les Damnés de la terre*, 1961; Harmondsworth: Penguin, 1967): 169.

Armah's depiction of Baako in *Fragments* maps his progress from an isolated artist in the Western tradition he has imbibed abroad, to an anguished recognition of his own failure to be relevant to his society, and, towards the end
of the novel, on to a nascent understanding of the absolute need to connect
with the past. The influence of Fanon on Armah needs to be emphasized because the intricate symbolic structure of *Fragments*, together with its frequent
use of Akan myth, might suggest detachment from actual reality. Armah has
not only made use of myths from the Akan tradition but he has also established links between a wider African nation and ancient Egypt in his novels
*Osiris Rising* and *KMT: In the House of Life,* as well as in his non-fiction. He
has done this to counter the insidious thrust of Western scholarship, which has
created corrosive assumptions, or stereotypes, that have been handed down to
Africa from Europe, and which many Africans have come to accept.

The perception of myth as being concerned exclusively with timeless
contradiction on a purely metaphysical level feeds into treatments of Armah's
novels that see them as embodying a pessimistic view of a static and abstract
human condition, rather than as representations of a specific nation with particular problems to be addressed. This has not infrequently damaged Armah's
credentials as a writer committed to the amelioration of society in Ghana and
in Africa. The definition of myth as expressive of what is unchanging in
human experience is also unsatisfactory, in that a writer may explore ontological, psychological, and physical contradictions through myths that, nevertheless, are also grounded in history. As Gregory L. Lucente points out, history
and realism often interact with myth in the novel:

> In narrative fiction, the transcendent fullness of myth, which locates its signi-
> ficance not in the world of time and matter, but in a realm beyond temporal and
> spatial limitation, thus complements the worldly plenitude of the realist sign, as
> it recodes on an idealized level what realist representation codes on the material
> one. Realism's dependence on the conventions of shared worldly knowledge
> mixes with myth's requirement of shared belief in a transcendent system of
> signs.[9]

---

[9] Gregory L. Lucente, *The Narrative of Realism and Myth: Verga, Lawrence, Faulkner, Pavese* (Baltimore MD: Johns Hopkins UP, 1979): 40.

Generally, in fiction, we do not encounter myth in isolation, but most often as thoughts and emotions pertaining to character. In *The Beautyful Ones Are Not Yet Born* and in *Fragments*, Armah utilizes native myth without giving it the privileged status of a cosmos that exists independently of the novels. Akan myth in the novels is presented from the point of view of particular characters, in a fictive world where other different or even contrasting perceptions are also represented. In *The Beautyful Ones Are Not Yet Born* the man perceives Maanan as Mame Water, and in *Fragments*, too, Baako relates to Juana as the same mythic water spirit. In both cases, the representation of the myth is ironical, and far from being a powerful influence over the world of the novels as a whole, the myth is part of a perception that is finally overturned or discarded. This is similar to what happens in *The Beautyful Ones Are Not Yet Born*. As John Lutz has shown, the novel actually questions the validity of the pessimism emerging from a static view of humanity, even if this has often been ascribed to Armah as its author:

> In the novel's vision, the very conditions that produce a cynical view of the social world as doomed by natural, unchangeable forces to degeneration, corruption, and cyclical eruptions of violence are interrogated, and the pessimism that these conditions produce rejected as an historically contingent, surmountable obstacle to positive social development.[10]

In *Fragments*, there is a similarly degenerate and corrupt society. Just as with *The Beautyful Ones Are Not Yet Born*, however, some readers fail to see that this is the protagonist's perception of his community and should not be understood as being Armah's own pessimistic view. I believe that, in *Fragments*, Armah presents the psychological contradictions experienced by Baako in order to go beyond them. The reader sees the social conditions producing the protagonist's alienation, and these are presented as problems that can be tackled. *Fragments* questions Baako's perceptions through his relationship with Juana, whom he sees as embodying the West African myth of Mame

---

[10] John Lutz, "Pessimism, Autonomy, and Commodity Fetishism in Ayi Kwei Armah's *The Beautyful Ones Are Not Yet Born*," *Research in African Literatures* 34.2 (Summer 2003): 95.

Water, but who spills over the mythic mould to become a psychologically convincing character.

The Mame Water myth, well-known throughout West Africa, concerns spirits, mermaids and mermen, who appear on earth in the shape of beautiful people to entice human beings to become their spouses. Once married to a Mame Water spirit, a person cannot marry or have children, but in compensation for the forfeiture of sexual reproduction, a Mame Water spouse receives riches derived from the bottom of the ocean. It is worth noting here that when traditional myths came into contact with Christianity, there were important changes in the way they became generally known. Early Christian missionaries attempted to gain converts by undermining native religion. A fictional example of this is to be found in Achebe's *Arrow of God*, where the python, sacred to the goddess Idemili, is demonized.[11] The Mame Water myth has been similarly demonized in Ghana by Christians in general and by Pentecostalists in particular.

I believe that Pentecostalist discourse is highly significant in *Fragments*, so I will go into some detail about this missionary activity before applying it to the novel. The anthropologist Birgit Meyer, working in Accra and in Peki, notes that the influence of Pentecostalism has grown in proportion to poverty, on the increase since independence. There are several similarities between the Pentecostalist prophets described by Meyer and Armah's prophet in *Fragments*. Pentecostalists preach mostly to "middle-aged women, who often are thrown back upon themselves and have to take care of their children without receiving much assistance from their (absent) husbands."[12] In *Fragments*, the crowd of worshippers listening to the preacher in chapter two are mostly needy women roused to hysteria by the bearded and white-robed preacher.

---

[11] In Achebe's novel, Mr Goodcountry tells his listeners: "If we are Christians, we must be ready to die for the faith [...] you must be ready to kill the python as the people of the rivers killed the iguana. You address the python as Father. It is nothing but a snake, the snake that deceived our first mother, Eve." Chinua Achebe, *Arrow of God* (1964; London: Heinemann, 1974): 47.

[12] Birgit Meyer, "Commodities and the Power of Prayer: Pentecostalist Attitudes Towards Consumption in Contemporary Ghana," *Development and Change* 29.4 (October 1998): 759.

Meyer notes the frequent contacts between preachers and European or American Pentecostalist associations. Armah's "prophet" is no exception, since his "message is in English," and he needs an interpreter to speak to the crowd on the beach.[13] Meyer further observes an obsession with demonology in the new Pentecostalist churches, while Armah's prophet "spoke mainly of fire. Different kinds of fire, fire from the Old Testament Bible, the fire of God's anger and his glory, matched with the burning unending fire of the devil in his hell" (29).

Meyer goes on to note that "money and goods are important themes in pentecostalist discourse" and the idea that the consumption of sophisticated Western goods is fraught with danger is often reiterated. These dangers are incorporated in the objects themselves. Meyer refers to a widely distributed booklet written by a Nigerian, Emmanuel Eni, describing the writer's arrival "in the realm of the Mami Water spirits at the bottom of the sea, which, as everybody knows, abounds with goods." Eni goes into the "scientific laboratory" under the ocean where scientists and psychiatrists joined forces in designing "flashy cars, the latest weapons, cloth, perfumes and assorted types of cosmetics, electronics, computers and alarms."[14]

Armah's *Fragments* shows the influence of Pentecostalism on a powerless and impoverished society. Writing of *The Beautyful Ones Are Not Yet Born*, John Lutz has suggested that, although Armah rejected Marxism as eurocentric, Armah's first novel "presents a world riven by contradictions that can best be understood through Marxian categories."[15] While I consider Marx's notion of commodity fetishism to be very important for an understanding of Armah's depiction of post-independence Ghanaian society, I think it is insufficient for an understanding of society in *Fragments,* as in Armah's second novel the author's treatment of commodities also shows the strong influence of

---

[13] Ayi Kwei Armah, *Fragments* (1969; London, Heinemann, 1988): 33, 29. Further page references are in the main text.

[14] Emmanuel Eni, *Delivered from the Powers of Darkness* (Ibadan: Scripture Union, 1987). Quoted in Meyer, "Commodities and the Power of Prayer," 765.

[15] Lutz, "Pessimism, Autonomy, and Commodity Fetishism in Ayi Kwei Armah's *The Beautyful Ones Are Not Yet Born,*" 95.

Pentecostalism. The fear and rejection of commodities in *Fragments* comes from both a Marxist perspective and from the American Pentecostalism encountered through the preacher in the novel's second chapter.

Whereas for Marx the danger of commodity fetishism lies in the process of objectification that consumption sets in motion, for the Pentecostalist, the danger of owning "shiny things," as Foli does in *Fragments,* resides in the fact that they alienate man both from his community and from the supernatural (7). Baako's own perception of the danger of material possessions comes very close to the Pentecostalist view, although what he fears is not the fires of hell but spiritual death. Pentecostalists lay emphasis on the strange underwater origin of Western goods. As Meyer notes,

> By stressing that commodities may be dangerous because of their past, Pentecostalism suggests that the appropriation of Western goods through consumption is problematic and involves consumers in the danger zone of inverted possession: rather than possessing the commodity, the owner risks to be [sic] possessed by the commodity.[16]

Possession is also inverted in the Marxist sense. Owing to Western modes of production and consumption, Ghanaians only see manufactured goods in their finished state and never during any phase of production. In Marx's commodity fetishism, the neglect of the origin of a commodity leads to warped social relations, because goods are divorced from producers or manufacturers. In both Marxist and Pentecostalist discourse, the magical appearance of goods possesses the owner, so that he becomes alienated from his fellow men. One of the characters possessed by possessions in *Fragments* is Foli, "the shriveled soul" (7). As spiritual leader of the family, he officiates (and desecrates) the departure ritual for Baako. As the maternal uncle, Foli has a special responsibility towards Baako, as he himself does towards his sister Araba's baby. Foli uses "one of his many shiny things" to cheat the ancestors out of their share of the drink which he should have poured into the ground as libation (7).

Baako is deeply concerned about the warped relationship between consumer and product, about the lack of connection between production and consumption. We see this in the notes he makes on Melanesian cargo cults: "The

---

[16] Meyer, "Commodities and the Power of Prayer," 768.

most impressive thing in the system is the wall-like acceptance of the division. Division of labour, power, worlds, everything" (158). He sees contemporary Ghana caught up in the worship of gods whose gifts are Western goods.

Cargo cultism developed in New Guinea when the arrival of white people bearing seemingly magical gifts was mythologized and understood in terms of the arrival of emissaries from their ancestors.[17] According to this myth, the dead of the community travel to the spirit world and are expected to return with gifts. The "been-to" in *Fragments* functions in the same way, travelling to the land of the gods and expected to return with their gifts. This myth can be very negative in its effects, for the belief in the return of the god's messengers demands expressions of faith. If these messengers fail to return, it is because the community has not expressed its faith with enough sincerity. In Melanesian cults, crops were burnt and animals sacrificed in order to demonstrate absolute faith in the return of the intermediaries. As Baako notes, "kill the pigs, burn the crop and wait with faith. Throw the last coins, brokeman" (161). Cargo cultism undermines local production and development. Those that travel to the spirit world – the dead or the been-tos – are not gods themselves, but intermediaries, they carry goods; they do not make them. As Baako notes, "it is presumably a great enough thing for a man to rise to be an intermediary between other men and the gods. To think of being a maker oneself could be sheer unforgivable sin" (157).

The harm that cargo cultism does is not limited to the economy of postcolonial states. Cargo cultism affects cultural development by penetrating the aesthetic sense of the community. The community is offered ready-made foreign artefacts they have not been involved in forming or creating, artefacts that can only draw passive acceptance. In *The Beautyful Ones Are Not Yet Born*, Armah had presented this beauty as "the gleam" that "draw[s] onto itself the love of a people hungry for something such as this."[18] When the object of beauty comes from an alien culture, in a finished state, into a culture which cannot be

---

[17] See *God, Ghosts and Men in Melanesia*, ed. Peter Lawrence & Mervyn J. Meggitt (Melbourne: Oxford UP, 1965).

[18] Ayi Kwei Armah, *The Beautyful Ones Are Not Yet Born* (1968; London: Heinemann, 1988): 10.

aware of the process of its development, the admiration it attracts must inevitably be passive. The object will then be 'active', in that it draws its beholders willy-nilly into its surface. In contrast to this, artefacts that have evolved in the culture of the community maintain their proper places as objects so that the beholder can become involved in the creation of beauty through his active perception. An alien aesthetic destroys native culture as surely as Western goods undermine traditional economies. When Naana sees the objects carried by Baako's white fellow travellers, she is aware of the threat of death embodied in Western objects:

> And some of these people bore in their arms things of a beauty so great that I thought then in my soul this was the way the spirit land must be. Only it was a beauty that frightened also [...]. I had made in my fear a hurried asking for protection on Baako's head. (11)

Baako finds the beauty of Paris similarly threatening. He appreciates the architectural beauty of the French capital but he realizes that the education that makes the admiration possible has also isolated him from his own people:

> [...] but in the attraction of this beauty itself there was the thing that had made enjoyment impossible for him. He had not been able to perceive anything without having it deepen that unsettling feeling that was not only one of loneliness, but a much more fearful emotion, as if there never was going to be any way out of his giddying isolation [...]. (48–49)

Following Fanon's view of the isolating and alienating effects of Western education, Armah presents Baako as the black man who realizes that his education "was like being tricked into a trap" (80). Baako's sense of being irretrievably compromised as an artist in contemporary Ghana is worked out through his love for the Puerto Rican Juana, whom he sees as a Mame Water spirit. His perception of Juana indicates that he conceives of himself as a Mame Water spouse who has sacrificed his own creativity, as the myth goes, in return for material goods. Baako understands that "been-tos" like Brempong, along with their families, have become too materialistic in the newly independent Ghana. Artists, too, pervert art for material gain.

Baako fears that materialism will corrupt him as an artist and he becomes paranoid about material goods and benefits. This emerges by comparing his attitude in this matter with that of his grandmother Naana, a character of strong spirituality who nevertheless accepts the need for physical comfort. This is a traditional African attitude embedded in the "perfect words" of the departure ritual:

> Watch over him
> and let him prosper
> there where he is going.
> And when he returns
> let his return, like rain,
> bring us your blessings and fruits,
> your blessings
> your help
> in this life you have left us to fight alone. (6)

Baako's return is intended to bear fruit "like rain." Naana herself acknowledges her own desires:

> I too have had my dreams of his return, and they too have been filled with things to give rest to tired flesh, heavy things, things of heavy earth. I have also dreamed of riches and greatness for Baako, and they were not for him alone. (3)

Baako's notes on cargo cults show that his rejection of materialism comes from the fear of being depersonalized. As we have seen, this ties in with the danger of inverted possession as outlined by Pentecostalists. Baako fears he will himself become the possession of his family. His journey is "a beneficial death, since cargo follows" and the traveller becomes dehumanized, "a transmission belt for cargo" (157).[19] Baako's mother Efua regards him as a "huge present" to herself (68). Efua and Baako's sister Araba have become infected with the materialistic 'wisdom' of Ananse. The words of the departure ritual are addressed to the traveller, but it is Efua and Araba who become selfish and greedy, like Ananse:

> Gain the wisdom
> to turn your back on the wisdom

---

[19] See Palle Christiansen, *The Melanesian Cargo Cult: Millenarianism as a Factor in Cultural Change* (Copenhagen: Akademisk Forlag, 1969).

of Ananse.
Do not be persuaded you will fill your stomach faster
if you do not have others' to fill.
There are no humans who walk this earth alone. (4)[20]

Baako explains the problem that Efua and Araba represent when he goes to Juana's hospital clinic, where she works as a psychiatrist. The demands that Baako's mother and sister make "go against those of the larger society," as when they debase the outdooring ritual of Araba's child by using it as an excuse to fleece their friends by their expectation of large amounts of money as presents for the outdooring (102). Baako considers the possibility of taking on the role of the old mythic hero who saves the community but he feels that this can no longer function in contemporary Ghana, because the extended family has been replaced by the nuclear model:

> It's the myth of the extraordinary man who brings about a complete turnabout in terrible circumstances. We have old heroes who turned defeat into victory for the whole community. But these days the community has disappeared from the story. Instead, there is the family, and the hero comes and turns its poverty into sudden wealth. And the external enemy isn't the one at whose expense the hero gets his victory; he's supposed to get rich, mainly at the expense of the community. (103)

Baako registers the insidious effect of colonialism on the African community and family structure but, despite his knowledge of the ravages of colonialism, he fails to connect with Naana and with tradition. Naana speaks about traditional relationships, of Baako's bond with Araba's child, and of his responsibility towards him. Baako washes his hands of his important role in the

---

[20] In West African folklore, Ananse is the "chief official of God" who brings Him a hundred slaves. He is portrayed as one who desires power absolutely. He asks God for one corn cob and a stick of maize and he promises a hundred slaves in return. Ananse sets off from heaven to earth, where he goes from one village to the next, always managing to deceive villagers into exchanging what he has for an object of much greater worth. Eventually he tricks a village into handing him a hundred young men. He gives these men to God as slaves and in return, God makes him chief. See Geoffrey Parrinder, *African Mythology* (London: Hamlyn, 1967): 137.

child's ritual, arguing that it was up to the father of the child, Kwesi, to stop Araba from outdooring the child before the proper time and that he himself, as Araba's brother, is "only a relative" (98).

Although Baako knows that both he and his community have been undermined, he is not able to connect this with his own self-image as an artist at this point. Baako does not know much about how his community functioned in the past. This is most evident when he projects Mame Water as the source of artistic inspiration, in an interpretation of the myth that shows the influence of Western education:

> The singer goes to the beach, playing his instrument. These days it's become a guitar. He's lonely, the singer, and he sings of that. So well a woman comes out of the sea, a very beautiful goddess, and they make love. She leaves him to go back to the sea, and they meet at long, fixed intervals only. It takes courage. The goddess is powerful, and the musician is filled with so much love he can't bear the separation. But then it is this separation itself which makes him sing as he has never sung before. Now he knows all there is to know about loneliness, about love, and power, and the fear that one night he'll go to the sea and Mame Water, that's the woman's name, will not be coming anymore. The singer is great, but he's also afraid, and after those nights on the shore, when the woman goes, there's no unhappier man on earth. (120)

In his interpretation of the Mame Water myth, Baako projects the artist as an isolated being in the tradition of twentieth-century Western art. As Gerald Moore has shown, "Africa does not possess the mythology of the lonely, neglected and misunderstood genius in his garret."[21] Baako makes isolation the condition of artistic inspiration. The student who had sold Baako the guitar he brings to Ghana tells him that "his wanting a guitar meant that he had begun to run from human beings" (65). Baako himself is aware of the falsity of his position, and as he prepares to play the guitar, "the theatricality of all these gestures he had made came nauseatingly to him, and he rose to put the guitar away" (65).

---

[21] Gerald Moore, "The Writer and the Cargo Cult," in *Common Wealth*, ed. Anna Rutherford (Aarhus: Akademisk Boghandel, 1972): 73.

Armah distances himself from his protagonist at this point in the narrative. After giving Juana his misrepresentation of the Mame Water myth, Baako comments that "the myths here are good [...] only their use..." Baako stops in mid-sentence and "his voice die[s]" because he does not know enough about his own culture (120). He admits to Naana that he does not "fully understand the ceremony" of the outdooring of Araba's child. In Akan belief, the blood-bond between a child and his maternal uncle is even closer than that between the child and his own father, because it is through the blood of the mother, which a brother shares, that the spirit of the child is formed. Since he is the central figure in that ritual, it is indeed "a shame," as Naana tells him, that he does not understand the central role he should take in the outdooring ceremony (97).[22]

It is clear that Baako has become alienated from his family. Isolation as the effect of Western influence affects both artists, and the community that learns to be passive and to expect bounty from outstanding, successful individuals. It is "THE INHABITANTS OF THE CIRCLE, A CHORUS OF QUIET, DENSE DEFEAT" that select and isolate prospective climbers, as Baako notes in his script, *The Brand* (150). The sculptor Ocran has the ability to remain comfortable in his isolation from the community; in Africa, it follows that he will be sterile. Ocran's sculpture replicates the "old anonymous sculpture of Africa," which could have evolved anywhere, even in Europe or America (78). What is so terrible about the anonymity of Ocran's sculpture is that its repetition reinforces the colonial idea of Africa as a single presence, defined only by and against Europe.

The practice of art that requires withdrawal from society is rejected in *Fragments*. The scene in chapter six, entitled "Gyefo" or "Redeemer," is central to Armah's presentation of aesthetics and community in Ghana. In this chapter, Baako watches the boy, who finds a double gong on the beach and who plays and sings during the hauling of the bag-net full of fish. When the fishermen begin their work, they lack unison, and their power is threatening:

---

[22] See Eva Meyerowitz, *The Sacred State of the Akan* (London: Faber & Faber, 1951): 174.

The men came back pulling on the rope with a casual hostility [...] legs and
thighs bulging with too much packed-in power, arms filled with rigid muscle,
moving all at once in too many undecided directions. It was very much like
fear, the look in Baako's eyes. (127)

The boy picks up "a double gong" from the sand and uses it as a musical instrument. Initially irritated by the song, by what seems a useless exercise in
the work of bringing in the fish, one of the fishermen kicks sand at the boy
and shouts at him. The boy stops only briefly, recovers, and continues singing and beating the gong. On the next return from the boat to the beach, one
fisherman joins him in the singing, and then, one by one, they all join in.
This creates a sense of community so that "the pulling took a rhythm from
the general song" (128).

The scene encapsulates an important element of art in Africa. The artist is
simply one of the workers, and they all participate in art. The occasion for
artistic effort is not display or even expression – the singing is needed to create
harmonious cooperation, a sense of community. The artist may initially be
treated in a hostile manner, but he does not nurture his alienation. The boy accompanying the fishermen simply "recovered and continued" (128). The boy's
song reverses Baako's interpretation of the Mame Water myth. In Baako's
model, the goddess stands apart while the lover despairs, whereas the boy's
song is like "a woman's long lament for one more drowned fisherman" (128).
Furthermore, for the boy on the beach, art is not an abstract or intellectual
exercise – the net full of fish is an image of the materiality of artistic endeavour.

Baako looks on "like a man on the point of finding something he has
grasped and lost and fears he will lose again" (127). He has, in fact, almost
found and lost again (at least, for the moment) not only the significance of
the boy's singing but also of Juana, the woman through whom he could heal
his relationship with society. The sense of an elusive knowledge haunts Baako, and he reaches for Juana, who cannot save him yet. She cannot save him
until he sees her as a woman rather than as his own particular Mame Water
spirit, the embodiment of an alienation from the community that is required
for his art.

The failure of art to be relevant in *Fragments* can fall either more heavily on a crassly materialistic society, or on the hero's alienation from his community. Baako's sense of failure is apprehended differently by himself and by Naana. Armah privileges Naana's point of view – the novel begins and ends with her; she is the last of Nananom, the ancestors. Through Naana, the reader becomes aware of the danger of Baako's hasty actions. In his premature actions, he is like Araba's child, "one of the uncertain ones" who dies because he is not protected from the hungry desires centred on him (97). Baako, too, returns "in a hurry," as Brempong notes (45). Like Araba's child, Baako is uncertain; "everything about his attitude was unfixed, free-floating, potential" (100). As Naana tells him, Baako expects to change his society too quickly. "It was too sudden, whatever you did [...] everything is wrong now" (187). He was "like single flowers that shone too unwisely soon and too hastily alone" (197). For Naana, Baako's failure is prefigured in his inability to save the child, and this happens because he does not root himself securely through knowledge of the past. He is thus unable to connect his problems in art with the undermining of traditional familial relationships. Being ignorant of the past and its traditions, Baako cannot use his social and artistic vision effectively for the amelioration of his community. His inability to connect with his grandmother means that his vision of and for contemporary Ghana remains fragmented.

Although Armah maintains enough distance from Baako to let the reader see the protagonist's deficiency, Armah shows that the greed and corruption of contemporary Ghanaian society are as much to blame for the morass in which it is mired. Traditional life is undermined through the introduction of Western goods and mores, but the novel does not present the desire for material goods as reprehensible. There is nothing necessarily corrupt about the ambition to fulfil the loved ones' desires for material goods on the part of the young man, Bukari, whose story is inserted precisely at the point where Baako fails to provide spiritual leadership for his family. Baako is sitting in a bar with his brother-in-law, Kwesi, who has "pleaded" for his help in dissuading his wife Araba from outdooring their child prematurely (90). Baako remains detached – in sharp contrast to Bukari, who weeps for being denied, through the death of his mother, the possibility of becoming her provider and therefore the leader of his family:

> I have traveled and suffered and it was all for you. Doing work and taking insults into my throat and running near my hope. Next year at Christmas I would have come back and given you many things you have dreamed about but never had. Did I not tell you? Was I a bad son to you? Why did you have to go so hatefully just when I was getting ready to come again? What have I done that you should have thought to do this thing to me? What did I do to you that was wrong? (93)

Bukari feels cheated out of the possibility of fulfilling himself by returning from abroad to help his family, and goes "deep into his sorrow" (93). Bukari's sense that he has been denied relevance is similar to Baako's own need to serve the community through his art. He has not yet, however, learnt to do away with the separation between spiritual and material benefits, and this again betrays his Western education. Unable to learn from Bukari, Baako washes his hands of familial responsibilities, leaving Araba's child to its fate. The unity between material and spiritual good is later enacted before Baako by the boy with the double gong on the beach, who "was giving those men something they didn't have" and which they needed even to achieve the practical and material purpose of hauling in the nets full of fish (129). Baako still has not learnt the essence of Naana's wisdom – that the real change needed in the present is not from the material to the spiritual, as Baako mistakenly supposes. Baako – and the educated elite – in Ghana need to re-learn the communalism of traditional life that dispersed wealth through the extended family and the community. Such dispersal would repair some of the ravages of colonialism and modernization, to be seen in the intense competitiveness and in the avarice of some families and small groups in newly independent states.

Baako finally begins to construct a bridge to the community through his love for Juana. Significantly, it is when he is travelling between places: i.e. becoming a connecting factor, that he becomes aware of Juana as a person rather than a goddess. The importance of this moment is marked by Baako's efforts to remember "precisely where, between which two names," he had stopped thinking of Juana as a mythological creature and started seeing her as a vulnerable flesh-and-blood woman (133). The image of connection is further developed in the quayside accident that follows in the narrative. The truck driver, Skido, dies when his vehicle, carrying badly needed food supplies, plunges into the river as he tries to reach the departing ferry. For a "long, sus-pended moment," the lorry bridges land and water, only to fall into the river as the ferry moves off. Skido's death, however, is not in vain (137). The sacrifice of the one who bridges and connects in order to nourish, transforms the com-munity. Before the accident, the truck drivers rush recklessly onto the ferry boat, bullying the smaller and the weaker to get onto the vessel. The same place is described again, this time by night, in terms of a sacred place, with the community carrying "dozens of oil lamps" as they make their way to the river to retrieve Skido's body from the water. The community has been completely transformed by Skido's sacrifice:

> The screeching rush was gone, together with the curses of sweating, angry men. A heavy breeze rose off the water, turning the misty drizzle into a fine sporadic spray and finally blowing out the little oil lamps one after the other. There were several people, but there was no noise, except now and then a short word, a request or a reply, coming from one of the men. (141)

The retrieval of Skido's body recalls the fishermen's hauling of the net full of fish in chapter six, "Gyefo," where the song initiated by the boy artist enables the men to work in unison to succeed in hauling in the net full of fish. Like the boy with the fishermen, Baako has "something" the others "didn't have" (129). Baako now takes the attitude of the boy, in that when he is told roughly to stand back, he does not retreat from society into isolation as he did before. Like the boy, Baako recovers and asks to be allowed to help. When the ropes being used to haul the truck up break, Baako contributes by suggesting that the ropes should be wetted, so that the second time the ropes do not break and the divers can reach Skido's body. Baako has started to learn about the ab-solute need for the intellectual and the artist to connect with society in Africa, even if this connection entails the sacrifice of more sophisticated intellectual and artistic forms that would seem to offer greater personal satisfaction.

The figure of the "gyefo" or "redeemer" is explored in *Fragments* through the deaths of Skido and of Araba's child, as well as through Baako's descent into madness. Just as the drowning of Skido transforms the truck drivers, the death of Araba's child is also redemptive for Baako. Baako's recollection of the outdooring ceremony of Araba's child while he is at the asylum shows Baako that it is through Naana's knowledge of the past that he must seek to restore his society. For Armah, salvation in Ghana and in Africa will not be found in the myth of the Promethean hero who "brings about a complete turn-about in terrible circumstances" (103). Rather than the dazzle of a brilliant mind, the redemption of the community requires connection between the intellectual or the artist and his society.

Artists and intellectuals in Ghana, however, often think of themselves in terms of God's anointed, like the biblical Zechariah, "a brand plucked from the burning" (147). Baako calls this the "Aggrey kind of attitude [...]. The educated really thinking of the people here as some kind of devils in a burning hell, and themselves the happy plucked ones, saved" (148).[23] In *Fragments*, the artist's ability to find satisfaction in art-forms that are irrelevant to society is associated with the "salutary cynicism of Protestants," which allows them "to kill all empathy, to pull in all wandering bits of self into the one self, trying for an isolated haven in the shrinking flight inward" (123). This attitude is contrasted with that of Juana, who is, as Baako tells her, "a Catholic, or better still a pagan," and concerned with the salvation of the community:

> Too much of her lay outside of herself, that was the trouble. Like some forest woman whose gods were in all the trees and hills and people around her, the meaning of her life remained in her defeated attempts to purify her environment, right down to the final, futile decision to try to salvage discrete individuals in the general carnage. (123)

The figure of Juana suggests the diffusion of the personality, the altruism that characterized many Africans communities before colonization. Juana finds it impossible to remain detached and her empathy makes her a splintered being, a positive embodiment of the title – *Fragments* – complemented by Naana, who stands for wholeness and circularity in the novel. Armah suggests that, by connecting with the two women, Baako may learn to put together the skills he obtained through his education abroad with aspects of his society that

---

[23] Baako is here referring to James Emman Kwegyir Aggrey (1875–1927), co-founder of Achimota School.

have been all but obliterated. The work of salvation will be hard, uneven, and piecemeal but never hopeless.

Armah's artist-figure fails as a Promethean artist to show readers that Baako must learn to question some of the assumptions he has gathered through his education and to reconnect with his society's traditional culture and with the community. Armah presents Baako as having a view of Akan myth that has been skewed by foreign education. Through his deepening love for Juana, however, Baako learns to question myths originating both in Africa and in the West, so that he can come to a valid understanding of the artist in his society. Utilized within the characterization and the thematics of *Fragments*, myth does not lead beyond a temporal referent. On the contrary, the author uses myth both to validate and to challenge the artist in African societies. In using myth critically for social direction, Armah shows that myth and realism, myth and politics are not necessarily antithetical.

## WORKS CITED

Achebe, Chinua. *Arrow of God* (1964, 1974; London: Heinemann, 1986).

——. *Things Fall Apart* (1958; London: Heinemann, 1987)

Armah, Ayi Kwei. *The Beautyful Ones Are Not Yet Born* (1968; London: Heinemann, 1988).

——. *Fragments* (1969; London: Heinemann, 1988).

——. *KMT: In the House of Life* (Popenguine, Senegal: PER ANKH, 2002).

——. *Osiris Rising* (Popenguine, West Africa: 1995).

Christiansen, Palle. *The Melanesian Cargo Cult: Millenarianism as a Factor in Cultural Change* (Copenhagen: Akademisk Forlag, 1969).

Eni, Emmanuel. *Delivered from the Powers of Darkness* (Ibadan: Scripture Union, 1987).

Fanon, Frantz. *The Wretched of the Earth*, tr. Constance Farrington, preface by Jean–Paul Sartre (*Les Damnés de la terre*, 1961; tr. 1963; Harmondsworth: Penguin: 1967)

Goody, Jack, & Ian Watt. "The Consequences of Literacy," in *Literacy in Traditional Societies*, ed. Jack Goody (Cambridge: Cambridge UP, 1975): 27–68.

Lawrence, Peter, & Mervyn J. Meggitt, ed. *God, Ghosts and Men in Melanesia* (Melbourne: Oxford UP, 1965).

Lucente, Gregory L. *The Narrative of Realism and Myth: Verga, Lawrence, Faulkner, Pavese* (Baltimore MD: Johns Hopkins UP, 1979).

Lutz, John. "Pessimism, Autonomy, and Commodity Fetishism in Ayi Kwei Armah's *The Beautyful Ones Are Not Yet Born*," *Research in African Literatures* 34.2 (Summer 2003): 94–111.

Meyer, Birgit. "Commodities and the Power of Prayer: Pentecostalist Attitudes Towards Consumption in Contemporary Ghana," *Development and Change* 29.4 (October 1998): 751–76.

Meyerowitz, Eva. *The Sacred State of the Akan* (London: Faber & Faber, 1951).

Moore, Gerald. "The Writer and the Cargo Cult," in *Common Wealth*, ed. Anna Rutherford (Aarhus: Akademisk Boghandel, 1972): 73–84.

Ogundele, Wole. "Devices of Evasion: the Mythic versus the Historical Imagination in the Postcolonial African Novel," *Research in African Literatures* 33.3 (Autumn 2002): 125–39.

Parrinder, Geoffrey. *African Mythology* (London: Hamlyn, 1967).

Priebe, Richard. *Myth, Realism, and the West African Writer* (Trenton NJ: Africa World Press, 1988).

◄❖►

CHRISTIANE SCHLOTE

# Oil, Masquerades, and Memory
## Sokari Douglas Camp's Memorial of Ken Saro–Wiwa

The map of my homeland has changed.
The cartographers blot out forests and rivers.
Oil wells and flares dot the new landscape –
now nobody recognises the beauty queen's face.[1]

U PON ENTERING THE SAINSBURY AFRICAN GALLERIES at the British
Museum, a visitor is first greeted by an impressive steel sculpture
called "Otobo (Hippo) Masquerade" (1995).[2] The masquerade,
which is almost two metres high, is made of wood, steel, and palm-stem
brooms, often used to "sweep away evil." According to Kalabari mythology, it
is a fierce and dangerous character in its mixture of animal and human features. A little further to the right, the visitor encounters an equally magnificent
figure, labelled "Big Masquerade with boat and household on his head"
(1995). This two-and-a-half-metres-high masquerade, made of steel, wood
feathers, and mirrors, is clad in a bloody apron and is wielding two machete-

---

[1] Tanure Ojaide, *The Tale of the Harmattan* (Cape Town: Kwela & Snailpress,
2007): 17. Special thanks are due to Tanure Ojaide for the reference to his poetry collection *The Tale of the Harmattan*, and to Geoffrey Davis and Ganesh Devy for having
provided the great opportunity for meeting at the "Chotro: Indigenous Peoples in the
Post-Colonial World" conference at the Indira Gandhi National Centre for Arts in
Delhi, India, in January 2008, in the first place.

[2] For an illustration of the masquerade, see http://www.sokari.co.uk/work.asp?a=32
(accessed 16 January 2009).

like knives.[3] In Kalabari society, swords "show power, violence, control," and the boat and the house signify wealth. At the same time,

> there is also a reminder of the religious side of masquerading. The stomach area of the masquerade has a white apron, the white apron is spattered with blood. This mark is a sacrifice to the gods that play in any performance.[4]

Furthermore, as part of Britain's "Africa 05" season in 2005 the museum's forecourt was transformed into an Africa Garden by the BBC's garden-make-over show *Ground Force*, temporarily displaying sculptures by contemporary African artists such as Rachid Koraïchi, Emmanuel Taiwo Jegede, and Adam Madebe. The garden also included a colourful water-sculpture with the name "Asoebi, or Lace, Sweat and Tears" (2005), which showed "five galvanised steel figures of Nigerian women, each nearly 2.5 metres in height and brightly painted in pink and green" which are "collectively described by the Yoruba concept of 'Asoebi'. The nearest English equivalent might be 'blood, sweat and tears', suggesting the beauty, suffering and indomitable spirit of the Kalabari people."[5] The creator of all these works, "Otobo," "Big Masquerade," and "Asoebi," is the Nigerian-born British artist and sculptor Sokari Douglas Camp, who mainly works in galvanized steel and who describes her transnational upbringing as follows:

> I was one of these colonial children that was mailed back and forth to school. So did I live in Nigeria? Quite honestly, not really. But then did I really live in England in boarding school? I'm not really sure about that either. I'm Kalabari[6]

---

[3] For an illustration of the figure, see http://www.sokari.co.uk/work.asp?a=27 (accessed 16 January 2009).

[4] Notes for the exhibition "Spirits in Steel" at New York's American Museum of Natural History, http://www.amnh.org/exhibitions/sokari/gallery.html (accessed 16 January 2009).

[5] For an illustration of Camp's "*Asoebi*" installation, see http://www.britishmuseum .org /explore/highlights/highlight_image.aspx?image=com13886.jpg&retpage=21980 (accessed 16 January 2009).

[6] Camp was born in Buguma in the Niger Delta. For an interdisciplinary overview of the history, culture, identity, and art (including the work of Camp and Bruce Onobrakpeya) of the different Delta groups, see *Ways of the Rivers: Arts and Environment*

and I don't feel strange when going back to Nigeria but I feel comatosed because, you know, our society is in such a state that women are maybe not meant
to do as much as I've done in my lifetime. [...] What is wonderful about being
there is that you don't stick out. You can go to any event and there's a sea of
black people and you just become part of a big crowd. Wherever I go here, I
stand out. And it's not just a feeling, it's real. Well, I mean, you can be running
in the countryside [...] and the countryside is lovely because there are all these
beautiful walks and things and I run out of the bushes and there's some poor
white couple and they get such a look of fear on their face and you think, I'm
sure if I was a white person running they'd just say hello. But because I'm a
black person they go, "Oh, shock". And that's a drag [...] because fancy just
being a shock. That doesn't tell you anything about a person. [...] I don't really
feel like a Londoner. I lived here nearly twenty years. I feel very much part of
South East London. I really like the idea of being Kalabari which is a minu-
scule tribe in Nigeria, and I like the idea of coming from a bad part of London.
[...] But it is very funny to be called British because most of the time I'm not
accepted.[7]

The presence of Camp's work in prestigious institutions such as the British
Museum, the Metropolitan Museum of Art, and the American Museum of
Natural History in New York and the Smithsonian Institution in Washington
DC, as well as in numerous galleries worldwide, indicates the increased visibility and recognition of the work of non-European artists compared, for example, to 1988, when, according to Juginda Lamba, a "visit to any state, municipal, or commercial art gallery in Britain will invariably produce the same
impression – that there is little or no representation of contemporary non-European art."[8]

Olu Oguibe explains the emergence of a new generation of Nigerian artists
in the late 1980s and the 1990s (including Camp, Folake Shoga, Osi Audu,
Yinka Shonibare and others) with their "physical presence in the West" and

---

*of the Niger Delta*, ed. Martha G. Anderson & Philip M. Peek (Los Angeles: UCLA
Fowler Museum of Cultural History & Seattle: U of Washington P, 2002).

[7] Author's interview with Sokari Douglas Camp, London, 25 May 1999.

[8] Eddie Chambers, Juginda Lamba & Tam Joseph, *The Artpack: A History of Black
Artists in Britain* (Bristol: Chambers & Joseph, 1988): 27.

"their ability to understand and master strategies of alignment and proper positioning [...] equipped with the advantage of familiarity with the techniques
and discourses of new forms" and also with the emergence of "an equally new
generation of more receptive, forward-looking, globalist powerbrokers, especially curators and critics" and, perhaps even more importantly, African curators such as Okwui Enwezor.[9] In Camp's case, in particular, Oguibe attributes
her comparatively high visibility in the British and global art scene to "her
privilege of graduating from Central School and the Royal College of Art in
London" (before that Camp also studied at the California College of Arts and
Crafts in Oakland) and "the growing interest of ethnographic and natural
history museums."[10] In fact, on the occasion of the return of the African collection from the Museum of Mankind in Burlington Gardens to the British
Museum in 2001, the May 2001 editorial of the *Burlington Magazine* viewed
the Sainsbury African Galleries' dedication to Henry Moore at the entrance as
"a curatorial intent to treat their contents as works of 'art' and 'culture'" and
praised them for "setting the works in their functional and cultural contexts,
while focusing the visitor's initial attention on their beauty and power"
(Camp's masquerades are accompanied by a video).[11] According to Polly
Savage, the appeal of Camp's work for curators is not limited to the observation that her sculptures are "visually striking and technically assured" but that

> they apparently do much to resolve the longstanding dilemmas of display. In-
> stalled alongside collections of Gelede and Kalabari masks, their presence in

---

[9] Michael D. Harris and Moyosore B. Okediji trace the interaction between African
and African-American artists in *Transatlantic Dialogue: Contemporary Art in and Out
of Africa* (exh. cat., Ackland Art Museum, University of North Carolina; Seattle: U of
Washington P, 2000).

[10] Olu Oguibe, "Finding a Place: Nigerian Artists in the Contemporary Art World,"
in *The Nsukka Artists and Nigerian Contemporary Art*, ed. Simon Ottenberg (Washington DC: Smithsonian National Museum of African Art & Seattle: U of Washington
P, 2002): 257–78. For the art versus ethnography debate, see also Carol Thompson,
"Slaves to Sculpture: A Response to Patricia Penn Hilden," *TDR: The Drama Review*
44.3 (Autumn 2000): 37–50.

[11] "Beyond the Great Court," *Burlington Magazine* 143.1178 (May 2001): 267.

the museum gallery seems to undermine the stability of troublesome binaries such as traditional/contemporary, art/artifact, aesthetic/didactic, and gallery/ museum. Because Camp's masquerades are intended for gallery audiences rather than performance audiences, the dilemma of removing the object's context is apparently eased, and her Kalabari background ostensibly qualifies her with what Said (1984) terms the "permission to narrate" partly relieving curators from the uncomfortable position of speaking for an "other."[12]

Yet, despite Camp's success and on a more sombre note, her personal experiences as a black artist in Britain still strikingly recall W.E.B. Du Bois's words from his classic *The Souls of Black Folk* (1903) more than a century earlier:

> Between me and the other world there is ever an unasked question: unasked by some through feelings of delicacy; by others through the difficulty of rightly framing it. [...] They approach me in a half-hesitant sort of way, eye me curiously or compassionately, and then, instead of saying directly, How does it feel to be a problem? they say, I know an excellent colored man in my town [...] I smile, or am interested, or reduce the boiling to a simmer [...]. To the real question, How does it feel to be a problem? I answer seldom a word. And yet, being a problem is a strange experience [...]. It is a peculiar sensation, this double-consciousness, this sense of always looking at one's self through the eyes of others.[13]

Camp's work and position as a British woman artist of Nigerian descent working in the rather male-dominated field of metal sculptures is a poignant example of the fusion of different identities and aesthetics and the transgression of various boundaries, not least in regard to the reception of her work in Nigeria, as she concedes herself: "They'd probably think someone else did it. They wouldn't know what to make of it. I mean banging metal and you're a sophisticated woman? What's the matter with you?"[14] But like many artists of her

---

[12] Polly Savage, "Playing to the Gallery: Masks, Masquerade, and Museums," *African Arts* 41.4 (Winter 2008): 75–76.

[13] W.E.B. Du Bois, *The Souls of Black Folk*, intro. Randall Kenan (1903; New York: Signet Classics, 1995): 43–45.

[14] Author's interview with Camp, London, 25 May 1999.

generation who were born and raised in Nigeria yet live abroad and who, nonetheless, possess "a deeper familiarity with Nigerian artistic traditions,"[15] Camp strongly draws on her Kalabari heritage and she is particularly concerned with what she perceives as Western misconceptions of Nigerian (and African) culture:

> I'm very happy to keep this Kalabari heritage and aesthetic things that Kalabari people are supposed to like. I find that great fun. I keep on adding things to my work while thinking here the highest art form is to peel everything off, take everything off to the bare. It's an aesthetic that they think is the highest form of art.[16] But you know I love things that are complicated [...] just because I don't think that there's a clear answer to everything. I think it might be my Nigerian soul basically talking to me. [...] I've got to break into museums because museums are giving the wrong interpretation of my culture. I mean, there are wonderful curators that I've come across in New York and Washington and realised that museums actually have a mission. [...] I'm just telling you that like, for example, some masks that are in museums, are actually not meant to be on your face like a Venetian mask. They're meant to be on your head, on top of your head. And I just think I'm lucky enough to be able to be in the press or

---

In Kalabari culture, as in many parts of Africa, women are not allowed to make masks or perform in masquerades. As a woman, Sokari Douglas Camp observes the masquerade from the perspective of the audience. [...] As an artist, Sokari Douglas Camp crosses the boundary between male and female domains, just as she blurs the boundaries between Africa and the West.

— Notes for the exhibition "Spirits in Steel" at New York's American Museum of Natural History, http://www.amnh.org/exhibitions/sokari/gallery.html (accessed 18 January 2009). On the issue of gender in African art, see Lisa Aronson, "African Women in the Visual Arts," *Signs* 16.3 (Spring 1991): 550–74.

[15] Oguibe, "Finding a Place: Nigerian Artists in the Contemporary Art World," 274.

[16] Camp clearly advocates an awareness of the constant danger of the aesthetic "as a tool of divisiveness, enmity, and oppression" when people making an aesthetic judgment are "in a dominant position politically, legally, or economically" and declare the cultural production of others as inferior in comparison with their assumptions of "universal standards of beauty"; Emory Elliott, "Introduction: Cultural Diversity and the Problem of Aesthetics," in *Aesthetics in a Multicultural Age*, ed. Emory Elliott (Oxford: Oxford UP, 2002): 3.

in writing saying that and it will hopefully inspire somebody else to do more elaborate work about this idea that you can have another head on top of a head. You can have a whole conversation, have something to do with a figure that changes proportions and does exciting things in art. That's all it is about. It's about communication.[17]

This essay takes up Camp's preference for "things that are complicated" and layered by focusing on Camp's series of sculptures which reflect her concern with the environmental destruction of the Niger Delta and its people caused by multinational oil companies, partly in complicity with the Nigerian government. In an attempt to examine Camp's form of artistic activism in connection with the politics of commemoration, particular attention will be paid to Camp's memorial for the Nigerian writer, environmental and political activist, and president of MOSOP (Movement for the Survival of the Ogoni People) Ken Saro–Wiwa, who was hanged (together with eight fellow Ogonis) on 10 November 1995, by the military regime of General Sani Abacha.[18]

---

[17] Author's interview with Camp, London, 25 May 1999. — Apropos the remark that some masks are meant to be "on top of your head," Camp explains as follows:

Some Kalabari masks have faces that are worn on top of the head so the face looks directly toward the sky, an impossible position to keep for a four-hour performance, naturally, but with the help of a carved face, simple. 'Otobo' hippo is one such masquerade. This spiritual character does not perform for the audience but concentrates on performing to God. I like this idea. Having your feet on the ground but conversing with the sky. Only when Otobo looks down do you get the full impact of his facial expression and see that he is a powerful animal that can eat men, turn over canoes. So he has a garland of skulls around his head.

— Notes for the exhibition "Spirits in Steel" at New York's American Museum of Natural History, http://www.amnh.org/exhibitions/sokari/gallery.html (accessed 18 January 2009). See also Robin Horton, "The gods as guests: An aspect of Kalabari religious life," in *The Performance Arts in Africa: A Reader*, ed. Frances Harding (London: Routledge, 2002): 117–37.

[18] For a bio-bibliography of Saro–Wiwa, see *Ogoni's Agonies. Ken Saro–Wiwa and the Crisis in Nigeria*, ed. Abdul Rasheed Na'Allah (Trenton NJ & Asmara, Eritrea: Africa World Press, 1998): 363–366. See also *Ken Saro–Wiwa: Writer and Political*

In 1993, the "Year of Indigenous Peoples" and the year of a large Ogoni demonstration against Shell (later known as 'Ogoni Day'), Ken Saro–Wiwa, who had been repeatedly arrested and detained, wrote:

> God created Ogoni to be a Little Paradise. He gave us, in Ogoni, flat, fertile land with fresh and salt water. He gave us oil and gas and he gave us brains with which to defend his great gift. [...] However, when I turned round to examine closely what is happening to our Little Paradise [...] I found that international oil companies and the rulers of Nigeria had conspired to turn our Little Paradise to a hell on earth and that in the process, Ogoni people are dying out.

For the Ogoni nation, of Nigeria's Rivers State, this "hell on earth" takes the form of an "ecological war," as Saro–Wiwa describes in agonizing detail what Tanure Ojaide alludes to more subtly in the lines from his poem "Quatrain suite" in the epigraph to the present essay:

> If you go to Korokoro, Kegbara Dere, Ebubu, Yorla, Lekuma (Afan) and other oil fields, you will see gas burning noisily. These fires have been burning 24 hours a day, 365 days a year since 1958. They have been pouring dangerous gases such as carbon dioxide, carbon monoxide, methane and soot into the air. Living near them is like being at the end of one million exhaust pipes from lorries. The noise and heat which they emit are equally poisonous. The soot goes into the air and comes down as what is called 'acid rain'. [...] Thus, all the water which the Ogoni people drink as well as the air they breathe has been poisoned. [...] The most cruel action of the oil companies, especially Shell, which has almost 99 per cent of the mining concession in Ogoni, is the greedy seizure of land. For Shell, agricultural land, residential land, forests, sacred land, all mean one thing: available land for the extraction of oil. Everything on top of the land, – men, trees, plants and animals – has to be killed off.[19]

---

*Activist*, ed. Craig W. McLuckie & Aubrey McPhail (Boulder CO: Lynne Rienner, 2000) and Sanya Osha, *Ken Saro–Wiwa's Shadow. Politics, Nationalism and the Ogoni Protest Movement* (London: Adonis & Abbey, 2007).

[19] Ken Saro–Wiwa, *Second Letter to Ogoni Youth* (Port Harcourt: Saros International, 1993): 3–7. See Wiwa's prison memoir *A Month and a Day: A Detention Diary* (1995), *Genocide in Nigeria: The Ogoni Tragedy* (1992), and *The Ogoni Nation Today and Tomorrow* (1993) for a detailed account of the Ogoni struggle.

The story of the exploitation of the Niger Delta is not at all a new one; it has been addressed and problematized by Nigerian and other artists throughout the decades: from Ben Okri's short story "What the Tapster Saw" (1988) and John Pepper Clark's play *All for Oil* (2000) about the palm-oil trade at the beginning of the twentieth century and the work of Ken Saro–Wiwa to Tanure Ojaide's poetry collections such as *The Tale of the Harmattan* (2007) and his novel *The Activist* (2006) and Sandy Cioffi's recent documentary film *Sweet Crude* (2008), which not only portrays the pollution but whose cinematic parade of the Delta's stakeholders also includes armed resistance groups such as MEND (Movement for the Emancipation of the Niger Delta) and other militants.[20]

## Integration Busing

Questions of how to artistically represent traumatic experiences such as those described by Saro–Wiwa and war, genocide, exploitation, and violent destruction in general have haunted past and contemporary artists and critics alike, especially since representations of violent events can be implicated in promoting and reaffirming the very violence they seek to decry. As Margot Norris argues, even

> in sincere and compassionate poetic and narrative strategies for representing mass killing, we find that omissions, repressions, disavowals, and displace-

---

[20] For recent studies of the historical, political, and economic background of the oil industry in the Niger Delta, see, for example, John Ghazvinian, *Untapped: The Scramble for Africa's Oil* (Pontypridd: Harvest, 2008), the articles in the "Portfolio" section of the *Virginia Quarterly Review* 83.1 (Winter 2007), Augustine Ikelegbe, "The Economy of Conflict in the Oil Rich Niger Delta Region of Nigeria," *Nordic Journal of African Studies* 14.2 (2005): 208–34, and Sonia Shah, *Crude: The Story of Oil* (New York: Seven Stories, 2004). In the "Foreword" to Ike Okonta & Oronto Douglas's *Where Vultures Feast: Shell, Human Rights, and Oil in the Niger Delta* (London: Verso, 2003), Nnimmo Bassey echoes Saro–Wiwa's accusation: "Royal Dutch/Shell is more than a colonial force in Nigeria. A colonial power exhibits some measure of concern for the territory over which it lords. This is not the case with this mogul, which goes for crude oil in the most *crude* manner possible" (xi).

ments may inadvertently produce verbal or discursive violence to suffering populations.[21]

The politics of representation becomes yet more complex when exploring the role of oil in times of large-scale violence and "high globalization," as Arjun Appadurai has termed the 1990s.[22]

In a pioneering essay, Amitav Ghosh maintains that, despite its dramatic nature, any literary engagement with the oil encounter and its main protagonists (especially America and the Arabian Peninsula) has remained "imaginatively sterile," and he concentrates on Abdelrahman Munif's quintet *Cities of Salt* (1984–89) as the most significant example of petrofiction:

> to the principal protagonists in the Oil Encounter [...] the history of oil is a matter of embarrassment verging on the unspeakable, the pornographic. [...] A great deal has been invested in ensuring the muteness of the Oil Encounter: on the American (or Western) side, through regimes of strict corporate secrecy; on the Arab side, by the physical and demographic separation of oil installations and their workers from the indigenous population.[23]

---

[21] Margot Norris, *Writing War in the Twentieth Century* (Charlottesville & London: UP of Virginia, 2000): 5. See also, for example, *Terror and Text: Representing Political Violence in Literature and the Visual Arts*, ed. Gerritt–Jan Berendse & Mark Williams (Bielefeld: Aisthesis, 2002), Laurie Vickroy, *Trauma and Survival in Contemporary Fiction* (Charlottesville: UP of Virginia, 2002), *The Media of Conflict: War Reporting and Representations of Ethnic Violence*, ed. Tim Allen & Jean Seaton (London: Zed, 1999), *The Violence of Representation: Literature and the History of Violence*, ed. Nancy Armstrong & Leonard Tennenhouse (London: Routledge, 1989), and Elaine Scarry's pioneering study *The Body in Pain: The Making and Unmaking of the World* (Oxford: Oxford UP, 1985).

[22] Arjun Appadurai, *Fear of Small Numbers: An Essay on the Geography of Anger* (Durham NC & London: Duke UP, 2006): 2. In his analysis of the linkage between globalization and ethnic cleansing and terror, Appadurai also examines "an excess of hatred that produces untold forms of degradation and violation, both to the body and the being of the victim" (10).

[23] Ghosh, "Petrofiction: The Oil Encounter and the Novel," in *The Imam and the Indian* (Delhi: Ravi Dayal, 2002): 75, 77. See also Claire Chambers, "Representations of the Oil Encounter in Amitav Ghosh's *The Circle of Reason*," *Journal of*

Camp's 'oil masquerades' can be read as attempts to artistically address this crisis of representation and "the muteness of the Oil Encounter," particularly in the light of the politics of commemoration. In 2005, Platform, an organization which, according to its website, "works across disciplines for social and ecological justice" by combining "the transformatory power of art with the tangible goals of campaigning," together with the British Arts Council, Amnesty International, and Greenpeace initiated a competition, inviting artists to design a memorial for Ken Saro–Wiwa. Forty-seven activists, artists, and architects submitted their proposals, and out of a shortlist of five Camp's design was chosen.[24] On 10 November 2006, Camp's 'Living Memorial' in the form of a bus (over three metres high and five metres long) was unveiled "outside the Guardian's offices in central London" before its tour to British historical sites linked to the slave trade such as Liverpool, Birmingham, and Bristol.[25] As with most of her sculptures, Camp's 'mobile memorial' is made out of steel, and it is adorned with a steel band with Saro–Wiwa's own words: "I accuse the oil companies of practicing genocide against the Ogoni." Its roof is filled with oil barrels, bearing the names of the eight Ogoni activists who died with Saro–Wiwa. The barrels were played by African musicians as part of a live music event in London on the occasion of the twelfth anniversary of Saro–Wiwa's execution. Only a few days earlier, in October 2007, the bus caused a stir when it was put in front of Shell's London headquarters: "When

*Commonwealth Literature* 41.1 (March 2006): 3, to whom thanks are due for sending me her essay, and Jennifer Wenzel, "Petro-magic realism: Toward a political ecology of Nigerian literature," *Postcolonial Studies* 9.4 (December 2006): 449–64.

[24] See http://www.platformlondon.org/ (accessed 20 January 2009). Camp's full proposal for the Ken Saro–Wiwa memorial (including pictures) is available at http://www.platformlondon.org/remembersarowiwa/pdfs/Sokari_Douglas_Camp.pdf (accessed 20 January 2009).

[25] See http://www.sokari.co.uk/ (accessed 20 January 2009) and Paul Arendt, "Say it with buses," *The Guardian* (9 November 2006). In 2007, the "The World is Richer: Sculpture and Maquettes. Sokari Douglas Camp" exhibition at Wallspace in the City of London also included Camp's proposal for a memorial in Hyde Park to mark the 2007 bicentenary of the abolition of the slave trade; see http://www.wallspace.org.uk /exhibitions/world-is-richer/index.html (accessed 15 January 2009).

three tonnes of steel parks on your doorstep in a rare display of protest you might well take notice."[26]

The mobility of the living memorial and its accessible spaces, which also serve as educational facilities for film screenings and exhibitions, add an interesting dimension to Pierre Nora's notion of *lieux de mémoire* and are essential elements of Platform's concept of a "travelling memorial [...] as an antidote to the colonial notion of fixed, figurative monuments": "The Living Memorial will inform, agitate and inspire, and claim its space in the landscape of multicultural Britain." Camp explains her inspiration for the memorial and her unusual choice of a bus, seen "as a pollutant, a carrier of supplies and information, and as a metaphor for Saro–Wiwa's activism,"[27] as follows:

> A bus of hope. A bus carrying information. A bus carrying some of the humour and terror of the people of the Niger Delta. [...] I thought of the information services I had seen in Port Harcourt, billboards with stiff characters [...]. Then I thought of the medicine buses that would arrive with people cured by the product being sold.[28] [...] I constructed a bus because I wanted a mighty vehicle to tour the streets of London and to be noticed, rather like a campaigning 'Battle Bus' in an election [...]. It is ironic that it is a fuel-guzzling object, coming from a country without MOT for vehicles [...]. I wanted something familiar but interpreted in a third world way. Can we have a lorry commemorating a campaigner against oil exploitation? Things are never black and white and intuitively I think Ken would like the irony of this because oil brought about his death but it is also playing a part in educating the world about the Ogoni peoples [sic] plight and the other people's of the Niger Delta.[29]

---

[26] See http://www.remembersarowiwa.com/ (accessed 21 January 2009).

[27] Arendt, "Say it with buses" (2006) and http://www.remembersarowiwa.com /what why.htm (accessed 21 January 2009).

[28] Camp further states that there "is an element of theatre and humour in the medicine men but what they deliver is relief and hope. Ken and his companions [sic] bravery had an element of this tonic"; http://www.remembersarowiwa.com/sokari.htm (accessed 21 January 2009).

[29] See http://www.platformlondon.org/remembersarowiwa/pdfs/Sokari_Douglas _Camp .pdf (accessed 21 January 2009).

## Memories in (Crude) Oil

As recent studies have shown,[30] analyses of (war) memory and commemoration have mainly been done within two theoretical frameworks, which T.G. Ashplant, Graham Dawson and Michael Roper specify as a "practice bound up with rituals of national identification, and a key element in the symbolic repertoire available to the nation-state for binding its citizens into a collective national identity" and, "for psychological reasons, as an expression of mourning [...] to the death and suffering that war engenders."[31] While these two functions have often been seen as unrelated, Ashplant et al. argue for a "more complex, integrated account of the interacting processes that link the individual, civil society and the state."[32] Although not strictly marked as a war memorial, Camp's living memorial requires an equally integrated approach, already hinted at in the last lines of the above quotation, which reflect the ambiguity of protest and public commemoration. In a similar vein, Andrew Apter traces the connection between Saro–Wiwa's environmental battle and ethnic politics which made him a Nigerian *cause célèbre*, while previously most Nigerians had not cared for the Ogoni tribe, "a mere half million people who were considered scarcely human, happy to be fishing their mangrove

---

[30] See, for example, Carol Acton, *Grief in Wartime: Private Pain, Public Discourse* (Houndmills: Palgrave 2007), *Memory and Memorials: The Commemorative Century*, ed. William Kidd & Brian Murdoch (Aldershot: Ashgate, 2004), *The Politics of War, Memory and Commemoration*, ed. T.G. Ashplant, Graham Dawson & Michael Roper (London: Routledge, 2000), Serguisz Michalski, *Public Monuments: Art in Political Bondage 1870–1997* (London: Reaktion, 1998), Jay Winter, *Sites of Memory, Sites of Mourning: The Great War in European Cultural History* (Cambridge: Cambridge UP, 1995), James E. Young, *The Texture of Memory: Holocaust Memorials and Meaning* (New Haven CT & London: Yale UP, 1993), and James M. Mayo, *War Memorials as Political Landscape: The American Experience and Beyond* (New York: Praeger, 1988).

[31] Ashplant, Dawson & Roper, "Introduction" to *The Politics of War, Memory and Commemoration*, ed. Ashplant et al., 7.

[32] Ashplant, Dawson & Roper, "Introduction" to *The Politics of War, Memory and Commemoration*, 12.

creeks and planting their gardens."[33] Owing to its educational conceptualiza-
tion, the 'memorial bus' clearly contributes to the revelation of the close links
between individuals, civil society, and the state in its overtly public commemoration of Saro–Wiwa, further complemented by an accompanying website (www.remembersarowiwa.com/).

Yet, in regard to its function as "a mourning site for lost loved ones [...] a
memorial to tragic loss,"[34] the bus differs significantly from Camp's other
memorial work and her smaller oil sculptures. Camp had already made head-
lines with a memorial called "No-o-war-r No-o-war-r" (2003), which honours
ordinary people and their contributions to democratic rights. She submitted a
proposal (which was eventually not chosen) for it as a model for the Fourth
Plinth in Trafalgar Square, which was empty from 1841 until 1999 but has
since been the temporary location for commissioned works by contemporary
artists. The memorial, according to Camp inspired by August Rodin's "The
Burghers of Calais" (1884–88), shows a group of people, demonstrating and
waving banners.[35] One of Camp's earlier memorial works, "Cross We Bear"
(1999), commemorates the life of Stephen Lawrence, an eighteen-year-old
British student of Jamaican descent who was stabbed to death on 22 April
1993 by a gang of white youths while he was waiting for a bus in the South
London district of Eltham. It is much more personalized, with a photograph of
Lawrence superimposed on the Union Jack, from which a crucified figure is
suspended:[36]

---

[33] Andrew Apter, "Death and the King's Henchmen: Ken Saro–Wiwa and the Poli-
tical Ecology of Citizenship in Nigeria," in *Ogoni's Agonies: Ken Saro–Wiwa and the
Crisis in Nigeria*, ed. Abdul Rasheed Na'Allah (Trenton NJ & Asmara, Eritrea: Africa
World Press, 1998): 122.

[34] Young, *The Texture of Memory. Holocaust Memorials and Meaning*, 3.

[35] Commissions chosen include works by Marc Quinn, Thomas Schütte, Antony
Gormley and Yinka Shonibare, http://www.london.gov.uk/fourthplinth/content/about-
programme (accessed 21 January 2009). See an illustration of "No-o-war-r No-o-war-
r" at http://www.sokari.co.uk/work.asp?a=59 (accessed 21 January 2009).

[36] See http://www.sokari.co.uk/work.asp?a=8 (accessed 21 January 2009).

There is this young black boy who was killed just because he was standing at the wrong place at the wrong time. He was killed by young boys. And they never organised to prosecute these people and there's great confusion still. I got his picture out of the paper and I put it on to this acetate thing just because it was something that was happening at the Elephant [Elephant & Castle tube station] and everyday passing it, it reminded me and as a mother or whatever you become very conscious of things like that. So it's not just different fabrics in my life, I'm thinking of my children's future. So I put Stephen's picture with the British flag and I put it in a glass container and so it became a kind of protest item as well and I didn't put oil in because I had air. I like the idea of glass acetate and 1990s air and this picture sealed in this picture. Somebody was just talking to me about the black legacy in this country and sort of saying, "Well, it's the cross we bear." And that's how that piece came on and I put a crucifix in it. It's very graphic and not quite like me. But there are instances where you do little things that just mark a point and from there I went on to wanting to make more elaborate things with the flag.[37]

Apart from these memorial works, the 'bus' can also be seen as part of Camp's series of "oil masquerades," including the sculptures "Beauty Flame Head" (2000), "Aged Flame Head" (2000), "Oil Nigeria Prayer" (1998), "Rumble in the Jungle" (1998), "Assessment" (1998), "Guns and Oil" (1998), "Close to My Heart" (1998), "Self" (1998), and "My World Your World" (1997), some of which formed part of the exhibition "Knots of the Human Heart" at London's Morley Gallery in 2000.[38] In most of these sculptures, Camp actually uses oil (often contained in glass containers) as material for the masquerade. Her interest in representing and addressing the oil encounter in the Niger Delta is not only politically motivated but stems from personal experience:

From my hometown we can see six oil flames that are like constant sunsets and the air has more soot than the busiest cities in the world; we only have ten cars in the town. One feels that the area is unhealthy, but the people go about their

---

[37] Author's interview with Camp, London, 25 May 1999.
[38] For illustrations, see the sections "Selected Work" and "Archived Work" on Camp's website at http://www.sokari.co.uk/about.asp (accessed 21 January 2009).

daily lives, the only indication that things are wrong is that we do not have
many older people in our community.[39]

Perhaps not surprisingly, her attempt at a self portrait, also entitled "Self"
(1998), is a reflection of her interest in two of the Niger Delta's most prominent features, oil wells and masquerades, and the sculpture shows a small
figure holding up a photograph of a burning oil well. Moreover, her focus on
and use of oil, particularly in combination with photography, further allows
her to depict past and present life in the Niger Delta in a conscious attempt to
"sculpt back" to the ethnographic gaze of non-Kalabari curators and museum
visitors, as exemplified in captivating sculptures such as "Close to My Heart"
(1998) and "My World Your World" (1997):

> At one time, for example, for an exhibition in Japan they wanted a picture of
> my home or my people. You know, your usual ethnographic picture of natives.
> [...] So I decided that I would take a picture of my home. And the pictures of
> my home that I chose were the pictures of an oil well just because in the Delta
> region in Nigeria you have these blazing fires which are rather fantastic to look
> at but they are polluting and you have an L.A.-cloud of pollution in the Delta
> now. And yet people are still in traditional clothes and stuff. It's kind of the
> modern and traditional all in the same breath. So I made a piece that had a
> picture of an oil well with a person in very traditional, beautiful clothes and she
> held up this picture made of glass and acetate and a photo negative. I thought
> that was great because you can see through the plate and see the metal work
> and you can see the image as well and you can go back and forth which I find
> very interesting. It's not just perspective, it's like layers [...] because we have
> displays of people that you feel very close to that have died. We have pictures
> of them and the children and the relatives. [...] Rather wonderful. It was like
> modern technology with something very, very human, very, very vulnerable
> but you celebrate it. And putting my landscape into that kind of context – I
> really care about the landscape, so it's a way of kind of documenting my life
> and a way of doing art at the same time. [...] And because of this oil well
> people couldn't really see what I was thinking about because it doesn't look
> like a British oil well, which are towers in the sea. In Nigeria you have a plat-

---

[39] http://www.platformlondon.org/remembersarowiwa/sokari.htm (accessed 21 January 2009).

form on the Delta coast. So it's slightly different but it's the same thing except that over there it's really pollutant because Shell and companies don't bother to cap the gases that come off. I think everyone should know that this is what's going on.[40]

While the 'bus' (which Camp calls "a practical sculpture" in her proposal) displays elements of the same "vitality, originality, and boldness" which Oguibe has identified as trademarks of Camp's work and which "gave British sculpture a jerk" in the 1980s and 1990s, her semi-abstract and figurative oil sculptures will in all likelihood elicit more personal responses from viewers.[41] On the one hand, this can be attributed to Camp's use of photographs which function as memory media per se and which have been highly influential in regard to the tradition of Kalabari ancestral screens (*duein fubara*, 'the foreheads of the dead'),[42] as Nigel Barley explains:

> Modern Kalabari constantly refer to photographs [...] when interpreting the *duein fubara*. [...] Did the conventions of the group photograph derive from the *duein fubara* screens or vice versa? [...] It is an interesting thought that contact with other ways of seeing and the invention of the camera led Africans toward more naturalistic sculpture as firmly as it encouraged Western artists in the opposite direction.[43]

As such, Camp's fusion of different techniques and materials and her inspiration drawn from "Buguma festivals or Brixton markets"[44] as well as other

---

[40] Author's interview with Camp, London, 25 May 1999.

[41] Oguibe, "Finding a Place: Nigerian Artists in the Contemporary Art World," 268.

[42] "Typically they consist of three main wooden figures that are carved in low relief and assembled from separate pieces of wood. [...] The frame of a screen, however, defines a self-contained space within which meaningful relationships are depicted. [...] The entire screen is surrounded by a wooden or bamboo frame"; Nigel Barley, *Foreheads of the Dead: An Anthropological View of Kalabari Ancestral Screens* (Washington DC: Smithsonian Institution & London: National Museum of African Art, 1988): 23.

[43] Barley, *Foreheads of the Dead: An Anthropological View of Kalabari Ancestral Screens*, 44–46.

[44] See the programme notes for the exhibition "The Essential Art of African Textiles: Design Without End" (September 2008–April 2009) at New York's Metropolitan

global influences is exemplary of what Elizabeth Harney calls "the poetics of diaspora," where "mythologized, partially remembered motifs serve as markers of belonging within the unfamiliar cultural terrain of the diaspora," yet where these "are never quoted directly but rather incorporated into a highly syncretic aesthetic that draws as much from the experiences of displacement as from nostalgia for home."[45] Drawing on Stuart Hall's division of the history of black-British art into three periods, Ingrid von Rosenberg also emphasizes the "mixture of influences" and the "transcultural trajectory" which have marked the third wave of black-British art in the 1990s.[46] At the same time, however, Camp remains acutely aware of the confrontational potential of transcultural art practices, which continue to distinguish her work:

> In terms of aesthetics I do have that feeling that I have to make myself clear to people. [...] The people that I was fascinated by [...] in the Delta, did things like kill dogs which is really bad form in England. So if I had wanted to discuss that in my work I have to put a zip on it just because no one would listen. They'd describe it as too outrageous. So I kept away from putting blood on the costumes. But when I worked with the Museum of Mankind I decided to really just go for it.[47]

On the other hand, the assumed greater effect of Camp's smaller oil sculptures and her memorials "No-o-war-r No-o-war-r" and "Cross We Bear," compared

---

Museum of Art, which also featured Camp's sculpture "Nigerian Woman Shopping" (1990) at http: //www.metmuseum.org/special/african_textiles/more.asp (accessed 19 January 2009). As Robin Horton points out, her massive yet open sculptures owe a great deal to the "complex basketry of storage vessels, fishdrying racks and fish traps which surrounded her as a young child"; "Sokari Douglas Camp: Ekine Woman in London?" in *Play and Display: Steel Masquerades from Top to Toe* (exh. cat.; London: Museum of Mankind/Silvara, 1995): 2.

[45] Elizabeth Harney, *Ethiopian Passages: Contemporary Art from the Diaspora* (London: Philip Wilson, 2003): 19. See also Amna Malik, "Conceptualising 'Black' British Art Through the Lens of Exile," in *Exiles, Diasporas and Strangers*, ed. Kobena Mercer (Cambridge MA: MIT Press, 2008): 166–88.

[46] Ingrid von Rosenberg, "Transformations of Western Icons in Black British Art," *Journal for the Study of British Cultures* 15.1 (2008): 70.

[47] Author's interview with Camp, London, 25 May 1999.

to the starker aesthetic of the Saro–Wiwa memorial, may hinge not least on the presence of the sculpted body in the conception of these masquerades which is missing from the 'bus', because, as Gerrit–Jan Berendse and Mark Williams conclude in their study of representations of violence in literature and the visual arts,

> At its most positive, the artist's role is perhaps simply to protest the value of physical being which terror denies. Ideology, ethnicity, religion – all abstract causes which justify terror must be measured against the mutilation of the human body that terror affects.[48]

## WORKS CITED

Anderson, Martha G., & Philip M. Peek, ed. *Ways of the Rivers: Arts and Environment of the Niger Delta* (Los Angeles: UCLA Fowler Museum of Cultural History & Seattle: U of Washington P, 2002).

Anon. "Beyond the Great Court," *Burlington Magazine* 143.1178 (May 2001): 267.

Appadurai, Arjun. *Fear of Small Numbers: An Essay on the Geography of Anger* (Durham NC & London: Duke UP, 2006).

Apter, Andrew. "Death and the King's Henchmen: Ken Saro–Wiwa and the Political Ecology of Citizenship in Nigeria," in *Ogoni's Agonies: Ken Saro–Wiwa and the Crisis in Nigeria*, ed. Abdul Rasheed Na'Allah (Trenton NJ & Asmara, Eritrea: Africa World Press, 1998): 121–60.

Arendt, Paul. "Say it with buses," *The Guardian* (9 November 2006).

Aronson, Lisa. "African Women in the Visual Arts," *Signs* 16.3 (Spring 1991): 550–74.

Barley, Nigel. *Foreheads of the Dead: An Anthropological View of Kalabari Ancestral Screens* (Washington DC & London: National Museum of African Art/Smithsonian Institution, 1988).

Berendse, Gerritt–Jan, & Mark Williams, ed. *Terror and Text: Representing Political Violence in Literature and the Visual Arts* (Bielefeld: Aisthesis, 2002).

Chambers, Claire. "Representations of the Oil Encounter in Amitav Ghosh's *The Circle of Reason*," *Journal of Commonwealth Literature* 41.1 (March 2006): 33–50.

Chambers, Eddie, Juginda Lamba & Tam Joseph. *The Artpack: A History of Black Artists in Britain* (Bristol: Chambers & Joseph, 1988).

Clark, John Pepper. *All for Oil* (Lagos: Malthouse, 2000).

---

[48] Berendse & Williams, *Terror and Text*, 32.

Du Bois, W.E.B. *The Souls of Black Folk*, intro. Randall Kenan (1903; New York: Signet Classics, 1995).

Elliott, Emory. "Introduction: Cultural Diversity and the Problem of Aesthetics," in *Aesthetics in a Multicultural Age*, ed. Emory Elliott (Oxford: Oxford UP, 2002): 3–27.

Fischer, Michael M.J. "Museums and Festivals: Notes on the Poetics and Politics of Representation Conference, the Smithsonian Institution, September 26–28, 1988," *Cultural Anthropology* 4.2 (May 1989): 204–21.

Ghazvinian, John. *Untapped: The Scramble for Africa's Oil* (Pontypridd: Harvest, 2008).

Ghosh, Amitav. "Petrofiction: The Oil Encounter and the Novel," in *The Imam and the Indian* (Delhi: Ravi Dayal, 2002): 75–89.

Harney, Elizabeth, with contributions by Jeff Donaldson, Achamyeleh Debela & Kinsey Katchka. *Ethiopian Passages: Contemporary Art from the Diaspora* (London: Philip Wilson, 2003).

Harris, Michael D., & Moyosore B. Okediji. *Transatlantic Dialogue: Contemporary Art in and Out of Africa* (exh. cat. exh. cat., Ackland Art Museum, University of North Carolina; Seattle: U of Washington P, 2000).

Horton, Robin. "The gods as guests: An aspect of Kalabari religious life," in *The Performance Arts in Africa: A Reader*, ed. Frances Harding (London: Routledge, 2002): 117–37.

——. "Sokari Douglas Camp: Ekine Woman in London?" in *Play and Display: Steel Masquerades from Top to Toe* (exh. cat.; London: Museum of Mankind/Silvara, 1995): 1–8.

Ikelegbe, Augustine. "The Economy of Conflict in the Oil Rich Niger Delta Region of Nigeria," *Nordic Journal of African Studies* 14.2 (2005): 208–34.

Malik, Amna. "Conceptualising 'Black' British Art Through the Lens of Exile," in *Exiles, Diasporas and Strangers*, ed. Mercer, 166–88.

McLuckie, Craig W., & Aubrey McPhail, ed. *Ken Saro–Wiwa: Writer and Political Activist* (Boulder CO: Lynne Rienner, 2000).

Mercer, Kobena, ed. *Exiles, Diasporas and Strangers* (Cambridge MA: MIT Press, 2008).

Na'Allah, Abdul Rasheed, ed. *Ogoni's Agonies. Ken Saro–Wiwa and the Crisis in Nigeria* (Trenton NJ & Asmara, Eritrea: Africa World Press, 1998).

Norris, Margot. *Writing War in the Twentieth Century* (Charlottesville & London: UP of Virginia, 2000).

Oguibe, Olu. "Finding a Place: Nigerian Artists in the Contemporary Art World," in *The Nsukka Artists and Nigerian Contemporary Art*, ed. Simon Ottenberg (Washington DC: Smithsonian National Museum of African Art, 2002): 257–78.

Ojaide, Tanure. *The Activist* (Lagos: Farafina, 2006).

——. *The Tale of the Harmattan* (Cape Town: Kwela & Snailpress, 2007).

Okonta, Ike, & Oronto Douglas. *Where Vultures Feast: Shell, Human Rights, and Oil in the Niger Delta* (London: Verso, 2003).

Okri, Ben. "What the Tapster Saw," in *Stars of the New Curfew* (New York: Penguin, 1988): 183–94.

Osha, Sanya. *Ken Saro–Wiwa's Shadow: Politics, Nationalism and the Ogoni Protest Movement* (London: Adonis & Abbey, 2007).

Rosenberg, Ingrid von. "Transformations of Western Icons in Black British Art," *Journal for the Study of British Cultures* 15.1 (2008): 59–74.

Saro–Wiwa, Ken. *Genocide in Nigeria. The Ogoni Tragedy* (Port Harcourt: Saros International, 1992).

——. *A Month and a Day: A Detention Diary* (Harmondsworth: Penguin, 1995).

——. *The Ogoni Nation Today and Tomorrow* (1968; Port Harcourt: Saros International, 1993).

——. *Second Letter to Ogoni Youth* (Port Harcourt: Saros International, 1993).

Savage, Polly. "Playing to the Gallery: Masks, Masquerade, and Museums," *African Arts* 41.4 (Winter 2008): 74–81.

Shah, Sonia. *Crude: The Story of Oil* (New York: Seven Stories, 2004).

Thompson, Carol. "Slaves to Sculpture: A Response to Patricia Penn Hilden," *TDR* 44.3 (Autumn 2000): 37–50.

Wenzel, Jennifer. "Petro-magic realism: Toward a political ecology of Nigerian literature," *Postcolonial Studies* 9.4 (December 2006): 449–64.

Young, James E. *The Texture of Memory. Holocaust Memorials and Meaning* (New Haven CT & London: Yale UP, 1993).

◄❖►

## Monika Reif–Hülser

# Ways of Transition

## Truth and Reconciliation Commissions: Controversial Strategies for Dealing with Past Violence in Societies in Transition

> It will sometimes be necessary to choose between truth and justice. We should choose truth [...]. Truth does not bring back the dead, but releases them from silence.[1]

LITERARY SCHOLARS AND PHILOSOPHERS have become increasingly interested in transitional justice, restoration, memory, and forgiveness. Inevitably connected with memory is the topic of the past, the weight that we are ready to ascribe to it, and its influence on the present. This is by no means a new debate; it acquires new significance, however, when applied to political processes of transition which we witness in so many countries today.

Literary texts mirror the societies from which they spring; they evoke the life-world, the politics, the moral systems, and the land of which they are a part. Hence, processes of transition, their forms, and the emotional strain they put on people's lives have moved to centre stage in literatures of and about cultures in distress. I want to discuss two of those texts – one from South Africa and one from Zimbabwe – and compare their approach to questions of narrative, truth, reconciliation, and forgiving.

Memory is the mode in which past events are reconsidered in these processes. I will accordingly begin with some reflections on the intricate relationship between memory and history.

---

[1] Antjie Krog, *Country of My Skull* (London: Jonathan Cape, 1998): 23.

## I.    Untimely Reflections

> To determine this degree, and through it the limit beyond which the past must
> be forgotten if it is not to become the gravedigger of the present, one would
> have to know precisely how great the *plastic power* of a man, a people or a
> culture is. I mean the power distinctively to grow out of itself, transforming and
> assimilating everything past and alien, to heal wounds, replace what is lost and
> reshape broken forms out of itself.[2]

Thus Friedrich Nietzsche writes in the second section of his *Untimely Meditations*, titled *On the Advantage and Disadvantage of History for Life*. He
published his *Meditations* in the year 1874, at a time when his mind was still
sharp and he wanted to draw attention to what he thought were the dangerous
consequences of the heyday of historicism. The historicists' argument that
everything in human life and thought had its causes in historical processes, and
the claim that it would therefore be the knowledge of history that held the promise of answers to a problematical present, was unacceptable to Nietzsche. He
turned the focus around, and claimed that overburdening human action and
human life with history would hinder creativity. By making the relativity of
existence an ever-present issue, young people would rather choke on history
than experience it as enabling.

Nietzsche, a fervent admirer of Ralph Waldo Emerson's ideas about the
damaging impact of history on the human mind, was strongly influenced by
the American poet and philosopher. In his essay *Nature*, published in 1836,
Emerson warned his fellow countrymen against making too much room for the
memory of old times and forgetting the future. "Our age is retrospective," is
the laconic first sentence of the whole essay. With the following lines Emerson
creates one of the most memorable literary passages about the Janus-faced
phenomenon of history. He writes:

> It [our age] builds the sepulchres of the fathers. It writes biographies, histories,
> and criticism. The foregoing generations beheld God and nature face to face;
> we, through their eyes. Why should not we also enjoy an original relation to the

---

[2] Friedrich Nietzsche, *On the Advantage and Disadvantage of History for Life*, tr. &
intro. Peter Preuss (*Vom Nutzen und Nachteil der Historie für das Leben*, 1874;
Indianapolis IN & Cambridge: Hackett, 1980): 10.

universe? Why should not we have a poetry and philosophy of insight and not
of tradition, and a religion by revelation to us, and not the history of theirs?[3]

Reading both passages, one can sense the community of concern between the
two writers, although they write from an historical distance of forty years and
out of somewhat different cultural and political contexts.

In Emerson's text, the main focus lies on authenticity of experience. His
attack is directed at scholars who supplant physical and sensual experience
through book learning – a kind of knowledge Emerson does not reject entirely,
but wants to be seen as only one possibility among others to experience the
world. For him, the immediate confrontation with Nature is the desirable, because fertilizing, way to learn; books mediate knowledge and present thoughts
that other minds had thought before, and so do not hold fresh promise for the
imminent future.

This is the point where Emerson and Nietzsche meet. The young generation
should be builders, creators, those who take over where the older generation
had to leave off. They are the ones who should not content themselves with
building "the sepulchres of the fathers"; rather, they should venture to build a
new nation.

Sixty years after the Declaration of Independence, Emerson feels it necessary to tell his compatriots that the country needs rebuilding, the political system needs restructuring, and the spirit of reform needs to be regenerated.
Hence Emerson becomes the spokesperson for what in retrospect was called
the 'American Renaissance'. This, as the term suggests, refers to a daring new
beginning in the course of which 'the fathers', though still honoured for their
achievements in the past, are no longer the norm-givers for the times to come.

When we look at countries in distress, when we see how they struggle with
the question of how to repair what was left after a period of political oppression and, as in Zimbabwe today, what is still there after decades of wholesale
exploitation of the land, Nietzsche's and Emerson's reflections do not sound
untimely at all. Reading the above passage closely, however, we realize that
Nietzsche does not wholly discard the workings of memory or remembrance –

---

[3] Ralph Waldo Emerson, "Introduction" to *Nature* (1836), in Emerson, *Essays &
Lectures*, notes by Joel Porte (New York: The Library of America, 1983): 7.

even if he wanted to oppose what he considered the pitfalls of historicism. On the contrary: he points out how difficult it is to decide at what point in the work of memory it would be healthier, more necessary, and perhaps even more healing, to forget than to remember.

According to him, the cultural task consists of "reshaping" ("*umzubilden*") by integrating into one's personal identity both the agreeable and the more shameful aspects of the past – indeed, to absorb these aspects ("*einzuver-leiben*") and recuperate or restore new forms out of the shattered fragments or unconnected left-overs of the past ("*zerbrochene Formen aus sich nachzu-formen*"). I understand this to be a personal as well as a public task, an individual as well as a cultural and a political challenge.

The violence implicit in the image of the "shattered fragments" which are to be reorganized into a new coherent form capable of holding under pressure re-calls an expression used by Michael Ignatieff in his article "Digging up the Dead," where he describes the hearings of the Truth and Reconciliation Com-mission as a "restitching together of a moral world."[4] It also reverberates with Toni Morrison's idea of a threshold between the compulsion to remember and the need to forget, which she puts in the following words: "What do we have to remember – and what are we allowed to forget?"[5] Her choice of words is less physical than Nietzsche's but it is all the same revealing: she expresses the constant tension between voluntary and involuntary acts of consciousness, and sees forgetting as grace, whereas remembering or re-remembering, as she sometimes calls it, corresponds more to an obligation, a duty even.

Quite differently, another writer, Salman Rushdie, under the immediate im-pression of Indira Gandhi's assassination in 1984 by her own Sikh body-guards, calls for "the clearest possible analysis of the mistakes of recent years." He closes his political statement with George Santayana's warning: "Those who forget the past are condemned to repeat it."[6] In his essay "Imagi-nary Homelands," which circles around the questions of why, what, and how

---

[4] Michael Ignatieff, "Digging up the Dead," *New Yorker* (10 November 1997): 93.

[5] From an unpublished interview.

[6] Salman Rushdie, "The Assassination of Indira Gandhi" (1984), in Rushdie, *Imagi-nary Homelands: Essays and Criticism 1981–1991* (London: Granta, 1992): 41.

we remember, Rushdie reflects on the connection between memory, truth, and narrative. He wanted to create an India that would be as authentic and as truthful as possible in his novel *Midnight's Children*. But in the process of writing he had to admit to himself that *"imaginative truth* is simultaneously honourable and suspect," that "the distortions of memory" produced a kind of "broken mirror, some of whose fragments have been irretrievably lost."[7] Like Nietzsche and Emerson, he holds remembering to be a vital necessity for the reconstruction of a shattered nation; it should come together, however, with the keen awareness that memories change in the course of time, so that looking back presents a different image each time.

Although different in context, the passages discussed here converge around the idea that there is a constant tension between memory and oblivion which can only be partly influenced by wilful action. Should we consider the past as a foreign country to which we have no access except through imaginative re-creation, as Rushdie argues?[8] Should we distance ourselves from the past, at least so far that the knowledge of it will not inhibit our present actions, as Emerson seems to suggest? Should we commit ourselves to discovering or defining the line that sets limits to our assumed sovereignty over remembering or forgetting, as Nietzsche meditates?

These questions raise intricate issues from the moment that the past becomes synonymous with authoritarian, dictatorial regimes – for human rights abuses, for mass atrocities, or for other forms of severe traumata.

In view of the memory-boom that has shaken the humanities over the last twenty years or so, remembering Nietzsche and his insistence on the dialectical movement between remembering and forgetting might seem an 'untimely meditation' in itself. It is crucial, however, for any reflections on Truth Commissions, and especially on Truth and Reconciliation Commissions and their efficiency in enabling transitional justice. It highlights the relationship between memory and oblivion not as an 'Either/Or' but, rather, as a 'One-never-without-the-Other' kind of relationship.

---

[7] Rushdie, "Imaginary Homelands" (1982), in *Imaginary Homelands: Essays and Criticism 1981–1991* (London: Granta, 1992): 10–11.

[8] Rushdie, "Imaginary Homelands," 9.

Truth and Reconciliation Commissions formed by analogy with the South African model ground their notion of justice and their factual jurisdiction on individual or collective memory; the remembered events are conveyed in the form of narratives which in some cases date back twenty or thirty years in time. Hence, in these proceedings, the interdependency of memory, narrative, and truth – a crucial issue, relevant not only for individual cases or stories but also as a general, systemic problem.[9]

## II.   Truth and Reconciliation Commissions

Several countries in different parts of the world decided to support the transition from an autocratic regime to a democratic policy through national commissions which had the mandate to clear the ground of violent actions committed in the past and to establish or re-establish justice among victims and perpetrators.

Jon Elster's study *Closing the Books* provides not only an extensive but also a systematic overview of the political processes worldwide which called for reparation, retribution, restitution or restoration.[10] In Latin America, for instance, such transitions were negotiated by the ceding military regimes, whose members quickly organized immunity for themselves. Some of the new democracies organized Truth Commissions which named the victims but left the perpetrators untouched.

---

[9] For a more detailed analysis of this question, see Monika Reif–Hülser, "Erzählen. Erinnern. Versöhnen? Beobachtungen zum Umgang Südafrikas mit den Folgen seiner traumatischen Geschichte und dem Versuch, die Demokratie zu wagen," in *Arbeit am Gedächtnis*, ed. Michael C. Frank & Gabriele Rippl (Munich: Wilhelm Fink, 2007): 229–49. See also Geoffrey V. Davis, *Voices of Justice and Reason: Apartheid and Beyond in South African Literature* (Cross/Cultures 61; Amsterdam & New York: Rodopi, 2003).

[10] Jon Elster, *Closing the Books: Transitional Justice in Historical Perspective* (Cambridge: Cambridge UP, 2004). See also Lucy Allais, "Forgiveness and Mercy," *South African Journal of Philosophy* 27.1 (2008): 1–9; "Forgiving without Forgetting," *SA Public Law* 22.1 (2007): 255–63; "Wiping the Slate Clean: The Heart of Forgiveness," *Philosophy and Public Affairs* 36.1 (2008): 33–68.

Argentina is one of the countries where high military ranks were accused, convicted, and put in prison. In addition to this, the new Argentine government organized a 'National Commission for disappeared persons'; the documentation is still going on and the numbers are growing steadily.

In Chile, the authoritarian military regime of General Pinochet was in power from 1973 to 1990. Military personnel, including Pinochet, tried their utmost to save themselves from prosecution, issuing a law of self-amnesty for all crimes committed between 1973 and 1978. Pinochet's authoritarian regime persisted until 1989, when, after the democratic candidate Aylwin won the elections, the Supreme Court blocked the latter's attempts to expose crimes against human rights committed in the past. Aylwin took another path and introduced a Truth Commission, whose members documented some three thousand human-rights violations and demanded that these crimes be compensated for. The trials, hearings, and commission-work lasted until 2002, the year in which Pinochet was finally declared unfit to stand trial.

In his book *Voices of Justice and Reason*, Geoffrey Davis also turns to the question of how reliable narrated memories can be and how closely they can be linked to truth claims as the basis for justice. Davis dedicates the last chapter in his book to these controversial debates around the workings of the South African Truth and Reconciliation Commission. He points out some of the most often mentioned dissatisfactions with the South African model, but he also underlines the fact that, more than any other Truth Commission – for example, the one in Chile, which bore many similarities to the South African situation – the proceedings in South Africa tried to make findings public, to issue amnesties and decide on punishment of the perpetrators. In Chile, by contrast, there were no such attempts to keep the public informed.

The regions of the world which dealt with this kind of retributive justice were mostly African countries. As Jon Elster shows, there were campaigns of genocide and human-rights violations in Eastern and South Eastern Europe, for some of which the investigations and trials are not yet finished. Srebrenica is only the most openly discussed case. But there are also countries which obviously never tried to raise the issue of a violent past in any way. Romania, for example, did not undergo such self-reflection. And although belief in the appeasing effect of Truth Commissions is not unanimously affirmative and optimistic, as we have seen, countries which did not try this "restitching of a moral world"[11] after the fact will perhaps have to face the consequences of this neglect in terms of social unrest.

## The Case of Zimbabwe

At this juncture, I want to turn briefly to Africa again, in particular to Rhodesia and South Africa, and intersperse a few observations on the different approaches to transition. The literary texts I want to discuss, then, will reflect on these differences in a significant way.

For both countries it is true that after the political turn to democracy there was still a white economic elite in power which organized the transition in such a way that white interests were secured.

As against what happened in South Africa, the political class in Zimbabwe decided explicitly against a *transitional* system of justice. The Lancaster House Agreement of 1979 which regulated the details of the power-shift did not include amnesty clauses for crimes and violations committed in the past. This Agreement ended biracial rule in Rhodesia and guaranteed the independence of Zimbabwe in accordance with international law. Prime Minister Robert Mugabe held a speech in which he declared himself prepared to end the struggles of the past in order to be able to reconcile the country and to satisfy foreign investors.

After this, the British assisted in setting up the Zimbabwe conference on reconstruction and development in 1981. At that conference, more than £630 million in aid money was pledged. The first phase of land reform in the 1980s, which was partly funded by the UK, successfully resettled around 70,000 landless people on more than twenty thousand square kilometres of land. After this, however, land distribution ceased and decisions about land ownership rested exclusively in the hands of Robert Mugabe. Whether the present situation in Zimbabwe is a long-term consequence of this transition remains very much an open question.

---

[11] See Ignatieff, "Digging Up the Dead," 93.

## The Case of South Africa

Among the many countries that tried to achieve the transformation from totalitarianism to democracy through 'transitional justice', South Africa is a singular case.

Before Mandela's release from Robben Island (the notorious prison island off the shore of Cape Town) in 1990, there had been negotiations going on between the then Prime Minister de Klerk, the ANC (whose leader Mandela still was) and Bishop Tutu about the parameters which would help effect Mandela's release as a relatively smooth transition – instead of throwing the country into a civil war and reviving the old antagonism between white and black people.

The establishment of the Truth and Reconciliation Commission (TRC) was meant to break the vicious circle of violence. By introducing new notions of how to deal with past violence, new ideas came into play – such as 'forgiveness', 'reconciliation', 'memory', 'truth', and 'narration'. I will come back to this aspect later.

The Commission took up its work in 1996, two years after Nelson Mandela was elected President of the new South Africa, for which Bishop Tutu was to express his political and cultural utopia, the 'rainbow nation'. The Commission organized so-called 'hearings' all over the country, from crowded small towns to the most rural places. TV, radio, journals, and daily papers reported and documented the stories recounted by the victims about torture, killings, rape, and murder committed in the name of justice. Indeed, the South African Parliament asked the TRC to provide a true picture "of the whole extent of cruelties, violations of human rights, torture committed in South Africa between 1960 and 1994." To verbalize, to witness, and to recognize past crimes publicly, to ask forgiveness for these deeds from the victim face-to-face and publicly, was meant to shame the wrong-doers and thus have a cathartic effect. The victims were asked whether they felt prepared to forgive or not. One criterion in favour or against was to be the decision whether the demand as well as the repentance were credible – and therefore true – for everyone witnessing the process. If these emotions could not be felt, everyone present could object to the perpetrator's plea for forgiveness. Enveloping everyone present in waves of emotion, the hearings established a collective experience which then turned into a collective memory. 'Truth hurts but silence kills' was one of the slogans of the TRC; again there was the evocation of truth without enquiring into the forms of its appearance.

The declared aims of the TRC were twofold:

1. to break the silence, not to hush up what had happened over the years of apartheid, hence to evade splitting the society into winners and losers; and
2. to avoid the effects the Nuremberg Trials had produced: namely, to criminalize the whole population through denazification.

In March 2003, Bishop Tutu handed the final report to Parliament. There were 22,000 documented cases which had come before the Tribunal between 1996 and 1998. The report lay open not only individual hearings but also the violence committed on both sides – by the apartheid regime as well as on the part of the resistance.

In the published version for the South African people, Tutu stressed his conviction that the only way to heal the wounds was to remember the traumatizing wrongdoings together, to create a collective memory which made every individual an integral part of the whole. Thus, sharing in emotional involvement was meant to create a community in the true sense of the word.

Geoffrey Davis titles the last chapter of his book "Doing justice to the TRC." He is aware of the many points of criticism brought against the hearings, the forgiving, and the reconciliation. The sharpest criticism was certainly the reproach that there was too much theatricality involved; the staging could only find acclaim with the people in the countryside, whereas in the big cities the hearings of the TRC did not draw much attention. But Davis also points out that, during the 1990s, it was perhaps the right procedure for channelling people's emotions and helping South Africans of every colour to understand that wrongdoers and victims could, in a certain framework, meet each other as human beings. In this sense, at least for the crucial time of the beginning of transition, the TRC was successful. Right from the beginning, however, there were also sceptical voices, particularly those writers and intellectuals such as Breyten Breytenbach and J.M. Coetzee.

## III. Literary Reflections of Narratives, Truth, and Reconciliation

In the last section of my essay, I want to discuss two textual examples, both of them dealing with the basic premises of the TRC procedure – one of them coming out of South Africa in 1999, the other out of Zimbabwe in 2005.

J.M. Coetzee's novel *Disgrace* was published in 1999 under the immediate impression of the TRC hearings. It tells the story of fifty-two-year-old David Lurie, twice divorced and dissatisfied with his job as an English professor specializing in Romantic literature and teaching Lord Byron in post-apartheid Cape Town. One day he gets involved with one of his female students. Knowing that this affair is likely to get him into trouble, he does nothing to protect himself from its consequences. He is dismissed from his teaching position, after which he remembers that he has a daughter somewhere in the country, with whom he then seeks refuge. The rhythm of nature, the quietness of the country life – genuine themes in Romantic writing – seem to calm him in his messed-up life. But there is unrest in the country. Shortly after he reconciles himself with his daughter's life-style the farm is attacked, Lurie assaulted, his daughter raped and impregnated. The perpetrators are not accused, the police are not informed; indeed, the whole affair is hushed up. In *Disgrace*, those who feel disgraced are also those who are punished.

Crucial for our purposes is the dispute at the heart of the story between Lucy and her father about the question of what to do about Lucy's pregnancy, resulting as it does from her being brutally raped by each member of a gang of black youngsters, one of whom turns out to be a relative of Petrus, Lucy's foreman on the farm. The debates with her father revolve around the following questions: should she go to the police and seek their support? Should she have her father seek revenge for her violation? Should she have an abortion? Should she sell the farm and leave the country? She rejects each of these suggestions, all of which her father calls the only "reasonable solutions." Trying to communicate to her father what the experience of the attack means to her, she enters the following dialogue:

> "But you are right. I meant nothing to them, nothing. I could feel it."
> There is a pause. "I think they have done it before," she resumes, her voice steadier now. "At least the two older ones have. I think they are rapists first and foremost. Stealing things is just incidental. A side-line. I think they *do rape*."

"You think they will come back?"

"I think I am in their territory. They have marked me. They will come back for me."

"Then you can't possibly stay."

"Why not?"

"Because that would be an invitation to them to return."

She broods a long while before she answers. "But isn't there another way of looking at it, David? What if [...] what if *that* is the price one has to pay for staying on? Perhaps that is how they look at it; perhaps that is how I should look at it too. They see me as owing something. They see themselves as debt collectors, tax collectors. Why should I be allowed to live here without paying? Perhaps that is what they tell themselves."

"I am sure they tell themselves many things. It is in their interest to make up stories that justify them. But trust your feelings. You said you felt only hatred from them."[12]

It cannot be overlooked that a sentence like "It is in their interest to make up stories that justify them" is a writer's comment on storytelling as a basis to legitimate actions. Significantly, Coetzee gives this sentence to Lurie. As we have learned to see him as biased on these questions, his contribution can be read as a 'true' statement, but need not be read as such. The author indicates a possible reading of this sentence but at the same time distances himself as author.

A little further on in the story, Lucy tells her father that the rape has had consequences:

They sit together at the kitchen table. She pours tea, passes him a packet of ginger snaps. "Tell me about the Durban offer," she says.

"That can wait. I am here, Lucy, because I am concerned about you. Are you all right?"

"I am pregnant."

"You are what?"

"I'm pregnant."

"From whom? From that day?"

---

[12] J.M. Coetzee, *Disgrace* (London: Secker & Warburg, 1999): 156–58. Further page references are in the main text.

"From that day."

"I don't understand. I thought you took care of it, you and your GP."

"No."

"What do you mean, no? You mean you didn't take care of it?"

"I have taken care. I have taken every reasonable care short of what you are hinting at. But I am not having an abortion. That is something I am not prepared to go through with again."

[…]

"Are you telling me you are going to have the child?"

"Yes."

"A child from one of those men?"

"Yes."

"Why?"

"Why? I am a woman, David. Do you think I hate children? Should I choose against the child because of who its father is?" (197–98)

As the story draws to a close, we learn that there are plans for Petrus to marry Lucy and take over the farmland step by step as his possession. In the same way he owns his wives, Lucy included, he will become the owner of the land, too. This is the truth, as the story tells us – but is this retribution? Restoration? Justice?

Apart from being Lucy's father, in his capacity as a literary character Lurie takes on the voice of 'common sense', arguing on that basis with his daughter, whose choice in this Benjaminian 'state of emergency'[13] is transition and the creation of new values. Is there common ground for understanding? Lucy repeats again and again not only that her father does not understand her, but also that he "cannot understand" her. Is this because there are different approaches to the role of the past? To the possibility of transition?

---

[13] Particularly in his protracted debate (1928–40) with the ideas of the political philosopher Carl Schmitt, Walter Benjamin posits a 'divine' or 'revolutionary' violence beyond state sovereignty and the law as a response to systemic states of emergency (such as fascism). See, for example, Benjamin, "Theses on the Philosophy of History" (1940), in Benjamin, *Illuminations*, ed. & intro. Hannah Arendt, tr. Harry Zohn (1968; London: Collins/Fontana, 1973): 259.

The novel has often been interpreted as a story with an allegorical ending: the unborn child symbolizes hope, future, and reconciliation for people with different ethnic backgrounds, different skin colour, different social classes. In my view, this constitutes a forceful closure of an open literary work, as the novel opens up more questions than it provides answers to the question of justice in South Africa in 1999.

Coetzee does not allow us to make distinctions between emotional response, reasoning, rational discourse, utilitarian argument in the dialogue of his characters. Even if we do not agree with Lucy when she tells her father that her decisions about land, blacks, and pregnancy are her very personal affair, we realize that the personal is political. But what does this insight bring to the question of staying on or leaving the country, of having the child or having an abortion?

Taking the many other narrative strands of the novel into account, it is obvious that Coetzee is pessimistic about Tutu's utopia, and also that, at a very early stage in post-apartheid history, he wishes to raise the question of what will happen when the strong symbolic figure of liberation, Nelson Mandela, is no longer active. Ten years later, as I write this essay, Mandela is still around, but more as a mythical figure than as a representative of political power. And, since he withdrew from active political life, power is shifting in South Africa.

Ian Holding's first novel from and about Zimbabwe, *Unfeeling* (2005), is dedicated *"For the victims."* Holding is a young Zimbabwean author who is familiar with the debates about the TRC in South Africa. He is also aware of the very close interrelationships among the political leaders of the two countries; Mandela and Mugabe were members of the ANC, and both fought for the independence of their countries. This is a heritage that weighs heavily on both sides. In other words, here the past is present in the minds of the people; it cannot be discarded, because it determines political decisions.

In this novel, the author creates a literary space to reflect the political and social situation in contemporary Zimbabwe as well as the controversial debates inside and outside the country about avenues of transition after Mugabe goes. As in the case of Ruanda, the model of the South African TRC meets with more criticism than consent, as its potency relied on individual face-to-face contact between victim and perpetrator. In countries where vast numbers of people and ethnic or religious groups are afflicted with a traumatic, state-imposed violent history, this format would not work. It would turn into an even more symbolic performance than the TRC.

In contrast to Coetzee's literary representation in *Disgrace*, Holding's novel appeals directly to the emotional if not the affective response of the readers. His literary means are the interior monologue (presented through a third-person narrator) and the effective use of the narrative present, flashbacks, and foreshadowings of events – so that, when plunged into the story, the reader finds herself in a true turmoil of indecisiveness, indeterminacy, disorientation. The only stable factor in the whole narrative is the land, the places of retreat, so that an imaginative topography of the protagonist's movements can be drawn in the reader's mind.

The protagonist is a sixteen-year-old boy, Davey Baker, who has lost both his parents in a massacre on the farm that his family had owned for several generations. As the novel opens, Davey has found his parents killed in a brutal attack by the local militia seeking to 'redistribute' the Bakers' land. The story is set in Zimbabwe just a few years ago, when President Mugabe passed a law allowing the mass seizure of white-owned farmland without due compensation, reimbursement, or payment. The militia took hold of key parts of the country and it is against this social and political upheaval that the story unfolds.

One of the minor characters comments on this situation. Marsha, a close friend of the Bakers', takes care of Davey after the killing, and tries to come to terms with the land question and the different feelings between Davey and herself:

> Although she wouldn't admit it, she hasn't got his fight, the simple refusal to give up and let go if they arrived tomorrow, crawling up the driveway in some ominous expensive car and demanding the farm. She knows they probably will one of these days, and when the time comes, then she's more than prepared to accept reality and quietly depart. But then, she wasn't born here.[14]

---

[14] Ian Holding, *Unfeeling* (London: Simon & Schuster, 2005): 22. Further page references are in the main text.

Without informing the Baker family, the government has given the farm to a black woman who gives the order to execute the Bakers so that she will not have to bother with the people who built the land. Roaming around on the farm, Davey is saved from meeting the same bloody fate as his parents, and the novel explores what Holding calls, with respect to his traumatized young protagonist, "the plight of the survivor":

> Poor Davey, she thought, was a walking, talking, breathing nightmare for them all, an icy plunge into that deep level where trauma and dread and violence are kept locked away. He stripped back layers of their own blindness to show what the future might hold, the plight of the survivor. (16)

After the murder, Marsha and her husband, who live on the neighbouring farm, take care of Davey. After some time, they decide to send him back to boarding school, so that he might be able to forget or be distracted from his haunting memories. It is at school, however, that Davey's traumatization begins to manifest itself. He begins to fight, smoke, and drink, and becomes a disturbing presence for his schoolmates as well as the teachers. His uncontrollable and at times unforeseeable behaviour causes general unrest. The individual story of Davey becomes the synecdochic representation of a tragedy involving the whole nation. "The pitiless scope of tragedy hits her," the narrator comments with reference to the killing, "such a vast act so insignificant to the wider world, a small entry in the catalogue of brutality" (45).

In one scene, Davey is forced to listen in church to a sermon on forgiveness; this brings him back to reality and makes him realize how utterly irreconcilable the words from the pulpit and his own emotions are. "We must never underestimate the blessing of forgiveness, the one true gift of the Lord to mankind," Pastor Fellows says, and his words make the tension in Davey rise.

> [Marsha] looked across to see him clenching his hands, flexing his jaw, his cheeks flushed. Jesus, she thought, please make him stop. But no: Pastor Fellows ploughed on, driving home his point.
> "Forgiveness is a powerful tool, indeed in the hands of mankind."
> At each intoned phrase Davey inhaled more audibly, drawing his face into a pained, angular tightness until Marsha saw a vein surface and bulge in his temple. As she reached out to put a comforting hand on his knee, he snapped. Swearing loudly he rose to his feet. (15)

One night, he escapes from school and makes his way back to Edenfields, where he wants to take revenge on the new owner. On his journey back to his former home, Davey meets some people who enter the stage of the narrative as if Holding wanted his readers to listen to a few voices representing average Zimbabweans uprooted from their native soil and alienated from their usual way of existence through the circumstances. He meets a poor but literate teacher who naively hopes that one day he will be given a tract of land; later he is picked up by a white-trash petrol-station owner who speaks his mind on the rich farmers "who've had it good for years" and should know that "one day it's all going to be pulled from underneath their feet." And he goes on to express his personal consolation for the bad times: "It's people like me who're going to be bloody laughing in a few years' time. We're the ones who're going to be spared all this bullshit" (143). The poor whites will keep their little businesses; it will be the white rich landowners who will lose everything. The scene at the gas-station makes it clear to Davey that the problem of justice or injustice is as much a question of social class as it might be of skin colour. The black-and-white metaphor brings no insight or solution. Davey's resolve to take revenge on the new black owner of his family's land is not a way to restoring justice, either. He feels trapped.

In this section of the novel, the difference between Lucy's controversy with her father and Davey's hopelessness in an inescapable prison of hatred and unending violence becomes very obvious. Coetzee's truth-seeking strategy is inspired by the philosophical genre of the Platonic dialogues where the pros and cons are discussed but the final solution is left to the enquirer. In Holding's novel, too, there is no way out of Davey's inner turmoil. He is still the victim of traumatization with no medium in his power to give words to his wounds. He is encapsulated in silence, alone with himself and the land, which can only offer space but no language to convert trauma into memory.

Early on in the novel, it is Marsha who gazes at the African sky, contemplating her place – as a white farmer's wife – under it:

> There is a kind of sanctity in this blue dome. Its purity holds her in so that despite the brutality and the killings, the fear and trauma raging below, she wants to stay here, do her best to hold onto her life. (22)

Again, these are very similar reflections to the ones Lucy engages in when she decides "maybe that is the prize we have to pay for staying on."

Davey does not have a language for these impressions; they remain images in his mind. Although the protagonist of Holding's novel cannot bear the idea of forgiveness, still having the images of his slaughtered parents in front of his eyes, the end of the novel suggests that he cannot think of any other way to cope with the past, either. He goes back to the farm, prepared to kill the black woman who is now occupying his house, inhabiting the memory of the life he had when he was a child. Revenge seems the only possible way to gain peace. However, when he comes to the farm he has to realize that

> someone else has "beaten him to his prize," or how it can be that she'd just died suddenly before his arriving to shoot her, he is overwhelmed by the whole flat, disappointing thing. Well, what does it matter? She's dead. (240)

He wanders aimlessly around the house until he takes his gun and a bottle of rum, and climbs up the hill in front of the house where he used to sit when he was a boy.

> He's alone. Invisible. Inaudible. Surrounded by trees, bush, rocky outcrops, he's just a tiny speck of nothingness lost against the vast, unfeeling wilderness. A cry will bring no response. Another gunshot will alert no one. It'll only send scurrying the birds, bush mammals, feeding beasts. And he's been in their domain once too often as it is. To them, he's a trespasser, an encroacher, an assailant. He knows what he knows.
>
> So he sits in the dark, lonely and regretful and unappeased, but with only the night lying before him, he breaks the seals on the rum bottle and waits patiently for Aunt Marsha to come in the morning to find him. (243)

The end of *Unfeeling* is as open and without answers to the questions raised as Coetzee's *Disgrace*. Both narratives show their protagonists in a transitional phase where remembering the past offers no more consolation than projecting a life in the future. Both novels point to the importance of language by re-capturing the remembered fragments of the past through narration, giving it coherence in the narrative flow. Hence, language and narrative provide a means of transgressing the boundaries between the literary, the political, and the ethical, but also as a means to reach out for the other by reaching out for oneself.

I want to close my untimely reflections with a poem by Antjie Krog, the poet, writer, and journalist who documented and accompanied the workings of the TRC in South Africa better than anyone else. In the poem that closes her book *Country of My Skull*, she evokes the 'truth' about the human condition:

> so much hurt for truth
> so much destruction
> so little left for survival
>
> where does one go from here?
>
> voices slung
> in anger
> over the solid cold length of our past
> how long does it take
> for a voice
> to reach another
>
> in this country held bleeding between us.[15]

## WORKS CITED

Allais, Lucy. "Forgiveness and Mercy," *South African Journal of Philosophy* 27.1 (2008): 1–9.

——. "Forgiving without Forgetting," *SA Public Law* 22.1 (2007): 255–63.

——. "Wiping the Slate Clean: The Heart of Forgiveness," *Philosophy and Public Affairs* 36.1 (2008): 33–68.

Benjamin, Walter. "Theses on the Philosophy of History" (1940), in *Illuminations*, ed. & intro. Hannah Arendt, tr. Harry Zohn (1968; London: Collins/Fontana, 1973): 255–66.

Coetzee, J.M. *Disgrace* (London: Secker & Warburg, 1999).

Davis, Geoffrey V. *Voices of Justice and Reason: Apartheid and Beyond in South African Literature* (Cross/Cultures 61; Amsterdam & New York: Rodopi, 2003).

Elster, Jon. *Closing the Books: Transitional Justice in Historical Perspective* (Cambridge: Cambridge UP, 2004).

---

[15] Antjie Krog, "Country of Grief and Grace," in Krog, *Country of My Skull*, 430.

Emerson, Ralph Waldo. "Introduction" to *Nature* (1836), in Emerson, *Essays & Lectures*, notes by Joel Porte (New York: The Library of America, 1983): 7–8.

Holding, Ian. *Unfeeling* (London: Simon & Schuster, 2005).

Ignatieff, Michael. "Digging up the Dead," *New Yorker* (10 November 1997): 84–93.

Krog, Antjie. *Country of My Skull* (London: Jonathan Cape, 1998).

Nietzsche, Friedrich. *On the Advantage and Disadvantage of History for Life*, tr. & intro. Peter Preuss (*Vom Nutzen und Nachteil der Historie für das Leben*, 1874; Indianapolis IN & Cambridge: Hackett, 1980).

Reif–Hülser, Monika. "Erzählen. Erinnern. Versöhnen? Beobachtungen zum Umgang Südafrikas mit den Folgen seiner traumatischen Geschichte und dem Versuch, die Demokratie zu wagen," in *Arbeit am Gedächtnis*, ed. Michael C. Frank & Gabriele Rippl (Munich: Wilhelm Fink, 2007): 229–49.

Rushdie, Salman. "The Assassination of Indira Gandhi" (1984), in Rushdie, *Imaginary Homelands: Essays and Criticism 1981–1991* (London: Granta, 1992): 9-21.

——. "Imaginary Homelands" (1982), in Rushdie, *Imaginary Homelands: Essays and Criticism 1981–1991* (London: Granta, 1992): 9–21.

◄❖►

FRANK SCHULZE–ENGLER

# Freedom vs. Anticolonialism in Zimbabwe
## Subversions of the 'Third Chimurenga' Myth in African Literature

A NTICOLONIALISM WAS NOT ONLY A KEY POLITICAL FORCE in twentieth-century world history, but has also been a major inspiration for the emergence of postcolonial theory and criticism; even today, the idea that 'postcolonialism' is essentially concerned with deconstructing the legacies of colonial discourse and with dismantling 'Western imperial narratives' remains highly popular among many of its academic practitioners. Yet, in many formerly colonized parts of the world, particularly in Africa, anticolonialism has turned into a new ideology utilized by incumbent power elites to legitimate their oppressive regimes. Present-day Zimbabwe offers one of the most blatant examples of an anticolonialism transformed into a stifling ruling-class 'truth' in the context of the so-called 'Third Chimurenga', the self-declared third war of liberation contrived by the present political regime under President Mugabe to thwart the opposition within the country, to divert national and international attention from the social and economic destitution into which the country has been led by its ruling party, and to cover up the massive violation of human rights that has become the hallmark of the Mugabe presidency.

The following essay will outline the bizarre suturing of anticolonialism and authoritarian oppression in 'official' political discourse in Zimbabwe and discuss the short-story collections *Writing Still* (2003), *Writing Now* (2005), and *Laughing Now* (2007) to highlight various modes in which Zimbabwean authors have attempted to unpick that suture and to project a democratic politics of civil society and human rights.[1] Finally, it will look at Chielo Zona Eze's recent novel *The Trial of Robert Mugabe* (2009) to highlight the pan-African dimension of the struggle against the pernicious legacies of authoritarian anti-colonialism, Zimbabwe-style, in contemporary African literature.[2]

What, then, is the 'Third Chimurenga', when did it begin to impact on Zimbabwean society, and how can its ideological underpinnings be related to the pervasive authoritarianism that has characterized the regime of Robert Mugabe, the former freedom fighter turned dictatorial president? The social and political background to this peculiar 'war of liberation' ostensibly targeting the former colonizers but effectively directed against vast sections of Zimbabwe's population is well-known. Immediately after Mugabe's ZANU government had come to power in 1980 in the wake of the collapse of the racist Rhodesian settler regime that had been defeated in the so-called 'Second Chimurenga' (the first Chimurenga having been the ultimately unsuccessful war against the British of 1896–97), internal divisions in the victorious 'Patriotic Front' composed of the nationalist parties ZANU and ZAPU and their respective guerrilla armies ZANLA and ZIPRA led to violent attacks by former ZIPRA guerrillas (so-called 'dissidents') in Matabeleland. These revolts were violently repressed by the notorious 'Fifth Brigade' sent into Matabeleland to 'restore order' in what became known as 'Operation Gukurahundi' ('Spring Rain' or 'Clear away the Rubbish'), a campaign of indiscriminate terror against the civilian population that left thousands dead and that – as Jocelyn Alexander and JoAnn McGregor put it in their contribution to a volume of essays on *Democracy and Human Rights in Zimbabwe* – led to a pervasive "feeling of alienation from the national body politic" in Matabeleland persisting to the present day.[3]

---

[1] *Writing Still: New Stories from Zimbabwe*, ed. Irene Staunton (Harare: Weaver, 2003); *Writing Now: More Stories from Zimbabwe*, ed. Irene Staunton (Harare: Weaver, 2005); *Laughing Now: New Stories from Zimbabwe*, ed. Irene Staunton (Harare: Weaver, 2007).

[2] Chielo Zona Eze, *The Trial of Robert Mugabe* (Chicago: Okri, 2009).

[3] Jocelyn Alexander & JoAnn McGregor, "Democracy, Development and Rural Conflict: Rural Institutions in Matabeleland North after Independence," in *The Historical Dimensions of Democracy and Human Rights in Zimbabwe*, vol. 2: *Nationalism,*

After an enforced period of 'national unity' in the 1980s and 1990s, the Mugabe government faced a major challenge in the late 1990s with the emergence of a popular democratic opposition and the founding of the Movement for Democratic Change (MDC) led by Morgan Tsvangirai. As a response to this challenge, the ZANU regime unleashed what became known as the 'Third Chimurenga': it expropriated the white farmers whose status had been protected under the settlement agreed upon during the independence negotiations, redistributed their land (often to party members and so-called 'war veterans'), and began a campaign of ruthless political violence directed against the opposition.[4] In May 2005, the Zimbabwean government embarked on 'Operation Murambatsvina' ('Drive Out Trash') and destroyed the homes of some 700,000 poor in Zimbabwe's urban slums, areas suspected of harbouring sympathy for the opposition.[5] Other 'operations' followed, such as 'Operation Dzikisai Madhishi' ('Pull Down Your Satellite Dish') in 2008, a campaign carried out by the Army to dismantle private satellite dishes to prevent the population from receiving foreign TV programmes,[6] the massive intimidation of voters before the election in 2008 which left over a hundred people dead and some 200,000 people homeless,[7] or 'Operation Mavhoterapapi' ('Where

---

*Democracy and Human Rights*, ed. Terence Ranger (Harare: University of Zimbabwe Publications, 2003): 129. For an incisive account of the Matabeleland crisis and the long-tabooed massive human rights violations during "Operation Gukurahundi," see The Catholic Commission for Justice and Peace in Zimbabwe, *Gukurahundi in Zimbabwe* (London: Hurst, 2007).

[4] See Zimbabwe Human Rights NGO Forum, "Their Words Condemn Them: The Language of Violence, Intolerance and Despotism in Zimbabwe" (May 2007), http://www.hrforumzim.com/frames/inside_frame_special.htm (accessed 1 September 2010).

[5] See Francis Musoni, "Operation Murambatsvina and the Politics of Street Vendors in Zimbabwe," *Journal of Southern African Studies* 36.2 (2010): 301–17.

[6] See Zimbabwe Civic Support Group, "Zanu-PF regime launches 'Operation Dzikisai Madhishi'," This Is Zimbabwe – Blog (11 June 2008), http://www.sokwanele.com/thisiszimbabwe/archives/1044#more-1044 (accessed 1 September 2010).

[7] See Susan Booysen, "The Presidential and Parliamentary Elections in Zimbabwe, March and June 2008," *Electoral Studies* 28.1 (2009): 150–54.

You Put Your X'), a nation-wide harassment campaign to punish voters who had voted for the MDC in the 2008 elections.[8]

As a result of this 'Third Chimurenga', which continues even after the settlement between Mugabe's ZANU/PF and the MDC negotiated after the elections in 2008,[9] Zimbabwe's economy has plummeted (with unemployment levels estimated at 94 percent at the end of 2008 and a rate of inflation running at 231 million percent in October 2008 before the Zimbabwe dollar was abandoned in favour of foreign currencies such as the US dollar in December 2008).[10] The health sector in the country with the world's fourth highest rate of HIV/AIDS has virtually collapsed,[11] political violence directed against the

---

[8] See Human Rights Watch, "'Bullets for each of you': state-sponsored violence since Zimbabwe's March 29 elections" (2008), http://www.hrw.org/reports/2008 /zimbabwe0608 /index.htm (accessed 1 September 2010); on post-2008 political violence in Zimbabwe, see also Zimbabwe Human Rights Watch, "Political Violence Reports: January–June 2009," http://www.hrforumzim.com/frames/inside_frame _monthly.htm (accessed 1 September 2010), and Amnesty International, "Zimbabwe progress on human rights woefully slow" (June 2009), http://www.amnesty.org/en /news-and-updates/news/zimbabwe-progress-human-rightswoefully-slow-20090 618 (accessed 1 September 2010).

[9] See Brian Raftopoulos & Shari Eppel, "Desperately Seeking Sanity: What Prospects for a New Beginning in Zimbabwe?" *Journal of Eastern African Studies* 2.3 (July 2008): 369–400; Nic Cheeseman & Blessing–Miles Tendi, "Power-Sharing in Comparative Perspective: The Dynamics of 'Unity Government' in Kenya and Zimbabwe," *Journal of Modern African Studies* 48.2 (2010): 203–29.

[10] "Zimbabwe's Unemployment Rate Hits 94 Per Cent," *Brisbane Times* (30 January 2009), http://www.brisbanetimes.com.au/news/world/zimbabwes-unemployment-rate- hits-94-per-cent/2009/01/30/1232818680519.html (accessed 1 September 2010); Chris McGreal, "Zimbabwe's Inflation Rate Surges to 231,000,000%," guardian.co.uk (9 October 2008), http://www.guardian.co.uk/world/2008/oct/09 /zimbabwe (accessed 1 September 2010).

[11] See Clare Kapp, "Health and Hunger in Zimbabwe," *The Lancet* 364.9445 (30 October 2004): 1569–72; Clare Kapp, "Health Crisis Worsens in Zimbabwe," *The Lancet* 369.9578 (16 June 2007): 1987–88; Clare Kapp, "Humanitarian Crisis Worsens in Zimbabwe," *The Lancet* 373.9662 (5 February 2009): 447; Peter Moszynski, "Health Crisis in Zimbabwe is 'Man-Made' and Needs Intervention from All UN

democratic opposition has reached unprecedented levels,[12] millions of refugees have flocked into neighbouring countries in Southern Africa, mainly South Africa,[13] and Zimbabwe now has one of the worst human-rights records on the African continent.[14]

What, then, are the ideological underpinnings of this 'Third Chimurenga'? Brian Raftopoulos has characterized the political project of the Mugabe regime in the following manner:

> Any reference to liberal concerns with human rights and democratic space that once informed the demands of the nationalist movement, was increasingly erased from the selective history of nationalism espoused by ZANU-PF, and increasing emphasis was placed on the commandism that had dominated liberation politics. [...] One of the most disturbing features of the Zimbabwean crisis has been the manner in which the Mugabe regime has articulated a repressive national politics to a broad anti-imperialist, pan-Africanist appeal, with essentialist notions of race as the central markers of conflict. [...] The Mugabe regime has been very effective in broadening its appeal through its use of an anti-imperialist ideological offensive, while domestically carrying out a very specific, repressive class project. The language of anti-imperialism has mobilised the collective language of the nation, in 'nationalist forms of globalisation politics' that attempt to conceal elite accumulation, and use popular mobilisation for authoritarian politics.[15]

---

States, Report Says," *British Medical Journal* 338 (13 January 2009), http://www.bmj.com.proxy.ub.uni-frankfurt.de/content /338/bmj.b100.full (accessed 1 September 2010).

[12] See Peter Godwin, *The Fear: The Last Days of Robert Mugabe* (London: Picador, 2010).

[13] See *Zimbabwe's Exodus: Crisis, Migration, Survival*, ed. Jonathan Crush & Daniel Tevera (Cape Town: Southern African Migration Programme & Ottawa: International Development Research Centre, 2010).

[14] See Zimbabwe Human Rights Commission, "Political Violence Reports: January–June 2009," http://www.hrforumzim.com/frames/inside_frame_monthly.htm (accessed 1 September 2010), and *Zimbabwe in Crisis: The International Response and the Space of Silence*, ed. Stephen Chan & Ranka Primorac (London: Routledge, 2006).

[15] Brian Raftopoulos, "The Zimbabwean Crisis and the Challenges for the Left," *Journal of Southern African Studies* 32.2 (2006): 209, 212, 214; on the significance of

Anticolonialism and the idea that the modern nation is inextricably and perennially linked to a history of resistance to outside forces are thus prime ingredients of the 'patriotic history' underlying 'Third Chimurenga' ideology:

> There is a public history in Zimbabwe that is still insistently propagated on
> state-controlled television, radio and in the state-controlled daily and Sunday
> press. This version of the country's past – now generally described as 'patriotic
> history' – assumes the immanence of a Zimbabwean nation expressed through
> centuries of Shona resistance to external intrusion; embodied in successive
> 'empires'; incarnated through the great spirit mediums in the first chimurenga
> of 1896–7; and re-incarnated by means of the alliance between mediums and
> ZANLA guerrillas in the second chimurenga of the liberation war. [...] the
> legitimacy of the Zimbabwe state, and of the Mugabe regime which embodies
> it, derives from this historic fusion of violence and spirituality.[16]

In his own justifications of 'Third Chimurenga' ideology, Mugabe himself has
time and again claimed that any political opposition to his own policies necessarily aids and abets the return to white settler rule and that the state terror
against the oppositional Movement for a Democratic Zimbabwe (MDC) is
thus a direct continuation of the anticolonial liberation struggle:

> The MDC should never be judged or characterised by its black trade union
> face; by its youthful student face; by its salaried black suburban junior profes-
> sionals; never by its rough and violent high-density lumpen elements. It is
> much deeper than these human superficies; for it is immovably and implacably
> moored in the colonial yesteryear and embraces wittingly or unwittingly the
> repulsive ideology of return to white settler rule. MDC is as old and as strong
> as the forces that control it; that converge on it and control it; that drive and

---

the Zimbabwean crisis in a wider Southern African context, see John S. Saul, *The Next
Liberation Struggle: Capitalism, Socialism and Democracy in Southern Africa*
(Toronto: Between the Lines; Scottsville: U of KwaZulu–Natal P; New York: Monthly
Review; London: Merlin, 2005), and John S. Saul, "The Strange Death of Liberated
Southern Africa," in Saul, *Decolonization and Empire: Contesting the Rhetoric and
Reality of Resubordination in Southern Africa and Beyond* (Johannesburg: Wits UP,
2008): 147–79.

[16] Terence Ranger, "Constructing Zimbabwe," *Journal of Southern African Studies*
36.2 (2010): 505.

direct it; indeed that support, sponsor and spot it. It is a counter revolutionary
Trojan horse contrived and nurtured by the very inimical forces that enslaved
and oppressed our people yesterday.[17]

A prime feature of 'Third Chimurenga' discourse has thus been the peculiar
suturing of anticolonialism and anti-imperialism, on the one hand, and an
authoritarian invocation of racial and ethnic exclusion and political uniformity,
on the other. As Lene Bull Christiansen put it in a recent essay on Yvonne
Vera's *The Stone Virgins*:

> ZANU(PF) has used a specific narrative of the liberation war to delimit the
> nation's imagined community discursively by defining different agents in
> relation to a schema of inclusion and exclusion [...]. By declaring a 'Third
> Chimurenga', which is defined as a final decolonization, ZANU(PF) defines
> itself as the liberator of the nation and its political opponents as agents of the
> colonial oppressors. This discursive appropriation of the First Chimurenga and
> the liberation war articulates the history of the First Chimurenga and the libera-
> tion war into a temporal schema that equates the Chimurengas with an on-going
> struggle against neo-colonial forces. [...] Thus, in ZANU(PF)'s political dis-
> courses President Mugabe's authority relies on defining the present time as a
> state of emergency, which is signified by the war against the neo-colonial
> forces that threaten the Zimbabwean nation with regression into a colonial
> state. In that way the Third Chimurenga discourse deems the current 'state of
> the nation' irrelevant for political debate and the government unaccountable for
> its mismanagement of the country, because the prime object of the government
> is to defend the nation against the neo-colonial enemy [...].[18]

How, then, has Zimbabwean literature responded to this suturing of anticolonialism and authoritarian repression? Putting the question in this manner immediately demands a critical caveat: of course there is no uniform Zimbabwean literature that could speak with one voice, and, as Ranka Primorac has

---

[17] Robert G. Mugabe, *Inside the Third Chimurenga* (Harare: Department of Information and Publicity Office of the President and Cabinet, 2001): 88, 89.

[18] Lene Bull–Christiansen, "Yvonne Vera: Rewriting Discourses, History and Identity in Zimbabwe," in *Versions of Zimbabwe: New Approaches to Literature and Culture*, ed. Robert Muponde & Ranka Primorac (Harare, Weaver: 2005): 204, 205.

argued, "the current 'patriotic' master fiction may be seen to have been antici-
pated, rehearsed and reinforced by popular adventure novels of ordeal published locally since 1980."[19] Nevertheless, a number of African writers in
Zimbabwe and beyond have made significant contributions to countering the
uniformity of 'patriotic' Third Chimurenga ideology, and it is these writers
and their literary responses that the present essay aims to explore.

I would like to frame my readings of contemporary fiction with two statements from Zimbabwean writers that embody two salient features of these
responses. The first statement comes from an interview with Chenjerai Hove
published in 2008:

> For me, even the financial, economic corruption begins with the corruption of
> language. Look at people talking about "American interests", or Mugabe talk-
> ing about "sovereignty" and "patriotism". All of a sudden there is a new defini-
> tion of patriotism. Suddenly, some of us who are critical of the system are no
> longer patriots or nationalists. [...] All of a sudden these words are being given
> a new meaning. So the corruption of language, for me, psychologically and
> emotionally, is the beginning of a multiplicity of other corruptions.[20]

The second comes from an essay by Brian Chikwawa which casts Mugabe as
"the blue-stomached lizard" and depicts the peculiarities of his regime thus:

> Here, there is a way in which life takes on a surreal hue, a way in which the
> state's voice, pitched against the ordinary folks' existential cries, has become
> detached from the realities of life. Here, the blue-stomached lizard and common
> people not only see things differently, but where this difference becomes clear-
> ly unbridgeable, appropriate corrective means are employed: the sound of the
> military boot on the street. [...] In Shona folklore, the lizard and the chameleon
> are objects of suspicion: a lizard became a chameleon by biting people and
> other creatures and sucking the color out of their bodies. Because the lizard has
> been a color thief, it is perhaps logical that today ordinary Zimbabweans –

---

[19] Ranka Primorac, "The Poetics of State Terror in Twenty-First Century Zimbabwe," *Interventions* 9.3 (2007): 434.

[20] Ranka Primorac, "'Dictatorships Are Transient': Chenjerai Hove interviewed by
Ranka Primorac," *Journal of Commonwealth Literature* 43.1 (March 2008): 139.

Shona speakers and non-Shona speakers alike – find that their lives have lost color and their story is altogether a distorted one.[21]

These two statements give voice to a twin desire which arguably also figures prominently in the story collections *Writing Still*, *Writing Now*, and *Laughing Now*: a desire to counter what is perceived as a corruption of language by an official 'patriotic' discourse of power and a desire to "give the colour back" to public and private life by countering the desiccation of public discourse with a diversity of viewpoints and a multiplicity of texts.[22] As the editor of *Writing Still* put it in her foreword,

> while writers may be social commentators, their role differs from that of journalists or historians in that good writing, by definition, offers multiple meanings and invites multiple interpretations; it allows us to perceive situations from many different points of view. Indeed, fiction, to paraphrase Iris Murdoch, is a way of telling the truth, and is sometimes the only way of telling a complex truth.[23]

If, as Flora Veit–Wild put it in an overview article on Zimbabwean writing, a major concern of Zimbabwean literature and criticism alike has lain in "de-silencing the past,"[24] the stories in *Writing Still, Writing Now*, and *Laughing Now* thus testify to a vibrant commitment of many authors to engage in 'de-silencing the present'. While Veit–Wild is certainly right in pointing out that maintaining literary life in the face of oppression is itself a major achievement and that the persistent literary creativity in Zimbabwe testifies to the fact that

---

[21] Brian Chikwawa, "Free Speech in Zimbabwe: The Story of the Blue-Stomached Lizard," *World Literature Today* 80.5 (September–October 2006): 19.

[22] For an exploration of these concerns through the medium of interviews and life-writing, see *Hope Deferred: Narratives of Zimbabwe Lives*, ed. Peter Orner & Annie Holmes (San Francisco: McSweeney's, 2010).

[23] Irene Staunton, "Introduction" to *Writing Still: New Stories from Zimbabwe*, ed. Staunton, xv.

[24] See Flora Veit–Wild, "De-Silencing the Past – Challenging 'Patriotic History': New Books on Zimbabwean Literature," *Research in African Literatures* 37.3 (October 2006): 193–204.

"Zimbabwe is not just crisis,"[25] many of the stories in these three volumes do also have an immediate political dimension of responding to this crisis, and it is this dimension that the present essay aims to explore.

In terms of a preliminary survey, this response can be differentiated into two distinct modes which, of course, overlap in many of the stories: in the first mode, topics and themes tabooed in 'patriotic' discourse are brought into the focus of literary attention; in the second mode, 'Third Chimurenga' ideology is directly addressed and criticized and the ethnic and racist divisions characterizing 'official' political discourse are challenged.

A number of topics and themes in these stories serve to illuminate the "complex truth" of contemporary Zimbabwean society. A major concern of many writers is the rapid deterioration of social and economic life. Thus, soaring inflation and social destitution are a focus of attention in stories such as Adrian Ashley's "Tables Turned Over," Edward Chinhanu's "These Are the Days of Our Lives," Shimmer Chinodya's "Queues," Rory Kilalea's "Unfinished Business," Christopher Mlalazi's "Pay Day Hell," and Erasmus Chinyani's "A Land of Starving Millionaires," while other authors target the economic, social, and political blunders involved in the enforced take-over of white farmlands (Lawrence Hoba, "The Trek," Charles Mungoshi, "The Sins of the Fathers," Vivienne Ndlovu, "Kurima," Julius Chingono, "Minister without Portfolio," or Lawrence Hoba, "Specialization"), the HIV/AIDS crisis (Vivienne Ndlovu, "Homecoming," or Derek Huggins, "The Lost Generation") or the plight of Zimbabwe's economic and political refugees in neighbouring countries; as the protagonist in Farai Mpofu's "The Letter" puts it, "it is always better to be treated like a dog in a foreign country than to be treated like a dog in your own" (205). Another major concern in many stories is political authoritarianism and violence. Thus, several stories deal with the 1980s mass killings in Matabeleland and their legacy in contemporary Zimbabwe (these are thematized, for example, in Gugu Ndlovu's "Torn Posters" and William Saidi's "The Winning Side"); in many stories, the political authoritarianism embodied in an ineffective, corrupt, and overbearing state bureaucracy is highlighted (for example, in Brian Chikwava's "Seventh Street

---

[25] Veit–Wild, "De-Silencing the Past," 204.

Alchemy" and "ZESA Moto Muzhinji," in William Saidi's "A Fine Day for a Funeral" and Edward Chinhanu's "The Chances and Challenges of Chiadzwa"), while other stories such as Freedom Nyamubaya's "That Special Place" focus on human-rights violations in the guerrilla camps in Mozambique during the 'Second Chimurenga'. In many of the stories, the connections between political oppression and a despotic gender ideology directed against women are thematized; yet others (such as Annie Holmes's "When Samora Died" and Rory Kilalea's "Mea Culpa") focus on homosexuality and lesbianism, both heavily tabooed in a 'patriotic' discourse of power that from the early 1980s has made homophobia a central pillar of its war against 'colonialism'.

Irony plays a major role in those texts that undermine authoritarian discourse without directly confronting 'Third Chimurenga' ideology. In Shimmer Chinodya's "Last Laugh," the humorous banter enacted in the dialogues among the customers waiting at a foodstall ridicules the pompous terminology of 'Third Chimurenga' propaganda and highlights the corruption of language effected by 'patriotic' discourse:

> 'Fish-mouth, I'm in a hurry. Can I liberate this plate?
>
> 'Eh, eh comrade, I thought we had long finished with this liberation business. Stay away from that plate.'
>
> 'Yes, stay away.'
>
> 'Stay away from stay-aways.'
>
> 'Off with you! You think this is sadza prepared by City Council labourers, ready in two minutes and stiff like a Shangaan staple.'
>
> 'Say, Mai George, are your chicken broilers, off-layers, good country road-runners or border jumpers?'
>
> [...]
>
> 'Don't jump the queue, Petros. You didn't buy nappies for Baby Jesus.'
>
> 'Now that you've finished taking over white farms, whose bedroom are you invading tonight, comrade?'
>
> 'I'm not a comrade.'
>
> [...]
>
> 'You're not a comrade? What's your real name, then? Donewell? Golden? Takesure? Toffee? Two-Boy? Obvious? Putmore? Forget? Definite?'
>
> 'Try Again!'

> 'No, he's not Try Again. He's Doughnut.'
> 'You would think this country has run out of names, sometimes. No water,
> no petrol, no electricity, no cooking oil, no bread, no soap and now no names.'
> (28–29)

Satire and irony also play a major role in those texts that engage in a direct
critical confrontation with 'Third Chimurenga' ideology. Thus, in Brian Chikwava's "ZESA Moto Muzhinji" the servants and workers of the new elite
composed of MPs, party bureaucrats, and businessmen refer to their masters
gathering in bouts of conspicuous consumption as "murungus" ('whites'),
while in Julius Chingono's "Kachasu – A Killer," the deadly effect of cheap
locally brewed alcohol is explained by the fact that, in former times, it would
have been drunk "on stomachs full of […] thick, white sadza," while today,
"sovereignty has replaced sadza" and "alcohol taken on a stomach full of
sovereignty tended to make us both offensive and aggressive" (53).

A prime example of political irony is to be found in Edward Chinhanu's
"These Are the Days of Our Lives," where the aptly named central character
Freedom can be seen to struggle through a day dominated by poverty, inflation, and unemployment. Returning home from a once more unsuccessful
attempt to make ends meet and confronted with a power cut (because he
couldn't pay his electricity bills) and a hungry family, Freedom exhaustedly
falls asleep only to be woken by the news on his next-door neighbours' radio
lambasting imperialist interference and extolling the virtues of the government:

> He heard about the brain drain, and how the British were financing the op-
> position so that it would win the next elections. That, of course, would never
> happen, because Zimbabwe would never be a colony again. Besides, Freedom
> thought, with every worker now becoming a millionaire, who would want
> change?
>
> Later in the news, he also vaguely heard the Minister of Agriculture talking
> about the country having enough stocks of maize to feed the whole country for
> the whole year.
>
> Indeed, with such promises of plenty and bumper harvests to come in the
> next years, who would want change? The whole world could go to hell. Zim-
> babwe would never be a colony again.

In Erasmus R. Chinyani's "A Land of Starving Millionaires," 'Third Chimurenga' tropes such as the perennial recourse to colonialism as the source of all social evils are turned around and brought to bear against the oppressive ZANU(PF) regime and the hyperinflation caused by its mismanagement of the economy. When Baba vaAlphabet, the eponymous protagonist of the story, who has been lugging a sack of worthless banknotes around which, it turns out, will not even buy him a single loaf of bread, is run over by the luxury car of a Member of Parliament, the banknotes printed by the regime which blames all social evils on colonialism are ironically transformed into symbols of the very colonial propaganda that the regime claims to be at work in every instance of social criticism or political opposition:

> The millionaire staggered towards the long line of tuckshops. The stagger of an inveterate beer-drinker after one bottle too many. Only he hadn't gulped anything for quite a long time. [...] He hadn't eaten anything either, or nothing but the national staple they now call air-pie – a euphemism for one big slice of *nothing*!
>
> Hunched under the weight of a huge plastic sack, the millionaire had the look of a man who carried the world on his back. [...] (38, emphasis in the original)

> Like a fiery bat straight out of hell, the legislator's blood-red luxury Mercedes turned the corner in the typical fashion of a well-fed politician with inexhaustible amounts of fuel to burn. Baba vaAlphabet flew into the air on impact, his sack of money with him, dying long before he hit the ground. His bag burst and the dollars flew into the air, scattered like colonial propaganda pamphlets dropped from a plane. And when they did flap down to join their owner, who lay prostrate on the ground, no one rushed to pick them up. (42)

A second line of direct confrontation with 'Third Chimurenga' ideology to be found in many of the stories is the undermining of the ethnic and racial exclusions characteristic of 'patriotic' discourse. This is not only true for a number of 'white' authors who attempt to come to terms with the legacy of white racism and the 'culture of superiority' it has given rise to and whose stories often feature characters seeking to explore possible avenues of (re)defining themselves as citizens of a 'new Zimbabwe,' but also for a 'black' author like Alexander Kanengoni, whose main character in "The Ugly Reflection in the

Mirror" discovers startling similarities between himself and the white commercial farmer on whose former land he has begun to farm. A particularly
striking example of what might be called an implied transcultural perspective
can be found in Charles Mungoshi's "The Sins of the Fathers," where the
views of Mr Rwafa, a successful nationalist politician and former minister, are
confronted with those of his family and of his son's father-in-law. In a key
scene in the story, Mr Rwafa (who, it turns out later, instigated the ethno-
politically motivated "death by accident" of his son's father-in-law and even
of his own grandchildren) is asked to talk about his memories of the liberation
struggle at a birthday party and starts on an increasingly furious hate-speech
combining anticolonialist rhetoric centering on "enemies of the state" and
"traitors" with a murderous ethnic divisiveness centering on ethnic purity:

> Mr. Rwafa talked of betrayals. He talked of traditional enemies of the people
> since time immemorial. Enemies of the state. Enemies of the clan, of the
> family. Looters and cattle thieves. Personal enemies. People who spat in the
> faces of their own people. Child thieves. Baby snatchers. He talked of his
> waking up to his mission. [...] His voice rose higher, hurt – terribly, terribly
> hurt – by effeminate, spineless sons of the family who marry into the families
> of their enemies, poisoning the pure blood of the Rwafa clan.[26]

The implicit and explicit delegitimization of 'Third Chimurenga' discourse to
be found in *Writing Still* and *Writing Now* forms part of a much longer and
broader literary tradition, of course, to which some of the authors in these volumes themselves previously contributed.[27] Yvonne Vera's novels form part of
that tradition of writing against anticolonialism as oppressive state ideology
(particularly her last finished novel, *The Stone Virgins*, set against the back-

---

[26] Charles Mungoshi, "The Sins of the Fathers," in *Writing Still*, ed. Staunton, 157.

[27] For recent overviews on the development of Zimbabwean writing, see *Versions of
Zimbabwe: New Approaches to Literature and Culture*, ed. Mponde & Primorac;
Ranka Primorac, *The Place of Tears: The Novel and Politics in Modern Zimbabwe*
(London: I.B. Tauris & New York: Palgrave Macmillan, 2006); and *Zimbabwean
Transitions: Essays on Zimbabwean Literature in English, Ndebele and Shona*, ed.
Geoffrey Davis & Mbongeni Z. Malaba (Matatu 34; Amsterdam & New York: Rodopi,
2007).

drop of 1980s political violence in Matabeleland), as do the writings of Dambudzo Marechera, which Maurice Taonezvi Vambe has characterized as "subversions of the allegory of nationalist models of resistance" that "dismantle the privileges of nationalist signifying processes."[28]

But political oppression Zimbabwean-style has repercussions far beyond Zimbabwe itself. In an ironic mirroring of 'Third Chimurenga' discourse (which presents the Mugabe regime as spearheading a pan-African confrontation with neocolonialism), intellectuals and writers in other parts of Africa have also taken up the Mugabe dictatorship as a pan-African issue – but as an exemplary case of a blatant political malaise rather than as a shining example of political resistance. A striking example of such a pan-Africanist revision of oppressive anticolonialism is to be found in Chielo Zona Eze's *The Trial of Robert Mugabe* (2009), a Nigerian writer's blend of fictionalized eyewitness accounts of murderous repression, political satire, and philosophical essay that not only exposes the disastrous consequences of Mugabe's regime for Zimbabwean society, but also explores the significance of the political ideology generated by that regime in a pan-African setting.

This setting is already invoked by the title of the novel, alluding to at least two major works of African literature, Ngũgĩ wa Thiong'o's and Micere Mugo's *The Trial of Dedan Kimathi* (1977) and Ali Mazrui's *The Trial of Christopher Okigbo* (1971). While Eze's novel follows a very different trajectory from Ngũgĩ's and Mugo's play extolling the heroic anticolonialism of the leader of Kenya's Land and Freedom Army who was hanged by the British during the 'Mau Mau War' in 1957, it abounds with intertextual references to Mazrui's "novel of ideas" exploring the ethical responsibility of one of Nigeria's foremost poets, who became a major in the Biafran Army during the Biafra War in Nigeria and was killed in action in 1967.

---

[28] Maurice Taonezvi Vambe, "The Instabilities of National Allegory: The Case of Dambudzo Marechera's *The House of Hunger* and *Black Sunlight*," *Current Writing: Text and Reception in Southern Africa* 13.1 (2001): 84–85; see also Maurice Taonezvi Vambe, "Dambudzo Marechera's *Black Sunlight*: Carnivalesque and the Subversion of Nationalist Discourse of Resistance in Zimbabwean Literature," *Journal of Literary Studies / Tydskrif vir Literatuurwetenskap* 16.3–4 (2000): 76–89.

Just like Christopher Okigbo in Mazrui's novel, Robert Mugabe is put on trial in the "Hereafter," and just like "After-Africa" in Mazrui's novel, "God's Court" in Eze's text is a decidedly pan-African venue closely interlinked with other non-African "Hereafters" that lend a pan-human quality to the judicial proceedings. While Mugabe's racialized logic ("no white God will ever preside over my trial," 13) is thus deflated by contrasting it with the universal scope of human-rights ethics embodied in the audience ("thousands of white and black faces – children, youth, men, women – all mixed together: black people of different skin hues, some as dark as charcoal, others as light as ripe banana," 14), the text nevertheless stages the trial as a distinctly pan-African event that systematically delegitimates the claim of oppressive anticolonialism to represent the spirit of resistance and liberation in Africa. As Mugabe nervously fingers his green-and-yellow-striped shawl bearing the inscription "Freedom Fighter," the court proceedings are opened by a collective singing of "Nkosi Sikelel'iAfrika," the pan-African hymn that not only became a globally acknowledged hallmark of the struggle against the apartheid regime in South Africa, but also served as independent Zimbabwe's first national anthem before being replaced in the mid-1990s by a more 'patriotic' hymn focusing on Zimbabwe rather than Africa. This emphatic subversion of oppressive anticolonialism's pan-African credentials is reinforced by the personalities of the judges conducting the trial: only one of them, Dambudzo Marechera, the non-conformist *enfant terrible* of Zimbabwean letters, actually hails from Zimbabwe itself; the other two judges are Steve Biko, the famous Black Consciousness leader killed by the South African apartheid regime in 1977, and Olaudah Equiano, the renowned spokesman of the movement for the abolition of the slave trade in eighteenth-century Britain and the author of one of the first black autobiographies published in the English language. Both the abolitionist movement and the anti-apartheid struggle, two archetypal instances of African resistance to colonial and racist oppression, are thus mobilized to counter the fallacious equation of oppressive authoritarianism with African liberation propagated by 'Third Chimurenga' ideology.

*The Trial of Robert Mugabe* is undoubtedly a book about individual responsibility: it is Mugabe the individual who is on trial, after all, and the principle of personal accountability on the part of Africa's political leaders is strongly invoked throughout the text. The fictional eyewitness accounts presented in the court (modelled on human-rights violation reports such as *Gukurahundi in Zimbabwe*, compiled by the Catholic Commission for Justice and Peace in Zimbabwe, but also staged as a congenial spin-off from the literary work of Yvonne Vera, presented by herself) all point to the fact that as Zimbabwe's President and Chairman of ZANU, Mugabe has been personally responsible for political mass murder, rape, and a deterioration of Zimbabwe's economy and infrastructure that cost hundreds of thousands of lives. Yet the novel refrains from vilifying Mugabe and putting the blame for the Zimbabwean tragedy on his shoulders alone. When Joshua Nkomo, Mugabe's former ally and latter-day political opponent, officially formulates the charges laid against Mugabe in the first chapter of the novel, he accuses Mugabe of "Guku Africanus" – a satirically conceived political disease named after the campaign of military terror unleashed by the Zimbabwean government in Matabeleland in the early 1980s that has since spread to various other parts of Africa and produces a skewed victimological logic employed to justify each and every act of political violence:

> *Guku Africanus*? It's a difficult term to define. The first thing to know, however, is that Zimbabweans knew it as *Gukurahundi*, or cleansing. It is a Shona word meaning the first rain of the season that cleanses the earth of chaff and dirt.
>
> That is the original meaning, but, as our dear readers would attest, over time, words acquire more meanings than originally intended. So, the current and most important meaning of *Guku Africanus* is that it is a curse, the original African curse, a *juju* hovering over the African sky whose potency lies in the fact that it intoxicates the African mind, especially that of their leaders. (20)
>
> *Guku* is born of the spirit of *ressentiment*, in which case a person develops a *gukunized* personality. The logic of a gukunized personality runs thus: I am a victim, therefore I cannot be blamed for any wrong, therefore I am right. A *gukunized* mindset finds nothing wrong in killing or harming other people because he already justifies this on the grounds of his having been harmed earlier. (33)

The personal tragedy of Mugabe highlighted in his fictional trial is thus grounded in the fact that he has become immured in the very 'Chimurenga' ideology that he had mobilized as freedom fighter; as Marechera puts it in the final verdict, he fell prey to an ideology of vengeance that consumed the spirit of freedom he had once struggled for:

> Frothing in your frenzy of vengeance, you became the archetypal African freedom fighter, who believed to have wrenched the torch of civilization from the gods for his people who, he thought, brooded in total darkness. You proclaimed yourself Prometheus. But in order that your torch might shine bright, you squelched your people's candles. Sir, you brooked no other light beside yours. You were lost in delusions of grandeur because your people wallowed in misery and fear. Is that greatness? (150)

In a final satirical twist, the novel extends its critique of anticolonial authoritarianism from the arena of African politics to global academic discourse by aligning the very term 'postcolonial' with the political malaise diagnosed as "Guku Africanus." In a satirical encyclopedia entry at the end of the novel, "postcolonial fever" is diagnosed as a "mental degradation" based on a victimological stance:

> *Postcolonial Fever*: mental disease. It is the condition of mental degradation rampant among the formerly colonized or oppressed people of the world.
>    Symptoms:
>    [...]
>    b) state of paranoia that the world consists of strings of conspiracy against the victim and his people.
>    c) the victim's unwillingness to emulate the path of progress from some other people; the victim sees this inability as being true to his roots.
>    [...]
>    d) the illusion that resistance per se is a virtue which implies the inability to transition to nation-building. (156)

While the satire at this point develops a polemical thrust that leaves little room for a more nuanced perspective on the 'postcolonial', the argument underlying these and similar passages in Eze's novel does, in fact, provide an important insight into the genesis of what Amartya Sen has called "postcolonial disaffection towards the West."[29] As Sen has argued in *Identity and Violence*, "one of the oddities of the postcolonial world is the way many non-Western people today tend to think of themselves as quintessentially 'the other',"[30] and thus generate identity constructs that remain perennially linked to the colonial past:

> While these "non-Western" – and sometimes "anti-Western" – views involve an emphatic seeking of independence from colonial dominance, they are, in fact, thoroughly foreign-dependent – in a negative and contrary form. The dialectics of the captivated mind can lead to a deeply biased and parasitically reactive self-perception. (91)

> The dialectics of the colonized mind can impose a heavy penalty on the lives and freedoms of people who are reactively obsessed with the West. (92–93)

In conclusion, the texts discussed in this essay provide a clear indication that we need to reconsider the habitual glorification of anticolonialism that continues to inform much of contemporary postcolonial theory and criticism. The idea that so-called 'postcolonial' literature is characterized by its resistance to colonial or imperial master-discourses has a rather hollow ring to it once it is confronted with the sociopolitical realities of contemporary literature in Zimbabwe – as has Fredric Jameson's well-meant, but theoretically, aesthetically, and politically counterproductive notion that so-called 'Third World literature' is necessarily an "allegory of the nation."[31]

---

[29] Amartya Sen, *Identity and Violence: The Illusion of Destiny* (New York: W.W. Norton, 2007): 85.

[30] Amartya Sen, *Identity and Violence*, 91.

[31] See Fredric Jameson, "Third-World Literature in the Era of Multinational Capitalism," *Social Text* 15 (Autumn 1986): 65–88, and Aijaz Ahmad's critical response, "Jameson's Rhetoric of Otherness and the 'National Allegory'," *Social Text* 17 (Autumn 1987): 3–25. For a critique of more recent attempts to re-install Jameson's 'national-allegory' hypothesis as a 'postcolonial metacritique', see Frank Schulze–Engler, "Transcultural Modernities and Anglophone African Literature," in *Transcultural Modernities: Narrating Africa in Europe*, ed. Elizabeth Bekers, Sissy Helff & Daniella Merolla (Matatu 36; Amsterdam & New York: Rodopi, 2009): 87–101.

What is at stake in deromanticizing anticolonialism in contemporary critical discourse is arguably a question of relevance – with regard to political responsibilities as well as to professional ethics. As Richard Werbner pointed out more than a decade ago, privileging anticolonialism in academic discourse can easily slip into a justification of oppression and end in a total failure of ethical responsibility:

> Silence is complicity, mainstream postcolonial studies often remind us in rightly speaking out against the living force of our heritage of colonial racism. But what about the impact of and responsibility for state violence against internal 'enemies', genocide and quasi-nationalism? Who, among the diasporic spokespersons for postcolonial studies, puts that on the critical agenda?[32]

Meanwhile, many Zimbabwean writers continue to confront the monological bleakness of 'patriotic' discourse with the stubborn hope that the defence of the freedom of speech and of human rights embodied in their work may one day become a resource that a post-authoritarian society will be able to draw upon. The chances of literature's making its voice heard in the face of a seemingly overwhelming oppressive apparatus may seem slim indeed, but as Ken Saro–Wiwa, who himself fought against another murderous dictatorship, has reminded us, "literature bides its time, waiting for the ripe moment – whenever that may be."[33] In raising its voice against an anticolonialism that has morphed into a vicious ideology of domination, the literature presented in this essay testifies to the hope that the ripe moment envisaged by Saro–Wiwa will not be indefinitely deferred.

---

[32] Richard Werbner, "Introduction: Multiple Identities, Plural Arenas," in *Postcolonial Identities in Africa*, ed. Richard Werbner & Terence Ranger (London: Zed, 1996): 13.

[33] Ken Saro–Wiwa, "A Cannibal Rage," in Saro–Wiwa, *Similia: Essays on Anomic Nigeria* (Port Harcourt: Saros International, 1992): 167.

## Works Cited

Ahmad, Aijaz. "Jameson's Rhetoric of Otherness and the 'National Allegory'," *Social Text* 17 (Autumn 1987): 3–25.

Alexander, Jocelyn, & JoAnn McGregor. "Democracy, Development and Rural Conflict: Rural Institutions in Matabeleland North after Independence," in *The Historical Dimensions of Democracy and Human Rights in Zimbabwe*, vol. 2: *Nationalism, Democracy and Human Rights*, ed. Terence Ranger (Harare: University of Zimbabwe Publications, 2003): 113–33.

Amnesty International. "Zimbabwe progress on human rights woefully slow" (June 2009), http://www.amnesty.org/en/news-and-updates/news/zimbabwe-progress-human-rightswoefully-slow-20090618 (accessed 1 September 2010).

Anon. "Zimbabwe's Unemployment Rate Hits 94 Per Cent," *Brisbane Times* (30 January 2009), http://www.brisbanetimes.com.au/news/world/zimbabwes-unemployment-rate-hits-94-per-cent/2009/01/30/1232818680519.html (accessed 1 September 2010).

Ashley, Adrian. "Tables Turned Over," in *Writing Now*, ed. Staunton, 7–15.

Booysen, Susan. "The Presidential and Parliamentary Elections in Zimbabwe, March and June 2008," *Electoral Studies* 28.1 (2009): 150–54.

Bull–Christiansen, Lene. "Yvonne Vera: Rewriting Discourses, History and Identity in Zimbabwe," in *Versions of Zimbabwe: New Approaches to Literature and Culture*, ed. Robert Muponde & Ranka Primorac (Harare: Weaver: 2005): 203–15.

Catholic Commission for Justice and Peace in Zimbabwe. *Gukurahundi in Zimbabwe* (London: Hurst, 2007).

Chan, Stephen, & Ranka Primorac, ed. *Zimbabwe in Crisis: The International Response and the Space of Silence* (London: Routledge, 2006).

Cheeseman, Nic, & Blessing–Miles Tendi. "Power-Sharing in Comparative Perspective: The Dynamics of 'Unity Government' in Kenya and Zimbabwe," *Journal of Modern African Studies* 48.2 (2010): 203–29.

Chikwawa, Brian. "Free Speech in Zimbabwe: The Story of the Blue-Stomached Lizard," *World Literature Today* 80.5 (September–October 2006): 18–21.

——. "Seventh Street Alchemy," in *Writing Still*, ed. Staunton, 17–30.

——. "ZESA Moto Muzhinji," in *Writing Now*, ed. Staunton, 41–51.

Chingono, Julius. "Kachasu – A Killer," in *Writing Now*, ed. Staunton, 53–61.

——. "Minister without Portfolio," in *Laughing Now*, ed. Staunton, 7–15.

Chinhanu, Edward. "The Chances and Challenges of Chiadzwa," in *Laughing Now*, ed. Staunton, 16–22.

——. "These Are the Days of Our Lives," in *Writing Now*, ed. Staunton, 63–70.

Chinodya, Shimmer. "Last Laugh," in *Laughing Now*, ed. Staunton, 23–37.

——. "Queues," in *Writing Still*, ed. Staunton, 43–61.

Chinyani, Erasmus. "A Land of Starving Millionaires," in *Laughing Now*, ed. Staunton, 38–42.

Crush, Jonathan, & Daniel Tevera, ed. *Zimbabwe's Exodus: Crisis, Migration, Survival* (Cape Town: Southern African Migration Programme & Ottawa: International Development Research Centre, 2010).

Davis, Geoffrey, & Mbongeni Z. Malaba, ed. *Zimbabwean Transitions: Essays on Zimbabwean Literature in English, Ndebele and Shona* (Matatu 34; Amsterdam & New York: Rodopi, 2007).

Eze, Chielo Zona. *The Trial of Robert Mugabe* (Chicago: Okri, 2009).

Gagiano, Annie. "Entering the Oppressor's Mind: A Strategy of Writing in Bessie Head's *A Question of Power*, Yvonne Vera's *The Stone Virgins* and Unity Dow's *The Screaming of the Innocent*," *Journal of Commonwealth Literature* 41.2 (June 2006): 43–60.

——. "Reading *The Stone Virgins* as Vera's Study of the Katabolism of War," *Research in African Literatures* 38.2 (Summer 2007): 64–76.

Godwin, Peter. *The Fear: The Last Days of Robert Mugabe* (London: Picador, 2010).

Hoba, Lawrence. "Specialization," in *Laughing Now*, ed. Staunton, 69–75.

——. "The Trek," in *Writing Now*, ed. Staunton, 115–20.

Holmes, Annie. "When Samora Died," in *Writing Still*, ed. Staunton, 83–92.

Huggins, Derek. "The Lost Generation," in *Writing Still*, ed. Staunton, 121–35.

Human Rights Watch. "'Bullets for each of you': State-sponsored violence since Zimbabwe's March 29 elections" (2008), http://www.hrw.org/reports/2008/zimbabwe 0608 /index.htm (accessed 1 September, 2010).

Jameson, Fredric. "Third-World Literature in the Era of Multinational Capitalism," *Social Text* 15 (Autumn 1986): 65–88.

Kanengoni, Alexander. "The Ugly Reflection in the Mirror," in *Writing Still*, ed. Staunton, 105–108.

Kapp, Clare. "Health and Hunger in Zimbabwe," *The Lancet* 364.9445 (30 October 2004): 1569–72.

——. "Health Crisis Worsens in Zimbabwe," *The Lancet* 369.9578 (16 June 2007): 1987–88.

——. "Humanitarian Crisis Worsens in Zimbabwe," *The Lancet* 373.9662 (5 February 2009): 447.

Kilalea, Rory. "Mea Culpa," in *Writing Still*, ed. Staunton, 109–26.

——. "Unfinished Business," in *Writing Now*, ed. Staunton, 143–67.

Mazrui, Ali Al'Amin. *The Trial of Christopher Okigbo* (London: Heinemann, 1971).

McGreal, Chris. "Zimbabwe's Inflation Rate Surges to 231,000,000%," guardian.co.uk (9 October 2008), http://www.guardian.co.uk/world/2008/oct/09 /zimbabwe (accessed 1 September 2010).

Mlalazi, Christopher. "Pay Day Hell," in *Writing Now*, ed. Staunton, 189–99.

Moszynski, Peter. "Health Crisis in Zimbabwe is 'Man-Made' and Needs Intervention from All UN States, Report Says," *British Medical Journal* 338 (13 January 2009), http://www.bmj.com.proxy.ub.uni-frankfurt.de/content/338/bmj.b100.full (accessed 1 September 2010).

Mpofu, Farai. "The Letter," in *Writing Now*, ed. Staunton, 201–205.

Mponde, Robert, & Ranka Primorac, ed. *Versions of Zimbabwe: New Approaches to Literature and Culture* (Harare: Weaver, 2005).

Mugabe, Robert G. *Inside the Third Chimurenga* (Harare: Department of Information and Publicity Office of the President and Cabinet, 2001).

Mungoshi, Charles. "The Sins of the Fathers," in *Writing Still*, ed. Staunton, 137–60.

Musoni, Francis. "Operation Murambatsvina and the Politics of Street Vendors in Zimbabwe," *Journal of Southern African Studies* 36.2 (2010): 301–17.

Ndlovu, Gugu. "Torn Posters," in *Writing Still*, ed. Staunton, 179–89.

Ndlovu, Vivienne. "Homecoming," in *Writing Still*, ed. Staunton, 199–203.

——. "Kurima," in *Writing Now*, ed. Staunton, 263–74.

Ngugi wa Thiong'o, & Micere Githae Mugo. *The Trial of Dedan Kimathi* (London: Heinemann, 1977).

Nyamubaya, Freedom. "That Special Place," in *Writing Still*, ed. Staunton, 217–28.

Orner, Peter, & Annie Holmes, ed. *Hope Deferred: Narratives of Zimbabwe Lives*, ed. (San Francisco: McSweeney's, 2010).

Primorac, Ranka. "'Dictatorships Are Transient': Chenjerai Hove interviewed by Ranka Primorac," *Journal of Commonwealth Literature* 43.1 (March 2008): 135–46.

——. *The Place of Tears: The Novel and Politics in Modern Zimbabwe* (London: I.B. Tauris & New York: Palgrave Macmillan, 2006).

——. "The Poetics of State Terror in Twenty-First Century Zimbabwe," *Interventions* 9.3 (2007): 434–50.

Raftopoulos, Brian. "The Zimbabwean Crisis and the Challenges for the Left," *Journal of Southern African Studies* 32.2 (2006): 203–19.

——, & Shari Eppel. "Desperately Seeking Sanity: What Prospects for a New Beginning in Zimbabwe?" *Journal of Eastern African Studies* 2.3 (July 2008): 369–400.

Ranger, Terence. "Constructing Zimbabwe," *Journal of Southern African Studies* 36.2 (2010): 505–10.

——, ed. *The Historical Dimensions of Democracy and Human Rights in Zimbabwe*, vol. 2: *Nationalism, Democracy and Human Rights* (Harare: University of Zimbawe Publications, 2003).

Saidi, William. "A Fine Day for a Funeral," in *Writing Now*, ed. Staunton, 275–86.

——. "The Winning Side," in *Writing Still*, ed. Staunton, 229–36.

Saro–Wiwa, Ken. "A Cannibal Rage," in Saro–Wiwa, *Similia: Essays on Anomic Nigeria* (Port Harcourt: Saros International, 1992): 165–67.

Saul, John S. *The Next Liberation Struggle: Capitalism, Socialism and Democracy in Southern Africa* (Toronto: Between the Lines; Scottsville: U of KwaZulu–Natal P; New York: Monthly Review Press; London: Merlin, 2005).

——. "The Strange Death of Liberated Southern Africa," in Saul, *Decolonization and Empire: Contesting the Rhetoric and Reality of Resubordination in Southern Africa and Beyond* (Johannesburg: Wits UP, 2008): 147–79.

Schulze–Engler, Frank. "Transcultural Modernities and Anglophone African Literature," in *Transcultural Modernities: Narrating Africa in Europe*, Elisabeth Bekers, Sissy Helff & Daniella Merolla (Matatu 36; Amsterdam & New York: Rodopi, 2009): 87–101.

Sen, Amartya. *Identity and Violence: The Illusion of Destiny* (New York: W.W. Norton, 2007).

Staunton, Irene, ed. *Laughing Now: New Stories from Zimbabwe* (Harare: Weaver, 2007).

——, ed. *Writing Now: More Stories from Zimbabwe* (Harare: Weaver, 2005).

——, ed. *Writing Still: New Stories from Zimbabwe* (Harare: Weaver, 2003).

Staunton, Irene. "Introduction" to *Writing Still*, ed. Staunton, xv–xvii.

Sugnet, Charles. "*Nervous Conditions*: Dangarembga's Feminist Reinvention of Fanon," in *The Politics of (M)othering: Womanhood, Identity, and Resistance in African Literature*, ed. Obioma Nnaemeka (London: Routledge, 1997): 33–49.

Vambe, Maurice Taonezvi. "Dambudzo Marechera's *Black Sunlight*: Carnivalesque and the Subversion of Nationalist Discourse of Resistance in Zimbabwean Literature," *Journal of Literary Studies/Tydskrif vir Literatuurwetenskap* 16.3–4 (2000): 76–89.

——. "The Instabilities of National Allegory: The Case of Dambudzo Marechera's *The House of Hunger* and *Black Sunlight*," *Current Writing: Text and Reception in Southern Africa* 13.1 (2001): 70–86.

Veit–Wild, Flora. "De-Silencing the Past – Challenging 'Patriotic History': New Books on Zimbabwean Literature," *Research in African Literatures* 37.3 (October 2006): 193–204.

Vera, Yvonne. *The Stone Virgins* (Harare: Weaver & New York: Farrar, Straus & Giroux, 2002).

Werbner, Richard. "Introduction: Multiple Identities, Plural Arenas," in *Postcolonial Identities in Africa*, ed. Richard Werbner & Terence Ranger (London: Zed, 1996): 1–25.

Zimbabwe Civic Support Group. "ZANU-PF regime launches 'Operation Dzikisai Madhishi'," This Is Zimbabwe – Blog (11 June 2008), http://www.sokwanele .com/thisiszimbabwe/archives/1044#more-1044 (accessed 1 September 2009).

Zimbabwe Human Rights Forum. "Political Violence Reports: January–June 2009," http://www.hrforumzim.com/frames/inside_frame_monthly.htm (accessed 1 September 2010).

——. "Their Words Condemn Them: The Language of Violence, Intolerance and Despotism in Zimbabwe" (May 2007), http://www.hrforumzim.com/frames/inside _frame_special.htm (accessed 1 September 2010).

◄❖►

GARETH GRIFFITHS

# Narrative, Identity, and Social Practice in Tanzania
## Abdulrazak Gurnah's Ironic *Paradise*

I N LATE-NINETEENTH-CENTURY COLONIAL TEXTS, TANZANIAN ETHNIC identities were frequently expressed through the discourse of race. These racial signifiers were often conflated with religious affiliations (e.g., by the simplistic conflation of Muslim and Arab identities). In reality, identities were rarely as clearly defined as the colonial texts of the period suggest. Such identities also employed a taxonomy intended to reflect the roles of various groups within the economic and material practices of Tanzania. These roles reflected the trade networks of East Africa and the economic and social relations that obtained between the littoral and the interior. Slaving and ivory trading were predominant. Zanzibar itself was the most important source of cloves in the period and maintained extensive plantations of spices. Group relations established by the slavers and traders continue to influence later constructions of identity by European colonialists, and those of the accompanying Christian missions. Colonial texts dramatized contemporary social practice, casting different ethnic and religious groups in fixed and exclusive roles. These roles persist across the very diverse and seemingly contradictory social performances that have been enacted since on this complex multicultural regional stage. As a result, these historical characterizations have shaped in various ways the formation of modern ideas of identity and so are crucial to understanding how contemporary Tanzanian writers such as Abdulrazak Gurnah have represented ethnicity.[1]

---

[1] The depiction of this region in late-nineteenth-century imperial narratives, briefly referenced here, is detailed in a number of my earlier published essays. These are: "Appropriation and Control, the Role of the Missionary Text," in *Missions and Colonies in the English-Speaking World*, ed. Gerhard Stilz (Tübingen: Stauffenburg, 2001): 13–23; "'Trained to tell the truth': Missionary Narratives and Christian Converts," in *Missions and Imperialism*, ed. Norman Etherington (New Oxford History of

In text after text disseminated by the colonial authorities and the missions in the region during the late-nineteenth and early-twentieth centuries, the slaver is identified exclusively as an Arab (occasionally inscribed as a Mussulman), the enslaved subject as an African, and the anti-slaver as a European. Groups such as the small but influential Indian community, which did not play what the narratives define as a principal role in this 'dramatization' of the region, were often ignored.[2] The identification of ethnicities with these fixed and separate roles allows the texts of the period to establish a radically simplified model of a society in which Arab slavers brutally attack and enslave innocent Africans who are then rescued by heroic European missionaries and colonial officers or officials. In fact, it was hard to draw any absolute line between the two ethnicities of Arab and African. Also, slavery in the region took many forms. While chattel slavery did exist, so did many other forms of slavery, notably pawning, a common form of debt payment in which a relative was 'pawned' as a servant until the debt was re-paid, a process which might take many years. Slaves were frequently converted to Islam, married, and integrated into the Arab/Islamic community. For example, Tipu Tib, whose African/Arab lineage is well-established, was also the most successful Zanzibari slave trader of the late-nineteenth century.[3] All these subtler distinctions are collapsed in the classic anti-slavery imperial narratives. Importantly, though, recent fiction from the region has opened up these issues in illuminating ways.

The Zanzibari-born writer Abdulrazak Gurnah's novel *Paradise* (1994) goes behind these colonial period representations and exposes their gross simplifications of East African social life. Its young protagonist, Yusuf, is subject to the widespread practice of 'pawning', a far more reciprocal arrangement than chattel slavery. The receiver of the pawn had clear obligations of care

---

The British Empire, Companion Volumes; Oxford: Oxford UP, 2005): 153–72; and, most recently, "Sites of Purchase: Slavery, Missions and Tourism on Two Tanzanian Sites," in *Economies of Representation 1790–2000*, ed. Leigh Dale & Helen Gilbert (London & New York, Ashgate, 2007): 17–29.

[2] To complicate matters even further, even the Indians ('Mhindi') were made up of several distinctive groups, including the Muslim Shamsi community, the Gujerati Hindu and the Sikh communities, even though, when represented at all, these differing ethnicities are usually homogenized in these texts.

[3] A further complication is that Christian missions often purchased slaves to 'free' them, and then resettled them in new multi-ethnic communities of converts. See Griffiths, "Sites of Purchase: Slavery, Missions and Tourism on Two Tanzanian Sites."

towards the pawned relative. In fact, it was frequently the pawned persons themselves who entered into such an arrangement as a means to reconcile debt.[4] Gurnah's novel questions the simplistic presentation of slavery and slave-trading in the colonial texts, but it also clearly condemns the excesses of chattel slavery and the brutality of its practice in East Africa. "Uncle" Aziz, as Yusuf is taught to address him, the successful trader who takes Yusuf as a pawn for his father's debt, eschews such slaving as "dishonorable" trade, and sees the pawn relationship as very different. What is Gurnah's purpose here? It is not, I suggest, to construct a defence of any of these forms of slavery but, rather, to show that slavery, like most other human abuses, is part of an overlapping set of practices that are not exclusive to any one group. Thus, chattel slavery is an extreme form of a practice of ownership and control of others which includes the pawn relationship, the gendered control of men over women (women can be bought, sold, and have no economic independence within the walls of Yusuf's master's house, the main correlative of the ironically entitled "Paradise" of the title[5]), the economic control of others as colonial master and servant. As the ending of the novel shows, this network of overlapping social control extends to the soldiers (*askaris*) in the armies of the Europeans at the outbreak of the 1914–18 War. During the war, tens of thousands of Africans were conscripted into military service against their will, an event which Gurnah's novel presents as yet another form of enslavement:

> When all the askaris had returned, and all the captives were gathered unsmiling in the middle, the sergeant marched up to the terrace to receive his order. The German officer nodded and the sergeant barked with satisfaction before turning back to the men. The captives were formed into two silent lines, and in the gathering darkness were marched off in the direction of the town. The German officer marched at the head of the shuffling column, his body upright and his movements precisely understated. His white uniform glowed in the fading light.[6]

---

[4] It is also, perhaps, worth noting that pawning and European post-slaving practices such as the indentured labour system, which was widespread in East Africa as Indians were brought there to serve the developing colonies, have more in common than is often recognized.

[5] The European term 'Paradise' is, of course, itself derived from the Arabic word for a garden, redoubling the ironic implications of the title.

[6] Abdulrazak Gurnah, *Paradise* (London: Hamish Hamilton, 1994; Harmondsworth: Penguin, 1995): 246–47. Further page references are in the main text.

The journey or safari is also a compelling metaphor in the novel for the idea of the penetration of a territory by external forces. In colonial-period texts, the Arab invasion is represented as brutal and rapacious enslaving and exploitation while the European invasion is depicted as enlightened interest (scientific exploration) or enlightened patronage (civilizing missions to modernize and convert the savage nations). *Paradise* revisits these prevalent representations of these two cultural incursions (Arab and European) and brings them into a closer and more nuanced relationship.[7] It also acknowledges the involvement of African ethnic groups in the enterprises of slaving and trade, as well as the role of Indians in the complex economic structures which emerged in the period. On the trading journey into the interior on which Uncle Aziz takes Yusuf, he explains to him the history of the region. After he finishes his story of the Omani sultans, he concludes:

> "You'll be thinking: how did so many of these Arabs come to be here in such a short time? When they started to come here, buying slaves from these parts was like picking fruit off a tree. They didn't even have to capture the victims themselves, although some of them did so for the pleasure of it. There were enough people eager to sell their cousins and neighbours for trinkets. And the markets were open everywhere [...]. Indian merchants gave credit to these Arabs to trade in ivory and slaves. The Indian Mukki were businessmen. They lent money for anything, so long as there was profit in it. As did the other foreigners, but they let the Mukki act for them [...]." (131–32)

As this passage shows, Gurnah records the prejudices that Arabs and Africans themselves display, in this case against the Indian minority. Nor does Gurnah gloss over the racism of both Europeans and Arabs towards other races and their similar divisions of peoples into 'civilized' and 'savage'. The violence and bigotry of the safari leader Mohammed Abdalla towards the peoples of the interior, with whom they trade on their journeys, clearly illustrates the racist attitude of the coastal Arab elite towards the 'savages' and unbelievers of the interior. The novel addresses the tendency to create demonized Others as a general human flaw and not an exclusively Arab or European practice.[8]

---

[7] I have discussed the possibilities of comparing these two events and the records that they have left in an earlier article: Gareth Griffiths, "Writing, literacy and history in Africa," in *Writing and Africa*, ed. Mpalive–Hangson Msiska & Paul Hyland (London & New York: Longman, 1997): 139–58.

[8] For a useful reading of this text, see David Callahan, "Exchange, Bullies and Abuse in Abdulrazak Gurnah's *Paradise*," *World Literature Written in English* 38.2

Thus, the novel acknowledges that the complex, multi-racial coastal dwellers have cast their own progenitors from the interior in the role of racialized Other, while they themselves exist in an uneasy inferiority towards the small group of aristocratic families (the Omani aristocracy of the coastal cities) who continue to claim a direct, unmediated descent from the people of the Arabian peninsula.[9] So, for Gurnah, such essentialisms are a feature of many forms of human discourse and racism is not a phenomenon that can be restricted to any one group. Despite this, Gurnah's novel clearly presents European colonialism as a far more destructive and divisive force than the earlier internal conflicts, which he also acknowledges were already present in the region. Thus, for example, when the German officer forces Chatu, the chief who has beaten Mohammed Abdalla and stolen their trade goods, to restore the latter, Uncle Aziz "lamented that they had been unable to settle matters between themselves and the sultan. 'Now that the European has arrived there, he will take the whole land,' he said" (172). This suggests that before the Europeans intervened negotiation between the different ethnicities was easier, since neither sought to completely dispossess the other. European colonization, by contrast, is seen as potentially destructive of the rights of all those who had shared the territory of modern Tanzania in the previous four centuries. The complicated relations between the various peoples of the region is suggested in the discussion that the local sultan and Uncle Aziz hold about the Europeans and their claim that their presence is in order to suppress the slave trade:

> "Your caravan trade is finished," the sultan of Mkalikali said. "These Mdachi! They have no mercy. They have told us they don't want you here because you will make us slaves. I tell them no one will make us slaves. No one! We used to sell slaves to these people from the coast. We know them, and we're not afraid of them."

---

(2000): 55–69. Callahan argues that Gurnah's novel "destabilizes our drive to found an originary zone of authenticity and harmony. Yusuf's world is one in which ultimately there is no conflict-free zone, and implicitly there never has been. This is not principally an account of European colonialism or its effect, although increased European intervention is viewed at the end of the novel with no approbation either" (57).

[9] It is especially ironic, as the great Belgian scholar Albert Gérard noted many years ago, that in many Arabic texts from the region people of Arab descent are self-described as 'white' as opposed to the presumably inferior 'black' indigenes, proving once again that the grotesqueries of chromatic racism are not restricted to any one society. Gérard, *African Language Literatures: An Introduction to the Literary History of Sub-Saharan Africa* (Harlow: Longman, 1981): 51.

> "The Europeans and the Indians will take everything now," the merchant
> said, making the sultan smile. (176)

In the words of Hussein, a Zanzibari who owns a small store in the interior
and in whose company Yusuf has an encounter with a racist European settler,
"'it isn't trade they're after, but the land itself. And everything in it … us'"
(86). The idea that the colonizer wishes to possess not just the land but the
people themselves brings it into much closer alignment with the idea of enslavement. Indeed, since Western domination is presented as a hold exercised
by the colonizer over the very minds of subjected peoples in this context, the
colonizer assumes the attributes of a surrogate father before whose power the
colonized child had no option but to bow. The parallel with Yusuf's relations
with "Uncle" Aziz is obvious.

Gurnah thus clearly reverses the hierarchy of demonization inherent in
late-colonial discourse, making the European the most savage and dangerous
group. In support of this, it is they who are exoticized in the text, and they
who are the subject of popular myths concerning their magical power and
their essential alienness, again reversing the usual pattern of colonial-period
discourse:

> One of the traders swore that he had seen a European fall down dead once and
> another one come and breathe life back into him. He had seen snakes do that
> too, and snakes also have poisonous spit. So long as the European's body was
> not ruined or damaged, had not started to rot, another European could breathe
> life back into him. (72)

Yet Gurnah does not merely reverse the categories of the colonial binary, but
also implies that they need to be addressed as existing in varying degrees and
in their different guises across all the ethnic and social formations of the region.

The choice of the young boy Yusuf as narrator in this text is crucial to this
wider aim. Child-narrators have been very common in postcolonial texts.
These young narrators present the society not as fully formed but as forming
in the text as their own consciousness of their world unfolds. They act to dismantle the idea of the naturalized subject and to highlight the role of cultural
and historical forces in bringing subjectivity into being. The reader is aware of
the child-narrator both as innocent and open observer and as the product of
shaping discursive and ideological forces. As children mature, so they
struggle to make sense of the practices that surround them, allowing author
and reader to open up the hidden spaces that the ideologies of their societies

cannot address. Thus, when we first encounter the idea of discrimination in *Paradise* it is through a child's eyes and we see (though he does not, at least initially) how forms of ethnic and racial discrimination are also bound up with others such as those based on gender:

> That was his first foreboding. When he saw the tears in his mother's eyes his heart leapt with terror. He had never seen his mother do that before […].
>
> Perhaps his father had said how fine his other family had been […]. Once he heard him say to her that she was the daughter of a hill tribesman from the back of Taita who lived in a smoky hut and wore stinking goatskin, and thought five goats and two sacks of beans a good price for any woman. "If anything happens to you, they'll sell me another one like you from their pens," he said. She was not to give herself airs just because she had grown up on the coast among civilized people. (13)

In fact, his mother's tears are because she has just heard that her child (Yusuf) is to be sent away as a pawn for her husband's debts. Our ignorance of the process and what it entails is shared by the young boy. As he learns over the next weeks what his fate is to be as a pawn, so we gradually also learn about that institution and how it interrelates with the other patterns of exclusion, discrimination, and control that make up the weave of this complex society. Thus, we cannot escape into some easy outsider stance which allows us access to a superior judgment. In these and other ways, Gurnah has succeeded in presenting us with a challenging alternative to the simplified views of an outsider exemplified in colonial texts and to the equally simplified view of those early 'insider' postcolonial texts written to refute them. As we enter a new and challenging stage of the postcolonial experience, this rich novel illustrates how terms such as 'outsider' and 'insider' have become more difficult to define and the speaking-positions of the subjects of the colonial encounter more complex to articulate.

It might therefore be useful if we begin to think, as the writing of Gurnah has implied, less in fixed racialized or ethnicized groupings than in shifting roles: i.e. interchangeable and overlapping functions in a continuum of social practices. These roles are enacted within a distinctive set of spatial and cultural (geo-cultural) formations – in this case, the formation of the coast (or littoral) versus the interior. The discursive economies of representation reflect the material practices of the engagement of these two regions in various forms of ongoing trade exchange in which the bodies of the interior peoples ('Africans') are the commodity and the people of the littoral ('Arabs', 'Europeans',

and 'Indians') are the purchasers, controllers of commerce, and interveners in
its regulation.

If colonial representations of Arab and African ethnicity is problematized
in *Paradise*, other recent texts have drawn attention to further issues in the
complex interweave of cultures along the East African coast.[10] Visibility in
representation is a factor of the public acknowledgement of the existing and
competing subject-positions of ethnic groups. Some groups that exercised a
very important role in the economies binding together littoral and interior in
the region, such as the small but wealthy Indian merchant community, hardly
feature at all in the written discourse of the colonial period. And this is despite
the fact that Indians frequently served as the chief economic and financial ad-
visers to the Omani Sultans, and as financiers it was their lending capacity
that underwrote many of the Arab slaving ventures, as *Paradise* makes clear.
They played a similar role in financing and underwriting the later 'exploration' journeying of Europeans, whose disruptive and often violent incursions
into the interior were legitimized as part of the process by which commerce
would open up the interior to trade, a trade that would replace and override
the need for a slaving economy in the region.

Nor has the practice of Gurnah's fiction been restricted to this revisionary
reading of the historical period and its narratives. His next novel after *Para-*

---

[10] Notable in this connection are the early writings of M.G. Vassanji detailing the
life of the Shamsi, the Ismaili Muslim Indian community of East Africa. Vassanji's
collection of stories entitled *The Gunny Sack* (1989) records the open prejudice that
characterizes the representation of the Indian minority in contemporary political discourse, reflecting the continuing prejudice in the modern period that Gurnah records in
*Paradise* as existing in the colonial era. Vassanji describes the reactions of a Tanzanian
crowd to a politician explicating the colours of the Tanzanian flag (black, blue, green,
and yellow), as part of his attempt to describe how the two republics of Zanzibar and
Tanganyika, originally separate at independence, are now re-unified in a single country
in which green represents its fertile land, blue the sea that borders its coast, and black
its people. What about the yellow? someone asks. Before the official explanation can
be given (that it represents the mineral wealth of the country), another voice interjects
that the yellow streak is for the Mhindi (the Indian minority). By recording this taste-
less joke, Vassanji's text reinforces the fact that even narratives such as Gurnah's
*Paradise* which consciously seek to undermine the simplifications involved in collap-
sing Arab and African identities into a single contemporary signifier such as 'black-
ness', underplay the role of the Indian minority communities, a role that is still largely
ignored in the contemporary official discourse of the nation.

*dise, Admiring Silence* (1996), showed how ideas of a racially distinct and even superior cultural heritage by 'Arab' Zanzibaris have again surfaced as Zanzibar becomes increasingly wealthy from modern cultural heritage tourism. The novel, which traces the return of its expatriate hero, who, like Gurnah himself, has lived most of his adult life in exile in England, records the period of brutality following the mainland government's overthrow of the separatist revolt by Zanzibaris, a revolt which seeks to reassert Zanzibari Arab identity as distinct from African mainland identity. For Gurnah, the revolt is simply a means of allowing local politicians, both on Zanzibar and on the mainland, to retain personal power and wealth by invoking racial, ethnic, and regional signifiers. Gurnah is also cynical about the way in which the post-independence regimes continue to blame colonialism as a way of avoiding responsibility for their own recent failures and excesses, even though he is equally clear that colonialism is an ongoing part of that failure and he in no way excuses it or its role. He does, however, question both forms of self-serving narrative – that of the locals who long for the colonial past and its nostalgic reassertion, and that of the postcolonial decolonizers, who appeal for unity and sacrifice while enriching themselves and their specific, ethnic cohorts and supporters:

> History turns out to be a bundle of lies that covers up centuries of murderous rampage around the globe – and guess who the barbarians are supposed to be. The most gentle of stories are interpreted as cunning metaphors that turn them into beasts and sub-humans, miserable creatures and slaves. Even their evident brutalities against each other can always be blamed on something else: slavery, colonialism, Christianity, a European education, anything but their own, unmasterable greed or their unregulated violence, or their artful dodges to escape the burden of having to do anything about anything.[11]

Similarly, although Indians played a vital role in sustaining the Omani Sultanate through almost a century of domination of the littoral trade, as Gurnah's *Paradise* suggests, the later novel shows how they have been largely excluded from a public role in the construction of the identities of the modern Tanzanian state, whether internally or in its public face through the discourse of tourism. Increasingly, Zanzibar stresses only its Arab heritage in the buildings of the Omani Sultans and in the old houses of the capital, Stone Town, now a World Heritage site. Conversely, mainland Tanzania is represented as being the culture of only one specific group, the people of the interior, whose

---

[11] Abdulrazak Gurnah, *Admiring Silence* (London: Hamish Hamilton: 1996): 7.

status as slave has now been reversed into that of sole authentic indigene. But such a reversal of their position on the power map of Tanzania does not acknowledge, let alone address, the ongoing problem of integration in a multiethnic region whose inhabitants have been anything but isolated genetically or culturally for five hundred years or more. It serves, rather, a specific political phantasm through which a certain limited, even myopic myth of cultural authenticity can be defended, a myth increasingly fashioned to support a limited and exclusionary idea of authentic heritage. This might matter less if it did not set the stage for a development of further racial and religious antagonism. In this climate, literary texts such as *Paradise* can play a vital role in questioning these hidden assumptions, tracing and exposing their origins and their persistent potential for reinforcing prejudicial constructions of ethnicity and identity in contemporary social practice.

## WORKS CITED

Callahan, David. "Exchange, Bullies and Abuse in Abdulrazak Gurnah's *Paradise*," *World Literature Written in English* 38.2 (2000): 55–69.

Gérard, Albert. *African Language Literatures: An Introduction to the Literary History of Sub-Saharan Africa* (Harlow: Longman,1981).

Griffiths, Gareth. "Appropriation and Control, the Role of the Missionary Text," in *Missions and Colonies in the English-Speaking World*, ed. Gerhard Stilz (Tübingen: Stauffenburg, 2001): 13–23.

——. "Sites of Purchase: Slavery, Missions and Tourism on Two Tanzanian Sites" in *Economies of Representation 1790–2000*, ed. Leigh Dale & Helen Gilbert (London & New York: Ashgate, 2007): 17–29.

——. "'Trained to tell the truth': Missionary Narratives and Christian Converts," in *Missions and Imperialism*, ed. Norman Etherington (New Oxford History of The British Empire, Companion Volumes, Oxford: Oxford UP, 2005): 153–72.

——. "Writing, literacy and history in Africa," in *Writing and Africa*, ed. Mpalive–Hangson Msiska & Paul Hyland (London & New York: Longman, 1997): 139–58.

Gurnah, Abdulrazak. *Admiring Silence* (London: Hamish Hamilton, 1996).

——. *Paradise* (London: Hamish Hamilton, 1994; Harmondsworth: Penguin, 1995).

Vassanji, M.G. *The Gunny Sack* (Oxford: Heinemann International, 1989).

⟨❖⟩

JANE PLASTOW

# Finding Children's Voices
## Using Theatre to Critique the Education System in England and Eritrea

T HIS ARTICLE EXPLORES TWO PROJECTS WHICH USED PERFORMANCE, in Leeds and Eritrea, to seek to encourage creative learning and to understand children's feelings and thoughts about the educational experience they were being offered.[1] In Eritrea these were the central objectives of the work, while in Leeds the root of the project had been a performative

---

[1] The project in Leeds, *Encounters with Africa*, was the University of Leeds centenary theatre project and was funded with support from the Vice-Chancellor, the Workshop Theatre and The West Yorkshire Playhouse. Carried out in 2004 it brought together pupils from the inner-city City of Leeds School, students and staff from the Workshop Theatre along with specialist professionals employed for the project. Over a period of some five months the production was devised out of a workshop process privileging the ideas and experiences of the volunteer performers. The production was toured to a number of high schools in the Leeds area, to the West Yorkshire Playhouse and was finally shown at the international *Performing Africa* conference at Leeds University.

The Eritrean project was carried out in December 2005 and January 2006. The project, funded by the British Academy, the University of Leeds, and the Eritrean Ministry of Education, was led by Jane Plastow and John Holmes in conjunction with the Asmara Teacher Training Institute and the Eritrean Bureau of Cultural Affairs. Working with teachers from six schools and pupils from two, in She'eb and Bogu, the project introduced child-centred teaching and theatre methodologies and explored the attitudes of children to their educational experience. For more information on the project, see Jane Plastow, "Finding Children's Voices: a pilot project using performance to discuss attitudes to education among primary school children in two Eritrean villages," *Research in Drama Education* 12.3 (November 2007): 345–54, and John Holmes, "Culture and Identity in Rural Africa: Representation Through Literacy," *Language and Education* 22.6 (2008): 363–79.

exploration of young peoples' understandings of Africa from within a Leeds context, and this led organically into an engagement with the educational experience of the children concerned. In both cases the work sought to raise children's self-esteem in relation to their ability to create meaningful, valued work, and to challenge adult audiences to take their sometimes critical views of the educational establishment seriously.

The conception of both projects was mine, although I only facilitated the work in Eritrea; in Leeds I acted as producer. The driving impetus for the projects was both experiential and theory-based. In terms of theory, I have long been led by the work of Paulo Freire and his ideas on education as an exchange of ideas between learner and teacher driven by what learners find relevant to their situation as opposed to the dominant 'banking' conception of teaching where pupils passively receive what the authorities consider useful for them to know.[2] This perspective has been augmented by the ideas of A.S. Neill and Rudolf Steiner about creative and child-led learning.[3] Experientially, my growing doubts about contemporary education models have been fed by my experiences as a high-school teacher in the 1980s in the Gambia, West Africa, where I experienced at first hand authoritarian models of neocolonial education; by interaction with a number of schools in Leeds where I have been involved in drama-based projects; and, probably most profoundly, by my own son's at times highly confrontational interaction with a British education system that demands obedience without feeling the need to explain why pupils should act in particular ways, and where the exam system appears to militate against enquiry outside the narrow limits of what is required to achieve good grades.

The children concerned in the projects I am discussing were aged between ten and fifteen. In the Eritrean case we worked with sixth-year children in two primary schools, each of which used a different language medium, since primary education in that country is in the mother tongue, and in Leeds we worked in the City of Leeds School, an inner-city institution close to the Uni-

---

[2] See Paulo Freire, *Pedagogy of the Oppressed*, tr. Myra Bergman Ramos (*Pedagogía del oprimido*, 1970; Harmondsworth: Penguin, 1996).

[3] See A.S. Neill, *Summerhill: A Radical Approach to Child Rearing* (New York: Hart, 1960), Paul Adams et al. *Children's Rights: Toward the Liberation of the Child* (New York: Praeger, 1971), and Rudolf Steiner, *The Education of the Child in the Light of Anthroposophy*, tr. George & Mary Adams (*Die Erziehung des Kindes vom Gesichtspunkte der Geisteswissenschaft*, 1907; London: Rudolf Steiner, 1965).

versity that is highly multicultural and has many children from challenging backgrounds. In both cases, the children themselves devised the pieces they produced for a public audience with the support of leading theatre directors and facilitators, so that the work reflected as truly as possible insights and opinions developed during a workshop process that used a variety of creative mediums.

## City of Leeds – Encounters with Africa

The project I produced in 2004 at City of Leeds School brought together a voluntary group of pupils and theatre students (both undergraduate and master's level) of the Workshop Theatre at Leeds University, with facilitation by two directors, Gail McIntyre of the West Yorkshire Playhouse and Chuck Mike, a leading American-Nigerian director. We also employed a leading theatre designer, Ian Somerville, and Sunduza, a Sheffield-based dance and music ensemble of Zimbabwean origin. I think it is hugely important that we give people from deprived communities the opportunity to work with the best professionals available, both in order to nurture creative talents and to demonstrate to the wider world that community arts are potentially equal to any other art-form. The brief I gave was to create a piece of theatre that explored the participants' understanding of Africa from being positioned in Leeds. The school environment was therefore not our only concern. We wanted to take into account the experience of pupils and students of African origin living in Leeds as well as understandings of non-Africans about the continent and how this led them to react to African people.

We ran a number of preparatory workshops in a range of mediums – art, music, and dance – to seek to engage children's interest in the project. The form that excited most pupils was African dance, as taught by Sunduza on a weekly basis for a term before formal rehearsals began. The high-energy, technically demanding dance workshops attracted a slightly shifting group of around twenty-five young people, backed by half a dozen others who learned to play drumming accompaniments. When rehearsals began we therefore already had a committed group ready to go on to the more analytically challenging work of exploring their understandings of Africa and how this influenced their lives.

The devising process ran for five weeks, including an intensive two weeks over the Easter holidays. We began with games asking children what their ideas of Africa were, before leading on to series of role-play exercises challenging perceptions about various 'outsiders'. Later participants were asked to undertake web-based research into learning about aspects of African history and politics that interested them. Most of the children involved were not academically oriented; several had already been excluded from other schools and others had minimal expectations of acquiring academic qualifications, but as they gradually realized that the ideas and information they brought to the creative process were being incorporated into the play they became much more confident about the value of what they could offer. As some of the children involved explained in post-performance interviews carried out by two postgraduate students, Chomba Njeru and Victoria Shaskan, who also participated in the production:

CHANTAL:     You think how can we make it up, that's a lot of work.
VICTORIA:    It felt weird. Felt like it was our play [...]. Cos if you do school plays, you get a script and you have to pretend to be someone, but being yourself. This is like our play because we all thought of it as well as yous. It was good.
WILL:        When I heard 'devising', I thought we'd put a few ideas forward and then they'd basically tell us it was all rubbish and make it up for us. At first I thought it was going nowhere, there seemed to be no structure at all. But actually it seemed to go quite well.
CHRISTINA:   Everyone put into it.
JADE:        Not like school lessons where no-one listens.[4]

The responses reveal not only the initial self-doubt of participants as to whether they could offer something which might be valuable, but also a depth of cynicism about processes that claim to be participatory in a school environment and as to whether adults ever really listen to children. These doubts were only gradually overcome by our alternative process of learning and creation.

We then found that the children were starting to offer their new learning to teachers and that this was leading them to critique classroom situations. The result was the specific scene I am focusing on for this essay. The situation was an imagined history lesson where the teacher has very narrow ideas about what can be included in the notion of African history and continually closes

---

[4] All interviews were carried out by Chomba Njeru and Victoria Shaskan, postgraduate students at the Workshop Theatre, University of Leeds, as part of the impact assessment of the project. Only children's first names have been used in order to protect their identity.

down children who say what she does not want to hear, to their increasing frustration. She notably fails to 'hear' the contributions from the only black child in the group, and says that other offerings do not come under the heading of what she chooses to designate history and are therefore irrelevant. The scene ends with a subversion of the teaching process where the children stop trying to please their teacher and get into a discussion of evolution that leads them to the conclusion that, whatever their race, they are all 'brothers' of the same origin. At this point the teacher is simply faded out by the dynamic of the play.

I should emphasize that this was only one scene in a much bigger piece of work and it was from a very particular viewpoint, not taking at all into account the constraints under which teachers work. I am in no way seeking to attack individual teachers in this essay but, rather, systems that strip children of creativity, confidence, and a spirit of enquiry.

Some children did drop out of the very demanding process en route, but others valued the responsibility that this freedom to choose gave them.

> JADE:        You always gave us the choice to drop out and do what we
>              wanted to do, because you always had expectations of us but
>              you never told us, which made us want to get it up and then
>              you told us it was really good. We started to get better.

It should also be taken into account that many teachers were amazed at what children were able to accomplish through the playmaking process. A teaching mentor with a strong professional performance background of his own, Raymond, who was eventually inveigled into joining the cast, told our interviewers:

> RAYMOND:     At first I didn't think they were gonna be able to do it. Be-
>              cause when you're in a system like the school, you're always
>              told what to do, what to think. For them to think for them-
>              selves and come up with a good piece, it was nice to see.

One thirteen-year-old boy whom I shall call Kyle – not his real name – was hyperactive and continually being thrown out of class and suspended. He was widely seen as unteachable. In the play Kyle became a leading actor, amazed at his own ability to learn and deliver lines based on research he had conducted. He also stopped getting into nearly as much trouble at school and his mother was hugely proud of his achievement. Kyle was surprised at his own ability, as was his head teacher, David.

KYLE:     I never knew I'd be that good, speak so long and keep it in my head, cos I thought I'd just forget it all. I did most of the time, but the last three or four I did okay. I was more determined to do it better next time. Since after the school one I got them all right.

DAVID:    One [thing] double surprised me [...]. That was Kyle's performance where he had long parts to deliver, quite technical as well. I was doubly surprised when I found out that he had to learn that in a very short space of time. So his ability was really tested and that was quite captivating.

This is just one example. When we carried out a process of post-production single-student and focus-group interviews, we kept hearing that children felt they had gained confidence and self-esteem, that they had gained a voice, and that they believed much more strongly in their ability to achieve their goals.

VICTORIA:   School's okay. I'm not that keen on it. Took me ages to settle in. Not my type of school. Because my Dad's in the army – and I'm not being racist – I've never gone to school with coloured people. I've never had Asian friends. Now I've made some friends that are Coloured and Asian. And they're really nice. I didn't think they'd be like that. I didn't think they'd want to talk to me.

ZOE:      I learned new African songs. And it kinda seems stupid but confidence. Cos I never used to be confident.

DONALD:   When I started, five days later on I started skiving. Then I came cos I was getting bored.

WILL:     I thought dancing was stupid, I couldn't do it. I was useless at it and I really didn't need to bother trying. Now I'm prepared to give it a go. That's probably the main thing, I'm more prepared to give something like that a go now.

DONNA:    (*Music teacher and main teaching support of the project.*) I don't know if you know, but afterwards we had a poetry competition at Leeds College of Music. And some of the students from your production wrote poems about Africa, and 'Where do I belong?' I think it was Christina. Fantastic. It opened up something in her.

## Eritrea – Being Blin

This project came out of an involvement in Eritrea and Eritrean theatre training that has lasted for me since the country became independent in 1991.[5] In this instance, I was running a pilot project with a colleague in the Leeds University School of Education, John Holmes, who had a similarly long-running commitment to Africa's newest nation, and we were bringing our skills together in the interests of: a) exploring the success of the country's policy of mother-tongue language learning at primary level; b) exploring children's views of their education as part of a national strategy of promoting more child-centred learning; and c) looking at how local arts forms could be incorporated into the educational syllabus as part of a national plan to include the arts in the primary-school curriculum.[6]

We ran the pilot project in two schools from different language areas. In each case, while John Holmes ran a workshop on child-centred learning as inset training for teachers from a group of schools I worked for a week with a group of around thirty children from the top year of primary school to explore their impressions of the education they were receiving. During this time I collaborated with two Eritrean cultural activists, Mesmer Andu and Yakim Tesfaye,[7] but no other adults were allowed to view the workshop process, and we had no plans for what the final performance would include. At the conclusion of both our weeks' work we showed the children's plays to all the teachers and local education officials on the child-centred learning workshop and held a discussion about their views of the findings.

---

[5] I was first invited to Eritrea in 1991 just after the country had gained its independence, in order to discuss setting up a national community arts training programme. This, *The Eritrea Community-Based Theatre Project*, then ran throughout the mid-1990s. I have also directed plays for the Eritrean government and led a number of theatre-training and research initiatives.

[6] These objectives were arrived at in consultation with the Eritrean Ministry of Education, which has been a major supporter of mother-tongue language learning and is concerned to develop more child-centred teaching methods and to incorporate more local culture in the primary-school curriculum.

[7] Mesmer Andu and Yakim Tesfaye were both originally trainees on the Eritrea Community-Based Theatre Project. They subsequently came to Leeds to study for the M A in Theatre Studies and since that time have been employees of the Bureau of Cultural Affairs. They have collaborated with me on a number of projects in Eritrea.

In the first village we worked in, we had uncovered a previously undiscussed problem with excessive corporal punishment (corporal punishment in some form is widespread in African schools). When we moved on to Bogu village, which I am concentrating on for this essay, we were working with a different linguistic group and a different culture towards children. The Blin (pronounced B'leen) people are a small minority in Eritrea. Only around sixty thousand people have Blin as their first language, and thirty primary schools work in the language. Blin was only written down in recent years, and the children we were working with were the very first group to have had all their primary education in their own language. Previously the community had been taught in the dominant language of the country, Tigrinya.

Bogu is a village around five miles from Eritrea's second biggest, and very multicultural, town of Keren. The children we encountered were understandably shy of the incoming group of three facilitators, but quite quickly relaxed as we opened the first morning by playing games under the shade of a large tree we had established as our headquarters, since no classroom was big enough to hold a theatre workshop. We explained to the children the broad aims of the project and then asked them to draw pictures first of the things they liked about school and then of things they found more problematical.

The drawing provoked great concentration. Art is supposed to be on the curriculum in Eritrean primary schools, but lack of supplies and trained teachers meant that we did not find it actually happening anywhere. We provided the children with bright felt pens and A4 sheets of paper and they scattered to lean the paper on rocks or exercise books and produce lovingly created drawings. We then laid all these drawing out as an open-air art gallery to discuss.

On the positive side, as in our previous school, we got lots of pictures of the Eritrean flag. This is flown prominently at all schools, and nationalistic pride is instilled in all children. We also got lots of pictures of football and volleyball – interestingly, sport had not figured on the curriculum of the mountain village of She'eb. The final group showed pictures of classes and teachers the children particularly liked; English was notably the most popular subject – the international language taught in all schools – and many children had written English captions on their pictures, although Blin and maths were also mentioned.

Showing things that were not popular was much more difficult for children in both of the villages we visited. Children are not only unused to having their opinions sought in relation to adults, they are particularly unused to critiquing adults or authority. However, a range of images were produced. Several showed the school as dirty, while others focused on subjects children did not like. In some cases these were the same subjects other young people had said they particularly did appreciate, but a notable minority picked out Blin as a subject they disliked. When we discussed this surprising result we found that the problem was at least in part teacher-related. Last year, the children said, they had enjoyed learning Blin because the teacher was nice and helpful, but this year they were not getting the same support and found the writing of the language difficult.[8]

We moved on from art to music and asked the children to sing for us a song they knew. This was partly because we planned to value local culture, but also to transfer some ownership of skills to children. In She'eb, children had immediately and confidently relaxed into singing a number of songs with great gusto, but here the result was tentative and weak. We asked what the problem was and were told that, culturally, singing was something that happened in the evenings and that it needed to be accompanied at least with a drum and preferably also with a *famfam* (mouth organ). We asked if they would feel happy singing if they brought a drum in the next day and were told that would be okay. Since they had no *famfam*, we bought them one that evening in Keren.

The next morning we moved on to asking the children, in groups, to sculpt still images of their lives. We got some good pictures of huts and games, but our universal favourite was a wonderful image of drawing water from the village pump. I just knew it would have to get into the final play somehow. The children practised animating some of these images, before we went on to ask them to provide similar living sculptures of good and problematical things at school. 'Good' included sport, nice teachers, friends, and learning; 'bad' was again dirt, learning Blin, and problematical teachers. What was becoming intriguing to the facilitation team was the problematization the children were

---

[8] Learning to write is especially problematical in Eritrea because there are three scripts in common use. Arabic is used widely by Muslim peoples (around fifty percent of Eritreans) while traditionally the highland peoples used a script derived from the Ethiopian Orthodox Christian script of Ge'ez for their languages of Tigrinya and Tigre. Older people, if literate at all, will use one of these scripts. When the government decided to write Blin down in Latin script, along with some other minority languages, they thought this would make learning international Western languages such as English easier, but the script is alien to villagers and is also seen as inferior, as it is not associated with religion as are both Ge'ez and Arabic.

displaying about attitudes to two subjects – teachers and language learning –
and we decided to use the art and images to lead into a discussion to try to
understand the children's perspectives on these subjects better.

Unfortunately, only one in our facilitation group was a native Blin speaker,
so it fell to Mesmer Andu to conduct the discussion. Since he had previously
worked as a teacher as well as being a drama worker, he had excellent rapport
with the children and a long discussion ensued. What we were told was fascinating.

On the subject of teachers, the problem was definitely not the excessive
physical punishment we had been shocked by in She'eb. In fact, we had
quickly noted how much more relaxed this group of children were around
school and adults than the Tigrinya children up the mountain, and in subsequent discussions with many people we came to the conclusion that Blin society is simply not as aggressive as is Tigrinya, but also that the school community has a much greater sense of camaraderie because, being such a small
ethnic group, everyone feels much more personally connected.

However, what the children did identify was a huge difference in teacher
attitudes and how strongly they responded to encouragement, while feeling
disheartened by the attitude of some teachers who were careless of their work,
often took cigarette breaks outside the classroom, and sometimes even disappeared for days at a time to Keren. To gloss this situation, it should be noted
that many teachers are on national service, which is supposed to last only
eighteen months but is often extended indefinitely; their pay can be as low as
£6 per month, which is barely sufficient to survive on, and even this is often
paid late. Given these circumstances, it is perhaps less surprising that some
teachers lack motivation than that many are still highly committed.

The discussion regarding language was equally interesting and quite complex. On the one hand, the children were proud of their ethnic identity, telling
us:

> I love to speak Blin, because we have not to ignore our language.
> I live in the culture.
> Blin language is useful, because we have not to ignore our language.

However, Blin was not seen as useful or prestigious in relation to the outside
world. We were told:

> I am proud of being Blin only among my people, but I feel bad when I am
> among others and I don't know their language.

> Our parents do not like us to learn Blin. Blin will not be helpful to you, they say.
>
> I love to speak English.

The problem, as perceived by the society, appeared to be that Blin had little status or economic value when it came to the wider world. The children did not want to be divorced from their culture, but they claimed that the three languages more widely spoken in the country, Tigrinya, Arabic, and English, all had higher status, and all aspired to be able to speak at least one of these.[9]

We ended that day with renewed efforts at music. Once the drum and *fam-fam* appeared, the children responded with huge enthusiasm and gave us an impromptu concert, culminating in a big circular dance that all confidently participated in – as well as drawing in a range of other children not taking part in the project but enticed to us by the music.

That night we discussed creating a playlet that would have two themes, both double-sided. On the one hand, we wanted to look at the importance children attached to encouragement from teachers, as opposed to the significant effect poor or careless teaching had on their motivation – especially in learning and valuing Blin. Discussion with colleagues from the teacher-training college revealed that teacher attitude to pupils was not a topic discussed, and certainly the importance of encouraging and rewarding pupils was not recognized. We felt that the insights revealed by the children could be hugely helpful to both teachers and teacher trainers in considering this question.

Secondly, we wanted to look at language issues. The liberal orthodoxy is that mother-tongue language learning must be best, at least at primary level, because it does not alienate children from their culture. However, the wider issue of how to operate in the nation as a whole was of great concern to parents and children alike. Although the importance of having a strong cultural, linguistic, and ethnic culture was recognized, learning in Blin was being seen as, at best, a waste of time. Once again children demonstrated what a strong influence teachers could have on attitudes to language learning, with good

---

[9] The State supports mother-tongue language learning at primary schools both to support policies of recognizing all Eritrean ethnic groups as important and because research has shown that children do much better throughout their school lives and are less alienated from their roots if they learn in their mother tongue – at least initially. However, few Eritreans speak Blin beyond village boundaries and many would like to learn a more widely spoken tongue in order to promote economic chances and engagement with wider Eritrean society.

teachers encouraging an enthusiasm for Blin while poor teachers reinforced feelings of uselessness. As with the teaching-attitude question, we felt that the authorities could learn from the insights revealed by the children – that it was not enough to teach a language but that the whole community needed to be involved in a debate about why and whether mother-tongue language learning was best for their children.

Since we had only a week, the facilitation team came up with the outline for a play drawing on the imagery shown by children and the issues they had raised. This we took to the children to check whether it fitted their perceptions, and for them to flesh out with dialogue.

The play, *Being Blin*, began with the beautiful water-pump image, which came alive as a young boy discussed his frustration at not being able to read a letter from his older brother abroad who had learned to write in Tigrinya. A second scene then moved to the town of Keren and illustrated children's linguistic embarrassment as a girl was unable to communicate with a shopkeeper. We then moved to the classroom situation, where we paralleled two Blin classes. In one, the teacher encouraged and supported his pupils, while in the second he ignored their work, went outside for a cigarette, and finally booted them out of class.

In the final scene, we moved to a family home where mother and father debated the usefulness of Blin in school while brother and sister – each from one of the class groups – demonstrated how different teaching methods affected their ability to do their homework. Finally, we heard the letter that had begun the play, in which the older brother said he was pleased his younger siblings were learning in their own language and when he soon came home he wanted to learn, too. This led into a final celebratory Blin dance and song, in which all the actors participated.

We showed our play to all the teachers on the training scheme – for whom I had also run a workshop on using theatre methods in the classroom – and they were very appreciative of the children's talent and interested in their observations, which led to a long discussion on language teaching; the problems and benefits of learning in a minority language, and the need to involve parents in understanding the pedagogical reasons for giving primary education in the mother tongue. Teachers were also concerned to express their frustrations with teaching conditions and their interest in the value children put on encouragement. In a final evaluation of the weeks' work, all the teachers said the drama was the most enjoyable and interesting aspect of the training, and the children went on to give us an impromptu concert and dance that lasted for hours into the early evening.

## Extrapolations

My sample from these two projects is hardly scientific, but what made me interested in writing this essay was a number of parallels I was able to draw between two projects carried out in nations which could hardly be further apart in terms of affluence, educational opportunities, and cultural and political heritage.

In both cases, we found children were prepared to work very hard and in their own time when they felt that they were appreciated by adult mentors and when the process and product were fun and something they felt proud of. Above all, in both places they loved the sense of ownership of the final product and the unusual sense that adults were listening to their voices. Moreover, all the children involved showed they were capable of complex and nuanced understanding of issues such as language debates and concepts of history that went far beyond simple factual learning and beyond what their teachers often thought they were capable of.

However, in relation to this level of debate, I would argue that the form of the projects was crucial in facilitating such complex thought. In both projects, when children were simply asked their opinions about a range of issues they tended to be either shy and tongue-tied or to come up with simplistic, sound-bite, received opinions. Our processes asked children to explore and test their ideas in a number of ways: through art-works, games, images, discussion, research, and performance. This matrix of approaches prevents the process of working becoming stale and boring, continually challenges the easy acceptance of received ideas, allows for creativity and imagination, and, finally, gives recognition and value to the process that has been undertaken in an immediate and concrete manner. It also allows learning to take place intellectually, through the body, and experientially, so that what is learned feels real, not abstract. Further, such a process allows the individual to have the support and safety of working within a community and to contribute in ways in which they can feel comfortable. Above all, learning is fun. It is evident to any parent that young children have an avid appetite for learning, but in conventional education all too often that appetite is removed as tasks become abstract, repetitious, and without apparent application to the day-to-day life of the child.

Conventional school education, certainly at high-school level, and in Africa even at primary level, aims to 'fill' children with knowledge aimed at enabling them to pass exams, so that they will be equipped to pass more exams. This approach is generally easy for teachers and educational examining bodies, because it is a matter of getting children to conform and accept whatever they are taught as 'truth' and 'valuable'. Yet we all know that in later life most of us will use very little of what we learn in high school and even at the time see little relevance in our learning to our 'real life' beyond the classroom. Such systems cannot want children who are questioning or think independently. Indeed, exams at high-school level often penalize children who answer questions outside a very strict framework of valued information or who make links between subjects. Children unable or unwilling to work within this narrow framework are deemed to be 'failures', their self-esteem and potential crushed at an early age. In both the projects discussed, we were working with children from non-privileged backgrounds who might not be expected to have very bright educational prospects; yet in both situations very few children chose to leave a process which required them to give up considerable amounts of time and to work hard. They came up with ideas new to adult facilitators and teachers, prompting fascinating discussion, and time and again their teachers told us they were amazed not only at the capacity for concentrated work shown by these children but by the high level of technical skill and ability to deal with complex ideas that the children demonstrated.

Our fundamental ideas were not new. Steiner was talking about creative education in British schools a hundred years ago and arts-education activists have long known about the extraordinary capacity of young people to act creatively. Yet education systems remain desk- and exam-bound, and learning generally continues to be seen as a one-way process rather than as a dynamic of interactive exploration. As I write this, I am planning further projects on a larger scale in both Eritrea and the UK that I hope will take learning through arts further to include all stakeholders in educational processes – children, teachers, educational authorities, and parents – so that we may think creatively about what constitutes real learning and how it can be accomplished using more than pens, paper, desks, and a teacher seen as the fount of all wisdom.

## Works Cited

Adams, Paul, et al. *Children's Rights: Toward the Liberation of the Child* (New York: Praeger, 1971).

Freire, Paulo. *Pedagogy of the Oppressed*, tr. Myra Bergman Ramos (*Pedagogía del oprimido*, 1970; Harmondsworth: Penguin, 1996).

Holmes, John. "Culture and Identity in Rural Africa: Representation Through Literacy," *Language and Education* 22.6 (2008): 363–79.

Neill, A.S. *Summerhill: A Radical Approach to Child Rearing* (New York: Hart, 1960).

Plastow, Jane. "Finding Children's Voices: a pilot project using performance to discuss attitudes to education among primary school children in two Eritrean villages," *Research in Drama Education* 12.3 (November 2007): 345–54.

Steiner, Rudolf. *The Education of the Child in the Light of Anthroposophy*, tr. George & Mary Adams (*Die Erziehung des Kindes vom Gesichtspunkte der Geisteswissenschaft*, 1907; London: Rudolf Steiner, 1965).

◄❖►

WHAT IT'S ALL ABOUT

RICHARD MARTIN

# Three poems for Geoff from around the world

## Birds of East Africa
Bujumbura, Burundi

In the walled garden, five guinea fowl spread out
in line across the lawn like beaters at a Victorian
shooting party, until one looks aside, and halts –
three others group around with squawks and calls,

they appear to exchange wicked gossip about the fifth;
five elderly ladies out on errands, in grey dresses
with white polka dots, heads nodding and weaving
as they chatter through tall flowers to the pool fence –

with a hop and a flap of wings, they land on the handrail,
perch unsteadily, plump round bundles nattering,
chattering, and mewling to each other beneath
the shadowy trees in the fading light –

it's not just that they resemble old ladies or ragbags,
but that, exotic as they may be, they serve as reminders
of the familiar, to soften the view of walls, gates, spikes,
and razor-wire against future uncertainties.

## Not Quite the Outback
Queensland, Australia

After driving for two days west and north,
we passed yet another
'Gateway to the Outback',
where the grass was burnt
bleached beige and white,
trees were silver grey grotesques,

where occasional trustful cows
still gathered in the one tree shade,
or noiselessly grazed where no grass grew –
I waited for homesteads called 'Heartbreak'.

At empty crossroads stood pub-hotels,
where bored barmaids
tided over white afternoons
with simple crosswords – a clue an hour;
where a clutch of seasoned men
chased whisky with beer,
laughed over threadbare jokes,
and bandied slander and stale dreams –
I began to fear what more
the outback might offer.

## More Than Sand
Rajasthan, India

On either side of the irrelevant road,
scrubby bushes and spindly trees seem
to thrive on sand; the desert is full of green,
from young peanut bushes to dusted thorns –

it comes alive in the afterglow of the setting
fireball sun, in the deep blue moonlit sky,
in the uncertain flickering of oil lamps
hung in branches round a dancing fire.

The desert unfolds towards its own infinity –
its vastness denying the planning
needs of fussy men, but space is suddenly
enlivened by a fleck of yellow, red, or green:

flowing saris worn by women who walk
from nowhere to nowhere with grace
and stateliness, jugs, or bulging sacks
balanced on their heads – the desert
contains so much more than sand.

◄❖►

## JACQUES ALVAREZ–PÉREYRE

## Les revenants

Une tête de taureau apparaît par-dessus le mur. De son échine surgit une armée de monstres. Ils allument des torches à partir des braises qu'ils ramassaient la nuit quand nous pensions avoir éteint les feux. Ils dansent: leurs mains aux doigts démesurés se tendent vers nous en un salut fraternel ou une invite à les rejoindre, nous qui sommes si proches d'eux quand la cruauté nous habite.

Jusqu'ici, ils restaient dans l'ombre, n'en sortant que lors de nos cauchemars. S'ils s'enhardissent, c'est qu'ils sentent venu le moment favorable. Et voilà maintenant qu'ils abaissent leurs masques : ils mettent leur visage tout contre le nôtre. Nous lisons dans leurs yeux le reflet de nos peurs, de nos tentations les moins avouables.

Pour les tenir à distance, il faudrait demeurer jour et nuit en alerte, placer des sentinelles à l'intérieur de nous-mêmes. S'ils s'emparent de notre âme, elle deviendra une chauve-souris aux ailes immenses qui volera de par le monde et qui mordra nos enfants.

## They are back!

A bull's head rears up above the wall. An army of monsters bursts forth from its neck. They light torches from the embers they had collected at night when we thought we had put out the blaze. They dance and stretch out their hands towards us with immeasurable fingers in a fraternal handshake or an invitation to join them: we are so close to them when possessed by cruelty.

Until now, they remained in the shadows, only appearing in our nightmares. If they become bolder, it is because they feel the time is ripe. And now they throw off the mask: we are face to face with them. In their eyes we can read the reflection of our fears, of our least savoury temptations.

To keep them at bay, we must be on the watch day and night, on sentry duty in the very depths of our being. If ever they capture our soul, it will become a bat with enormous wings flying around the world and infecting our children.

❖

## STEPHEN GRAY

## Interview with the Last Speaker

Here on the verge of this dry river lives:
Elsie Valbooi, in her hovel of sticks and sacks,
where the farmer lets her trespass for now.
Come out, Elsie, and greet my listeners,
speak into the microphone. She emerges
like a shy animal from its hideaway.
I offer the ritual greeting. She is still winding
her headscarf on, tucking down her skirt.
Meet Elsie. We're old friends by now, she is
becoming famous: the last speaker of a language
of the Southern San group, like Gri and !Ora,
Kxoedam and Nama. In her mouth lives
/'Auni, the gift she'll take when she goes.
Wants no radio (doesn't speak /'Auni),
no cell-phone or CD (don't speak her system).
Teach these visitors, Elsie, tell 'em how to say
'I want' in /'Auni, you can do it for us.
(She approaches the recorder she's used to,
lets off a disyllable, like no one else can do,
here it comes): "qtabba…" (She grins, no teeth
to get her tongue around.) Still able to manipulate,
though, that's the palatal click, back there.
"Qtabba tsamma," she says; she wants a melon.
"Qtabba taba" – a borrowing from our tobacco.
What else, Elsie? She concentrates: "Qtabba mili."
That's right, she wants corn on the cob, or maize.
What more, my dear, say it loud and clear?
(She hesitates, her eyes rove away with age,

rootle in her memory.) Her brain holds words
for every single thing she knows, but today she shares
all this knowledge with none. Her clan has gone,
her sisters and her man, like wind, like dust,
like ashes of her fireplace where she boils up
her tea. "Qtabba tsitsi …" – that's the dental.
She means water, she needs "tsitsi," the spring
out of which her folk all began. So say it after me:
"qtabba tsitsi, qtabba tsitsi, tsi, tsi, tsi …"
Not too bad for a first attempt. But it takes a lifetime
to master *l'*Auni and that whole world it holds.
How do we lose a language like the one Elsie
alone possesses? That's much easier. Just erase.

❖

KAREN KING–ARIBISALA

# The Nature of Tragedy

> When beggars die there are no comets seen;
> The heavens themselves blaze forth the death of princes[1]

B IG MEETING CALLED FOR TODAY, with both Housemistresses, Matron, with every single girl directed to be in attendance; it was taking place in the central common-room of St. Hilda's House; and I suspected that the reason for the meeting was that Mrs Perkins suddenly had a face.

Mrs Perkins is a maid, one of the domestic staff as we're told we should call them and I hadn't noticed she'd got a face until … her cheeks were bruised and swollen, one of her eyes had black and purple smudges round it as if she'd hurriedly applied the wrong sort of make up, or someone had done it for her; and she was always sniffling from a nose which seemed smashed in, and whenever she came up from the kitchens below she'd come at the wrong time, when she wasn't supposed to be there and she'd be, she'd be sniffling with the nose set in that face. If you attempted to speak to her she would walk away and return to the kitchen.

Sarah Ponsonby said that she'd tried to complain about the possibility of Mrs Perkins's snot getting into our food and had waited outside that awful kitchen cave, waited outside the tradesman's door for Mrs Perkins so she could do her complaining about the snot possibilities and Sarah Ponsonby said that after she'd complained, Mrs Perkins wouldn't even look at her.

And Mrs Perkins really was acting strangely, and somehow I guessed that we'd hear something to do with her face, the big meeting today would be about her face.

---

[1] William Shakespeare, *Julius Caesar* II.ii.31–32.

◄❖►

The common-room of St. Hilda's House wasn't expecting so many girls and the mistresses and matron to be in it at the same time, so it was fairly heaving with excitement when Miss Gramley came in with Matron and Miss Twist, and there was a sudden hush like when the curtain is about to go up before one of Shakespeare's plays begins or any entertainment but especially when its going to be tragedy. Miss Gramley's eyes roamed round the room and Matron decided to sit on a chair which Joey brought for her. The rest of us, with the exception of the Housemistresses, of course, were sitting on the carpet since most of the chairs and tables had been removed to allow for more room.

There's always a kind of build-up to these affairs I've noticed, but Miss Gramley didn't bother with any building up, she went straight to the heart of the matter and the matter was that – I suppose there was a build-up because she began by talking about a certain window episode and she said "Just because, girls, just because no one was disciplined when it was reported that the girls in dormitory F drew the curtains of their windows after the lights out bell, and waved at the village boys – who I'm told were laughing raucously having frequented a pub in the village – it appears that the discipline of St. Hilda's House has taken a turn for the worse. It has been going down hill."

I was in Dormitory F wouldn't you know?

"Not only did you disrespect, show no regard for school rules, but since it was night-time when this activity was engaged in the girls in the said dormitory would have had to have been clad in their night garments, with all of its suggestions of the lewd, the salacious. Perhaps you girls are unaware of the fact that there are certain women, women of a certain ilk, a certain extraction who … who draw their curtains open at night to look at men. Ladies certainly do not."

Miss Twist and Matron were now staring at the carpet with such concentration that I wondered if I'd gotten it wrong; perhaps I'd been so upset by the state of Mrs Perkins's face that I hadn't been able to think of much else; like most of the girls I'd been speculating. What could have happened? Apparently a prefect had questioned the mistresses on this very issue of Mrs Perkins's face and the mistresses were mum; it was a secret, so we'd got Mildred to threaten Alice to bring up the subject during dining-room conversation and sort of confront the Mrs Perkins's face problem and get the mistresses to face up to things openly – after Alice had made a few comments about the weather of course – and Alice knowing what Mildred's hockey stick could do, primed herself and said "Um Miss Gramley, we, I was wondering why Mrs Perkins's face is like that, swollen and she's got a black eye and also her nose is broken." Alice trailed off nervously. She knew full well that we weren't allowed to, as Miss Gramley was always saying, "fraternize" with the domestic staff. Gramley was livid but ignored her, ignored our curiosity, and simply expanded on Alice's earlier remarks about the weather; nothing was said about Mrs Perkins and her face.

Miss Twist and Matron looking embarrassed, soon excused themselves from the meeting and Miss Gramley had the floor, and for some reason, she decided to give us a little background information on the history of the school; she said that originally the school was made up of two separate schools, Lady Guinevere's School for Young Ladies and the School of St. Anne and that Lady Guinevere's School for Young Ladies was for the daughters of the gentry and St. Anne was for the others, the daughters of the clergy, trades people, and some others, some exceptionally clever working-class lower-class girls. The two schools had eventually been merged and today the entire school was Lady Guinevere's School for Young Ladies; however certain vestiges of the School of St Anne's former existence remained, like the kitchen door....

"Indeed" she said "that very door from which Mrs Perkins ... um, the kitchen door is actually quite historical, it is the door for tradesmen to...."

◄✧►

Windows and doors, doors and windows, but she'd mentioned Mrs Perkins at last and Gramley would have to tell us what happened with Mrs Perkins and her face – she'd better – Must be something ghastly because Mrs Perkins's face spoke of tragedy of some sort and we were missing our morning classes because of this meeting. But if Gramley did have Mrs Perkins's face on her agenda she was really building up to things. Miss Gramley had progressed from windows, to dormitories, to doors and was now talking about the kitchens. Course we're not allowed down there in the kitchens; whenever the girls of a particular table were on dining-room duty they'd just stack the dirty plates, glasses and cutlery on trays and put them on a shelf and then after they'd finished with that they would return to the dining-room for lunch time announcements – that sort of thing; and by the time we were done the trays with the dishes, everything would have disappeared unless for some reason the domestic staff were slow in removing them – like Mrs Perkins during the past few days or so; often she'd be there staring at the dishes and that's how I knew like if it was for the first time, that she had a face.

◄❖►

And Miss Gramley is talking about kitchens, the kitchens. "Girls the kitchens are below for a reason, the domestic staff is below for a reason. Of course they serve their purpose but you also have your own purpose in life and it is to live a life of lofty, higher ideals. The domestic class simply have no time to … to listen to Bach, Beethoven, Schubert for instance."

Most of my dorm squirmed at this aspect of lofty higher ideals because every Sunday – whether we liked it or not – our dormitory taking turns with the others was forced to go and spend a boring two hours with Miss Gramley in her study and listen to Bach, Beethoven and Schubert and she would beam and beam and say that if we listened carefully we'd become even more re-fined than we already were and that she'd treat us to Earl Grey tea and not those other plebeian teas – she didn't say plebeian but that's what she meant.

"The domestic class … ."

"Miss Gramley, if I might ask, where is all this leading to? Has it got any-thing to do with Mrs Perkins?"

"This is exactly my point, Candace. Already, you, a lover of Shakespeare, have begun to be influenced, unduly influenced in a most negative manner, by Mrs Perkins."

"All we … all I want to know is what happened to her face. I don't want to upset her by asking her myself and if it's something horrible she's going through we'd like to know about it; she's always snivelling these days and she's always late collecting the meal trays. I think most of us want to sym-pathize with her, Madam." I said and some girls nodded in agreement.

"There is no doubt" Miss Gramley continued in her most upper-class accent "that Mrs Perkins has undergone an unfortunate experience. From the look of her face it would appear that she has tripped, fallen, perhaps walked into a door; most unfortunate."

"A door, Miss Gramley? Could it by any chance be the tradesman's door?"

And the room was so quiet, couldn't have been more quiet, like the quiet of high tragedy when there's nothing left to hold on to and there's nothing more to say about the tragedy because it's so up there and high and you can't do anything because things are so very, very bad and low.

"Candace your constant interruptions reveal a lack of empathy with your parents' wishes and the parents and guardians of those girls who have been sent to Lady Guinevere's School for Young Ladies. You are being educated to be ladies, even you Candace with your slave ancestry."

"Sounds like we're being educated to be idiots" I muttered but she heard me and she couldn't afford to be lower class and scream at me at this precise juncture so she didn't.

"Candace" she said, and yet again she refers to Shakespeare; she knows I like him and his tragic plays; she believes she can get me to think like her by appealing to my Shakespearean sensibilities.

"Shakespeare Candace, Shakespeare – If you or any of the other girls wish to express your sympathy with regard to Mrs Perkins's condition – and this essentially is the purpose of our meeting – it would be appropriate to do so from a distance."

"What's this got to do with Shakespeare Madam?"

"Let us imagine my dear that Mrs Perkins has been involved in a tragedy of some sort – although naturally people like her are not the subject of trage-dies – can you imagine a tragedy entitled 'Mrs Perkins's Candace?" she laughed delicately, "Why, the very notion! Tragedy revolves around people of distinction, men of distinction, men of good breeding. They have to be above us in some way, so that when they do fall from their lofty pinnacles they will, they will fall; if one is at ground level, where is the tragedy in that? Why the need for inordinate sympathy for the groundlings?"

Well I never! Gramley has put Mrs Perkins on the groundling level; Mrs P is now one of the groundlings who according to Prince Hamlet of Denmark are "for the most part capable of nothing but inexplicable dumb show and noise."

Gramley continues by listing some of Shakespeare's tragic heroes – *Julius Caesar*, a biggie, *Macbeth* another biggie, *King Lear*, yet another biggie, *Hamlet the Prince of Denmark* and of course *Othello* a Black but a general, a Black biggie in his own right and Othello is Black like me and that is the nature of tragedy … tragedy only happens to biggies and therefore since tragedy only happens to biggies nothing too bad, certainly nothing tragic could have occurred in Mrs Perkins's groundling life.

We girls are listening intently, perhaps too intently and Miss Gramley dis-misses us reminding us that we are in this school to "emulate, subscribe to the

loftier pursuits of life" and that she "will do everything in her power to ensure" our "adherence to higher principles and ladylike behaviour". Miss
Gramley further promises to shortly convey our concern for Mrs Perkins's
condition to the woman herself and she says she hopes that will put an end to
the matter; and Miss Gramley and I are in the common-room looking at the
girls leave; Sarah Ponsonby raises her eyebrows at me and Lillian sticks up
her thumbs in the victory signal. I'm waiting behind because....

I am all ladylike politeness; could we please discuss this issue some more I
ask Miss Gramley, and she responds with ladylike politeness and she says
"My dear Candace you do understand don't you, I mean the point I was
making about Shakespeare and his heroes, lofty men with lofty ideals who ...
that's tragedy my dear."

"My dear Miss Gramley" I say to her face "Every one of those lofty men
died and they died because of a vicious flaw, they died because they thought
they were so high up and wanted to get higher, they died because of something bad in their character, some lackey thing, something lacking."

She colours.

"Very well, very well Candace, I suppose you want to come along with
me? But I must warn you of what you will face in the basement, the kitchens.
Let us go and see Mrs Perkins."

"And her face" I say.

◄❖►

Mrs Perkins is with her face when we see her and she's been crying. Miss
Gramley turns her head away from the face and asks Mrs Perkins to remain
sitting where she is and not to stand. Miss Gramley's eyes strain to the far end
of the kitchen and she tells the people there to go upstairs and when they begin to move to the stairs, Mrs Gramley says that they should not go up the
stairs, only Mrs Perkins and a selected few others are allowed to use that
facility; they should know that they should leave the kitchens through the
tradesman's entrance. They are not new to the system; only when the girls are
in their class-rooms, can the domestic staff clean the dormitories and the like
and make use of the stairs. She is aware however that certain circumstances –
the inordinate curiosity aroused by Mrs Perkins's apparent dilemma in St.
Hilda's House ... and that today being an unusual day that they might have
forgotten themselves.

The kitchen is a room of "Yes Madam" "Yes Madam" "Yes Madam" as the staff leave by the tradesman's entrance and shut the door and stand outside the door, behind the door.

Mrs Perkins probably thinks she's going to be sacked or something but when I smile at her she seems to relax. Miss Gramley isn't relaxed though.

"Mrs Perkins…" she begins.

"Won't you sit down Madam, Miss Candace … hope I haven't done wrong Madam? It's been so bad … so bad for me … hope…."

"You haven't done anything wrong" I say and drag a chair close to Mrs Perkins and sit beside her.

Miss Gramley winces.

"Mrs Perkins, no, you haven't done anything wrong, I am just doing my duty and Candace expressed … you know her temperament!" she attempted a smile.

"Cup of tea Madam?"

"No thank you Mrs Perkins I felt it incumbent upon me to come here and enquire as to your ailment – personally."

◄❖►

Mrs Perkins doesn't appear to be listening; there was a time when she was really feisty, when Sarah Ponsonby had complained about Sunday lunch and Mrs Perkins had got riled up and told off Sarah, but I guess things must be really bad for Mrs Perkins because she had been acting strangely and her face looked even more horrible up close; the black eye was … and her nose had been smashed; and it resembled my nose and I thought through some sort of violence we had become related kind of – me as a flat-nosed black, descendant of slaves linked to her smashed-in nose though white – and I thought that the brutality of the past showed on our faces, mine a historically brutalized face and hers featuring a present brutal brutality, a brutality much worse than whatever had caused the black eye, the smashed nose on her face; and our faces were stamped with that violence, with that brutality which caused my skin, my face to mourning-grieve with black colour and hers to be tired – drained of colour leaving her face colourless; her face.

"Candace I think we'd better go" says Miss Gramley.

I stay put and when I show anger, the anger is returned in a ladylike manner when Miss Gramley scowls at me with a ladylike scowl and Mrs Perkins notices it.

"I'm sorry, I'm sorry Miss Gramley. Don't be mad with Miss Candace she don't mean no harm do you luv?"

Mrs Perkins's face is contorted, and snot is running from her nose and she wipes the back of her hand across her nose, whimpers at the pain and wipes her hand on her apron.

Miss Gramley winces again.

"I'm sorry Miss Gramley ... don't go ... thank you for comin' down 'ere. It's not most toffs that'd come down 'ere to see the likes of me and it's been so bad you know with Bill – that's me husband – he beat me bad and then our John sees 'is dad cuffin me and next thing John's got a knife and John's stabbin an stabbin ... so much blood Miss ... and Miss Sarah says me snot's gettin in the food but I dint say nothin."

She laughed raucously as if she'd made a joke and Miss Gramley shivered, and removing a spotless handkerchief from her pocket she pressed her lips, her mouth, as if she'd tasted something vile, something lower.

"I am so very sorry about this Mrs Perkins. I have indeed come to express my deepest sympathy; very regrettable, the domestic accident. I do hope you are taking something for that cold?"

"Yes Madam, thank you Madam, thank you."

This other meeting, other, is over and Miss Gramley gestures for me to accompany her upstairs. She wants me to go back with her, go back, no doubt to lofty higher ideals which to me speak tragedy, the nature of tragedy, the tragedies which flaw and flow so undercurrent swift neither windows, nor doors, nor dormitories, nor kitchens, nor basements can stem the tide of their flowing so vicious flawed and so high-minded are these flaws so high-minded and yet so very low groundling low are these flaws which brought down men thought so high to groundling level. And ladies too; ladies....

I don't think Miss Gramley had ever come down to this level before, come up to this level before, and she seemed afraid, I don't know what of, but afraid. Shrugging her shoulders at my face she climbed back, up the stairs and looking at the face of her back as it went up the stairs I imprinted the nature of tragedy on my own face and it has been many years now that I have been sitting with my face and with Mrs Perkins's face in this kitchen downstairs as we talk of and share the nature of tragedy.

◄❖►

JÜRGEN JANSEN

## he made it – very much his story

New English Literatures
in Aachen?
oh yes.
New English Literatures
here, in that humanities hole?


indeed things happen.
oh well.
so may I ask
how come
here of all places?


is it to do with
that one person
and his master class
unPC once called
Man and Commonwealth Literature


originally so patronized by beautiful girls,
the occasional brainy boy?
and is it to do
with some pump-priming
from Political Science?

whichever. he's the one
who went global
in the process putting Aachen
on the map
pushing New English Literatures.

‹❖›

# Peter Stummer

## Stock-Taking in the Guise of Some Semantic Gymnastics

A raw poem for Geoff,
in honour of Hena and Anna

Could it be that relics of a half-digested reading of *Jumpers* wander
Through my mind? But that would prove that literature affects us
In a way, does it not? Anyway, I remember how it all began.
We prided ourselves on siding with the underdog and discovered
The fate of minorities. Some of us took refuge in the lean-to of
The Commonwealth, while others started to take issue with
English Studies, even degraded it to Eng.Lit. (downsizing had yet
To be invented) or dreamt up Cultural Studies of a particular kind.
It all started with the flag-independence of Ghana and professorial
Aggrandizement, which no longer convinced rebellious students.
The way Anglistics saw itself came more and more under fire.
Unwittingly we applied the core–periphery paradigm, worming
Away from the margins of the field, or so we were told. Some
Colleagues of our up-and-coming generation were eager to fawn
On profs in power positions, where they defined the rules of the
Game (defending the status quo of the system) and insisted that,
With us, it was just a matter of sour grapes. We extolled the periphery,
They maintained, because we lacked the ability to play ball with the core.
Could these be the times when unheard-of Soyinka might be a match
For time-honoured Shakespeare? No way, they thought, but they were
Already on the retreat.
For we had started to get organized. We got our act together and formed
Associations and thus became internationally active, before networking and
Globalization had become common coinage. We experimented with 'New
Literatures in English' and were proud of the non-totalizing plural, only to
End up in the maze of postcoloniality. For, in the meantime, another slur
Had appeared on the scene. Against a backcloth of postmodern trickery,

We were accused of lagging behind, inasmuch as we defended some sort
Of lingering partisanship. It took the mainstream a terribly long time to
Perceive, in its 'ethical turn', that some aspects of postmodernism had been
Nothing but a ploy to play into the hands of the neo-con revolt
Of 'depoliticizing the Culture Wars'.

Now, I fear, the maggots of success are in the process of feeding on the
Green leaves of our beginnings. We have made it, to a degree, and we have
Thus arrived. We have arrived in the centre of a field which seems to take
Many of the formerly marginal positions for granted, it is true. However,
The field as a whole is no longer what it was like at the outset. It has
Significantly diminished in its perceived importance for society. And the
Most alarming feature is not the decline in comparison to the new positivism
In the applied sciences, but the near absence of any historical awareness
Within the field itself.

Thus it was with considerable dismay that some of us discovered, at a recent
Conference, not so much that a remnant of commitment could be smeared as
Silly and benighted 'dogooderism' – which everybody who is with-it has long
Left behind – but that many among the next two generations took the notion
Of 'commodification' as something entirely and solely neutral or even
    positive.

In that sense an era has come to an end, and we, the old fogies of yesteryear,
Wonder what may lie in wait in a cloudy future. The organized and/or
Institutionalized reflection of reified literature might, perhaps, be dispensable,
As long as the writing itself in as many registers as possible, from, say – as far
As English is concerned – Indian and Nigerian English to Jamaican 'patwa'
And Caribbean 'creole', is still going strong, digitalization or no
    digitalization.


PS:
By all accounts, the courageous enterprise of the Rodopi publishing
Project, which has led to several high-quality publication series,
Must not go unmentioned. Instead it ought to be gratefully acknowledged.
Since it demonstrated that, given the necessary unflagging resolution,
Operations from the margin could still be successful after all.

◄❖►

# Coda

HAMISH WALKER and MICHAEL SENIOR

# A Personal Dedication to Dr. Geoffrey Vernon Davis

or, a socialite gentleman scholar, cosmopolitan workaholic, connoisseur of fine books, films, wines, beers, and spirits

## The Mists of Time ...

WELL, WHEN INGRID FIRST BROACHED THE SUBJECT of wanting to celebrate the occasion of Geoff's 65th and retirement with a festschrift, or, as Hancock would say in the vernacular, a liber amicorum, our initial reaction was to say, yes, of course, we would want to take advantage of this double celebration to pay tribute to an old (aren't we all these days?), dear, and generous friend. But then Ingrid went and put a bit of a damper on things by saying that contributions were usually of a somewhat more academic or 'wissenschaftliche' nature, which, as things stand, put us in our place right at the bottom of the list of potential scholarly contributors, so that when Ingrid eventually put out her call for papers (the 65th was long gone), we really felt we'd been put on the mailing list as a courtesy and that, in our case at least, a few pints and a pie with Geoff down the pub would have been a more suitable way of celebrating the occasion. But, scraping the bottom of the barrel, Ingrid must have changed her mind and decided we would, after all, be permitted to pay our own small tribute. So, here goes....

When and where we all met for the first time is beyond recollection, lost in the shrouds of history. It was, therefore, presumably in some pub in Aachen, and the most likely candidate would be the one we frequented most – Runi's (God bless her, she must be responsible for having ruined many a young liver).

## Bringing Culture to the Heathens....

Or, maybe it was at the English film club – Geoff must have got that going back in the very early 1970s – does anyone still run it, care about it, or even remember it in these days of video on demand? But it was a unique institution, probably still cherished in the thoughts of hundreds of ex-students when they recall their student days and one of Geoff's early victories achieved, presumably, after numerous battles with the RWTH authorities and for which we owe him a debt of gratitude. For many it was the highlight of a week of tedium, misery, and occasional moments of study.

Or could it have been, God forbid, in the Anglistik Institute? At the PH or in some greasy Greek restaurant? Who knows, who cares. After all, it was nearly four decades ago and friendships formed in youthful years last longer. Or was it just the clinginess of ex-pats huddling together in hostile climes?

## First Steps to Recognition...

So there we all were, back in the early 1970s, with Geoff revelling in the lap of luxury, sharing an apartment (well, Geoff always maintained it was just sharing) with the beautiful Fiseni twins in salubrious Burtscheid, the up-market, posh, spa area of Aachen, and then, taken unawares – FAME. Geoff, crack of dawn, 7.45 a.m., interviewed by WDR radio on the subject of his mate Richard Booth, successful purveyor of second-hand books, owner of a Rolls and room for a whole herd of ponies, lord and uncrowned king of Hay-on-Wye. Geoff's first public statement to the world, heard by millions! Ah, if only we'd known in advance and been up early enough. But, it was a first encounter with UDI.

And then there was the Spoken Word! Peter Pim and Billy Ball, central characters of one of the first English textbooks for the German 'Hauptschule', were revamped when language labs came into fashion (and let's hope those monotonous, uninspiring old machines have long disappeared again). The publishers asked us to speak the texts for the first P.P. & B.B. tapes. So, wet and wintry weekends were spent in the teacher training college studio recording mind-bogglingly stultifying sentences in every tense imaginable, past, present, and future, conditional, simple, and continuous, just to earn a few bob on the side and further our already established careers of boring as many students and pupils to tears in as short a time as possible.

## Journeys to the Heart of Europe...

And then there were more interesting and engaging events, like the trips 'abroad'. Prague was always a favourite. Within fairly easy reach of Aachen, a day's drive more or less and then – after the suspense of the border crossing – the city of spires, Disneyland, Dubček, Dvořak, Smetana, Jánaček, Kafka, Havel, products of this small nation steeped in culture nestling in the heart of Europe. Where else could East meet West? The city overrun by Ossis travelling to meet their Wessi relatives. Why not drop into the DDR bookshop for a few metres of Marx and Lenin. (The DDR bookshop was later taken over by the British Council, an irony worthy of Geoff's sense of humour.) Eterna, Supraphon, providers of fine music for impoverished Western tourists such as ourselves. But, Prague today, rich in culture, has become a popular destination for British louts bent on getting, well, pissed. Not us, though. We imbibed culture! Off to an organ concert in the Klementinum or the regular Monday recital in St James Church followed by a full-blown concert maybe in the Rudolfinum or the Municipal Hall or in the fabulous Estates Theatre where Mozart conducted his first performance of *Don Giovanni*. An afternoon concert followed by an evening performance – pretty average day. And then it really was time to sample that other great product of the Czech lands – beer! Where to? The Black Bull up at the castle? The 3 Ostriches on the Charles Bridge? The Two Cats – just across from Mozart's house? The Golden Tiger in the Old Town, the Golden Well hanging on to the cliffs below the castle? Ah, that refreshing challenge of debating and adjudicating the merits of the Smichov brewery, the sweet delights of Pilsener Urquell, or that most excellent of beers, Budweiser (Czech, that is). Fond memories! (Well, as far as anyone could remember anything the next morning!).

## First Steps Towards Asia...

The South African trip was to blame (and, have patience, we'll come to that momentous trip shortly). Our first evening in Jo'burg was spent at the outstanding Garden of Allah, little knowing what long-term effects this would have on our palates: the start of a lifelong passion for good Indian nosh. Back in the UK, Madhur Jaffrey had just published what was to become our bible for the ensuing decades – *An Invitation to Indian Cooking*. And if you haven't got a copy, you just don't know what you've been missing all these years! Back in Aachen, cooking with a vengeance, whose turn is it this week to spend Friday and Saturday slaving over a lamb korma or a mouth-watering sindhi gosht or struggling to get that murgh mussalam just right? And we still do it, though less frequently today, as curries, cathartic by nature, do tend to see us up with the dawn chorus a little more often than back then. But Madhur is nothing if not a purist, and just a whisper of 'curry powder' would have sent her howling all the way to Hyderabad. So, just where in the Aachen of the mid-1970s was one to find all those exotic and magnificent spices? Asafoetida, turmeric, cardamom, cumin? Asian shops? Not invented yet, still just a twinkle in a subcontinental eye. But, yes, sources were eventually found – a first tentative Asian wallah testing the market down on Annuntiatenbach and, for the even more exotic ingredients – the old apothecary!!

Many a sundowner and pleasant evenings spent in the company of Geoff and Rogan Josh et al.

## A Career Hiccough…

The life of a Lektor (English: dogsbody) was not too unpleasant in the 1970s. In the German university way of things, we enjoyed a status more or less on a par with that of a punkah wallah. 'We need regular infusions of fresh blood', chanted professorial Draculas unisono in English departments throughout the land! And the butchers had their way. Lektors were slashed, flailed, sacked for little obvious reason. So, off to court we all went, where reason prevailed and the downfall of these professorial slaughterers were the tribunals' findings of "no reasonable grounds for dismissal," 'Kettenverträge' – not legal. But justice moves at such a leisurely pace that, prior to reinstatement, long periods of unemployment were the norm. Litigation progressed through the judicial hierarchies at a pace even a lame snail on crutches would have found frustrating (one of the co-authors of this 'paper' fought the State tooth and nail all the way up to the Federal High Court of Labour/Bundesarbeitsgericht, after which he was never again called 'a right case', but progressed to gain recognition as a case of precedence. But, it took seven years!). Many just gave up. But Geoff, probably thanks to innate grit and his northern upbringing, was a man of action ('thur'll be trubble up t'Institute, mark my words') and it was to the word he turned, putting his literary talents to good use. In the belief that the pen is mightier than the sword, Geoff essayed into trade-union journals describing the sorry plight of the 'Lektor' in German tertiary education. But everything has a silver lining and unemployment was also accompanied by our first brief encounters with the 'Arbeitsamt' – Sorry, mate, come back in three months. If Geoff's lawyer hadn't been so inept, then surely he would have been reinstated much quicker than was the case, but, reinstatement, for better or worse, did happen, and all dreams of a career move to sunnier and perhaps more promising climes were dashed by the simple need for dough (like having to repay all those unemployment 'benefits'). But, a boon for many an aspiring author, unemployment bestows a breathing space to indulge in new activities and, in Geoff's case, first fruitful forays into the realms of Commonwealth Lit., not to mention trivial pursuits like doing a doctorate.

## Home Sweet Home...

After the life of Riley in Burtscheid, Geoff, in a fit of nostalgia for his student days in Teddy Hall, moved back into hall at Hasselholzer Weg to live and share a kitchen with a motley collection of Asian students from whom he learnt the uses and usefulness of chopsticks in Chinese and Asian cuisine.

Teddy Hall, Oxford, of course, dates back to the thirteenth century. And here we see an original illustration of that eminent dignity and scholar, St Edmund of Abingdon, Archbishop of Canterbury, taken from an ancient illuminated manuscript, the Book of Kells. This early manuscript was later published in a revised, abridged edition and, alas, all references to anything English were deleted and so, regrettably, this true portrayal of St. Edmund fell victim to the bloody Irish axe. However, later in his career, Geoff was to encounter the Book of Kells again as one of the first contributions to Commonwealth literature.

Then, next move, just across the road to Lütticher Strasse before the more enduring move to Johanniter Strasse. Permanency at last, we breathed with a sigh of relief, after having lugged countless boxes of books up countless flights of stairs. And the accumulation of books, videos, records, DVDs in the succeeding thirty years (not to mention Ingrid's stuff) discourages any thought of moving again. But are Geoff's neighbours aware of the literary tsunami looming above them every single day, a potential avalanche threatening to engulf them in mountains of books? What do they all weigh? An enormous collection just waiting for gravity to send them careering through the decks to crush those unsuspecting souls below. Suicidal to live under Geoff, really. Perhaps there should be a warning above the portal downstairs:

'Beware all ye souls below the fifth floor. The wrath of God, fire, brimstone and tons of Geoff's books are about to descend upon you'.

We suppose if there were a lift in the house it would just be marked: 'Fifth floor – rare books, records, DVDs, videos and Africana'.

## The Great Trip...

And this is how it all started: Sometime during the winter of 1974/75, Hamish quite innocently said, "My sister's getting married in Rhodesia in the summer. Anyone fancy coming along?" So we did. (There's that UDI again.)

And here they all are, those intrepid explorers of darkest Africa twenty-five years on:

And if you're wondering why we don't have any photos from the original safari (this later expedition pictured penetrated no further than the frontiers of eastern Eschweiler), this is simply because there were so few bearers available to transport the cumbersome photographic equipment of the time.

So, off on a jaunt through southern Africa. First impressions: amazing! there are parts of the world where you can invite people months in advance to a summer barbecue and you just know it's not going to rain! Absolutely jaw-dropping! From Jo'burg by rail through Botswana, past Gaborone, Francis-town, and picturesque Plumtree station with Rhodesian Railways serving scrumptious pumpkin pie in clerestory dining cars. The fascinating Railway Museum in Bulawayo (Beyer Garretts, would you believe?). Back to the 1950s: Sunday afternoon in downtown Bulawayo, Gray's Inn hotel bar,

"Sorry sir, we don't serve people without ties after 6pm." However, not a problem, this particular watering-hole did provide ties for the ingenuous visitor, so drinking continued. Until: "Sorry sir, we don't serve people wearing jeans after 7pm." Not much one can do about that, so our Sunday afternoon binge was thus prematurely terminated. The incomparable Wankie game reserve and first encounters with real wild animals. What a tremendous experience watching giraffes bending over themselves to drink. Off to Vic Falls for a few days to experience the delights of that most luxuriant and wonderful of colonial establishments – the Victoria Falls Hotel – not that we could actually afford to stay there, but day visitors were made most welcome: the Edwardian pool, sundowners, the evening brai, and then home to our cottage on the banks of the Zambezi. Back to Bulawayo, then on to Salisbury – should we pop in to Ian Smith's surgery and give him a good piece of our collective mind? Hitchhiking from Salisbury (Harare) to Jo'burg, how many hundreds of miles was that? Meeting up en route at the Zimbabwe ruins. Picking up a camper in Jo'burg and on to magnificent Swaziland, Mlilwane game park, white rhinos, ostriches flirting with Gerd. Durban, the Transkei, Garden Route, until, midday Saturday, petrol stations close for the weekend, shit!! Off to find a local magistrate to obtain permission to fill up after 12 noon on a Saturday. Flat Earthers! Over the Drakensberg and down to Cape Town to stay with our wedding hosts. Let's climb up Table Mountain! Last one up's a sissy! Not too difficult a climb, nor the climb back down again. However, it's only after the event they tell you about the seventeen different species of venomous snakes inhabiting the hillside! Oh, my God!!

Then the long drive back across the arid Karoo scrublands of central South Africa, Bloemfontein, Parys, Jo'burg, Frankfurt, Aachen. But then, let's do something about it, apartheid, discrimination, racism. Active in Third World groups, talks, presentations, creating teaching materials – until, one day, Geoff: "Why don't we write a book about it?" Daft idea, but that's what happens when you're unemployed with too much time on your hands. So, that's how it all started. Geoff's career as author, editor, scholar, and luminary of Commonwealth literature. *The Privileged and the Dispossessed* was the initial work, in two volumes, where Geoff did most of the work while kick-starting or, indeed, just kicking his slothful co-author into action. But at least we did get to know those two incredible publisher's readers at Schöningh – Jerry and Liam – with their absolutely peerless magnetic matrix board with *snails* depicting the progress of each of the twenty volumes in the series ("Teaching English and American Studies")!

And where did it get him in the end? Well, incumbent of the Chair of the Association of Commonwealth Literature and Language Studies (ACLALS) can't be that bad, something, indeed, to be proud of and must put the lad from Liverpool somewhere in line for the throne (hopefully in front of Basher Ernst August of Hanover) or, failing that, at least recognition in the form of an OBE. But, yes, without doubt an impressive achievement (though Geoff in all modesty would probably just claim no-one else wanted it).

## Decades of Change…

All good things must come to an end, and the 1970s eventually faded away. Perhaps not as exhilarating as the Swinging Sixties, but with a wealth of extraordinarily charismatic characters, Willy Brandt, Herbert Wehner, Helmut Schmidt (all socialists, you may notice). But, at the end of the decade, ominous clouds on the horizon. We spent the evening of 3 May 1979 in the Reuters pub in Aachen reading the ticker tape as it came in with the news of Margaret Thatcher's (not a socialist) impending election victory leading to monetarism and the destruction of the social fabric of many a northern mining community. Years of discontent and strife, but not even the Iron Lady dared touch the schools and hospitals of the North – an omission which the next Tory government has promised to remedy! Best not to be in the UK.

Parting may be such sweet sorrow, but for some of us the 1980s and 1990s saw the achievement of one of Geoff's lifelong ambitions – to leave Aachen, though it wasn't Geoff who moved but Mike and Hamish, and whether Geoff would have contemplated exchanging Aachen for the fogbound, endless plains of Lower Saxony, as we both did, is debatable. However, with Mike now at home in sunny Baden–Württemberg, a new tradition has recently been established with Geoff and Ingrid having become welcome guests each year for a bona fide English Christmas – turkey, stuffing, crackers, Queen's Speech, tinsel, and party hats! One episode springs to mind: with Geoff thumbing through some scholarly tome, the atmosphere abruptly electrified by an intense flash of that analytical mind and Geoff posing the only pertinent question possible, "But where are all the pictures, Missie?" Spoken like a true academic. But not wishing to disappoint Geoff in his desire for more graphical contributions, we include at this point, pictorial evidence:

Geoff entering into the true spirit of Christmas

But, for Geoff in the 1990s, there loomed a further and well-deserved academic award, his 'Habil', a second, professorial qualification.

## Pastures New ...

The end of an era...

Is there anyone out there who can actually remember the Rheinisch–Westfälische Hochschule at a time when Geoff wasn't on the staff? We're pretty certain only the very few will remember *this* Geoff.

Old academics never die, they just keep pontificating on and on and endlessly on, but, with retirement, a fresh opportunity to take up more esoteric challenges, to enjoy a new-found freedom, liberation from the stultifying constraints of having to teach increasingly distant generations suckled on the internet in the belief that books are just one of Amazon's minor product lines, to be avoided at all cost.

Or perhaps an opportunity to indulge in a completely new career:

Geoff being auditioned by Bill for the role of Ben
in Lloyd Webber's "The Flowerpot Men"

There are, of course, many more memories worthy of mention, trips to Ireland, Holland, snowball fights in Aachen, Geoff complaining to the police about his car having been towed away overnight (which it hadn't – Geoff had just driven it from one pub to the next and forgotten where he'd left it), reclining in MGBs, Mahler concerts spread across little Belgium; but we have to save something for his centenary.

So – the moment we've been waiting for: a toast to a friendship that has withstood the test of time:

Cheers, Geoff, lang may yer lum reek, and for God's sake let's get down the pub for that pie and a pint!

## (Epilogue...

Ah yes, on second thoughts, if Ingrid thinks we're going to sit down for Geoff's 100th and spend hours concocting a load of sentimental rubbish like this again, forget it! That telegram from the Queen will have to suffice.)

⊰❖⊱

# Notes on Contributors

JACQUES ALVAREZ–PÉREYRE studied at the universities of Bordeaux and Lille and taught at the Université Stendhal (Grenoble), of which he is now professor emeritus. He also spent two years as an assistant professor of French at Howard University (Washington DC) and Morehouse College (Atlanta GA). A writer of fiction and poetry, including *De ce côté-ci de la terre* (1968) and *L'arrière-saison* (2001), he has also published widely on South African theatre and poetry, including *Les Guetteurs de l'Aube: Poésie et apartheid* (1979), translated by Clive Wake as *The Poetry of Commitment in South Africa* (1984), as well as the socio-historical studies *Nelson Mandela: de la résistance à l'épreuve du pouvoir* (1997) and *Littérature et discrimination raciale en Afrique du Sud* (2003). He is also a translator, particularly of Fatima Dike Peter Horn, Wopko Jensma, Matsemela Manaka, Maishe Maponya, and Zakes Mda.

STELLA BORG BARTHET is a senior lecturer in the Department of English at the University of Malta, where she teaches courses in postcolonial literature and theory, and in eighteenth- and nineteenth-century English and American literature. She has functioned as an adjudicator for the Commonwealth Writers' Prize, and is the author of articles and book chapters, mostly on Australian and African fiction. Her current research interests include postcolonial and African-American writing. She is the editor of the companion volumes *A Sea for Encounters: Essays Towards a Postcolonial Commonwealth* (2009) and *Shared Waters: Soundings in Postcolonial Literature* (2009).

MARCIA BLUMBERG is an Associate Professor of English at York University, Toronto, where she teaches a range of drama and theatre courses. She was a Research Fellow at the Open University in England. Specializing in modern and contemporary theatre, she has presented numerous international conference papers, published many articles on theatre, and co-edited (with Dennis Walder) *South African Theatre As/And Intervention* (1999).

SHIRLEY CHEW is professor emerita of Commonwealth and Postcolonial Literatures at the University of Leeds, and currently Visiting Professor in the

Division of English, Nanyang Technological University, Singapore. She has published widely in the field of literatures from Commonwealth countries; and has co-edited *Unbecoming Daughters of the Empire* (with Anna Rutherford, 1993), *Translating Life: Studies in Transpositional Aesthetics* (with Alistair Stead, 1999), *Re-Constructing the Book: Literary Texts in Transmission* (with Maureen Bell, Simon Eliot, Lynette Hunter, and James L.W. West, 2001), and the *Blackwell Concise Companion to Postcolonial Literature* (with David Richards, 2010). Recent publications include essays on Nissim Ezekiel, Amitav Ghosh, Shashi Deshpande, V.S. Naipaul, and Olive Senior. She is the founding editor of *Moving Worlds: A Journal of Transcultural Writings* (2001–).

BRIAN CROW teaches in the Department of Drama and Theatre Arts at the University of Birmingham. He has also taught at universities in Nigeria, Scotland, and Australia. His area of academic specialism is postcolonial theatre, in particular drama and performance in sub-Saharan Africa. He is the author of *Studying Drama* (1983) and, with Chris Banfield, of *An Intro-duction to Post-Colonial Theatre* (1996). He is currently working on a book examining the relationship between tradition and modernity in African drama, and its implications for both form and content.

MARGARET DAYMOND is professor emerita and Fellow of the University of KwaZulu–Natal. Her research centres on writing by women, mostly African women, with a focus on autobiography, narrative, letters, and fiction. She has published on Bessie Head, Doris Lessing, Sindiwe Magona, Lauretta Ngcobo, Lilian Ngoyi, Yvonne Vera and others. Her books include *Women Writing Africa: The Southern Volume* and *South African Feminisms: Writing, Theory and Criticism, 1990–1994*. She was a founder editor of the journal *Current Writing: Text and Reception in Southern Africa*, which is now in its twenty-first year of publication.

HOLGER EHLING is a journalist, writer, broadcaster, and publishing industry consultant based in Frankfurt, Germany. He read English, German, and Philosophy at the Universities of Göttingen and Mainz. He has worked as a reporter in Africa, New Zealand, and Latin America and was a correspondent in London for many years. He was a vice president of the Frankfurt Book Fair until late 2005. He has initiated and developed the Cape Town International Book Fair and has consulted for book fairs in Zimbabwe, Ghana, Egypt, Korea, Mexico, and Argentina. For fifteen years, he was the founder-editor of

*Matatu: Journal for African Culture and Society* and the founder of the ANA–Matatu Award for Children's Literature in Nigeria. He is a regular contributor to book-industry journals in Germany, the USA, and Australia as well as being a commentator for a variety of newspapers and radio stations. He has written and edited numerous books on African literature, media studies, and England. He was recently involved in a study of international book industry statistics on behalf of the International Publishers Association and has contributed the chapter on the publishing industries to a report on the impact of digitization on the creative industries commissioned by the Culture Committee of the European Parliament.

JAMES GIBBS has recently retired from the University of the West of England, Bristol. Before that he taught at universities in Liège, Ibadan, Zomba, and Legon. His studies of African theatre include *Ghanaian Theatre: A Bibliography* (1995) and *Nkyin-Kyin: Essays on the Ghanaian Theatre* (2009), and (co-edited with Martin Banham and Femi Osofisan) *African Theatre in Development* (1999), *African Theatre: Playwrights and Politics* (2001), and *African Theatre: Companies* (2008). More generally, he is the editor of *A Handbook for African Writers* (1986) and co-editor (with Jack Mapanje) of *The African Writers' Handbook* (1999) and (with Kofi Anyidoho) of *FonTomFrom: Contemporary Ghanaian Literature, Theatre and Film* (2000).

STEPHEN GRAY was educated at the universities of Cape Town, Cambridge, and Iowa (where he was a member of the Writers Workshop, 1966–69). Until his early retirement in 1992, he lectured at Rand Afrikaans University in Johannesburg, where he became Professor of English. He lives in Johannesburg as a free-lance writer, concentrating on his creative work and contributing regularly to the *London Magazine* and to the book pages of the *Mail and Guardian* weekly, Johannesburg. His influential *Southern African Literature: An Introduction* was published in 1979; he has edited *The Penguin Book of Southern African Stories* (1985) and its companion, *The Penguin Book of Southern African Verse* (1989), along with numerous other collections and re-issues of prominent authors. His own works include *Selected Poems (1960–92)* (1994) and the novels *John Ross: The True Story* (1987), *War Child* (1993), and *Drakenstein* (1994).

GARETH GRIFFITHS is Professor of English and Cultural Studies at the University of Western Australia and a Fellow of the Australian Academy of the

Humanities. He has written and edited many books and articles on postcolonial literatures and cultures, and on modern drama. He has a long-established interest in African literatures in English. He is presently working on two research projects concerned with missions and their role in educating post-colonized subjects. His publications include *The Empire Writes Back: Theory and Practice in Post-Colonial Literatures* (1998, 2nd ed. 2000), *Post-Colonial Studies: The Key Concepts* (2000, 2nd ed. 2007), and the edited collection *The Post-Colonial Studies Reader* (1995, 2nd ed. 2005), all with Bill Ashcroft and Helen Tiffin; *African Literatures in English: East and West* (2000); *Disputed Territories: Land Culture and Identity in Settler Societies*, co-edited with David Trigger (2003); and *Mixed Messages: Materiality, Textuality and Missions*, co-edited with Jamie S. Scott (2005).

JÜRGEN JANSEN was born in Aachen, where he still lives, has taught English, French, and German, then political science; has brought a little knowledge of things Indian to the New English Literatures; and has resolutely resisted retirement.

KAREN KING–ARIBISALA is a professor in the Department of English, University of Lagos, Nigeria. As well as publishing a number of academic articles in various journals, she is a writer of fiction and is the recipient of several grants, awards, and prizes from such bodies as the British Council, the Ford Foundation, the Commonwealth Foundation, and the Camargo Foundation. Her most recent novel, *The Hangman's Game* (2007), won the Best Book prize (African Region) in the Commonwealth Literature Awards for 2008.

BERNTH LINDFORS, professor emeritus of English and African literatures at the University of Texas, Austin, has written and edited a number of books on anglophone African literatures, the latest being *Early Soyinka* (2008) and *Early West African Writers* (2010).

MBONGENI ZIKHETHELE MALABA is Professor of English Studies at the University of KwaZulu–Natal, Pietermaritzburg Campus. Prior to moving to South Africa, he lectured at the Universities of Zimbabwe and Namibia. He has published extensively on Shakan, Zimbabwean, South African, and Namibian literature. Recent publications include *Charles Mungoshi: Collected Essays* (ed. 2007), *Policy and Practice in English Language Education in Namibia* (ed. 2009), and, co-edited with Geoff Davis, *Zimbabwean Transitions: Essays on Zimbabwean Literature in English, Ndebele and Shona* (2008).

ANDREW MARTIN has a Bachelor's degree in social science and a Post-Graduate Diploma in library and information science from the University of Cape Town and is Bibliographer/Literary Researcher at the National English Literary Museum (NELM), Grahamstown, South Africa, and the compiler of *The Poems of Dennis Brutus: A Checklist, 1945–2004* (2005). Andrew, who has a sideline as a (published) poet, is currently doing bibliographic research into black South African literature in English. He has located and secured for NELM scarce and scattered literary resources by and on South African writers, and is of genial assistance to South Africanists worldwide.

RICHARD MARTIN taught English and American literature for many years as a colleague of Geoff Davis at the University of Aachen. Since taking early retirement, he has concentrated on his poetry, which has been published in magazines in England, Ireland, the USA, Canada, and Austria. He has published two collections, *Spider's Nets* (2008) and *Lucky Charm* (2011).

JÜRGEN MARTINI studied at the universities of Cambridge (BA, MA), Hamburg, Marburg, and Bremen (PhD), and has taught at secondary-school level (Magdeburg), in the adult-education sector (Bremen and Magdeburg), and at the universities of Bremen, Bayreuth, and Magdeburg. He has served on the juries of the German Juvenile Literature Prize and the Federal Foreign Languages Competition. His research interests have included children's literature, and African, Caribbean, and Pacific literature, and he has, with Helmi Martini–Honus, translated works of fiction by Francisco Sionil José, Meshack Asare, Buchi Emecheta, Patricia Grace, Meja Mwangi, and Flora Nwapa. He is the editor of *Leaflets of a Surfacing Response: 1. Symposium Canadian Literature in Germany* (1980), *Gesellschaft und Kultur der Karibik* (1982), and *Missile and Capsule* (1983), and co-editor of *Literary Theory and African Literature/Théorie littéraire et littérature africaine* (with Joseph Gugler & Hans–Jürgen Lüsebrink, 1993) and *Preserving the Landscape of Imagination: Children's Literature in Africa* (with Raoul Granqvist, 1997). He is on the advisory board of the journal *Matatu*.

CHRISTINE MATZKE has recently moved to the University of Bayreuth after teaching in the African Studies Department at Humboldt University, Berlin. Her research interests include African (specifically Eritrean) theatre, African literature in English, and postcolonial crime fiction. She is the co-editor of *African Theatre: Diasporas* (with Osita Okagbue, 2009), *Of Minstrelsy and Masks: The Legacy of Ezenwa–Ohaeto in Nigerian Writing* (2006, with

Aderemi Raji–Oyelade and Geoffrey V. Davis), and of *Postcolonial Post-mortems: Crime Fiction from a Transcultural Perspective* (with Susanne Mühleisen, 2006). Apart from being a co-member with her on the editorial board of *Matatu*, and a wonderful friend, Geoff Davis also belongs to her informal circle of crime-fiction scouts and aficionadoes.

JANE PLASTOW is Professor of African theatre in the School of English and Director of the Centre for African Studies, both at the University of Leeds. She has lived and worked in many African countries, but the primary focus of her work in more recent years has been the Horn of Africa, particularly Ethiopia and Eritrea. She is a theatre director, a trainer in the techniques of theatre for development, and an academic researcher. Significant publications include *African Theatre and Politics* (1996) and *Theatre and Empowerment* (2004), the edited collection *African Theatre: Women* (2002), an edition of *Three Eritrean Plays* (2005), and, co-edited with Richard Boon, *Theatre Matters* (1998).

MONIKA REIF–HÜLSER studied literature (English, American, and French), history, and sociology at the universities of Erlangen–Nürnberg, Paris (Rambouillet), Lyon, and Konstanz. Since 1980 she has taught and researched English and American studies, postcolonial literatures, and cultural studies at the University of Konstanz. She has held guest professorships at Guelph, Toronto, and Shanghai. Publications include *Film und Text: Zum Problem von Wahrnehmung und Vorstellung in Film und Literatur* (1984) and *Fremde Texte als Spiegel des Eigenen: Postkoloniale Literaturen und ihre Auseinandersetzung mit dem kulturellen Kanon* (2006), as well as the edited collection *Borderlands: Negotiating Boundaries in Post-Colonial Writing* (1999). An American studies monograph, 'Family Structures and Cultural Change', is in preparation.

CHRISTIANE SCHLOTE teaches drama and postcolonial literatures and cultures at the University of Zurich. She has published extensively on postcolonial and transnational literatures, British Asian theatre, postcolonial cityscapes, documentarism, war and commemoration, and Latina/o American and Asian American culture. She is the author of *Bridging Cultures: Latino- und asiatisch-amerikanisches Theater in New York* (1997) and co-editor of *New Beginnings in Twentieth-Century Theatre and Drama* (with Peter Zenzinger, 2003) and *Constructing Media Reality. The New Documentarism* (with Eckhart Voigts–Virchow, 2008). She is currently editing the manuscript for a book on transnationalism in the work of South Asian writers and playwrights and co-editing a study on literature from the Middle East and its diasporas and a volume on literary and linguistic representations of war and refugeehood.

FRANK SCHULZE–ENGLER has taught at the Universities of Frankfurt, Bremen, and Hanover. In 2002 he became professor of New Anglophone Literatures and Cultures at the Institute for English and American Studies at Goethe University Frankfurt. His publications include *Intellektuelle wider Willen: Schriftsteller, Literatur und Gesellschaft in Ostafrika 1960–1980* (1992), the co-edited volumes *African Literatures in the Eighties* (1993, with Dieter Riemenschneider), *Postcolonial Theory and the Emergence of a Global Society* (1998, with Gordon Collier and Dieter Riemenschneider), *Crab Tracks: Progress and Process in Teaching the New Literatures in English* (2002, with Gordon Collier), *Transcultural English Studies: Theories, Fictions, Realities* (2008, with Sissy Helff) and *Beyond 'Other Cultures': Transcultural Perspectives on Teaching the New Literatures in English* (2011, with Sabine Doff), as well as numerous essays on African and Indian literature, comparative perspectives on the New Literatures in English, transculturality, postcolonial theory, globalized modernity, and the cultural dimensions of globalization. He is currently Director of the Centre for Interdisciplinary African Studies at Goethe University Frankfurt.

JAMIE S. SCOTT is Director of the Graduate Programme in Interdisciplinary Studies and a professor in the Department of Humanities at York University, Toronto, Canada. His most recent publications include "Religions and Postcolonial Literatures," in the *Cambridge History of Postcolonial Literatures* (2012) and essays on missions and film and missions and fiction. He is the editor of, and contributor to, *"And the Birds Began to Sing": Religion and Literature in Post-Colonial Cultures* (1996) and *The Religions of Canadians* (2012), and co-editor of *Mapping the Sacred: Religion, Geography and Postcolonial Literatures* (2001, with Paul Simpson–Housley), *Mixed Messages: Materiality, Textuality, Missions* (2005, with Gareth Griffiths), and *Canadian Missionaries, Indigenous People: Representing Religion at Home and Abroad* (2005, with Alvyn Austin). He is working on a study of Christianity and popular film.

MICHAEL SENIOR, born and schooled in Yorkshire, moved to Wales, where he took a degree in history, graduating in 1968. He then left for Germany, where he worked as a teacher and in teacher-training in Aachen and Osnabrück for fifteen years, before, in 1985, pursuing a career in information technology. After retirement in 2004, he has lived in Baden–Württemberg, earning a living as a tourist guide to the palaces, gardens, and castles of Heidelberg, Schwetzingen, and Mannheim. He is co-author (with Geoff Davis) of the ground-breaking, two-volume study and reader *South Africa: The Privileged and the Dispossessed* (1983/1985).

JOHN A STOTESBURY has taught at the University of Eastern Finland (formerly Joensuu) since 1975. His study of the colonialist writer Joy Packer appeared as *Apartheid, Liberalism and Romance* (1996). Published anthologies, the majority co-edited, include *African Voices: Interviews with Thirteen African Writers* (1989); *Postcolonialism and Cultural Resistance* (1999); *Past and Present in Post/Colonial Literatures* (2002), *Cultural Identity in Transition: Contemporary Conditions, Practices and Politics of a Global Phenomenon* (2004); *Southern Women Write Africa* (2007); and *Aging, Performance, and Stardom: Doing Age on the Stage of Consumerist Culture* (forthcoming). From 2004 to 2009 he edited the ESSE newsletter *The European English Messenger*. He is on the advisory board of the journal *Matatu*.

PETER O. STUMMER has recently retired from teaching in the English Department of the University of Munich, where he concentrated on contemporary and postcolonial writing. He has published widely on English literature, political discourse, and African, Australian, and Indian literature in English. He edited *The Story Must Be Told: Short Narrative Prose in the New English Literatures* (1986) and co-edited, with Bernd Schulte–Middelich, *Die industrielle Revolution in England: Literarische Texte und ihre Kontexte* (1991) as well as (with Chris Balme) *Fusion of Cultures?* (1996). His most recent articles have examined fiction from Zimbabwe and South Africa.

HAMISH WALKER grew up in Bulawayo and studied mechanical engineering there before leaving to hitchhike around Europe in 1972, in the course of which he was offered a job in Aachen. After spending many very formative years in Aachen, much influenced by anti-apartheid activities and close friendship with Geoff Davis and Michael Senior, in 1996 he moved to Hannover, where he runs a technical consultancy; the friendship is still as strong as ever.

BRIAN WORSFOLD is professor emeritus of English at the University of Lleida (Catalonia, Spain). A graduate of Rhodes University (Grahamstown,

South Africa), he holds a PhD from the University of Barcelona, his doctoral dissertation focusing on the novels of black South African writers. He has published articles on various aspects of literatures in English from Africa, especially from Southern Africa, and is the author of *South African Backdrop: An Historical Introduction for South African Literary and Cultural Studies* (1999). Since 1999, he has undertaken research on aging as represented in literatures in English, especially as presented in anglophone African fiction. He is the editor of *Multi-Cultural Voices* (1998), *Women Ageing Through Literature and Experience* (2005), *The Art of Ageing: Textualising the Phases of Life* (2005), and *Acculturating Age: Approaches to Cultural Gerontology* (2011). He currently heads the research group Grup Dedal-Lit and is General Editor of the Dedal-Lit series published by the University of Lleida.

## The Editors

GORDON COLLIER (New Zealand/Germany) taught postcolonial literature, film, and cultural studies at the universities of Mannheim (1970–76) and Giessen (1977–2008). His research interests include postcolonial film, Caribbean literature, narratology, and iconography. He has published books on translation and on Patrick White (*The Rocks and Sticks of Words*, 1992) and is the editor of *US/THEM: Translation, Transcription and Identity in Post-Colonial Literary Cultures* (1992) and *Spheres Public and Private: Western Genres in African Literature* (2011). He has co-edited the critical anthologies *Shuttling Through Cultures Towards Identity/Vers une identité interculturelle* (with Judith Bates, 1996), *A Talent(ed) Digger* (with Hena Maes–Jelinek and Geoff Davis, 1996), *Postcolonial Theory and the Emergence of a Global Society* (with Dieter Riemenschneider and Frank Schulze–Engler, 1998), *Crabtracks: Progress and Process in Teaching the New Literatures in English* (with Frank Schulze–Engler, 2002), and *A Pepper-Pot of Cultures: Aspects of Creolization in the Caribbean* (with Ulrich Fleischmann, 2003). Forthcoming in 2012 are the edited collections *Sub-Saharan Cultures and Literatures, East and South* and *Focus on Nigeria* and the two-volume retrospective *John Kinsella – Spatial Relations: Essays, Reviews, and Commentaries*. He is co-general editor and technical editor of the book-series Cross/Cultures: Readings in Post/Colonial Literatures and Cultures in English and of the journal *Matatu: A Review of African Literature*. His co-edition (with Chris Balme) of Derek Walcott's earlier criticism, 'The Journeyman

Years: Occasional Journalism 1959–1974', is forthcoming. He is currently compiling a comprehensive bibliography and filmography of the African diaspora.

MARC DELREZ (MA Adelaide; PhD Liège) teaches literature in English (new and established) as well as comparative literature at the University of Liège, Belgium. In the postcolonial field, his publications include articles on Salman Rushdie, Randolph Stow, David Malouf, Robert Drewe, Nicholas Jose, Richard Flanagan, Andrew McGahan, and Janet Frame. He is the author of *Manifold Utopia: The Novels of Janet Frame* (2002) and co-editor (with Bénédicte Ledent) of *The Contact and the Culmination* (1997), a collection of essays on postcolonial literature. He also co-edited, in the Cross/Cultures series, the twin volumes entitled *Towards a Transcultural Future: Literature and Society in a 'Post'-Colonial World* (with Geoffrey V. Davis, Peter H. Marsden, and Bénédicte Ledent).

ANNE FUCHS (England/France) taught comparative literature and theatre studies at the University of Nice for twenty-eight years. She has collaborated with Geoff Davis on compiling two collections of essays, *Theatre and Change in South Africa* (1996) and *Staging New Britain: Aspects of Black British Theatre Practice* (2006), and on numerous other projects. In retirement she continues her interest in African literature, theatre studies, black-British literature, and literature of the Indian diaspora.

BÉNÉDICTE LEDENT teaches English language and Caribbean literature at the University of Liège (Belgium). She is the author of *Caryl Phillips* (2002) and of numerous articles on contemporary Caribbean fiction. She has edited *Bridges Across Chasms: Towards a Transcultural Future in Caribbean Literature* (2004), a special issue of the journal *Moving Worlds* on Caryl Phillips (2007), and (with Kathleen Gyssels) *The Caribbean Writer as Warrior of the Imaginary/L'Écrivain caribéen, Guerrier de l'imaginaire* (2008). A co-edited collection, with Daria Tunca, *Caryl Phillips: Writing in the Key of Life*, is forthcoming (2011). Bénédicte is co-editor of the book series Cross/Cultures: Readings in Post/Colonial Literatures and Cultures in English.

◄❖►